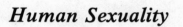

Human Sexuality

Human Sexuality

A Comparative and Developmental Perspective

Herant A. Katchadourian,
editor

University of California Press
Berkeley and Los Angeles, California
University of California Press, Ltd.

University of California Press
Berkeley   Los Angeles   London

Essay Index

University of California Press
Berkeley and Los Angeles, California
University of California Press, Ltd.
London, England
Copyright © 1979 by
The Regents of the University of California
ISBN 0-520-03654-9
Library of Congress Catalog Card Number: 77-93458
Printed in the United States of America

1   2   3   4   5   6   7   8   9

Contents

Part IV: Sociological Perspectives

Part V: Anthropological Perspectives 265

Introduction

Herant A. Katchadourian

In this book a group of biological and behavioral scientists consider the issue of human sexual development from alternative and complementary perspectives.

Broad statements about human sexual development are difficult to make because there is as yet no such discrete field of study. Information on the subject is scanty and scattered throughout various areas, and the available data are highly uneven in scope and quality.

To date, there has never been a comprehensive empirical investigation of the development of sexuality in childhood and adolescence. Freud's well-known views on infantile sexuality and psychosexual development were derived from the study of adults. Kinsey refocused attention on childhood sexuality by reexamining a sprinkling of investigations that had been conducted prior to the early 1950s, but like Freud, Kinsey worked predominantly with adults.

The psychological literature on child development clearly shows a general neglect of sexuality. What little work has been done on sexual development is hardly comparable to the extensive, painstaking research in areas such as cognitive development. Although sociologists have been preoccupied with issues like sex roles, they have usually managed to evade the implications of such issues for sexuality. But now we are beginning to recognize incongruity in the scant attention paid to sexuality by serious researchers and the often mindless popular preoccupation with sex.

Our scientific and scholarly concepts of human beings are often suggestive of statues with missing or covered genitals. Ignorance of such a pervasive aspect of life is bad enough, but even worse is the fact that such gaps cast doubt upon our assumptions about other aspects of behavior, since in the final analysis all behavior is integrated and indivisible. Whether we are dealing with the body, the mind, or the soul, sexuality confronts us at every turn as a biological, psychological, and moral issue. People and cultures have been willing enough to embrace or suppress sex, but few seem to have learned much about it. Ours certainly has not.

A precondition to knowledge about any type of behavior is an understanding of its genesis. We will never gain in-depth knowledge of sexuality, normal or abnormal, without studying its development throughout the life span. Substantial work in this field would have been difficult in the past and to some extent remains problematic. But under current social conditions it is reasonable to expect more active involvement on the part of serious investigators. If there are not many experts on human sexual development as yet, there certainly are many individuals whose expertise is relevant to this issue, and their insights should be brought together.

The central purpose of this book is to do just that. We have gathered here contributions from specialists representing the fields of primatology, biology, physiology, psychophysiology, developmental psychology, social psychology, psychiatry, and anthropology. The task is to address the issue of sexual development from a broad multidisciplinary perspective with particular focus on gender identity and sex roles.

Sexuality is far too complex to be dealt with in its totality at one sitting. Therefore, we have deliberately excluded consideration of many important aspects. For instance, we do not deal here with the structure and development of the reproductive system, the physiology of sexual response, or for that matter, many aspects of sexual behavior. Some may wonder if large sections of this book have anything to do with "sex." The answer to that query depends on whether or not one accepts the premise that there is more to sex than the manipulation and conjugation of the genitalia. That sexuality deals with more than "sex" has been clear for some time to many students of human behavior, and public awareness of this fact seems to be increasing. Beyond reproduction, beyond orgasmic pleasure, sexuality permeates our thoughts and feelings in countless ways, sometimes without our knowing it. The mutual invasiveness of the sexual and the non-sexual aspects of our lives is such that it is difficult, if not impossible, to make clear distinctions between the two.

Such a broad conception of sexuality is necessary as well as troublesome. Its necessity is self-evident if the above premises about its pervasive nature are accepted. It is problematic on several counts. For investigators of human sexuality, such a broad conceptualization can have a paralyzing effect. If sex permeates everything else, how does one begin to study it without taking on all of life itself? At a more personal level, there is a need for a more differentiated view whereby we restrict our perceptions of what is sexual to certain behaviors socially predefined as such. To those for whom sexuality is tinged with shame and anxiety, it becomes especially important to prevent sex from contaminating and soiling other aspects of life.

Quite obviously, reproductive behavior and sexuality are greatly influenced by the sex of the individual, that is, whether the person is male or female. Perhaps not as obvious is the fact that the psychological and cultural meanings of being masculine or feminine are also crucial to how we feel and behave sexually.

The need for a better understanding of these issues goes beyond academic curiosity. For all practical purposes, every single one of us belongs to one sex or the other, behaves under some conception of what it means to be masculine or feminine, and engages in a variety of sexual experiences. Setting aside the question of how these factors influence the rest of our lives, there is much to be said for understanding how they influence each other.

In an attempt to come to grips with these issues, this volume is the first of three installments. The two companion volumes in preparation will focus more specifically on the processes of sexual learning and the social contexts wherein such learning takes place. For the purpose of providing a broad multidisciplinary view of the concepts of sexual development and of gender identity and roles, this volume is intended to be able to stand alone.

This volume and the two that will follow are part of the Special Studies Program of the Project on Human Sexual Development. Elizabeth J. Roberts, executive director, describes the background and purposes of the project as follows:

> This national project was initiated in 1974 to (1) stimulate new thinking and develop new programs to expand the public's understanding of human sexuality; (2) provide forums and agendas for discussion of the many complex personal and social issues it raises; and (3) consider ways to improve the conditions of sexual learning in our society by suggesting social

and educational policies and priorities. The project is based on the assumption that sexuality and the ways in which we express it are not totally inborn, but that our maleness and femaleness is made up of a complex set of roles, behaviors, and attitudes that are in large part learned, developed, and limited by family, society, and culture. The project has taken as its focus the importance of early learning for sexual development and its influence on subsequent sexual behavior and relationships. Through this focus, it hopes to turn attention away from the limited view of sex as an isolated activity or as a source of personal or social problems, toward a view that emphasizes its positive potential and broader significance throughout our lives.

The project's research and policy activities were developed in response to concerns and issues raised by the National Commission on Population Growth and the American Future. The studies prepared for this commission stressed the importance of sexuality in everyday life and revealed that ignorance and myth about sexuality are widespread in our society. They suggested this lack of understanding contributes to negative self-images, to faulty communication between men and women, and to uninformed and irresponsible sexual decision-making. Despite our nation's preoccupation with "sex," there is considerable evidence that millions of Americans of all ages need help in understanding their sexuality.

But such understanding will not come easily. The term is imprecise, the content narrowly defined, and the issues emotionally charged. Human sexuality is a developmental process, a personal experience, and a behavioral expression. While the word *sexuality* is frequently equated with "sex" and brings to mind brief, transitory experiences isolated from the rest of living, the full meaning of sexuality in our lives is not confined to the bedroom, to the nighttime, or to any one part of the body. Our sexuality is part of our basic identity; it is expressed through our life styles, in our masculine and feminine roles, in the ways we express affection, as well as in our erotic behaviors. Our sexuality and the ways we express it are not totally inborn. Nor do we become sexual all at once at puberty. Rather, sexual development is a life-long process beginning in earliest childhood and continuing into old age. How children learn and develop early in life has an impact on how they will subsequently experience and express their sexuality. What is learned, how it is learned, and who the teachers are might be different throughout the life cycle; but we may be sure that learning about sexuality is going on. The information and attitude that affect our sexual development come from a myriad of formal and nonformal, intentional and incidental environments and sources—parents, teachers, peers, the media, health policies, leisure-time activities, the channels of touch, sight, conversation, and reading. It is this developmental process that needs most to be explored and that is the primary focus of the Project on Human Sexual Development and its action-research activities.

The contributors to this volume met at a conference sponsored by the project and funded by the Carnegie Corporation. The conference, held in January of 1977 at Stanford University, included a number of additional participants (who are listed in the appendix).

The conference discussions were organized primarily along disciplinary lines, which are also reflected in the organization of this volume. Five main perspectives are represented: evolutionary, biological, psychological, sociological, and anthropological. Each unit consists of three contributions, usually by specialists from the same discipline. The first contribution is the major statement representing the salient findings and viewpoints within the perspective in question. The second contribution may be either a response to the issues raised in the first, or a more independent approach that complements the first. The final contribution to each triad (written by the person who chaired the conference section) reacts to the first two contributions, adds additional considerations, and points to new directions for research in the field. Recommendations for new research are the outcome of discussions among the authors of the unit.

In view of the particular functions these various contributions are expected to fulfill, they could not be treated as equivalent chapters. Therefore, this volume is divided into five parts. In each part the three authors collectively state the case for a given perspective.

Two additional contributions complete the volume. One chapter attempts to provide a general context for the discussion of sex and gender by focusing on terminological issues and the other on models for the analyses of sexual behavior.

Given the range and diversity of the viewpoints represented here, it is only fair to state beforehand that they do not add up to an integrated and coherent view of the subject. The gaps and inconsistencies in this volume are an inevitable outcome of the complexity of the subject and a reflection of our current level of knowledge. Discourse in these issues is currently handicapped by a babel of disciplinary tongues, congeries of methodologies, a profusion of assumptions, presumptions, and plain old prejudice. Yet for the patient and discerning student there is also much of value to glean in the midst of apparent chaos.

A particular advantage of this volume is that its contributors come with impeccable professional credentials in their respective fields and can legitimately speak with the voice of authority on their subject matters. The views they express are of course their own, and they are worth listening to.

Acknowledgments

This volume is the first of several to be produced under the sponsorship and guidance of the Project on Human Sexual Development, the major current activity of Population Education, Inc. (PEI). The project was initiated by John D. Rockefeller 3rd and his associate, Joan Dunlop, and has evolved under the creative leadership of Elizabeth J. Roberts, executive director of the project and president of PEI. The board of directors of PEI is chaired by Philip R. Lee. Members of the board are listed in the Appendix.

I have been responsible for directing the Special Studies Program of the Project on Human Sexual Development. Funding for the Special Studies Program is provided by the Carnegie Corporation of New York—support which is especially meaningful in light of that organization's long and distinguished record of support for research and child development.

I was most ably assisted in the planning and management of the conference that provided material for this volume by Elizabeth J. Roberts. Many logistical details were handled by John A. Martin. I was also guided in the planning by several Stanford University colleagues, Robert Sears, Albert Hastorf, Alberta Siegel, and Julian Davidson. Carol King, who helped me edit the volume, went far beyond the unscrambling of syntax and contributed significantly to the organization and final clarity of the book.

6

We gratefully acknowledge permissions granted by the following:

P. M. Bentler, to reproduce "Development of Feminine Sex-Role in Males: A Theory" (table) from his paper published in *Archives of Sexual Behavior* (vol. 5) in 1976.

American Anthropologist, to reprint excerpts from "Head-Hunting Practices of the Asmat of Netherlands New Guinea" by G. Zegwaard, which first appeared in that journal (vol. 61) in 1959.

Archives of Neurology and Psychiatry, to reprint an excerpt from "Imprinting and the Establishment of Gender Role" by John Money, J. G. Hampson, and J. L. Hampson, which first appeared in that journal (vol. 77, pp. 333–336). Copyright 1957, American Medical Association.

Archives of Sexual Behavior, to reproduce "The Variety of Heterosexual and Homosexual Interactions Observed in Captive *Macaca arctoides*" (illustration), from "Male-Female, Female-Female, and Male-Male Sexual Behavior in the Stumptail Monkey, with Special Attention to the Female Orgasm" by S. Chevalier-Skolnikoff, which first appeared in that journal (vol. 3) in 1973.

The Counseling Psychologist, to reproduce "Sexuality-Achievement Scoring Mechanism" (figure) from "Vicarious and Direct Achievement Patterns in Adulthood" by Jean Lipman-Blumen and Harold J. Leavitt, which appeared in that journal (vol. 6) in 1976.

Duxbury Press, to reprint an excerpt from "Concealment of Ovulation, Parental Care, and Human Social Evolution" by R. D. Alexander and K. M. Noonan, from *Evolutionary Theory and Human Social Organization* (1978), edited by N. A. Chagnon and W. G. Irons.

The Terminology of Sex and Gender

Herant A. Katchadourian

It is a truism that sexuality is one of the more enigmatic and conflicted topics confronting investigators of human behavior. Perhaps not as obvious is the terminological confusion that characterizes professional discourse on sexuality. My purpose here is to examine terminological inconsistencies and to point out the wide range of meanings attached to key terms in our sexual vocabulary.

This is not an exegetical exercise to resolve all differences in usage and meaning; currently such consensus would be impossible. Nonetheless, terminological clarification is important on at least two counts. First is the obvious need for effective communication within and between disciplines. Second, and more important, as language reflects thought, one cannot hope for conceptual clarity in the presence of linguistic ambiguity. Likewise, one cannot meaningfully discuss terminology without some consideration of the concepts the terms are supposed to represent —hence the justification for occasionally straying into the arena of broader issues.

Given the paucity of knowledge in the field of sexuality, its terminology has not attracted much attention. In the past, too few people have said too little of value for the scientific community to take notice. But this situation has been changing significantly during the last several decades, and the serious study of sexuality with its psychosocial ramifications has now brought the field to the fringe of established behavioral disciplines.

In this discussion, our primary interest is not with sexuality in general, but with its *psychosocial derivatives*. At the risk of introducing one more term, it may be worthwhile to consider the

8

potential usefulness of such a designation to subsume such terms as *gender identity, gender role, sex role, sex-role identity,* and so on.

The reference to gender identity and such terms as *psychosocial derivatives* does not imply that these characteristics are psychosocially rather than biologically determined. What is psychosocial about them in this context is their manifestations and expression, rather than their derivation. Whatever biological and non-biological factors determine gender identity and sex roles, these entities are always manifested as psychosocial aspects of an individual. In other words, even though gender identity and sex role are by definition based on the biological sex of the person and may conceivably have biological determinants beyond genital anatomy, such concepts can be understood only as psychological and social phenomena.

The Many Meanings of Sex

The word *sex,* derived from the Latin *sexus,* has been in the English vocabulary for a long time. The *Oxford English Dictionary,* for example, includes a reference that dates back to the fourteenth century. But in modern times, the word has accumulated many different connotations. Formally defined, *sex* refers primarily to the two divisions of organic beings identified as male and female and to the qualities that distinguish males and females. But the multiple uses and derivatives (sexes, sexed, sexual, sexually, sexualism, sexualist, sexuality, sexualize) encompass so many meanings that the word has become quite diffuse. As commonly used, these various meanings can be outlined under two headings: *sex* as a biological or personality characteristic; *sex* as erotic behavior.

In the first sense, *sex* most commonly and least ambiguously refers to the fact of being male or female as determined by structural and functional characteristics. In this sense, sex is a biological fact that normally has an imperative presence in humans and a mutually exclusive dichotomy: a person is male or female and must be one or the other. To be more specific, sex in this sense is qualified sometimes as *biological sex.* But even this distinction does not isolate a single entity but one with a number of discrete components. It is important to differentiate among these components because in pathological conditions the aberration may involve one aspect but not another. Subsumed under biological sex are the following:

1. Genetic sex as revealed by the chromosome count (46XX or 46XY in humans) or the presence of the sex-chromatin mass (Barr body)
2. Hormonal sex: the androgen-to-estrogen balance
3. Gonadal sex: the presence of testes or ovaries
4. Morphology of the internal reproductive organs
5. Morphology of the external genitalia (Money, 1965).

One could add to this list the somatic dimorphism established definitively at the end of puberty, including the secondary sexual characteristics.

What has been described here is the normal maturational sequence. Abnormalities can be present at any stage: the sex chromosome pattern may be abnormal; the hormonal balance may be reversed; the gonadal structure may be inconsistent or mixed; the internal and external sex organs may be inconsistent with genetic sex; pubertal changes may not occur on schedule (Federman, 1968).

In a biologically normal individual (and the great majority of people are normal in this regard) biological sex entails a specific and consistent set of characteristics. The abnormalities, though rare, are of great importance for our understanding of sexual development.

Based on these biological givens, the word *sex* is put to other uses. For instance, it is widely used as a demographic variable and an index of social and legal status. Uses such as in *sex-typing, sexual identity,* and *sex role* are other examples. And so is *sexism,* the most recent addition to this vocabulary, patterned after *racism.*

Thus, in this first category of meaning, *sex* designates certain aspects of individuals, not restricted to who one is, but also including how one behaves or is expected to behave. Yet such behavior is not always sexual in the sense of being erotic, hence the justification of discriminating between this category of meanings and the category in which *sex* pertains more specifically to erotic behavior. This distinction is nevertheless tenuous since the meaning of *erotic* is itself problematic, and the two categories of meaning are closely linked.

The term *sexual behavior* becomes problematic when pressed beyond its informal, everyday meaning. *Sexual behavior* usually refers to what people "do" sexually ("having sex"). Activities like coitus or masturbation readily qualify. But what about sexual fantasy or nocturnal orgasm? People attach different degrees of erotic significance to such activities. The basic problem here is not specific to the sexual sphere because it hinges also on what we mean by *behavior*. Sexual fantasy may be erotic, but is it "behavior"?

To obviate this difficulty, some refer to *sexual experience*, on the assumption that experience includes private feelings and thoughts, while behavior can be limited to "outer," observable activity. But here again, more fundamental questions arise about what is "inner" and what is "outer" regarding behavior, and whether such distinctions make any sense.

Assuming we could agree on the more fundamental issues related to all behavior, we would still have the problem of defining which behaviors are to be considered "sexual" and on what grounds. Definitions based on physiological evidence of sexual arousal or orgasm have great merit but exclude vast areas of activity that could reasonably be regarded as sexual, such as sexual fantasy, without readily discernible manifestations of physiological arousal. Furthermore, physiological evidence would include manifestations like reflex erections in infants, the erotic nature of which is questionable.

Kinsey was quite aware of this difficulty, but for research purposes he defined sexual behavior as behavior leading to orgasm. This definition reduced sex to six main "outlets": masturbation, sex dreams, petting, coitus, homosexual activities, and animal contacts. The great majority of orgasms were found to be achieved through one or another of these means. This approach provides an empirical base but restricts reality to what can be readily counted and quantified.

In contrast, Freud perceived sexual behavior in far broader terms—far beyond what is commonly understood as being sexual. Freud's approach makes sexuality more a matter of interpretation than of observation. The issue is no longer a question of which categories of behavior are sexual and which are not, but whether a particular behavior in a given instance is sexually motivated. In this sense any form of behavior may be eroticized without being

11

consciously known as sexual to the person or recognized as such by others. In the Reichian vision, the entire cosmos becomes eroticized.[1]

In the first category of meanings, *sex* refers primarily to morphological and personality characteristics but also to behavior. In the second category of meanings, while *sex* refers primarily to erotic behavior, the term also pertains to physical and personality features with erotic association, such as in the word *sexy*.

In both categories where *sex* is used in descriptive or adjectival form, the level of precision with which it designates an entity varies widely. For example: *sex chromosome* denotes a specific and unambiguous entity; *sex hormone* is basically a misnomer, but conventional usage has defined it sufficiently to make its meaning clear to scientists; *sex roles* and *sexual behavior* are more ambiguous terms and may mean different things to different people.

Finally, *sexuality* as distinct from *sex* deserves some comment. As formally defined, *sexuality* is the quality of being sexual, the possessing of sexual capacity and the capability of sexual feelings. But in common usage the term is endowed with additional meanings. Whatever *sex* is, *sexuality* seems to imply something more. From a biologist's perspective, "there is the basic sex, which depends on the kind of sex gland present, and sexuality, which depends on the different structures, functions, and activities associated with the sex glands" (Berrill, 1976). In one ancient usage referred to in the *Oxford English Dictionary*, *sexuality* characterizes the male and female reproductive elements, the gametes (ova and sperm), which in turn determine the sex of the individual. In this sense, a man has sex, sperm has sexuality.

In sharp contrast, Beach views sexuality as an "emergent" in the evolution of *Homo sapiens*. In this sense, the relation of human sexuality to mating behavior of other species is comparable to the relationship of human language to animal communication (Beach, 1974).

Other writers are often unclear on what they mean by *sexuality*, but in current usage the term seems always to represent something more than *sex*. To some, sexuality encompasses more than

1. The nature of sexual behavior and sexual orientation or preference are discussed at greater length in the chapter by Katchadourian and Martin in this volume.

genital functions, coitus, or other "sexual behaviors." Some use the term to convey the broader and more subtle emotional, interpersonal, and nongenital components of eroticism. Others seem to use it because it sounds more refined and proper. All of these considerations have probably contributed to making *sexuality* part of the standard title of textbooks in this field (Gagnon, 1977; Goldstein, 1976; Katchadourian and Lunde, 1975; McCary, 1973).

It would seem legitimate to use *sexuality* as the broad, overarching term as long as we remember that it represents an abstraction and that what is meant by it tends to reflect the theoretical framework or value assumptions of the user. The issue of meaning thus remains problematic.

Sexual and Gender Identity

In its most elementary sense, *sexual identity* is synonymous with the sex of the individual, determined by the generally unequivocal biological fact of being male or female. But the term has also a more subtle and ambiguous meaning, namely sexual identity as a fundamental personality characteristic. In this sense it is often used synonymously with *gender identity*.

Identity is derived from the Latin word for "sameness" (*idem*), and its dictionary definition refers to the persistent individuality and sameness of a person or thing over time and under different circumstances. The central idea underlying the concept of identity is so fundamental that one can find numerous references to it under different guises.

Among philosophers, John Locke and David Hume have addressed themselves to this matter.[2] At the turn of this century, social psychologists began to emphasize the concept of the "self" as fundamental to personality development. Of particular interest are the views of William James, who differentiated between the material self, the social self, the spiritual self, and the pure ego as components of personality (James, 1892).[3]

During the last two decades the concept of identity has attained a remarkable popularity through the work of Erik Erikson. This

2. For their representative writings in this regard and additional commentaries by other philosophers, see Perry, 1975.

3. For a review of the work of other social scientists in this area, see Hall and Lindzey (1970).

popularity may have been due in part to Erikson's linking of identity formation with adolescence, a phase of life that has been a source of increasing social and professional interest since the 1950s.

Erikson's views on "ego identity" are difficult to summarize without seriously diminishing them, and even in their original form the meaning of *identity* remains somewhat unclear. Erikson distinguishes between *identity,* which is characterized by items like a person's name and station in the community; *personal identity,* which includes a "subjective sense of continuous existence and a coherent memory"; and *psychosocial identity,* which "has even more elusive characteristics, at once subjective and objective, individual and social" (Erikson, 1968b).

In everyday terms, *identity* refers to a person's individuality, the response to the question "Who am I?" But what Erikson means by *ego identity* is more complex. It includes a conscious sense of individual identity, an unconscious striving for a continuity of personal character, certain aspects of "ego synthesis," and the maintenance of an inner solidarity with a group's ideals and identity. The issue of identity is not settled permanently during adolescence. What occurs then is at best a clarification and reworking of earlier solutions and enough of a consolidation to provide the person with a selfsameness even though many aspects of personality continue to be refined in successive phases of the life cycle.

The emergence of a sense of personal identity progresses on multiple fronts including, of course, cognitive development. Important components are self-labeling and the labeling of oneself by others. Both are of particular importance to sexual identity since one of the earliest labels attached to a person pertains to his or her sex.[4]

The relationship of identity to personality is unclear. In one sense, identity would seem to be a facet or part of personality. Yet, in its broadest sense, identity becomes virtually synonymous with personality.

Without resolving this fundamental problem, we could assume that whatever identity is, sexual identity is part of it. Perhaps sexual identity should encompass everything that is sexual in a person: physiological functions, type and intensity of sexual

4. See Sears' comments on self-labeling in this volume.

behaviors, one's own and others' perception of oneself as a sexual being, and everything else that may have to do with being a man or a woman. Or is sexual identity only a part or a more differentiated aspect of this totality?

Erikson's own views are not entirely clear in this regard. The term *sexual identity* appears in only one version of Erikson's epigenetic scheme, along with its polar opposite, *bisexual diffusion.* The issue of sexual identity is the antecedent during adolescence of the phase-specific crisis of young adulthood, which is Intimacy vs. Isolation (Erikson, 1959). In later versions, *sexual identity* is replaced by *sexual polarization* (Erikson, 1968b). Unlike some other terms, those relating to sexual identity are not discussed in any detail by Erikson, but one fairly clear implication is that sexual identity involves the definition of sexual orientation or "polarization" along a heterosexual-homosexual axis as against confusion between such choices.

Erikson has not spelled out the antecedent stages of sexual identity during the preceding four phases of the life cycle, nor its derivatives beyond young adulthood. It would be interesting to know, for instance, what Erikson believes takes place in early childhood when, according to Money and others, the "gender identity gate" ordinarily shuts irrevocably. It would likewise be instructive to learn how Money and Ehrhardt's scheme of the sequential and interactional components of gender identity differentiation (Money and Ehrhardt, 1972) compare with Erikson's epigenetic model. Unfortunately, one is hard pressed to find specific comparisons or references by these and other authors to each other's views.[5]

Others also view sexual identity in rather global terms. For example, Sandra Bem attributes to the traditional view of the ideal or healthy personality a concept of sexual identity that has three basic components: (1) a sexual preference for members of the opposite sex; (2) a sex-role identity as either masculine or feminine, depending upon one's gender; and (3) a gender identity, a secure sense of one's maleness or femaleness (Bem, in press).

5. One glimpses Stoller's despair with *identity* from a footnote in which he quotes with seeming approval a colleague's conclusion that "the term 'identity' has little use other than a fancy dress in which to disguise vagueness, ambiguity, tautologies, lack of clinical data, and poverty of explanation" (Stoller, 1968, p. x).

Other authors use *sexual identity* much more narrowly, often as a synonym for *sex-role* or *gender identity*, reflecting masculinity and femininity.

Preoccupation with masculinity and femininity long antedates contemporary scientific interest in it. In Chinese philosophy and religion, the masculine principle called *Yang* and the feminine principle called *Yin* are attributed not only to men and women, but to everything in existence, including inanimate objects, spirits, and events. The doctrine, found in the Taoist text, the *Tao-te Ching,* is typical of Chinese dualism, which proposes that everything in existence is constituted by the interaction of two opposed but complementary modes of energy. The Yang is masculine, procreative, bright, solar, celestial, active, and positive. The Yin is feminine, fertile, lunar, terrestrial, passive, and negative. The Yin and Yang are present in varying degrees and interact in every human being, but men are predominantly Yang and women are predominantly Yin. And since good and evil are opposites that must also be accounted for in a dualistic doctrine, the *shen* (or good spirits) are Yang in character, while the *kwei* (or evil spirits) are Yin (Noss, 1963). Yet this bipolar world view, in its ancient, classical formulation, did not represent a struggle between elemental forces of good and evil. Rather, "Yang and Yin were equally essential forces in the ceaseless dynamic of an impersonal universe" (Thompson, 1969).

Although in this context the Yang and Yin cannot be equated with facets of sexual identity, some contemporary writers have used the Yang and Yin or some similar idea to represent the male and female points of view, which are present in different proportions in every individual of either sex. The Jungian concept of the animus and anima is a case in point.

Jung conceived the anima and the animus as archetypal figures that belong to the individual consciousness but are rooted in the collective unconscious. The *anima* represents the feminine personality components of the man and at the same time the image that he has of feminine nature in general—in other words, the archetype of the feminine. Likewise, the *animus* represents the masculine personality components of the woman and also her image of masculine nature. Normally, both masculine and feminine characteristics are present in every individual, but the person expresses outwardly the set of characteristics that are considered most appropriate to his or her sex and are therefore not disturbing to the ideal self-image (Jung, 1969).

Jung distinguished between the outer personality, which he called the *persona*, and the inner personality, which he called the *anima*, or soul. Comparing the personas of men and women, Jung said that logic and objective reality prevail in the outer attitude of man, or at least are considered ideal, but feeling prevails in the outer attitude or ideal of woman. "The conscious attitude of woman is in general far more exclusively personal than that of man. Her world is made up of fathers and mothers, brothers and sisters, husbands and children. . . . The man's world is the nation, the state, business concerns, etc. His family is simply a means to an end . . ." (Jung, 1953, p. 208).

But in the soul, the relations are reversed: The man feels and the woman reflects. "As the anima produces *moods*, so the animus produces *opinions*." Awareness of these inner psychic processes enables us to use them consciously as functions, according to Jung. So long as the anima or animus is unconscious, it is always projected, "for everything unconscious is projected," and life runs its course in inevitable opposition. In such cases, the soul is projected into a corresponding, real object—a member of the opposite sex—with whom a relationship of almost absolute dependence results (Jung, 1953, pp. 195–209).

Freud's views of sexual identity were embedded within his broader conception of sexuality. Even though he did not dwell on the concept of sexual identity as such, his preoccupation with the issues of masculinity and femininity pervade many of his writings.[6]

Fundamental to the Freudian view of gender is the concept of bisexuality: "Since I have become acquainted with the notion of bisexuality I have regarded it as the decisive factor, and without taking bisexuality into account I think it would scarcely be possible to arrive at an understanding of the sexual manifestations that are actually to be observed in men and women" (Freud, 18:220). According to Stoller, the concept of bisexuality remained central and relatively intact throughout Freud's psychoanalytic thinking (Stoller, 1974).

6. In the index of Freud's monumental collection of psychological writings, *sexuality* is referred to in over 80 different associations but *identity* is not one of them. For specific references to masculinity and femininity in Freud's writings, see Freud, 24:317.

Freud believed bisexuality was part of the biological "bedrock" underlying psychological functions. By the turn of this century the basic similarity of the ontogeny of the reproductive system in both sexes had been established and parallels were already being drawn with psychic bisexuality. In a lengthy footnote, Freud refers to a number of these views which state that masculine and feminine elements are to be found in every individual albeit in different proportions (Freud, 7:143). Freud also assumed that as a biological universal, bisexuality influenced the psychological realm. In Freud's thinking, as Stoller points out, *bisexuality* became a referent for

> overt homosexuality; pleasure in both homosexual and hetero-sexual intercourse; identification with aspects of the opposite sex; cross-gender non-erotic behavior, such as effeminacy; friendship; the capacity of certain cells and tissues to shift appearance or function, or both, from that typical of one sex to the other; embryological undifferentiation; vestigial tissues of the opposite sex in the adult; an innate "force" that can influence behavior toward that of the opposite sex. The an-lagen of bisexuality were the "bedrock" of behavior, and its psychological manifestation—homosexuality—was the nidus from which psychopathology arose. He felt more than com-fortable with such inclusive usage; he felt it was correct. To fail to see that these are all of one family was to throw away a con-cept of great power (Stoller, 1974, pp. 392–393).

Yet Freud was also uneasy about the potential of biological concepts and terminology dominating psychoanalysis. In a 1913 discourse on the relationship between psychoanalysis and biology, he wrote, "In spite of all our efforts to prevent biological termi-nology and considerations from dominating psycho-analytic work, we cannot avoid using them even in our descriptions of the phenomena we study . . . we speak, too, of 'masculine' and 'feminine' mental attributes and impulses, although, strictly speaking, the differences between the sexes can lay claim to no special psychical characterization" (Freud, 13:182). In another context, after referring to a female patient's "masculine" intel-lectual attributes, he adds that "these distinctions are conven-tional rather than scientific" (Freud, 18:147–172).

Freud wrote the first substantial exposition of his views on bisexuality in his "Three Essays on the Theory of Sexuality"

18

(vol. 7) in 1905 when dealing with the issue of homosexuality. Another major statement on gender also occurs in connection with homosexuality—this time in a case discussion of a homosexual woman (Freud, 18:147–172). In his "New Introductory Lectures on Psychoanalysis" (vol. 22) Freud chose "Femininity" as one of his main topics and based his remarks mainly on two earlier papers: "Some Psychical Consequences of the Anatomical Distinction Between the Sexes" (1925) and "Female Sexuality" (1931).[7]

Psychologists with more empirical and experimental orientations have also been long interested in masculinity and femininity. In the late nineteenth century, sex differences were beginning to receive professional attention, and by the 1920s formal studies had begun to appear with some regularity in the psychological literature.[8]

An early empirical study was undertaken in the 1930s by Lewis Terman and Catherine Miles, who devised a questionnaire-type "Masculinity-Femininity Test." Even though they do not use the terms *gender identity* or *sexual identity* in *Sex and Personality*, the authors are much concerned with this very issue. In the introduction to their book Terman relates that the idea of developing a test of masculinity and femininity occurred to him in 1922 in connection with his work with gifted male and female children with respect to their interest, practice, and knowledge of games.

The expectation underlying such masculinity-femininity tests is not that these personality dimensions and their manifestations consist of mutually exclusive alternatives, but rather that combinations of traits are distributed unevenly among males and females. As Terman himself pointed out, "Although practically every attribute alleged to be characteristic of a given sex has been questioned, yet the composite pictures yielded by majority opinion stand out with considerable clearness" (Terman and Miles, 1936). These tests, of course, merely try to identify existing differences between the two sexes without pretending to disclose how these differences come about.[9]

7. For further discussion of Freud's views on gender and bisexuality, see Stoller, 1972, 1974.

8. For a survey of this early literature, see Johnson and Terman, 1940.

9. For a review and critique of masculinity-femininity inventories see Constantinople, 1973.

Since Terman's pioneering work, an extensive psychological literature has developed in this area. At its broadest, this literature deals with the psychology of sex differences encompassing a large number of variables ranging from tactile sensitivity to intellectual functions, personality traits, socialization patterns, and so on (Maccoby and Jacklin, 1974). A more circumscribed approach focuses on personality and behavioral characteristics and various scales and inventories have been developed to differentiate the two sexes.

In most of these tests masculinity and femininity are implicitly perceived as bipolar and unidimensional. As Constantinople (1973) has pointed out, the unidimensionality of masculinity-femininity is clearly untenable as long as these tests are not measuring a unitary trait. Also, depending on the behaviors sampled, one will derive different estimates of a person's relative masculinity-femininity level. The bipolarity aspect implies that masculinity and femininity are at the opposite extremes of a single continuum whereby masculinity at one end represents not only a total absence of femininity but also its very opposite. While it may or may not be possible to resolve this issue to everyone's satisfaction, caution has been raised against viewing such a complex matter in terms of a simplistic bipolar continuum (Carlson, 1972). Furthermore, in current efforts, masculinity and femininity have been dealt with not as polar opposites but as two orthogonal dimensions, both representing positive domains of behavior optimally coexisting in the ideal person with an androgynous sexual identity (Bem, in press). To further emphasize this, some have invoked the ancient concept of the Yang and Yin (Cox, 1976).

The designation *sex-role identity* is often used in a sense similar to *gender identity*.[10] At least it is meant to confer some notion of identity as it "includes both cognitive and affective factors which reflect both self-evaluation and the evaluation of others as to one's adequacy as a male or female" (Constantinople, 1973).

The word *gender* is derived from the Latin *genus* meaning birth or origin, and hence representing a certain type. It is primarily a grammatical term representing the subclassification of certain words, usually nouns and pronouns, as masculine, feminine, or neuter. The terms *gender role* and *gender identity* are of recent

10. In the journal *Child Development* the *sex-role identity* term first appears in 1956 in an article by Harry Levin and Robert Sears.

origin. John Money, the first person to use *gender role*, defined it in print in 1955 (Money, 1973). Robert Stoller reports that *gender identity* "was arrived at" in discussions between himself and Ralph Greenson. Stoller used the term formally in 1963 in a paper presented at the Twenty-third International Psychoanalytical Congress (Stoller, 1964). Money also gives credit to Stoller for originating *core gender identity* (Money, 1973).

The justification for introducing *gender identity* was Stoller's concern that *sexual identity* was ambiguous since it also could refer to sexual activities or fantasies. Since *sex* had strongly biological connotations, Stoller proposed to use it to "refer to the male or the female sex and the component biological parts that determine whether one is a male or a female." He went on to explain that

the word *sexual* will have connotations of anatomy and physiology. This obviously leaves tremendous areas of behavior, feelings, thoughts, and fantasies that are related to the sexes and yet do not have primarily biological connotations. It is for some of these psychological phenomena that the term *gender* will be used: one can speak of the male sex or the female sex, but one can also talk about masculinity and femininity and not necessarily be implying anything about anatomy or physiology. Thus, while *sex* and *gender* seem to common sense to be practically synonymous, and in everyday life to be inextricably bound together . . . the two realms (sex and gender) are not at all inevitably bound in anything like a one-to-one relationship, but each may go in its quite independent way (Stoller, 1968, pp. vii–ix).

The concept of gender identity has proven useful in emphasizing the psychosocial components in sexuality. The contrast between maleness and femaleness as reflections of biological sex, and masculinity and femininity for its nonbiological aspects, has indeed helped refine discussions.

The separation of biological sex from gender takes on dramatic dimensions in the self-perceptions of transsexuals. This is expressed by Jan (formerly James) Morris, who writes:

To me gender is not physical at all, but is altogether insubstantial. It is soul, perhaps, it is talent, it is taste, it is environment, it is how one feels, it is light and shade, it is inner music, it is a spring in one's step or an exchange of glances, it is more truly life and love than any combination of genitals, ovaries,

21

and hormones. It is the essentialness of oneself, the psyche, the fragment of unity. Male and female are sex, masculine and feminine are gender, and though the conceptions obviously overlap, they are far from synonymous. As C. S. Lewis once wrote, "Gender is a reality, and a more fundamental reality than sex. Sex is, in fact, merely the adaptation to organic life of a fundamental polarity which divides all created beings. Female sex is simply one of the things that have feminine gender; there are many others, and Masculine and Feminine meet us on planes of reality where male and female would be simply meaningless" (Morris, 1974).

Unfortunately, the term *gender identity*, vague at its conception, has failed to be sufficiently refined as yet. In his first substantial discussion of this issue, Stoller noted that "while the work of our research team has been associated with the term *gender identity*, we are not militantly fixed either on copyrighting the term or on defending the concept as one of the splendors of the scientific world. It is a working term. We know that, though it deals with another realm of feelings, thoughts, and behavior than that encompassed by, say, *sexual activity*, the two terms are contiguous and at times inextricably intermingled. With *gender* difficult to define and *identity* still a challenge to theoreticians, we need hardly insist on the holiness of the term *gender identity*" (Stoller, 1968). Almost a decade later, the precise meaning of the term has not moved much further (Stoller, 1976).

Money, Ehrhardt, and Green have attempted to be systematic in the uses of the term, yet their statements, too, are seemingly tinged with ambiguities and differences. Money and Ehrhardt define *gender identity* thus:

> *Gender Identity*: The sameness, unity, and persistence of one's individuality as male, female, or ambivalent, in greater or lesser degree, especially as it is experienced in self-awareness and behavior; gender identity is the private experience of gender role, and gender role is the public expression of gender identity (Money and Ehrhardt, 1972).

It is unclear what is meant by gender identity being experienced in self-awareness *and* behavior. Can one experience behavior outside of self-awareness? If the word *behavior* is left out, then gender identity becomes more readily understandable as the self-perception of one's "individuality as male, female, or ambivalent." Richard Green in turn defines *gender identity* thus:

Sexual identity—also termed gender identity—is a fundamental personality feature. It may be considered as encompassing three components: (1) an individual's basic conviction of being male or female; (2) an individual's behavior which is culturally associated with males and females (masculinity and femininity); and (3) an individual's preference for male or female sexual partners (Green, 1974).[11]

Sexual identity now appears to encompass a few more things. First, it is a "basic conviction," which may be another way of saying that it is a persistent self-perception. But Green also attributes to it culturally sex-linked *behavior* and *sexual orientation preference*. That definitions can differ is in itself not surprising until one realizes that Money, Ehrhardt, and Green are long-time collaborators, who evolve their definitions from work with very similar forms of clinical data.[12]

Discrepancies in meaning widen further with the introduction of more authors. For example, while Green accepts *gender identity* as synonymous with *sexual identity,* Lief seems to distinguish between the two, yet without making this distinction quite clear. For Lief, *sexual identity* "may be defined as the person's inner feeling of maleness or femaleness continued over time." He then deals with *gender identity* separately, and while he does not define the term as such, we are told that with rare exceptions "the development of sexuality leads to a secure sense of maleness or femaleness, which is generally complete by the age of three years." Lief then cites homosexuality as "a special case of disturbance of gender identity; homosexuals do not have doubts about their maleness or femaleness (sexual identity)" (Lief, 1976).

Hooker, who has studied sexual identity and sexual patterns in male homosexuals, defines *male gender identity* as a reference to "*all* that distinguishes males from females: including patterns of skills, occupation, dress and adornment, gestures, demeanor, emotional expression, erotic fantasies, and sexual behavior." As to the gender identity disturbance of homosexuals, Hooker reports that "for the majority of the individuals in my particular sample there is no apparent correspondence between a conscious sense of gender identity and a preferred or predominant role in

11. Green also refers to three "developmental phases" that constitute sexual identity: (1) core-morphologic identity; (2) gender role behavior; and (3) sexual partner orientation (Green, 1975).
12. Ehrhardt also raises this issue in her chapter in this volume.

sexual activity. Except for a small minority, the sexual pattern cannot be categorized in terms of a predominant role, and the consciousness of masculinity or femininity appears to bear no clear relation to particular sexual patterns" (Hooker, 1965).

The infant's developing sense of self as a boy or a girl is sometimes referred to as *core gender identity*. Stoller states, "By the time of the phallic stage an unalterable sense of gender identity— a core gender identity ("I am male," "I am female")—has already been established in the normal person" (Stoller, 1964). "Core gender identity is the sense of maleness or the sense of femaleness . . . a psychological state, a part of identity, it is not synonymous with belonging to one's sex, but rather with the conviction that one does so belong." Core gender identity is "produced" by three "components": external genital anatomy; infant-parent relationships; and a hypothetical "biological force" (Stoller, 1976).

Core has been used also to qualify one of the components of gender identity. Green refers to *core-morphologic identity* as "the individual's earliest self-awareness of being anatomically male or female . . ." (Green, 1974). In this volume, Luria also uses the word *core* to describe gender identity established in early childhood.

Disorders of gender identity have been particularly significant to the study of sexual identity since they manifest the possibility of a discrepancy between biological sex and the self-perception of the person as male or female.[13] Such disorders are of two general categories. First is hermaphroditism or intersexuality, in which there is a failure in sexual anatomical differentiation of varying degree. The second group is biologically normal, so far as can be determined, but gender identity is not congruous with biological sex. Hence, such individuals are referred to as having cross-gender identification or being transsexuals.

A more recent term is *gender dysphoria*, a descriptive entity for certain conditions that have as their common denominator the rejection of one's biological sex and a persistent desire to appear, act, think, and feel like a member of the opposite sex.

13. Early publications in this area go back several decades. See, for instance, Hampson, 1955; Hampson, Hampson, and Money, 1955; Hampson and Money, 1955. John Money's doctoral dissertation on hermaphroditism is dated 1952.

The term *dysphoria* (in contrast to *euphoria*) designates unhappiness with one's own biologically imposed sex. Since these persons are unhappy not with their gender but with the incongruity between it and their biological sex, once again we have a misnomer.

The gender dysphoria syndrome as a medical entity has gained importance because of the feasibility of radical sexual transformations through surgery, hormones, and reeducation (Laub and Gandy, 1973). Those who deal with such individuals face a problem of differential diagnosis. The distinctions they need to make are among (a) psychotics who have a delusion about being members of the opposite sex; (b) "effeminate" male and "masculine" female homosexuals; (c) transvestites; (d) cases of biological intersex; (e) transsexuals.

These conditions have also been categorized by Money as gender-role transposition where a "total" transposition occurs "episodically" in transvestism and "chronically" in transsexualism. A "partial" transposition characterizes bisexualism when episodic, and homosexualism when chronic. Such transposition can also be "optional," occurring in recreational role transpositions episodically, and in occupational role transpositions chronically (Money, 1973).

Sex and Gender Roles

Because the concepts are closely related, and given the currently promiscuous use of terms, a substantial number of topics discussed under *sexual* or *gender identity* could be found just as easily in the literature under *sex roles* or *gender roles*. While some authors have attempted to define *sex roles* with sufficient specificity, many more use the term broadly enough either to include or to be synonymous with *gender identity* and related terms. For example, an extensive research bibliography on sex roles compiled for the National Institute of Mental Health ranges over descriptive studies of measured or observed sex differences in personality characteristics, cognitive functioning, and the like; studies in the origin of sex differences and development of sex roles; studies concerning the manifestation of sex roles in the world of work, the family, and educational institutions; historical accounts of the relative status of the sexes in various cultures; the process of socialization and development of sex roles, and methodological issues and concerns for research in this area (Astin et al., 1975).

In the following discussion we shall rely on a somewhat restrictive view of what is meant by sex roles and emphasize those aspects that set this concept apart from gender identity, even though the two entities are closely related.

The Concept of Role

The term as well as the notion of *role* originated in the theater. The Latin word *rotula* means a small wooden roller. The parchment containing the actor's script was rolled around this rod and hence was referred to as the *roll* (or *rowle*). The actor's role is thus defined by the script to be re-enacted in the play. By extension of meaning, people can be said to play certain roles in life.[14] As in the case of the actor, the role concept makes it possible to distinguish a particular role, such as physician, from the individual's other personal positions in life, such as spouse or parent. Napoleon Bonaparte in the role of emperor is different, of course, from Marlon Brando in the role of Napoleon as emperor.

Each person in a social context holds multiple roles that vary both in their degree of stability over time and in the extent to which they mark or define the person's self-perception and public position. They also vary, of course, in their degree of congruence and along other dimensions.

The concept of role was introduced into the social sciences in the 1920s by George H. Mead and the University of Chicago sociologists. Since then the concept of role has been among the central concerns of sociology, social psychology, and cultural anthropology. It has provided a conceptual bridge linking individual behavior to social organization. The role concept figures prominently in Parsons' analyses of social systems, Linton's attempt to link culture and social structure, and Mead's theory of the development of the self. Role concepts have been put to many other uses also (Gross, Mason, and McEachern, 1958; Sarbin and Allen, 1954).

In view of the multiplicity of its uses, it is not surprising that the role concept has been subject to various interpretations and definitional ambiguities. Reviewers have repeatedly pointed this

14. The *Oxford English Dictionary* has a 1692 reference that reads, "The methods of Government and of humane society must be preserved, where every man has his roll and his station assigned him."

out. For example, Neiman and Hughes, who surveyed the literature between 1900 and 1950, noted the seemingly hopeless tangle
of definitions and usages (Nieman and Hughes, 1951). These
discrepancies in meaning have tended to discredit the usefulness
of the role concept for some (Borgatta, 1960). Others have taken
a more positive approach and tried to develop a more systematic
language for role analysis (see chapter 4 in Gross et al., *op. cit.*).

Sociologists define *role* in terms of an individual's "position,"
by which they mean the "location" of an "actor" or class of actors
in a system of social relationships. Such a position is independent
of any particular incumbent and entails a more or less explicit set
of responsibilities and prerogatives. A *role* is then the set of social
expectations as to how the incumbent of a given position should
behave toward incumbents of other positions. Roles are in this
sense another variety of norms or shared rules about behavior.

In the above sense, roles are clearly social expectations. While
this view seems to be held by most sociologists, there are some
who view it as descriptive of what a person actually does, rather
than of what one is expected to do. Among nonsociologists and
in ordinary parlance, the latter case would seem to be the prevalent usage. This distinction between behavior and social expectation could be maintained simply by foregoing the use of *role* in an
unqualified manner and instead referring to *role expectations,
role behavior,* or *role enactment,* depending on which meaning is
intended in a given case. The term *role playing* is perhaps best
avoided since it connotes an element of pretense or sham.

Simply stated, *sex roles* are those roles that are determined by
sex. One further distinction is between *biological sex roles,* which
refer to "feeling tones, behavior, and impulses (functionally or
historically dependent upon gonadal stimulation and social recognition as a sexually mature person)," and *social sex roles,* which
refer to the "differential functions, status, and personality traits
characterizing the two sexes in a particular cultural setting"
(Ausubel, 1958, p. 447).

Societies have various systems of division of labor, and sex
has been a consistent factor in determining the resultant social
differentiation and stratification. Linton wrote in 1936, "The
division and ascription of statuses with relation to sex seems to be
basic in all social systems. All societies prescribe different attitudes and activities to men and women." Social theorists, including Karl Marx and Herbert Spencer, have suggested that the

economic division of labor began with the division of tasks between the sexes. Anthropologists have amassed a vast literature on sex roles, and there has been a marked increase of interest in their study in recent years.[15]

The use of *sex roles* in relation to social roles is quite clear. But *sex role* is also used to refer to personality traits and to sex-determined behaviors outside of social roles. The term includes but is not restricted to erotic responses and interactions. In this sense, its relationship to gender identity needs to be clarified. Another source of ambiguity is the erotic content imputed to the various meanings of *sex roles*. For all apparent purposes, the term has no erotic connotation when referring to various occupational and similar social roles. At the other extreme there are the sex roles in sexual interactions. Such distinctions are meaningful up to a point.

Money concluded that sex-role typing encompasses "anything that is sexually dichotomized, like jobs, clothing, etiquette and recreation, irrespective of eroticism and the sex organs per se"— all of which constitutes a heavy burden for a single term. It was Money who introduced *gender role* "so as not to confuse the sex of the genitalia and their activities with nonerotic and nongenital sex roles and activities that are prescribed culturally and historically." The term *gender role* includes

> all those things that a person says or does to disclose himself or herself as having the status of boy or man, girl or woman, respectively. It includes, but is not restricted to sexuality in the sense of eroticism. Gender role is appraised in relation to the following: general mannerisms, deportment and demeanor; play preferences and recreational interests; spontaneous topics of talk in unprompted conversation and casual comment; content of dreams, daydreams and fantasies; replies to oblique inquiries and projective tests; evidence of erotic practices and, finally, the person's own replies to direct inquiry (Money, Hampson, and Hampson, 1955).

Through the use of such an all-inclusive term (which, however, still excluded some of the areas covered by *sex roles*), Money

15. One of the early classics in this field is Mead, 1935. Also see Mead, 1961. And for reviews of this literature see D'Andrade, 1966; Brown, 1976; Lipman-Blumen, 1975; and Astin et al., 1975.

hoped *gender role* would "unite what the observer perceives and records with what the person knows and feels about himself or herself." In this way, gender role would also subsume gender identity and there would be no need for two terms (Money, 1973). But as *gender identity* continued to be used in the literature, Money subsequently redefined *gender role* in a more restricted sense to reflect this persistent dichotomy. The two terms now came to represent the two sides of the coin of identity. One side is the Money and Ehrhardt definition of gender identity quoted earlier; the other side is the following definition of *gender role*:

> Everything that a person says and does, to indicate to others or to the self the degree that one is either male, or female, or ambivalent; it includes but is not restricted to sexual arousal and response; gender role is the public expression of gender identity, and gender identity is the private experience of gender role (Money and Ehrhardt, 1972).

The focus on behavior, rather than on social expectation, is in fact the more usual usage outside of the sociological literature. For example, Sears states:

> For purposes of measurement, a gender role must be reduced to precise forms of behavior, the presence or absence of which can be noted in an experimental or naturalistic setting (Sears, 1965).

This is only one instance in which the language of the sociology of sex roles differs from that of the psychology of sex roles. In psychological usage, *sex-typed behavior* is defined as "role behavior appropriate to a child's gender" and *sex-typing* as "the developmental process by which behavioral components of one or another gender role are established" (Sears, 1965). Walter Mischel views sex-typed behaviors in social-learning theory terms as "behaviors that typically elicit different rewards for one sex than for the other. In other words, sex-typed behaviors have consequences that vary according to the sex of the performer" (Mischel, 1966).

Sex-typing is an important term in the psychological literature.[16] What others mean by *gender identity* or *sex role* is often

16. The earliest reference to "cultural sex typing" in *Child Development* is found in a 1946 article by George Bach.

subsumed under *sex-typed behavior*. For example, the terms *gender identity* and *sex role* do not appear in the index of the extensive review of the psychology of sex differences by Maccoby and Jacklin, but a whole chapter on "sex-typing" deals with the issue of masculine/feminine patterns of behavior (Maccoby and Jacklin, 1974). Maccoby points out that she prefers to reserve the term *sex roles* for "the sociological definition of a set of behavioral expectations." Sex-typing is also discussed in detail by Mischel in *Carmichael's Manual of Child Psychology* (Mischel, 1970).

Sex-role behavior is the counterpart of *sex-role identity*. As Kagan puts it, "The concepts of sex role, sex-typing, and sex role identity are closely related" (Kagan, 1964). The exact differences among these terms remain obscure. Furthermore, the occurrence of *role* and *identity* in the same term causes confusion for those who want to separate these two entities.

Finally, a potential source of confusion is the term *stereotype*, as in "sex-role stereotype." In its original sense, the word refers to a printing plate that produces identical imprints. Its derived meaning then extends to anything indistinguished by individual characteristics. In biology, a stereotypic response is the unlearned behavioral reaction of an organism to an environmental stimulus. In more ordinary usage, stereotypes are preconceived expectations about characteristics and behaviors supposedly manifested by members of a given category. They are presuppositions that may be true for some but not for all. For example, if the view is held that the majority of women in the United States do not work outside the home, that would be a stereotype because the statement is not true. But the view that women are more heavily responsible than men for child care is true and therefore not a sex-role stereotype, although the disparity does not necessarily represent a desirable situation.

The pervasive influence of sex-role stereotypes has been pointed out repeatedly. Maccoby and Jacklin (1974) emphasize this influence in their evaluation of the sex differences literature. There have been attempts to focus on the deleterious effects of such sex stereotyping in psychotherapeutic practice (Broverman et al., 1970; American Psychological Association, 1975). To the extent that stereotypes foster half-truths and falsehoods, they are obviously undesirable. On the other hand, as Jeanne Block has pointed out, stereotypes "may have encoded also certain culturally discerned and repeatedly validated truths" (Block, 1976), and hence cannot be categorically dismissed as "myths." However one feels about them, stereotypes certainly have to be contended with, either as part of the truth or as contaminants of it.

References

American Psychological Association. 1975. Report of the task force on sex bias and sex-role stereotyping in psychotherapeutic practice. *Am. Psychol.* 30:1169–1175.

Astin, H. S., Parelman, A., and Fisher, A. 1975. *Sex roles: A research bibliography.* Rockville, Md.: National Institute of Mental Health.

Ausubel, D. P. 1958. *Theory and problems of child development.* New York: Grune and Stratton.

Bach, George R. 1946. Father-fantasies and father-typing in father-separated children. *Child Dev.* 17:63–80.

Beach, F. A. 1974. Human sexuality and evolution. In *Reproductive Behavior,* ed. W. Montagna and W. A. Sadler. New York: Plenum Press.

Bem, S. L. In press. Beyond androgyny: Some presumptuous prescriptions for a liberated sexual identity. In *Psychology of women: Future directions of research,* ed. J. Sherman and F. Denmark.

Berrill, N.J. 1976. Sex and sexuality. In *Encyclopaedia Britannica,* 15th ed.

Block, J. H. 1976. Issues, problems, and pitfalls in assessing sex differences: A critical review of *The psychology of sex differences. Merrill-Palmer Quart.* 22:283–308.

Borgatta, E. F. 1960. Role and reference group therapy. In *Social science theory and social work research,* ed. L. Logan. New York: National Association of Social Workers.

Broverman, I. K.; Broverman, D. M.; Clarkson, F. E.; Rosenkrantz, P. S.; and Vogel, S. 1970. Sex-role stereotypes and clinical judgments of mental health. *J. Consult. Clin. Psychol.* 34:1–7.

Brown, J. 1976. An anthropological perspective on sex roles and subsistence. In *Sex differences: Social and biological perspectives,* ed. M. S. Teitelbaum. New York: Anchor Books.

Cameron, Norman. 1950. Role concepts in behavior pathology. *Am. J. Sociol.* 55:464–467.

Carlson, R. 1972. Understanding women: Implications for personality theory and research. *J. Social Issues* 28:17–32.

Constantinople, A. 1973. Masculinity-femininity: An exception to a famous dictum? *Psychol. Bull.* 80:389–407.

Cox, S. 1976. *Female psychology: The emerging self.* Chicago: Science Research Associates.

D'Andrade, R. G. 1966. Sex differences and cultural institutions. In *The development of sex differences,* ed. E. E. Maccoby. Stanford: Stanford University Press.

Erikson, E. 1959. Identity and the life cycle. *Psychol. Issues,* no. 1.

_____. 1968a. Identity: Psychosocial. In *International encyclopedia of the social sciences,* ed. D. L. Sills. New York: Macmillan.

_____. 1968b. *Identity: Youth and crisis.* New York: W. W. Norton.

Federman, D. D. 1968. *Abnormal sexual development.* Philadelphia: W. B. Saunders.

Freud, S. 1957–1964. *The standard edition of the complete psychological works of Sigmund Freud,* ed. James Strachey. London: Hogarth Press.

Gagnon, J. 1977. *Human sexualities.* Glenview, Ill.: Scott, Foresman.

Goldstein, B. 1976. *Human sexuality.* New York: McGraw-Hill.

Green, R. 1974. *Sexual identity conflict in children and adults.* New York: Basic Books.

_____. 1975. Sexual identity: Research strategies. *Arch. Sex. Behav.* 4:337–352.

Gross, N.; Mason, W. S.; and McEachern, A. W. 1958. *Explorations in role analysis,* New York: Wiley.

Hall, C. S., and Lindzey, G. 1970. *Theories of personality,* 2d ed. New York: Wiley.

Hampson, J. G. 1955. Hermaphroditic appearance in hyperadrenocorticism. *Johns Hopkins Bull.* 96:265–273.

Hampson, J. L.; Hampson, J. G.; and Money, J. 1955. The syndrome of gonadal agenesis (ovarian agenesis) and male chromosomal pattern in girls and women: Psychologic studies. *Johns Hopkins Bull.* 97:43–53.

Hampson, J. G., and Money, J. 1955. Idiopathic sexual precocity. *Psychosom. Med.* 17:43–53.

Hooker, E. 1965. An empirical study of some relations between sexual patterns and gender identity in male homosexuals. In *Sex research: New developments,* ed. J. Money. New York: Holt, Rinehart and Winston.

James, W. 1892. *Psychology.* New York: Henry Holt.

Johnson, W. B., and Terman, L. H. 1940. Some highlights in the literature of psychological sex differences. *J. Psychol.* 9:327–336.

Jung. C. G. 1953. *Two essays on analytical psychology,* trans. R. F. C. Hull. New York: Pantheon Books.

Jung, E. 1969. *Animus and Anima.* New York: Springer.

Kagan, J. 1964. Acquisition and significance of sex typing and sex role identity. In *Review of child development research,* vol. 1, ed. M. L. Hoffman and L. W. Hoffman. New York: Russell Sage Foundation.

Katchadourian, H., and Lunde, D. 1975. *Fundamentals of human sexuality,* 2d ed. New York: Holt, Rinehart and Winston.

Laub, D. R., and Gandy, P., eds. 1973. *Proceedings of the second inter-*

disciplinary symposium on gender dysphoria syndrome. Stanford: Division of Plastic Surgery.

Levin, H., and Sears, R. 1956. Identification with parents as a determinant of doll play aggression. *Child Dev.* 27:135–153.

Lief, H. I. 1976. Introduction to sexuality. In *The sexual experience,* ed. B. J. Sadock, H. I. Kaplan, and A. M. Freedman. Baltimore: Wilkins and Wilkins.

Linton, R. 1936. Status and role. In *The study of man.* New York: Appleton-Century-Crofts.

Lipman-Blumen, J. 1975. Changing sex roles in American culture: Future directions for research. *Arch. Sex. Behav.* 4:433–446.

Maccoby, E. E., and Jacklin, C. N. 1974. *The psychology of sex differences.* Stanford: Stanford University Press.

McCary, J. 1973. *Human sexuality,* 2d ed. New York: Van Nostrand.

Mead, G. 1934. *Mind, self, and society.* Chicago: University of Chicago Press.

Mead, M. 1935. *Sex and temperament in three primitive societies.* New York: Morrow.

————. 1961. Cultural determinants of sexual behavior. In *Sex and internal secretions,* 3d ed., vol. 2, ed. W. C. Young. Baltimore: Wilkins and Wilkins.

Mischel, W. 1966. A social learning view of sex difference in behavior. In *The development of sex differences,* ed. E. E. Maccoby. Stanford: Stanford University Press.

————. 1970. Sex-typing and socialization. In *Carmichael's manual of child psychology,* vol. 2, ed. P. H. Mussen. New York: Wiley.

Money, J. 1965. Psychosexual differentiation. In *Sex research: New developments.* New York: Holt, Rinehart and Winston.

————.1973. Gender role, gender identity, core gender identity: Usage and definition of terms. *J. Am. Acad. Psychoanal.* 1:397–403.

Money, J., and Ehrhardt, A. 1972. *Man and woman, boy and girl.* Baltimore: Johns Hopkins Press.

Money, J.; Hampson, J. G.; and Hampson, J. L. 1955. An examination of some basic sexual concepts: The evidence of human hermaphroditism. *Johns Hopkins Bull.* 97:301–319.

Morris, J. 1974. *Conundrum.* New York: Harcourt Brace Jovanovich.

Nieman, J. N., and Hughes, J. W. 1951. The problem of the concept of role: A re-survey of the literature. *Soc. Forces* 30:141–149.

Noss, J. B. 1963. *Man's religions,* 3d ed. New York: Macmillan.

Oakley, A. 1972. *Sex, gender and society.* London: Temple, Smith.

Parsons, T. 1951. *The social system.* Glencoe, Ill.: Free Press.

Perry, J., ed. 1975. *Personal identity.* Berkeley: University of California Press.

Sarbin, T. R., and Allen, V. L. 1954. Role theory. In *The handbook of social psychology,* 2d ed., ed. G. Lindzey and E. Aronson. Reading, Mass.: Addison-Wesley.

Scott, W. R. 1970. *Social processes and social structures.* New York: Holt, Rinehart and Winston.

Sears, R. R. 1965. Development of gender role. In *Sex and behavior,* ed. F. A. Beach. New York: Wiley.

Stoller, R. J. 1964. A contribution to the study of gender identity. In *The sexual experience,* ed. B. J. Sadock, H. I. Kaplan, and A. M. Freedman. Baltimore: Wilkins and Wilkins.

_____. 1968. *Sex and gender.* New York: Science House.

_____. 1972. The 'bedrock' of masculinity and femininity: Bisexuality. *Arch. Gen. Psychiatry* 26:207–212.

_____. 1974. Facts and fancies: An examination of Freud's concept of bisexuality. In *Women and analysis,* ed. J. Strouse. New York: Dell.

_____. 1976. Gender identity. In *The sexual experience,* ed. B. J. Sadock, H. I. Kaplan, and A. M. Freedman. Baltimore: Wilkins and Wilkins.

Terman, L. M., and Miles, Catherine. 1936. Sex and personality: Studies in masculinity and femininity, 1st ed. New York: McGraw-Hill.

Thompson, L. G. 1969. *Chinese religion: An introduction.* Belmont, Calif.: Dickinson.

Analyses of Human Sexual Behavior

Herant A. Katchadourian and John A. Martin

One of the more serious handicaps facing the scientific study of sex is the lack of consensus among researchers in providing a clear and concise statement as to what, precisely, constitutes sexual behavior. Conceptualizations of sexuality have ranged from the more or less narrow viewpoint that sex is made up of a set of specific and observable forms of physical activity to the broad notion of an erotically charged cosmos as in the writings of Wilhelm Reich. Perhaps the clearest contrast is between Freud's broad concept of the libido, a psychological entity that defies behavioral operationalization, and Kinsey's contention that orgasm, a physiological entity, is the most reliable yardstick with which sexual behavior can be measured.

Sex is complex, but so are most forms of human and animal behavior. In recent years there has been a substantial move in the behavioral sciences to clarify complex behavioral phenomena in order to facilitate empirical investigation. Assumptions about the behavioral phenomena in question are clearly laid out and formalized, then simplified so that only the most essential characteristics of these complex processes are preserved. We shall attempt clarification here by suggesting that the essential components of human sexuality can be characterized rather simply and illustrated schematically. We do not, of course, wish to pretend or imply that the imposition of this sort of conceptual framework or model is tantamount to a thorough understanding of the "essence" of sexuality in any profound philosophical sense.

For our immediate purposes, we shall define *behavior* as any clearly discernible activity of an organism or individual, including

The authors wish to thank Dr. Helena C. Kraemer for her comments and suggestions on an earlier draft of this paper.

both that which can be observed and verbal reports regarding subjective states and experiences. We assume that whenever behavior has a conscious erotic component in the form of a psychological state of arousal, with or without physiological concomitants, then such behavior is defined as "sexual." This definition is admittedly fragile, but to aspire to anything more decisive will only hopelessly distract us.

As a general conceptual model, it may be possible to summarize the essential characteristics of the organization of a given person's sexual behavior at a particular period in that individual's life with two bits of information: the "direction" of sexual striving and the "magnitude" of such behavior. We suggest, in addition, that both direction and magnitude can be scaled so as to yield continuous variables, x and y, respectively. It should then be possible to represent variability in sexual organization on a standard Cartesian coordinate plane as ordered pairs (x, y), so that each ordered pair represents the intersection of a particular value for direction and a particular value for magnitude.

Direction of Sexual Striving

Let us suppose that we were to compile a list of all the possible characteristics of all possible objects of sexual striving. Suppose, in addition, that we were to construct a geometric form so that each characteristic is represented by one of the dimensions that make up the form. If our list were complete, it would be possible, at least in theory, to characterize each possible sexual object as a point somewhere within the form. Points near one another in this multidimensional space would, thus, represent objects that are similar to one another along at least some of the dimensions. The notion of direction, as we use it here, rests on the assumption that there is a certain degree of homogeneity in the preferred attributes of any given individual's sexual choices. Thus, we assume that, for any given individual, the bulk of his or her sexual striving is *directed*, as it were, toward a particular cluster of objects in this multidimensional space—that is, toward objects that are similar to one another along one or more critical dimensions. The *direction* of sexual striving is meant to refer to that vector of sexual interest.

The number of possible characteristics of sexual objects is obviously very large. Although we want to avoid the temptation to posit dichotomies, it is simplest to think of these characteristics as occurring in contrasting pairs. Some of these pairs represent vast differences: for example, whether the object is living or non-living, human or nonhuman. Others are relatively trivial, such as plump or slim, dark or light. The specification of these dimensions is subject to both theoretical analysis and empirical investigation; and some dimensions, of course, are more salient than others. The writings of Havelock Ellis, Sigmund Freud, Harry Stack Sullivan, and Alfred Kinsey provide some idea of what the most important dimensions might be.

Perhaps at the most fundamental level, the distinction should be made whether the sexual impulse is aimed "inward" or is directed "outward." The term *autoerotic* was coined by Ellis, who meant by it ". . . the phenomenon of spontaneous sexual emotion generated in the absence of an external stimulus proceeding, directly or indirectly, from another person" (Ellis, 1905, vol. 1, p. 161). The basis of autoeroticism for Ellis was therefore the *origin* of the sexual impulse and its spontaneous generation in the absence of an external stimulus proceeding from another person, rather than the nature of the resultant sexual expression.

The more common understanding of the same term focuses on the mode of sexual expression, rather than on the origin of the sexual impulse. Thus, whatever the source of arousal, activities like sexual fantasy, nocturnal orgasm, and masturbation are considered to be autoerotic since they involve no actual interaction with another person. To further emphasize this distinction, Kinsey coined the term *sociosexual* to characterize sexual activities like petting, coitus, and homosexual relations that entail human interactions and "must depend upon some confluence of the capacities, interests, and desires of individuals, and on the willingness of each to adjust to the other" (Kinsey, 1953, p. 250).

The distinction between autoerotic and sociosexual "direction" of the sexual impulse has a certain face validity but becomes ambiguous if pressed further. Suppose several adolescents masturbate together in a group. Does this act entail a significant sociosexual component, even though the individuals are not touching each other? Or, when a person is absorbed in sexual fantasies extraneous to the coital act in which he or she is simultaneously engaged, is the coital act any less autoerotic than masturbation with an inanimate object?

In view of such considerations, it may be more realistic to think of sexual activities as variable mixes along a continuum of auto-eroticism and sociosexuality rather than as polar opposites. In this sense every sexual behavior may be thought of as a composite of "self" components and an interpersonal dimension. The latter may be at the level of fantasy, but it is by no means less "real" or significant. The distinction between autoeroticism and socio-sexuality should not be entirely disregarded, however. The model of a continuum still presupposes the existence of extremes: An episode of masturbation with the predominant motive of sexual release with little or no erotic imagery still remains in sharp contrast to an act of sexual intercourse between lovers who become so absorbed in each other that they "lose" themselves during the act.

The concept of direction of sexual impulse plays an even more elaborate role in Freud's formulations. For Freud, direction has two components: choice of sexual object and choice of sexual aim. All sexual behaviors necessarily reflect these two choices, which thus constitute the bases of Freud's classification of sexual behaviors (Freud, 1905).

Freud's sexual paradigm for normal adult sexual expression was heterosexual intercourse in which the object choice is an adult of the opposite sex (who is not a close relative) and the sexual aim is coitus. Deviations from this norm would involve aberrant choices of object or of means. In the first instance, the alternative object could be an adult of the same sex (homosexuality), a child (pedophilia), a close relative (incest), animals (zoophilia), inanimate objects (fetishism), or a dead body (necrophilia). In the second category of deviant aims, instead of seeking to engage in coitus the individual might prefer to watch others in erotic contexts (voyeurism), expose himself (exhibitionism), inflict pain (sadism), or suffer from it (masochism). When choice of both object and aim are deviant, the former would define the deviation.

Kinsey found such distinctions untenable when used to characterize persons rather than behaviors. Thus, one can clearly label a given act as heterosexual or homosexual depending upon the sex of the partners. But to call individuals one or the other was not nearly so meaningful to Kinsey because he found homosexual and heterosexual behaviors to coexist in a significant segment of the population. Kinsey therefore offered a seven-category heterosexual-homosexual rating scale ranging from group 0, consisting of persons with exclusively heterosexual expressions, to group 6 with exclusively homosexual histories (Kinsey, 1948).

Kinsey's report that only half of all males could be subsumed under group 0 raised an uproar, but neither that issue nor the validity of Kinsey's survey findings concerns us here. More pertinent is his suggestion that it is reasonable to construct a continuum among normal individuals along the heterosexual-homosexual directions of object choice. Pomeroy considers the heterosexual-homosexual rating scale among Kinsey's major contributions (Pomeroy, 1972). To Robinson the scale was "arguably the most pathetic manifestation of Kinsey's philosophical naivete," since from a theoretical standpoint a seven-way breakdown and a three-way breakdown (heterosexual, bisexual, homosexual) do not differ significantly. The presumption in both cases is that "at some point differences of degree become differences in kind" (Robinson, 1976, pp. 73–74). Kinsey's definition of sexual behavior was strictly behaviorist. For Kinsey, sexual identity is embodied in the nature and magnitude of the components of the person's various physical and sociosexual acts. This view disregards the feasibility that the gestalt of a person's sexuality might involve more than the sum of his actions. It also runs counter to the Freudian view that one may be "latently" homosexual without ever having committed a homosexual act.

Kinsey's decision to label acts rather than people can have a salutary effect in that labels tend to stereotype and dehumanize people. But this does not resolve the issue of sexual identity. Kinsey's heterosexual-homosexual scales can all too easily be reduced to three categories applicable to people: heterosexual, bisexual, homosexual, as was suggested above. Thus, sooner or later one must confront the issue of what defines a person sexually in a holistic, integrative sense. Paul Robinson, in raising many of the above considerations regarding Kinsey's position, compares Kinsey's views to the radical empiricism of David Hume: "Just as Hume had dissolved the self into a series of discrete moments of consciousness, Kinsey dissolved sexual identity into a series of discrete orgasms" (Robinson, 1976, p. 68).

Harry Stack Sullivan also employs the notion of a continuum in his theorizing on human sexuality, and his continuum may be thought of as an extended version of Kinsey's (Sullivan, 1953). Sullivan uses the term *intimacy need*, which is comparable to the concept of *direction*. He suggests that the manifestation of intimacy, in its integration with lust, can be categorized in terms of the distance from oneself of the preferred partner in interpersonal intimacy. Sullivan's continuum assumes that the individual progresses through specific childhood, preadolescent, and adolescent developmental phases en route to the sexual identity of adulthood. The *autophilic* individual has, for whatever reason, never fully assimilated the vicissitudes of the preadolescent phase, and thus, if he has a capacity for intimacy or arousal at all, the object of intimacy/arousal is concentrated within himself, or his personification of himself. The *isophilic* has passed through the preadolescent phase, but has not gone beyond it and therefore chooses as objects members of his own sex. The *heterophilic* has passed through preadolescence into the critical early adolescent phase, and thus chooses as an object that sort of person most essentially different from one's self, a member of the opposite sex. Whether or not passage from the autophilic to the isophilic to the heterophilic is tied, as Sullivan suggests, to psychological development from childhood to early adolescence, Sullivan's typology is of interest for the purpose of defining the dimension of direction.

Magnitude of Sexual Experience

Common observation and experience indicate that people vary among themselves and at different times in their lives in the "amount" of sexual behavior they manifest. Such variation presumably reflects the availability of opportunities as well as differences in the level of need, or motivational force. The notion of magnitude, while simple on the surface, is nevertheless rather difficult to pin down. The amount of sexual behavior, within a given direction of striving, seems easy enough to understand as a generality. But in specific terms, what constitutes amount? Frequency to orgasm? Frequency of contact? Number of partners? Degree of fantasizing? Intensity of arousal? All of these seem important.

In more formal terms, the same notions are readily discernible in the thinking of sexual theorists. Freud's concept of the libido has a fluid yet quantitative aspect to it whether viewed in biological terms or as a metaphor for psychological events. The libido fits a "hydraulic" model subject to shifts and transfers.

The difficulty in dealing with Freud's model of sexuality in quantitative terms is that he failed to define explicitly a "unit" of sexual behavior that could be counted. Kinsey tried to remedy this omission by taking orgasm as the unit and therefore being able to count behaviors that led to this discrete, discernible event. To describe how much sex a person was having, Kinsey combined all activities that led to orgasm over a given period of time and viewed them as that person's "total sexual outlet." As Kinsey was well aware, this approach leaves out countless manifestations of sexuality that do not culminate in orgasm, or even physical contact. Yet Freud's conception of the libido is so diffusely pervasive that it is impossible to quantify even in hypothetical terms. The dimension of magnitude is admittedly problematic, but the general notion of *amount* of sexual behavior nevertheless asserts itself with at least some common-sense validity.

Representation of the Model

When the dimensions of direction and magnitude are used to characterize human sexual organization, much of the complexity and richness of human sexual experience is drastically simplified and perhaps even, in some ways, trivialized. The model could, of course, have included three dimensions or thirty. In choosing to limit the model to these two dimensions only, we have made a number of implicit assumptions regarding the nature of human sexual experience.

Previous theory and research in human sexuality has, as suggested above, overwhelmingly indicated that direction and magnitude are crucial. No other descriptive dimensions of human sexuality have been afforded such uniformly concentrated attention in the scientific and theoretical literature. Yet, inasmuch as no explicit arguments exist, to our knowledge, that these two dimensions are, in fact, the critical dimensions of human sexuality, the validity of the model, the extent to which it reliably distinguishes individuals from one another, and the extent to which the two-number summary covaries with other variables of psychological interest in a predictable fashion are all subject to

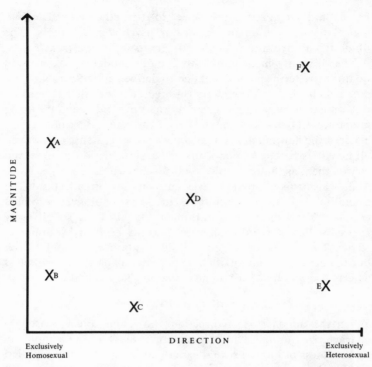

Fig. 1. Schematic diagram of the scores of 5 hypothetical individuals on the dimensions of Direction and Magnitude.

empirical investigation. Our contention is simply that previous theory and research do, in fact, indicate that direction and magnitude constitute, on at least a rudimentary level, necessary and irreducible dimensions for the characterization of a given individual's sex organization.

As previously indicated, the model naturally lends itself to schematic representation. In the above diagram, the x axis (horizontal) represents direction, and the y axis (vertical) represents magnitude. The labelled points may be thought of as scores of persons measured at similar ages. The diagram allows comparisons between different persons in both dimensions. Thus, one can readily see that A and B are nearly exclusively homosexual in organization, but A has a higher magnitude of sexual behavior. D is near the midpoint in direction, but has a higher

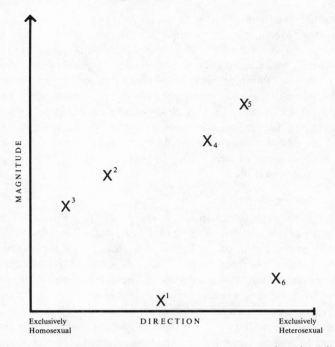

Fig. 2. An alternative version of the model, representing six points in the life of one hypothetical individual.

outlet than E, who is almost exclusively heterosexual. Comparisons of *exogenous* variables of interest would thus be possible between subsets of individuals by direction (A and B as opposed to E and F) or by magnitude (B, C, and E as against A, D, and F).

Alternatively, the developmental course of the organization of a given person's sexual behavior can be charted by introducing a third dimension, z, of time. Time is only one of many possible extensions of the model; particular extensions are indicated by the nature of the problem being investigated. For this particular example, the model provides ordered triples (x, y, z), with z being an index of the individual's stage in life, or age. Three-dimensional graphs are, of course, difficult both to draw in two dimensions and to visualize. However, the three-dimensional version of the model can be represented two-dimensionally if we consider only one person at a time. Figure 2 represents six points in a hypothetical individual's life. At the earliest point (labelled "1"), he is rather low in magnitude and near the middle of the scale in direction. At points 2 and 3, he becomes increasingly homosexual in direction, and the magnitude of behavior surges and then dips again slightly. Points 4 and 5 are characterized by steady increases in magnitude and movement toward heterosexuality. The final point (point 6) is slightly closer to the heterosexual end of the direction dimension, but magnitude of behavior has reduced drastically. With enough data, additional details could be used to provide a more or less complete picture of the course of an individual's sexual life.

The Value of the Model

What has been proposed thus far is a purely descriptive model of the organization of human sexual behavior. This sort of descriptive model can be useful in and of itself in terms of providing a theoretical anchor for discussions of sexual behavior insofar as its heuristic value and generality can be agreed upon. The real value of the present model, however, lies in its applicability to empirical problems.

Consider the following example: Suppose a researcher is interested in identifying a set of variables relevant to the *development* of sexual behavior. This problem could then be defined as a prediction problem in which an attempt is being made to specify a set of developmental predictors for the dependent variable (x,y). Suppose the researcher decided in advance that all possible predictors could be organized into five categories consisting of two crossed bipolar dimensions (making four categories), and a fifth category that is derivative of the previous four.

The first dimension might involve the distinction between variables and constants—that is, between predictors that are both more or less universal aspects of human development and also more or less universally contribute to the development of sexual behavior, and those predictors that vary considerably among individuals. The presence of a penis in the male is a good example of a constant. The size of the penis is a good example of a variable, inasmuch as genital size varies among individuals, as does the extent to which sexual development is affected by such variation".

The second dimension might distinguish those variables and constants that are fundamentally biological from those that are psychosocial in nature. As the presence of a penis in the male is a biological constant, and the size of the penis is a biological variable, likewise the fact of being reared by an adult is a psychosocial constant, but the particular sexual attitudes and degree of tolerance of the adult or adults responsible for an individual's rearing is a psychosocial variable.

The final category of predictors is exemplified by sex role and gender identity—predictors that affect the organization of sexual behavior both directly and indirectly. The effect is direct in the same sense as variables in the first four categories of predictors developmentally affect sexual organization in a direct manner, and *indirect* in the sense that these predictors are themselves *predictable* by some of the predictors in the first four categories. These predictors, then, ought to be afforded particular attention in the research that grows out of this hypothesized developmental model. Sex role and gender identity are, of course, only two examples of predictors in this fifth category: a number of other predictors might take the same role in the model.

In the present example, then, the dynamic model may be pictorially represented by Figure 3. Note that the role of gender identity and sex roles in the model is illustrated in that the boxes labelled "biological and psychosocial constants and variables" lead into the box labelled "(x,y)" by way of the boxes labelled "Sex Role/Gender Identity." Note also that the diagram allows for the possibility that the system may operate differently for the two sexes. Given sufficient data, the researcher could reasonably employ multiple regression techniques to identify which predictors of those chosen to study, when combined with one another, contribute significantly to the development of the organization of sexual behavior.

Variants of the suggested model could also be investigated. Clearly, in order to complete Figure 3, another set of arrows leading from the box labelled "(x,y)" to the boxes labelled "Sex Role/Gender Identity" would have to be included in order to reflect the feedback between the two. Formidable logical and methodological problems are introduced by assuming a nonrecursive model—that is, a model in which causation is bi-directional (Duncan, 1975)—but these problems are by no means insurmountable.

The point we wish to make here is a simple one. Given an

45

Herant A. Katchadourian and John A. Martin

The Organization of Sexual Behavior

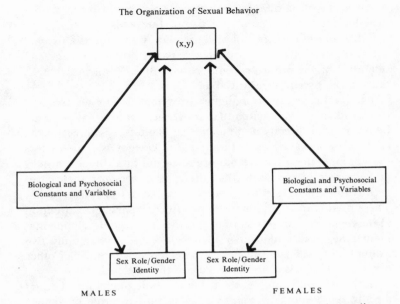

Fig. 3. A pictoral representation of the relationship between the predictors.

appropriate empirical realization of the model, it can be employed in a variety of specific contexts to answer an infinite variety of specific questions about human sexuality.

At this point, we should re-emphasize something we said at the beginning of this paper. We do not wish to imply that we have, with our model, encapsulated all that needs to be said about human sexual behavior. Sexuality is clearly an aspect of human experience too rich, too complex, and too varied to elucidate at one sitting. Like the shadows in Plato's cave, direction and magnitude can, potentially, tell us a great deal about sexual behavior, but fall short of telling us *everything* about sexual behavior because, simply, they are not the *reality* of sexual behavior. But as long as we are, as behavioral scientists, chained so that our vision is limited to the world of shadows, we must settle for whatever our limited vision can tell us until something better comes along.

There are many precedents in a wide variety of fields for highly simplified summaries of complex processes. The simple two-number characterization of heart function by "blood pressure" is perhaps one of the best known.[1] While the simple summary of systolic/diastolic blood pressure can by no means be considered an adequate representation of cardiovascular function, it tells us a great deal about the heart and about the person whose heart function has been so summarized. Thus, this relatively simple model and the extremely simple measurement technique developed to implement the model have proven to be valuable diagnostic and research tools. Similarly, although IQ fails to *define* intelligence or cognitive functioning in any profound sense, the single number that is the standardized score on an IQ test has provided educators and researchers a powerful means of predicting certain aspects of cognitive capacity and achievement. Both blood pressure and IQ are used extensively, and both are based on a relatively small number of simplifying assumptions about the nature of the underlying processes they attempt to model.

And both served their purposes well until more refined models and more precise techniques came along. The electrocardiogram provides a great deal more information about the heart than does simple blood pressure; likewise, the expanded battery of tests currently used in psychological testing centers provides a clearer and more concrete, culture-free measure of cognitive functioning than does the simple IQ test. Nevertheless, even with EKG and intelligence-test batteries, blood pressure and IQ are still quite useful in many contexts, and are still widely used. Our model of sexual behavior will undoubtedly fall somewhat short of the distinguished careers of blood pressure and IQ, but perhaps, like blood pressure and IQ, our model will serve some purpose until something better comes along.

References

Duncan, Otis D. 1975. *Introduction to structural equation models.* New York, Academic Press.

Ellis, Havelock. 1905. *Studies in the psychology of sex.* vol. 1. Philadelphia: F. A. Davis.

Freud, Sigmund. 1964. Three essays on the theory of sexuality (originally published in 1905). In *The standard edition of the complete*

1. There are, of course, many functional distinctions between the two models, the main one being that *diastolic* and *systolic* are not meant to be orthogonal dimensions as are *direction* and *magnitude*.

psychological works of Sigmund Freud. vol. 7, ed. J. Strachey. London: Hogarth Press.

Kinsey, Alfred C.; Pomeroy, Wardell B.; and Martin, Clyde E. 1948. *Sexual behavior in the human male.* Philadelphia: Saunders.

Kinsey, Alfred C.; Pomeroy, Wardell B.; Martin, Clyde E.; and Gebhardt, Paul H. 1953. *Sexual behavior in the human female.* Philadelphia: Saunders.

Pomeroy, W. B. 1972. *Dr. Kinsey and the Institute for Sex Research.* New York: Harper and Row.

Robinson, Paul A. 1976. *The modernization of sex.* New York: Harper and Row.

Sullivan, H. S. 1953. *The interpersonal theory of psychiatry.* New York: Norton.

Part I
Evolutionary Perspectives

There has been a remarkable upsurge of interest in recent years in the evolution of human behavior. In addition to biologists and anthropologists, virtually all students of human behavior and culture perceive a need for an evolutionary perspective in all comprehensive attempts at the exploration of human nature. The issue is not an arcane and esoteric academic concern. A better understanding of how we came to be who we are today can have a vital bearing on our understanding of how we behave and how best to manage our individual and communal lives.

Such concerns are especially significant to the realm of sexuality in general and gender identity and sex roles in particular. Claims of modernity and sexual revolutions notwithstanding, patterns of behavior in these areas have ancient roots indeed.

So, in order to begin at the beginning, the first part of this volume focuses on the evolutionary perspective. The central emphasis here is not on how individual humans behave, but rather on what we can learn about the phylogenesis of human sexuality by examining the behaviors of our closest contemporary primate relatives.

Jane Lancaster, the author of the primary paper, is an anthropologist who has specialized in the study of nonhuman primates. She introduces her contribution with an examination of the biases that distorted earlier views of the roles played by males and females in social organization and mating. The major areas she examines are those of orgasm in the female primate, cyclicity of primate sexuality, and the relationship of dominance to reproductive success. Her conclusions, derived from a review of more recent findings, shed new light on primate sexual behavioral patterns, which turn out to be more varied and extensive than mere coital activity between adults for reproductive ends. Sexuality seems to be a prominent feature of social interaction among nonhuman primates, as it is among humans. In these interactions, females emerge as more autonomous and sexually active than previously assumed: It is both sexes, not just males, that actively seek mating partners, consummatory responses, and sexual attachments. Even though much of the evidence is still fragmentary, it is possible to see the roots of human sexual behavior going farther back than has been appreciated.

In his response to Jane Lancaster's contribution, Richard Alexander views the issues from the perspective of an evolutionary biologist. He concurs that primate female sexuality is more complex, and female choice a more important factor in determining sexual and social behavior, than generally acknowledged. But Alexander also offers alternative interpretations to some of Lancaster's conclusions on functions of orgasm, male dominance, sex as an integrative mechanism, and incest avoidance. His discussion makes a careful distinction between the functions of "proximate mechanisms" (such as pleasure and pain) and the "ultimate function" of reproduction.

Frank Beach approaches these issues from yet another perspective—that of the comparative psychologist. His perspective is also that of a distinguished investigator of sexuality over a span of some four decades. There is, therefore, much wisdom in his comments on the use and abuse of animal models for understanding human behavior. For Beach, the cardinal rule is that intraspecific analysis must precede interspecific generalizations, and intraspecific analysis itself presupposes understanding of causes and consequences as well as external patterns of response. It is within this framework that he responds to the issues raised by Lancaster and Alexander.—H. A. K.

Sex and Gender in Evolutionary Perspective

Jane B. Lancaster

Many biologically oriented scientists attempt to make use of existing knowledge about the biology and behavior of nonhuman primates in an effort to understand the evolutionary background of human behavior. This information has been considered especially useful in the analysis of the evolution of human sexual behavior and sex roles, both in respect to similarities and continuities between animal and human behavior and in respect to presumed major adaptations that set humans apart from other species. The following quotations, drawn from recent summaries in the fields of psychology, psychiatry, anthropology, and biology, illustrate the kinds of interests in and uses of primate behavioral data in the current literature on the evolution of human behavior patterns:

> Primatological, ethnographic, and psychiatric data suggest the hypothesis that male dominance facilitates male-female copulatory behavior while female dominance inhibits it (Abernethy, 1974, p. 813).
>
> ... the weight of available evidence favors the theory that female orgasm is a characteristic essentially restricted to our own species (Beach, 1974, p. 359).
>
> All we need to assume is that the breeding system of the more successful populations was competitive and hierarchical. The

I am most grateful to the following people for their helpful comments and criticisms on early stages of this manuscript: Lyn Bromley, Frances Burton, Suzanne Chevalier-Skolnikoff, Glenn Hausfater, Chet Lancaster, Thelma Rowell, Don Symons, S. L. Washburn, and Adrienne Zihlman.

relevance of the primate data lies not so much in the models of our early social organization that it provides, as in the information it gives us on the primate biogram, many aspects of which we are heir to (Fox, 1972, p. 305).

The human pattern of reproduction does not resemble reproduction of any other primate. The human system is characterized by the absence of estrous cycles in the female and of the marked seasonal variations that appear to characterize reproduction in nonhuman primates. . . . The important similarities in the social lives of higher primates, such as living in year-round bisexual groups, cannot be attributed to nonexistent similarities in mating systems (Lancaster and Lee, 1965, p. 513).

In the language of sociobiology, to dominate is to possess priority of access to the necessities of life and reproduction. This is not a circular definition; it is a statement of a strong correlation observed in nature. With rare exceptions, the aggressively superior animal displaces the subordinate from food, from mates, and from nest sites. It only remains to be established that this power actually raises the genetic fitness of the animals possessing it. On this point the evidence is completely clear (Wilson, 1975, p. 287).

The reproductive advantages conferred by dominance are preserved even in the most complex societies (Wilson, 1975, p. 288).

These summaries, written in the late 1960s and early 1970s, are largely based on data developed during the 1960s in the first round of field studies on the behavior of free-ranging primates. The remarkable aspect of all the above summaries is that they are already out of date. Primatology is a fast-moving field, and early field studies suffered major biases resulting from inadequacies in sampling technique, selection of study groups, and duration of fieldwork, which distorted observations of many categories of behavior and especially those related to the roles played by both sexes in the social organization of the group and the roles played by individuals in the mating system (J. Altmann, 1974; Bernstein, 1976; Sade, 1972; Wrangham, 1974).

This chapter summarizes recent data mostly drawn from long-term field studies and developed using careful techniques of sampling the behavior of all individuals in a social system. These new data have important implications for the understanding of the role of sexual behavior in integrating primate societies, the importance of orgasm in female primate sexual behavior, the roles played by dominance and personal preference in mate selection in primate societies, and the question of avoidance of incestuous matings. The final section of the chapter discusses implications for the evolution of human sexual behavior.

Orgasm in the Female Primate

Considering that sexual orgasm in the human female was thought by many to be either a myth or an aberration and was poorly understood even by physiologists before the pioneer publication of *Human Sexual Response* by Masters and Johnson (1966), it is not surprising that little was known about the sexual responses of nonhuman female primates. In the first publication on the subject Zumpe and Michael (1968) reported their observations of the clutching reaction of female rhesus monkeys, which occurs during the ejaculatory mount of the male, most often immediately preceding ejaculation. The clutching reaction (a spasmodic arm reflex) is associated with other female responses including looking backward and lipsmacking at the moment of ejaculation, reaching back and biting, or postejaculatory pelvic flexions. Frame-by-frame analysis of 16:mm film showed that the onset of the clutching reaction occurred while the male was still thrusting and that it seemed to trigger the male's ejaculatory spasm.

In further experimental work the clutching reaction was depressed by ovariectomy or progesterone treatment but restored by estrogen. In females with regular access to males, the clutching reaction invariably occurred during the ejaculatory mount, but in females denied access to a male for many weeks, the clutching reaction occurred early in the mounting series before the male was ready to ejaculate. Zumpe and Michael found that of a total of 389 ejaculations experienced by three nonpregnant females, 97 percent were associated with the clutching reaction.

A few years later Burton (1971) described sexual climax in female rhesus monkeys brought to orgasm through stimulation of the clitoris and vagina with a simulated penis. Burton reported observable changes associated with the female rhesus sexual response that appear similar to those described by Masters and Johnson for the human female: an excitement phase, a plateau phase, sexual climax as evidenced by behavior patterns such as the clutching reaction, low-pitched grunting, rhythmic contractions of the vagina, and a resolution phase.

More recent descriptions by Chevalier-Skolnikoff (1971) and Michael, Wilson, and Zumpe (1974) on sexual behavior of captive macaques report female orgasmic responses that are not dependent on vaginal penetration. Chevalier-Skolnikoff (1971) reported that in homosexual copulations between female stumptail macaques, the mounting female performed about the same number of thrusts as males generally made in heterosexual copulations and on a number of occasions displayed all the behavioral manifestations observed in males during orgasm: a pause after a series of thrusts, muscular body spasms accompanied by a rhythmic, voiced expiration, and a characteristic facial expression. Michael, Wilson, and Zumpe (1974) noted similar behavior in heterosexual copulations of rhesus in which the female played the mounting role and rhythmically thrust her pelvic region along her male partner's back. A small number of these episodes appeared to result in sexual climax for the female.

The authors were particularly impressed by the fact that these malelike patterns of mounting, thrusting, and orgasm were so complete in wild-reared females in spite of the fact that the rate of rehearsal in play behavior is probably low (less than 1 percent the rate of males as measured in caged situations). They also noted that the highest frequency of this behavior was correlated with estrus, occurred only in older, more confident females, and was often associated with failure in male performance. Hanby, Robertson, and Phoenix (1971) reported similar instances of females mounting their male sexual partners in a captive group of feral Japanese macaques. In these cases too, the females involved were mature and sexually experienced, but the authors do not report responses suggesting orgasm.

Field studies are generally sketchy on female sexual responses although in one study on mating behavior of free-ranging chacma baboons Saayman (1970) reported copulation calls (a series of staccato grunts) given by females toward the end of a copulatory series in conjunction with male ejaculation. Saayman noted that the copulation call and a bounding-away reaction, which follows as the male ceases thrusting, appear to be involuntary movements, and he suggested they may represent an orgasmic response in the female. Like the rhesus clutching reaction, the copulation call is hormone dependent; that is, it occurs in greatest frequency during maximal genital swelling. The copulation call was most common with mature male partners, and Saayman thought that this fact may account for the high number of presentations to adult males by swollen females. The temporal relationship noted by Zumpe and Michael (1968), in which the female's orgasmic response usually preceded the male's by only a few seconds, may partly account for the failure of field workers to report female orgasm in nonhuman primates.

It is interesting to note that Kline-Graber and Graber (1975) consider contraction of the pubococcygeus muscle as the most important aspect of human female orgasm. Masters and Johnson (1966) refer to it as the "penile grasping reaction," which occurs during especially strong orgasm. Chevalier-Skolnikoff (1971) has noted that this response is found in one species of primate, *Macaca arctoides*, in which a postejaculatory "tie" is effected by an anatomical "lock and key" combination involving the enlarged pubococcygeus muscle in the female and the conelike projections on the penis of the male (Fooden, 1967; Kanagawa and Hafez, 1973).

A final consideration is the role played by swelling of sexual skin in primate copulation. Generally authors have considered sexual swelling from the perspective of the male as either an aid to mounting and penetration or as a sexual stimulus. However, laboratory studies and carefully sampled field studies indicate that the most potent sexual stimulus to the male is an estrogen-dependent pheromone-like agent secreted in the vagina, and that neither redness nor swelling of the sexual skin is stimulating to the male without the presence of the olfactory cue (Michael, Keverne, and Bonsall, 1971; Michael and Saayman, 1968; Saayman, 1973). The importance of sexual swelling to the stimulation of female appetitive behavior seems to be generally under-emphasized.

In general then, the evidence for sexual orgasm in the nonhuman female primate is not particularly good, but what evidence there is suggests that further research might be fruitful. A wide range of species differences exists in the copulatory behavior of the male nonhuman primate, including the patterns of precopulatory grooming, courtship, copulatory posture, mating time, and the number of mounts preceding ejaculation (Michael et al., 1966). Similar variability between species probably exists for females, and it is reasonable to look for differences in female arousal that correlate with variations in male behavior patterns such as the number of successive mounts preceding ejaculation. Implants to monitor brain activity or contractions of vaginal muscles would help to establish the existence of orgasmic responses in the nonhuman female primate. Further observations of the social and behavioral setting would then be warranted to establish an understanding of the role female orgasm might play in particular primate social systems.

Variations in Nonhuman Primate Sexuality

The tendency for nonhuman primates to form year-round bisexual social groups has impressed many theorists as providing a background for the evolution of human society. Zuckerman (1932) first formulated the proposition that the possibility of year-round sexual behavior in nonhuman primates provides the "social glue" for stable social groups by permanently attracting males to females and their young. Lancaster and Lee (1965) reviewed the available literature on primate mating from early field studies and found that the proposition as stated could not be correct since many primate societies have major seasonal limitations on mating so that primary sexual behavior between adults may occur during only three or four months a year. Recent reviews by Eaton (1973), Rowell (1972), and Saayman (1975) clearly indicate that, although there are seasonal limitations on primary sexual behavior, in some nonhuman primate species, females have long periods of sexual receptivity and such receptivity occurs under a variety of hormonal conditions.

Most field workers assumed originally that sexuality in nonhuman female primates was limited to a five- to seven-day period around the time of ovulation and that female primates were not receptive to males during other phases of the menstrual cycle, nor during pregnancy and lactation. If this were true, then an individual female's participation in mating activities could be limited theoretically to only a week every other year if she became pregnant during her first menstrual cycle after weaning an infant. Loy (1970, 1971) published the first careful study of female cycles in a free-ranging group of rhesus monkeys. At Cayo Santiago Loy found that in the mating season females copulated during all parts of the menstrual cycle, but there were two points when copulations reached their highest frequency: one during midcycle around the time of ovulation and another just before the onset of menstruation. This continuing receptivity during the menstrual cycle with two peaks of higher receptivity (coinciding with dual estrogen maxima) occurs in caged rhesus and is similar to frequency of intercourse in some studies of the human female (Michael and Zumpe, 1970). Furthermore, female rhesus continue cycling during the mating season even when they have become pregnant at the beginning. Loy found that females averaged 4.2 postconception estrous periods with a range of from 3 to 7. Some of the females that did not become pregnant during the mating season continued to show estrus of varying intensity during the entire annual cycle.

Similar observations on the menstrual cycle, but with a single peak in copulatory frequency, have now been reported for the chacma baboon (Saayman, 1975), the Japanese macaque (Hanby, Robertson, and Phoenix, 1971), the pigtail macaque (Eaton and Resko, 1974), and the olive baboon (Rowell, 1972). Sexual cycling during pregnancy has been documented for a variety of monkeys and apes such as gorillas, chimpanzees, vervet monkeys, langurs, and Japanese macaques (Rowell, 1972). These data imply that in at least some species of nonhuman primates, female sexuality is not restricted to a brief period of estrus but occurs throughout the menstrual cycle and during pregnancy with increased frequencies of copulations at one or two points in the menstrual cycle: the first around ovulation and the second around menstruation. Such a description includes the sexual behavior of human and some nonhuman female primates and suggests that previous distinctions emphasizing a unique emancipation of human female sexuality from hormonal states were overdrawn.

Saayman (1975), in discussing his study of the mating behavior of free-ranging chacma baboons, stressed that an over-focus on behavior around the period of ovulation gives an inaccurate description of the full range of sexual behavior. He prefers to describe chacma mating as a rotating system in which female sexual invitations to adult and immature males and mounting of females by juvenile, subadult, and adult males occur throughout the menstrual cycle, with an elevation of frequency during the follicular phase, particularly during the swollen cycle state. Saayman notes that previous workers have considered sex a generally disruptive agent in baboon social life. In contrast, his own field data suggest that sex may be a powerful integrating mechanism:

> The mating system, comprising rotating sexual partners, may well be adapted for the periodic reinforcement of social bonds between adult females and partners selected from those age classes of males which are capable of integrated copulatory responses. It is likely that such a system functions to promote, rather than to disrupt, friendly social relationships and consequently may contribute toward the maintenance of troop cohesion (Saayman, 1975, p. 184).

Other studies from both laboratory and field suggest that sexual stimulation may be one of the most powerful expressions of an emotionally bonded relationship in a number of primate species. For example, Hanby (1974) analyzed the importance of male-male mounting in Japanese macaques to amicable play relations among both adult and juvenile males and to recementing social bonds when the social group was stressed, rather than to affirm dominance relationships. Erwin and Maple (1976) described reciprocal copulation in a closely bonded pair of male rhesus raised alone together. Chevalier-Skolnikoff (1974, 1976) published descriptions of the wide variety of sexual activities in *Macaca arctoides,* such as homosexual and heterosexual copulations and mutual masturbation, which included reversals of sex roles as well as inclusion of both adults and young. She emphasized that this wide variety of sexual behavior occurred in an amicable social context and was most likely to occur between individuals with special friendships to each other (see Figure 1).

Chevalier-Skolnikoff's observations come from a single laboratory group. However, other investigators working with *M. arctoides* have noted similar behaviors, such as female-female copulation with orgasm (Kling and Dunne, 1976; Mass, 1972). Since there are no field studies on this species of macaque, it is not clear whether the relative openness of sexual behavior of *M. arctoides* represents a response to captive conditions or a species' specialization in social and sexual behavior.

Sexual behavior is clearly a very important way of expressing and maintaining special affectionate relationships in nonhuman primates. Its use is seen in two very different aspects of primate

Mounting with unilateral manual genital stimulation between two males.

The female-female homosexual mounting position.

Mounting with mutual oral genital stimulation between two males.

A supine position observed during both heterosexual coitus and female-female homosexual interactions.

Mounting with unilateral oral genital stimulation between two males.

Mutual presentations with manual genital stimulation between two males.

Fig. 1. The variety of heterosexual and homosexual interactions observed in captive *Macaca arctoides* (Chevalier-Skolnikoff, 1974).

behavior. First, it can be found in the relative emancipation of female sexual behavior from the restrictions of the mammalian estrous cycle in a number of, and perhaps most, Old World monkey and ape species. Second, it can be found in the widely occurring phenomenon of the use of either primary sexual behavior or of sexual behavior patterns, such as mounting, presentation, and genital investigation, in nonsexual contexts to express special affinity and affection between individuals. As Wickler argued in *The Sexual Code* (1973), sexual behavior patterns are a primary medium of primate social interaction irrespective of whether a fertile copulation is likely to occur. One final implication is clear: that the sex roles of male and female primates as manifested in copulatory positions, initiation of sexual activity, sexual responses, and variety of sexual contacts, are not strictly sex specific among nonhuman primates and that each sex may play the "opposite" role at particular points of the life cycle or in certain social contexts.

Dominance and Reproductive Success

The priority-of-access model pervaded most of the early field work on primate social behavior. The assumption was that high dominance status among males provided the individual with priority of access to all environmental incentives, ranging from food and sitting positions to choice of mates. Extending this further, researchers assumed that, if only one female were in estrus at a particular time, then the most dominant male of the group would control sexual access to her, especially during her most fertile days. Implicit in this assumption was either that females exercised little choice in who impregnated them, or that they naturally preferred males high in the dominance hierarchy for sexual partners. The first field studies on baboons (DeVore, 1965) and rhesus (Kaufmann, 1967) appeared to support the model, and subsequent generalizations as in Wilson (1975) and Fox (1972) were stated as if the case for natural selection favoring dominance through male reproductive success were a settled issue. However, a number of recent publications have discussed complex problems making the collection of adequate data extremely difficult because of a variety of built-in biases of early field work, in which data was collected on an *ad libitum* basis.

Problems Related to Sampling

One of the principal biases of *ad libitum* sampling is that it produces high frequencies of data on the behavior of easily observed animals, usually males, high status individuals, and females with young infants (Altmann, 1974). Often the behavior of other group members is hardly sampled at all. Drickamer (1974b) studied correlations between social rank, observability, and sexual behavior among male rhesus in a free-ranging colony at La Parguera. He found that the frequency of *ad libitum* behavioral observations on males was directly correlated to dominance status, with the frequency of appearance of high-ranking males being 82 percent, medium-ranking males 56 percent, and low-ranking 36 percent. When he sampled the rate of observability of females known to be in estrus, he found that on average only 37 percent were visible at any one time. Since dominant males control sexual access to estrous females mainly through visual control of the environment and harassment of subordinates' attempts to copulate, there are obviously numerous opportunities for subordinate, subadult, and juvenile males to copulate with estrous females out of sight of dominant animals.

Many field workers have noted that copulations by immature and subordinate males are usually secretive and sometimes hasty. Recent laboratory studies suggest that in some species it is only necessary for a dominant male to be visible for immature males to be sexually inhibited. Perachio, Alexander, and Marr (1973) found that the presence of a dominant rhesus male could inhibit electrically evoked mating activity by subordinate, wired males with receptive females. When the dominant male was removed from sight, both spontaneous and evoked mating behavior reappeared in the wired male. Similar observations have been made by Trollope and Blurton-Jones (1975) on captive *Macaca arctoides* in which subadult males demonstrated temporary inability to mount when paired with adult females in the presence of the adult male of the group. Removal of the adult male brought instantaneous recovery and normal copulatory patterns.

A number of field workers have reported on similar behavior patterns in which dominant males either inhibit or interrupt copulations between subordinate and immature males with estrous females. These interruptions do not prevent the pair from mating but simply alter the location of the copulation to an area beyond the visual control of the dominant animal (Hanby, Robertson, and Phoenix, 1971; Hausfater, 1975a; Stephenson, 1975). It seems obvious that the only really reliable data on copulatory success will come from studies that use careful sampling techniques, the best being continuous observation of a female throughout her entire period of fertility.

Another difficulty results from short-term sampling. The question is whether individual males have long-term, stable status or occupy different dominance positions during various periods of the life cycle. In general it seems that while status hierarchies among females are highly stable over long periods of time, the opposite is the case for males. Two major factors influence fluctuations in male status: the high rate of turnover among males attached to a stable group of females and the effects of maturation on individual status. During the first 400 days of his study on dominance and reproduction in the yellow baboon, Hausfater (1975a) found that there was a demographic change (because of birth, death, and migration) in the number of adult males in the study group once every 13.3 days; among adult females the comparable figure was every 57.1 days. Agonistically induced changes in the ranking of adult males occurred, on the average, once every 21.0 study days, while none occurred among the females during the entire period. In analyzing the duration of rank occupancy he found that the number of ranks occupied per adult male during the 400 days was 3.6 and that for ranks 1 to 9 in his study group there was an average of 8.5 changes in occupancy in each rank. He concluded:

> Thus, whether the rank occupancy data are ordered by rank of occupant or by identity of occupant, it is clear that adult males in the study group changed their rank frequently during the study period and, conversely, that no dominance rank was occupied exclusively by one particular male (Hausfater, 1975a, pp. 61–62).

Studies on Reproductive Success

Studies of reproductive success are likely to be useful only if they are designed to generate data on sexual behavior of all age/sex classes, with careful observation and sampling techniques. A number of studies that at least partly meet these criteria have been published recently: Lindburg (1971) on forest rhesus in India, Drickamer (1974a, 1975) on rhesus monkeys at La Parguera, Saayman (1970, 1975) on the chacma baboon, Hausfater (1975a, 1975b) on the yellow baboon, Enomoto (1974) and Stephenson (1975) on the free-ranging Japanese macaque, and Hanby, Robertson, and Phoenix (1971) and Eaton (1974) on a natural troop of Japanese macaques maintained at the Oregon Regional Primate Center. Although these studies hardly represent the full range of primate species, they represent the species in which dominance hierarchies seem particularly important in social life. Therefore, they constitute a good sample of societies that might provide support for the priority-of-access model.

There is only one study in this group that gives data on the reproductive advantages of high-dominance status, however, and that is Drickamer's investigation (1974a) summarizing ten years of reproductive data for adult female rhesus monkeys in a free-ranging colony. He found that a larger percentage of high-ranking females than low-ranking females gave birth each year, that daughters of high-ranking females produced their first infants at an earlier age than daughters of low-ranking females, and that infants born to high-ranking females had a higher rate of survival than the young of low-ranking females.[1] The other studies, all of which concentrated on male copulatory success, generally concluded either that there was no correlation between dominance and copulations or that the correlations were low and not consistent with a priority-of-access model. The summary findings of these studies follow.

Short-term Alternative Reproductive Strategies. Hausfater (1975a) gives the most cogent discussion of alternative male reproductive strategies in dominance-oriented social systems. He found that an individual male baboon tends to adopt the strategy most appropriate to his age and status. Mature, high-ranking males tend to concentrate their reproductive efforts on only a few

1. Rowell points out that Drickamer's data does not correct for age effects. Since the correlation between age and rank is consistent among rhesus females, it is likely that Drickamer's data attest to the success of the experienced mother in raising her young and in particular of older females with adult and subadult daughters as maternal helpers (personal communication).

mature females by forming consortships with them on approx-imately the two or three days around the time in the cycle that laboratory studies have shown to be optimal for insemination. This strategy maximizes the possibility of impregnating a female while minimizing the possible negative costs of consortship (such as loss of eating time, fights) by concentrating on only a few days of a female's cycle. Other mature males follow a reproductive strategy of forming consortships with any female showing estrous behavior; this would include copulations with adolescent, preg-nant, and young females as well as with mature females during the days of the menstrual cycle in which the likelihood of con-ception is reduced but still possible. A third strategy is carried out by subadult and juvenile males, who combine the strategies of the other two groups by concentrating their mating attempts on females about the time of ovulation, but without showing strong partner preferences. They avoid the negative consequences be-cause they do not form consortships. They are able to compete only by maintaining constant vigilance and copulating with other males' consorts during brief moments when the more dominant males are distracted. No one strategy is more effective than the others, but each strategy is more appropriate for a particular male at a particular time and place.

Personal Mating Preferences in Males. A number of authors were impressed by strong personal preferences in choice of mating partner found especially in fully mature, socially important males. Such preferences were so strong that dominant males often re-fused copulation to nonpreferred females even when they were the only females in estrus. What underlies such individual choices is not completely clear. Enomoto (1974) reported that Japanese macaque males showed strong preferences for mating with spe-cific lineages of females and avoidance of others; Stephenson (1975) found such choices in Japanese macaques related more to what he called "social class" than to lineage; for example, high-ranking males preferred females from high-ranking lineages; Hausfater (1975a) and Saayman (1970) found what they felt was simply personal favoritism on the part of individual male baboons for individual females.

In a laboratory study on pigtail macaques Goldfoot (1971) found that a male, when given choices between joining females of various social ranks and estrous conditions, showed that high rank in a female was more important than her ovarian condition in determining his choice of cage mate. Perachio, Alexander, and Marr (1973) also noted a male preference for dominant females, which partially overrode a preference to copulate with females in estrus. Among rhesus macaques and baboons, favorite partner relationships extend into nonmating contexts and throughout the year, strongly suggesting the development of personal attachments between particular males and females that include higher rates of sexual activity (Agar and Mitchell, 1975; Ransom and Rowell, 1972; Saayman, 1970). Most investigators have stressed that personal preferences work against the priority-of-access model because preferences tend to leave young, immature, low-status females or particular subsets of females free to mate with other males.

Correlation of High Status with Age. A number of authors have reported that the single most important correlate of high status is maturity, not fighting ability or social aggressiveness (Drickamer, 1975; Hanby, Robertson and Phoenix, 1971; Hausfater, 1975a; Stephenson, 1975). Saunders and Hausfater (in press) devised a computer simulation of differential reproduction with respect to dominance rank in males, using Hausfater's field data on the yellow baboon. They found that the highest correlations with a male's probability of consorting with a female during her most fertile day were longevity, then the initial rank of the male when he first began his reproductive career. In other words, the males that father the most offspring are those who live the longest, and since initial adult rank correlates most strongly with maternal rank in many primate societies, the second most important factor is likely to be the social status of a male's maternal lineage.

Among most species of Old World monkeys and apes as well as among humans, male social maturity is delayed several years beyond that of female age-mates. Reproductive maturity as measured by ovulation and presence of viable sperm roughly coincides in primate males and females, but most primate males take additional years to reach full adult body size. During this period female peers are raising their first young. In the most highly dimorphic species the difference between the sexes in reaching maturity is the greatest, and in species of low dimorphism the difference is usually the least.

In some species full social maturity may take even longer to reach than does adult size. For example, Stephenson (1975) found that among free-ranging Japanese macaques, leader or central males were usually between the ages of fourteen and twenty-five. If dominance really correlates with full social maturity—or even middle age—in many primate societies, then high status may be a normal part of the male life cycle. But considering the action of natural selection on such populations, it is important to remember that most males do not live long enough to gain high rank. Large numbers of juveniles and subadults die before reaching maturity. Because population explosions result when free-ranging monkey groups are fed artificially, these premature deaths have been attributed to limited food supply.

Dittus (1975) published demographic statistics on a stable population of free-ranging toque macaques in Sri Lanka. The highest probability of survival was found in animals that had attained effective breeding age: for young adult females (4½+ years) the probable average number of years of life remaining was 16.6, and for young adult males (7+ years) it was 10.5 years. Among juveniles the death rate of both males and females was very high. Only 15 percent of the females and 10 percent of the males reached effective sexual maturity. Mortality peaked during the first months of life for both sexes. For males the risks were equally high in adolescence: approximately 72 percent of males who reached adolescence died between the ages of four and seven years. Adolescence is a high risk point for males in many primate populations because at this age males leave the protective custody of their mothers and the play group and begin to circulate among other social groups in the area. Increased risks come from predators, wounds from fighting with male strangers, and probably from accidents. Demographic data suggest that competition between males for impregnation of females is best understood in relation to differential survival to full maturity, which includes many factors beyond aggressive potential and dominance, such as efficiency in food metabolism, resistence to disease and infections, ability to form positive social attachments, and just plain good luck.

Correlation of High Status with Time Spent in Group. In an analysis of status among rhesus macaques living in free-ranging colonies Drickamer and Vessey (1973) found that, besides the high correlation of rank with age, there was an even more significant relationship between status and length of time of group membership. Norikoshi and Koyama (1975), in a study of dominance rank and group shiftings of male Japanese monkeys over an eight-year period at Arashiyama, found that a total of fifty-four males moved out of their natal groups and eight remained. The authors found no correlation between social rank and body weight among adults but did find strong positive correlations with age and also with length of time in the troop. Several factors may lie behind these correlations. First of all, among both rhesus and Japanese macaques, males born into high-ranking lineages tend to stay in their natal groups. However, it appears that remaining in the natal group is an exceedingly rare event when the total male population is considered, even though the top leadership positions of a group are sometimes occupied by males born to the top-ranking female lineage (Enomoto, 1974; Itoigawa, 1975; Norikoshi and Koyama, 1975).

A migrating male is more likely to stay long enough with a group to build up seniority and high rank when he is accepted by the resident females and permitted access to the central part of the group. Rejection of migrant males by resident females has been reported by Neville (1968). Breuggeman (1973) noted that whether a male is central or peripheral in status among rhesus at Cayo Santiago depends on female acceptance. Neville (reported in Agar and Mitchell, 1975) found that the rhesus males who remained permanently with a newly joined group were those who had formed consortships during the mating season. The readiness with which group females form coalitions against males deemed threatening to an infant has been observed for many primate species, including the vervet monkey (Lancaster, unpublished data), the North Indian langur (Hrdy, 1976; Jay, 1965), and the rhesus macaque (Lindburg, 1971). There are few indications as to the specific status of these males (central, peripheral, newcomer, and so on), but in general, females with infants prefer the presence of fully mature, well-known males. Much of the data indicates that, among species in which males enjoy central social

67

positions (such as baboons, macaques, and vervets), access to centrality is based on acceptance by resident females. Males not accepted have difficulty staying with the group long enough to build up seniority and high status in the male ranks.

Female Choice. Few field workers have seriously studied the question of female choice in mating among monkeys and apes. However, field work publications are filled with reports of females soliciting copulations and refusing copulation attempts by keeping their hindquarters lowered. As Stephenson noted in discussing Japanese macaques:

> In the mounted position, the male probes for the vaginal opening with his penis. If the female has not raised her rump to the proper height, her vaginal opening will be at the wrong angle to the male's penile probes and he will not achieve intromission. This means that the female can control whether a male will succeed in his attempts at intromission; hence mounting with intromission is taken as evidence that the female is sexually receptive (Stephenson, 1975, p. 75).

Hausfater (1975a) found consistent female preference for mating with the higher-ranking male within the subset of group males with whom she mated. Saayman (1975) felt that female chacma baboons seek mature partners because these males stimulate them to orgasm. In his main study group, females showed sexual preference for the third-ranking mature male, who was the least aggressive and who frequently intervened on their behalf in agonistic situations. In a laboratory experiment on female sexual preference in pigtail macaques, Eaton (1973) found that females showed strong aversion to one highly aggressive male who frequently attacked them. Other preferences and aversions for particular males were highly idiosyncratic but important in understanding individual behavior patterns.

Tutin (1975) analyzed chimpanzee partner preferences in over one thousand copulations observed during a fifteen-month period at the Gombe Chimpanzee Reserve. The sexual behavior of nonparous and parous females differed widely. Nonparous females had a very low probability of pregnancy (chimpanzees cycle for several years before the first pregnancy), and such females most commonly copulated promiscuously with the local male population. Parous females, on the other hand, usually formed secluded consortships during estrus. Tutin reported that the frequencies of male involvement in consort behavior did not correlate with age, dominance, or the amount of agonistic behavior directed toward females. Instead, males that spent the most time grooming females in group situations and males that were generous to females in food-sharing were the most likely to form successful consortships. Tutin concluded that social and caretaking characteristics of male chimpanzees appear more important for their reproductive success than dominance status.

Modern evolutionary theory, particularly as stated by Goss-Custard, Dunbar, and Aldrich-Blake (1972), and Trivers (1972), makes a strong case for female selectivity in primate mating patterns. In contrast to the male, the female monkey or ape has a limited number of opportunities during her lifetime to pass on genes to succeeding generations. Also, the successful rearing of offspring demands considerable parental investment for female primates compared with many other mammals. For these reasons, natural selection must favor females who are selective in whom they permit to impregnate them. The most obvious choice is the fully mature male, one who has demonstrated his ability to survive when perhaps 90 percent of his birth cohort has succumbed to genetic unfitness, disease, malnutrition, infection, accidents, and fights.

In his analysis of mate selection by rhesus macaques in India Lindburg (1975) noted the preference for alpha males shown by estrous females, especially around the time of ovulation. Lindburg concluded that the higher-than-expected, observed success of alpha males in mating was related to female preference and not to the male's ability to dominate other males and limit their access to females. The correlation of alpha-male status with age and seniority in the group fits well with this concept. The alpha male's status demonstrates his genetic fitness in the sense that he has proven his ability to survive to middle-age, and his seniority and centrality in the group demonstrate his social skills in forming stable social relations and protecting weaker group members.

In a review article on dominance, aggression, and reproduction in primate societies, Bernstein (1976) emphasized the importance of the "control role" in primate social systems. This role consists primarily of behavior involving vigilance and buffering the group against various sources of disruption and disturbance. Because the salient features of the role relate to group protection and not to acquisition of personal incentives, the role can be observed even in species lacking evidence of a dominance hierarchy. Bernstein summarized the control role as follows:

> Alpha males, however, were noted to maintain their position through social skills as members of a central core or alliance, and high rank was related primarily to seniority. Moreover, alpha males responded actively to challenges to the troop and were judged to contribute significantly to the survival of infants. It was therefore hypothesized that increased genetic fitness related to the increased survival of immature animals in the troop, most of which would already be the offspring of senior (and hence alpha) males. Selection would then be for the social skills leading to successful alliances in troop defense. Such skills might also relate to female partner preferences thus increasing the reproductive effectiveness of alpha males at any point in their careers, including years prior to and following their assumption of alpha rank (Bernstein, 1976, p. 459).

Avoidance of Incestuous Matings

The anthropological and psychological literature picked up very quickly on a report published by Sade (1968) on the inhibition of son-mother mating among free-ranging rhesus monkeys. Generalizations usually had focused on the supposed presence of a precultural incest taboo for nonhuman primates. Subsequent studies show that the reality of incest avoidance in monkeys and apes is much more complex. The data are still very inconclusive—but intriguing.

Recent data published on a wide variety of Old World monkey species show that males are generally much more mobile than females in respect to social group membership: Gartlan (Gartlan and Brain, 1968) on the vervet monkey, Lindburg (1969) on the free-ranging rhesus in North India, Drickamer and Vessey (1973) on free-ranging rhesus colonies, Dittus (1975) on the toque macaque, Itoigawa (1975) and Norikoshi and Koyama (1975) on the free-ranging Japanese macaque, Parker (1975) and Hausfater (1975b) on the yellow baboon. All of these studies indicate that females form the stable, organized core of a long-term social group, and males compose a more or less shifting population within a neighborhood. Most agree that males may transfer a number of times during their lives and that all but a small minority leave their natal groups during adolescence and early adulthood. In groups in which mating is seasonal, much of this group shifting begins slightly before the onset of the mating season and continues until the beginning of the birth season. Higher rates of aggression and fighting also are apparent during this period. A number of authors have remarked on the importance of estrous females in attracting shifting males to join their group. For most nonhuman primates the likelihood of mother-son and brother-sister conceptions is extraordinarily low because they do not spend adult life in the same social group. The frequency of father-daughter incest is undetermined since paternity is unknowable (presumably to both the observer and the animals) in the vast majority of Old World monkeys and apes. One point that has not been carefully considered is whether males who have survived to full adult maturity avoid returning to their natal groups or simply circulate freely among all the social groups in the neighborhood. Although the data are inconclusive because of small samples and short-term observations, there are a few records of males returning to their natal groups.

The most recent field data on the closest living relatives of humans (the chimpanzee and gorilla) provide a very different pattern of group attachment than that reported for Old World monkeys. In the gorilla (Harcourt, Stewart, and Fossey, 1976) both young males and young females leave their natal group around puberty: the male to wander alone or establish a new group of his own, the female to join other groups until she finds one in which she can successfully rear young. Among chimpanzees at the Gombe Reserve Bauer (1976) found that females showed much lower intrasexual bonding than males of the same community and that young females often transferred out of their natal community, whereas males did not. The net result of these sex differences in group attachment is the same as that for Old World monkeys; high rates of inbreeding do not occur, because of differentials in mobility and group attachment between the two sexes.

Most interesting issues revolve around whether inbreeding is limited because strange females are more attractive to males than familiar ones and vice versa, or because there is some clear aversion to mating with close relatives. In his first observations on the subject of mating behavior of a group of free-ranging rhesus at Cayo Santiago, Sade (1968) formulated the hypothesis that an adult male who remained in his mother's group was inhibited from copulating with her by her higher dominance rank, although this inhibition did not apply to unrelated females who were dominant to him. A more recent study by Missakian (1973) on a different group at Cayo Santiago and subsequent observations by Sade (1972) on his original group indicate that son-mother copulations are not unusual during the late adolescent/early adult period of the male life cycle for those males who remain in the natal group. In fact, Missakian found the mother to be the preferred sex partner in some cases. The question of relative dominance rank is unclear since this is the time period when male rhesus become dominant over their mothers (by virtue of growth in size), but both Sade and Missakian observed copulations when the son was still subordinate to his mother.

By the time full adulthood is reached among Old World monkeys, the number of males of a birth cohort still living in their natal groups is very small. However, studies on a large number of groups of Japanese macaques (Enomoto, 1974; Itiogawa, 1975; Norikosi and Koyama, 1975) indicate that among the fully adult central males in a social group, the number of sons can be proportionally high. Enomoto found that the first three dominance positions in his study group were held by males belonging to the dominant female lineage. These males showed positive behavior toward females (mothers, sisters, aunts, cousins) of their own lineage when these females were in estrus, but the females showed strong preferences for mating with those central hierarchy males who had transferred into the group. This finding is opposed to the observations of Sade (1968) on rhesus and Goodall (1968) on chimpanzees. Both Sade and Goodall reported active sexual solicitation of sons by their estrous mothers and refusal to mount by the sons. Matings between brother and sister have been reported in the literature on rhesus: Loy (1971) found brother-sister matings at Cayo Santiago close to random frequencies, but Missakian (1973) found that, once brothers reached full adulthood, they no longer copulated with their sisters even if they stayed in their natal group.

The frequent observation that some males prefer or avoid mating with specific subgroups in baboon and macaque societies may indeed reflect preferences for mating between individuals from unrelated genealogies. Wade's laboratory study on the response to strangers by rhesus monkey social groups may be relevant. Wade (1976) found that, when given alternatives, males showed preference to forming social alliances with less-familiar over more-familiar females. Females, on the other hand, preferred to form alliances first with males, then with familiar females, and last with unfamiliar females. Females also showed reduced social tolerance of strange females when in the presence of a male. Such basic social preferences may underlie complex behavior patterns such as male transfers between neighborhood social groups or reduced frequencies of mating between closely related individuals.

Conclusions

Attempts to establish a primate background from which to view the evolution of human sex and gender have been based on meager scraps of data and observations without controls. Until recently, at least, we have known little about what nonhuman primate sexual behavior really is. Most generalizations have been based on presuppositions of what primate sexual behavior ought to be, backed up with the few supporting facts available. Since 1970 a number of more informative studies from both the laboratory and the field have been published. Some of these studies were performed specifically to gather data on reproductive behavior in nonhuman primates, and for the most part the data were gathered using carefully controlled sampling techniques. Some of these new data only raise more questions, but other data have important implications for developing a perspective on the evolution of human sexual behavior.

One of the most significant generalizations to come from the new data is that, like humans, Old World monkeys and apes do not engage in sexual activity only around the period of ovulation. Many different species use primary sexual activity or behavior patterns drawn from the sexual repertoire to express and cement positive social attachments. Primary sexual behavior between members of the same sex, between adults and young, and between adult males and pregnant, menstruating, or anovulatory females is not uncommon among nonhuman primates. In nonhuman primates the stimulation and rewards of sexual behavior appear to be important mechanisms of social attachment, in some species possibly comparable to behavior patterns like grooming. The evolution of human sexual behavior must be understood as derived from a primate background in which sexuality was already a prominent feature of social interaction. In a recent analysis of reproduction in the human female, Newton (1973) noted the importance of sexual stimulation and orgasm in all major aspects of a woman's reproductive role, including coitus, labor, and nursing. Because sexuality is one of the most potent biological stimuli and orgasm one of the most potent rewards, it is not surprising that this system should feature prominently in the social behavior of a species whose adaptations are so highly committed to long-term, individualized, social attachments.

A second major consideration is the notable lack of evidence that female behavior and social status in nonhuman primates are largely under the control of hormonal cycles. All of the recent field studies emphasize that under normal social circumstances there is no correlation between social status and sex hormone state. On the contrary, they emphasize the general stability of female social status and dominance rank irrespective of whether a female is in estrus, anovulatory, pregnant, or lactating. Furthermore, in some species of nonhuman primates, female sexual behavior appears to be very similar to that of humans in one important respect: Females can be active in seeking copulation during all parts of their sexual cycle, even though higher frequencies of coitus occur around ovulation and just before menstruation. Such a degree of emancipation of sexuality from sex hormone cycles might be expected in species using sexuality as a major means of forming social attachments. The ability to be selective in mating partners during estrus can also be viewed as an important step in the evolution of volitional control over personal sexuality. Continuous sexual receptivity in human females is not the same thing as continuous estrus. Continuous sexual receptivity provides the female with ready and regular options for sexual activity, an evolutionary development of great importance considering the high amount of parental investment a human female must give to rearing a child successfully.

A third important generalization is the lack of evidence for major sex role differences in regard to important aspects of sexual behavior. For example, field data suggest that both males and females play active roles in selecting mating partners, in seeking consummatory responses, and in forming sexual attachments. Furthermore, accumulating evidence suggests that the roles are not rigidly sex specific and that there is wide variation among species in the roles that males and females play during various periods of the life cycle and under different social circumstances.

Perhaps one of the most significant generalizations for the development of evolutionary theory is the relationship of dominance to reproductive success in complex social systems. Much more work needs to be done in long-term studies covering the entire life cycle of individuals, but it seems probable now that the elusive quality of "dominance" correlates most strongly with full social maturity and length of tenure in a social group and not with aggressive potential per se. As such, it is a part of the normal life cycle of those individuals who live long enough to become dominant. Competition between males for access to females is based mainly on ability to survive, and not on anything so stark as physical intimidation. Furthermore, being in a dominant role represents only one of several effective strategies for passing genes on to the next generation. Field data at present do not show that one strategy is more effective than another nor that an individual uses only one strategy during a lifetime. The probability is that these strategies are situation specific and can be used by most individuals according to their social circumstances.

The final generalization relates to the question of incest avoidance. The field studies to date strongly indicate that among Old World monkeys the male has a larger social field than the female. Typically, the male circulates among social groups in a neighborhood during various parts of his lifetime, whereas a female is most likely to spend her entire life in her natal group. This differential between the sexes in group attachment means that mother-son and brother-sister matings will be rare because they are unlikely to live in the same social group. However, a few such matings have been observed in free-ranging monkeys, particularly during the latter part of adolescence in the male. Field studies suggest that the stimulus properties of the less familiar female may have higher positive valence than those of females from the same social lineage. The attractions of the stranger may account for the lower-than-expected frequencies of incestuous matings. Similar mechanisms appear to reduce inbreeding among the African apes, but in their case it is the female who is more mobile than the male.

References

Abernethy, V. 1974. Dominance and sexual behavior: A hypothesis. *Am. J. Psychiat.* 131:813–817.

Agar, M. E., and Mitchell, G. 1975. Behavior of free-ranging adult rhesus macaques: A review. In *The rhesus monkey,* vol. 1, ed. G. Bourne. New York: Academic Press.

Altmann, J. 1974. Observational study of behavior: Sampling methods. *Behavior* 49:227–267.

Bauer, H. R. 1976. Sex differences in aggregation and sexual selection in Gombe chimpanzees. *Amer. Zool.* 16:209.

Beach, F. A. 1974. Human sexuality and evolution. In *Reproductive Behavior,* ed. W. Montagna and W. A. Sadler. New York: Plenum Press.

Bernstein, I. S. 1976. Dominance, aggression and reproduction in primate societies. *J. Theor. Biol.* 60:459–472.

Breuggeman, J. A. 1973. Parental care in a group of free-ranging rhesus monkeys (*Macaca mulatta*). *Folia Primatol.* 20:178–210.

Burton, F. D. 1971. Sexual climax in female *Macaca mulatta.* In *Proceedings of the Third International Congress of Primatology,* vol. 3. Basel: S. Karger.

Chevalier-Skolnikoff, S. 1971. Paper read at American Anthropological Association annual meeting, November 1971, in New York.

————. 1974. Male-female, female-female, and male-male sexual behavior in the stumptail monkey, with special attention to the female orgasm. *Arch. Sex. Behav.* 3:95–116.

————. 1976. Homosexual behavior in a laboratory group of stumptail monkeys (*Macaca arctoides*): Forms, contents and possible social functions. *Arch. Sex. Behav.* 5:511–527.

DeVore, I. 1965. Male dominance and mating behavior in baboons. In *Sex and Behavior*, ed. F. A. Beach, New York: Wiley.

Dittus, W. 1975. Population dynamics of the toque monkey, *Macaca sinica.* In *Socioecology and psychology of primates,* ed. R. Tuttle. The Hague: Mouton.

Drickamer, L. C. 1974a. A ten-year summary of reproductive data for free-ranging *Macaca mulatta. Folia Primatol.* 21:61–80.

————. 1974b. Social rank, observability, and sexual behavior of rhesus monkeys (*Macaca mulatta*). *J. Repro. Fertil.* 37:117–120.

————. 1975. Quantitative observation of behavior in free-ranging *Macaca mulatta*: Methodology and aggression. *Behavior* 55:209–236.

Drickamer, L. C., and Vessey, S. H. 1973. Group changing in free-ranging male rhesus monkeys. *Primates* 14:359–368.

Eaton, G. G. 1973. Social and endocrine determinants of sexual behavior in simian and prosimian females. In *Symposia of the 4th International Congress of Primatology,* vol. 2, ed. C. H. Phoenix. Basel: S. Karger.

————. 1974. Male dominance and aggression in Japanese macaque. In *Reproductive Behavior*, ed. W. Montagna and W. A. Sadler. New York: Plenum Press.

Eaton, G. G., and Resko, J. A. 1974. Ovarian hormones and sexual behavior in *Macaca nemestrina*. *J. Comp. Physiol. Psychol.* 86:919–925.

Enomoto, T. 1974. The sexual behavior of Japanese monkeys. *J. Hum. Evol.* 3:351–372.

Erwin, J., and Maple, T. 1976. Ambisexual behavior in male rhesus monkeys. *Arch. Sex. Behav.* 5:9–14.

Fooden, J. 1967. Complementary specialization of male and female reproductive structures in the bear macaque, *Macaca arctoides*. *Nature* 214:939–941.

Fox, R. 1972. Alliance and constraint: Sexual selection and the evolution of human kinship systems. In *Sexual selection and the descent of man*, ed. B. Campbell. Chicago: Aldine.

Gartlan, J. S., and Brain, C. K. 1968. Ecology and social variability in *Cercopithecus aethiops* and *C. mitis*. In *Primates: Studies in adaptation and variability*, ed. P. Jay. New York: Holt, Rinehart & Winston.

Goldfoot, D. A. 1971. Hormonal and social determinants of sexual behavior in the pigtail monkeys (*Macaca nemestrina*). In *Normal and abnormal development of brain and behavior*, ed. G. B. A. Stoelinga and J. J. Van Der Werff Ten Bosch. Leiden: Leiden University Press.

Goodall, J. 1968. The behavior of free-ranging chimpanzees in the Gombe stream reserve. *Anim. Behav. Monogr.* 1:165–311.

Goss-Custard, J. D.; Dunbar, R. I. M.; and Aldrich-Blake, F. P. G. 1972. Survival, mating and rearing strategies in the evolution of primate social structure. *Folia Primatol.* 17:1–19.

Hanby, J. P. 1974. Male-male mounting in Japanese monkeys (*Macaca muscata*). *Anim. Behav.* 22:836–849.

Hanby, J. P.; Robertson, L. T.; and Phoenix, C. H. 1971. The sexual behavior of a confined troop of Japanese macaques. *Folia Primatol.* 16:123–144.

Harcourt, A. H.; Stewart, K. S.; and Fossey, D. 1976. Male emigration and female transfer in wild mountain gorilla. *Nature* 263:226–227.

Hausfater, G. 1975a. Dominance and reproduction in baboons (*Papio cynocephalus*). *Contrib. Primatol.* 7:1–150.

————. 1975b. Estrous females: Their effects on the social organization of the baboon group. In *Proceedings from the Symposia of the 5th Congress of the International Primatological Society*, ed. S. Kondo, M. Kawai, A. Ehara, and S. Kawamura. Tokyo: Japan Science Press.

Hrdy, S. B. 1976. Hierarchical relations among female Hanuman langurs (*Presbytis entellus*). *Science* 193:913–915.

Itoigawa, N. 1975. Variables in male leaving a group of Japanese macaques. In *Proceedings from the Symposia of the 5th Congress of the*

International Primatological Society, ed. S. Kondo, M. Kawai, A. Ehara, and S. Kawamura. Tokyo: Japan Science Press.

Jay, P. 1965. The common langur of North India. In *Primate behavior: Field studies of monkeys and apes,* ed. I. DeVore. New York: Holt, Rinehart.

Kanagawa, H., and Hafez, E. S. E. 1973. Copulatory behavior in relation to anatomical characteristics of three macaques. *Am. J. Phys. Anthrop.* 38:233–240.

Kaufmann, J. H. 1967. Social relations of adult males in a free-ranging band of rhesus monkeys. In *Social communication among primates,* ed. S. Altmann. Chicago: University of Chicago Press.

Kline-Graber, G., and Graber, B. 1975. *Woman's orgasm.* New York: Bobbs-Merrill.

Kling, A., and Dunne, K. 1976. Social-environmental factors affecting behavior and plasma testosterone in normal and amygdala lesioned *M. speciosa. Primates* 17:23–42.

Lancaster, Jane B., and Lee, Richard B. 1965. The annual reproductive cycle in monkeys and apes. In *Primate behavior: Field studies of monkeys and apes,* ed. I. DeVore. New York: Holt, Rinehart.

Lindburg, D. G. 1969. Rhesus monkeys: Mating season mobility of adult males. *Science* 166:1176–1178.

————. 1971. The rhesus monkey in North India: An ecological and behavioral study. In *Primate behavior,* vol. 2, ed. L. Rosenblum. New York: Academic Press.

————. 1975. Mate selection in the rhesus monkey, *Macaca mulatta.* Paper read at American Association of Physical Anthropologists meeting, April 12, 1975 in Denver.

Loy, J. 1970. Peri-menstrual sexual behavior among rhesus monkeys. *Folia Primatol.* 13:286–287.

————. 1971. Estrous behavior of free-ranging rhesus monkeys (*Macaca mulatta*). *Primates* 12:1–32.

Mass, R. 1972. Effects of dorso-lateral frontal ablations on the social behavior of a caged group of eleven stump-tailed macaques. Doctoral dissertation, Rutgers University, 1972.

Masters, W. H., and Johnson, V. E. 1966. *Human sexual response.* Boston: Little, Brown.

Michael, R. P.; Herbert, J.; and Welegalla, J. 1966. Ovarian hormones and grooming behavior in the rhesus monkey (*Macaca mulatta*) under laboratory conditions. *J. Endocrinol.* 36:263–279.

Michael, R. P.; Keverne, E. B.; and Bonsall, R. W. 1971. Pheromones: Isolation of male sex attractants from a female primate. *Science* 172: 964–966.

Michael, R. P., and Saayman, G. S. 1968. Differential effects on behavior of the subcutaneous and intravaginal administration of oestrogen in the rhesus monkey (*Macaca mulatta*). *J. Endocrinol.* 41:231-246.

Michael, R. P.; Wilson, M. I.; and Zumpe, D. 1974. The bisexual behavior of female rhesus monkeys. In *Sex differences in behavior,* ed. R. C. Friedman, R. M. Richart, and R. L. Vande Wiele. New York: Wiley.

Michael, R. P., and Zumpe, D. 1970. Rhythmic changes in the copulatory frequency of rhesus monkeys (*Macaca mulatta*) in relation to the menstrual cycle and a comparison with the human cycle. *J. Reprod. Fert.* 21:199-201.

Missakian, E. Z. 1973. Genealogical mating activity in free-ranging groups of rhesus monkeys (*Macaca mulatta*) on Cayo Santiago. *Behavior* 45:224-240.

Neville, M. K. 1968. A free-ranging rhesus monkey troop lacking adult males. *J. Mammal.* 49:771-773.

Newton, N. 1973. Interrelationships between sexual responsiveness, birth and breast feeding. In *Contemporary sexual behavior,* ed. J. Zubin and J. Money. Baltimore: Johns Hopkins University.

Norikoshi, K. and Koyama, N. 1975. Group shifting and social organization among Japanese monkeys. In *Proceedings from the Symposia of the 5th Congress of the International Primatological Society,* ed. S. Kondo, M. Kawai, A. Ehara, and S. Kawamura. Tokyo: Japan Science Press.

Parker, C. 1975. Male transfer in olive baboons. *Nature* 255:219-220.

Perachio, A. A.; Alexander, M.; and Marr, L. D. 1973. Hormonal and social factors affecting evoked sexual behavior in rhesus monkeys. *Am. J. Phys. Anthrop.* 38:227-232.

Ranson, T. W., and Rowell, T. E. 1972. Early social development of feral baboons. In *Primate socialization,* ed. F. Poirier. New York: Random House.

Rowell, T. E. 1972. Female reproduction cycles and social behavior in primates. *Advanc. Stud. Behav.* 4:69-105.

Saayman, G. S. 1970. The menstrual cycle and sexual behaviour in a troop of free-ranging chacma baboons (*Papio ursinus*). *Folia Primatol.* 12:81-110.

————. 1973. Effects of ovarian hormones on the sexual skin and behavior of ovariectomized baboons (*Papio ursinus*) under free-ranging conditions. In *Symposia of the 4th International Congress of Primatology,* vol. 2, ed. C. H. Phoenix. Basel: S. Karger.

————. 1975. The influence of hormonal and ecological factors upon sexual behavior and social organization in Old World primates. In *Socioecology and psychology of primates,* ed. R. Tuttle. The Hague: Mouton.

Sade, D. S. 1968. Inhibition of son-mother mating among free-ranging rhesus monkeys. *Sci. and Psychoanal.* 12:18–37.

————. 1972. A longitudinal study of social behavior of rhesus monkeys. In *The functional and evolutionary biology of primates,* ed. R. Tuttle. Chicago: Aldine-Atherton.

Saunders, C., and Hausfater, G. In press. In *Proceedings of the 6th Congress of the International Primatological Society.* Basel: S. Karger.

Stephenson, G. R. 1975. Social structure of mating activity in Japanese macaques. In *Proceedings from the Symposia of the 5th Congress of the International Primatological Society,* ed. S. Kondo, M. Kawai, A. Ehara, and S. Kawamura. Tokyo: Japan Science Press.

Trivers, R. L. 1972. Parental investment and sexual selection. In *Sexual selection and the descent of man,* ed. B. Campbell. Chicago: Aldine.

Trollope, J., and Blurton-Jones, N. G. 1975. Aspects of reproduction and reproductive behaviour in *Macaca arctoides. Primates* 16:191–205.

Tutin, C. E. G. 1975. Exceptions to promiscuity in a feral chimpanzee community. In *Contemporary primatology.* Basel: S. Karger.

Wade, T. D. 1976. Effects of strangers on rhesus monkey groups. *Behavior* 56:194–214.

Wickler, W. 1973. *The sexual code: The social behavior of animals and men.* Garden City, N.Y.: Doubleday.

Wilson, E. O. 1975. *Sociobiology: The new synthesis.* Cambridge, Mass.: Belknap.

Wrangham, R. W. 1974. Artificial feeding of chimpanzees and baboons in their natural habitat. *Anim. Behav.* 22:83–93.

Zuckerman, S. 1932. *The social life of monkeys and apes.* London: Routledge and Kegan Paul.

Zumpe, D., and Michael, R. P. 1968. The clutching reaction and orgasm in the female rhesus monkey (*Macaca mulatta*). *J. Endocrinol.* 40:117–123.

Sexuality and Sociality in Humans and Other Primates

Richard D. Alexander

In the preceding chapter, Dr. Lancaster's review of primate sexual behavior raises issues of considerable importance in efforts to understand ourselves further through comparative study. For several years, I have thought that certain unique or uniquely exaggerated attributes of the human female—such as menopause and the concealment of ovulation (the latter as compared with its advertisement in other primates)—probably represent keys to the reconstruction of the history of human sociality, if we only knew how to interpret them. More recently I have wondered if they might not even represent the principal keys for understanding the entire question of how the human evolutionary line came to diverge so dramatically from the lines of all other primates. In this discussion I will try to combine an analysis of Lancaster's arguments with an explanation of the basis for these views and their meaning (see also Alexander and Noonan, 1978).

Comparisons of sexual and social behavior among different primate species allow us to see our own behavior in perspective with that of our closest contemporary relatives. There is also another kind of comparative study. It involves searches among even widely divergent taxonomic groups with parallel systems of, say, behavior, for correlations with other attributes which, by their independent appearance in the different groups, suggest cause-effect relationships not previously apparent. For example, Alexander and co-workers (1978) have demonstrated close correlations between harem sizes and degree of sexual dimorphism in body length in three mammalian groups with independently evolved variations in breeding systems. These findings are a quite powerful indication that varying intensities of male-male competition are responsible for relative amounts of sexual dimorphism in all three groups.

The above comparative procedures may contribute to reconstructions of the reasons for the divergences of the human line from those lines giving rise to other primates. In turn, clarifications of the reasons for humans becoming what we apparently are may yield new insight into countless observable but incompletely understood facts of everyday human existence, and suggest new possibilities for the adjustment of human behaviors toward the alleviation of many practical and painful problems.

Dr. Lancaster examines recent data with reference to female orgasm, mate selection, incest, and the role of sex in integrating primate societies. She reviews evidence that orgasm occurs in at least some nonhuman primate females, shows that females of some nonhuman primates are sometimes sexually active outside estrus, and concludes that nonhuman primates are sexually more plastic than has been supposed. She suggests that male dominance is not as important as had been supposed in determining who mates with whom, and that female preferences are much more important than has been supposed.

I certainly agree that female sexuality in primates is considerably more complex and important than previous studies have suggested, and that female choice is a much more potent force in determining sexual and social behavior than we have usually acknowledged. I also think that the arguments for the existence in nonhuman primates of female orgasm, anestrous sexuality, and the employment of multiple strategies toward success in sexual activities are amply documented.

Proximate and Ultimate Factors

My disagreements with Lancaster—or my opinion that different interpretations will be more useful in some cases—reflect my concern with what I regard as a common deficiency in the analyses of biological and social scientists. I refer to the failure to recognize or take into account continually that *proximate mechanisms* exist and are maintained only because in the past (at least) they have served the *ultimate function* of reproduction. By proximate mechanisms I mean things like pleasure and pain—and any and all kinds of responses that could be subsumed under learning or development, so long as the contingencies are historically relevant (and, therefore, the proximate "mechanism" is indeed a mechanism and not simply an accident or an incidental effect of some novel circumstance).

One reason why it is useful to think about the ultimate function behind a proximate mechanism is that proximate mechanisms are difficult things to understand, and we need all the help we can get. Another reason is that a proximate mechanism cannot (for long) be its own justification. Thus, the association between pleasure and, say, sex or eating does not exist because of some kind of physiological determinism: The association has evolved across our history because sex and eating have led, directly or indirectly, to reproduction. It follows that the particular manners or circumstances in which sex and eating bring the greatest pleasure ought to associate with events that in the past either most surely led to reproduction or led to the most reproduction. Bearing such thoughts in mind can assist us in analyzing the nature of physiological and ontogenetic phenomena.

There are some particularly confusing aspects of the relationship between proximate and ultimate mechanisms. For example, because we have evolved to associate pleasure with sex and eating, the connection may persist for a while even if the association with reproduction suddenly disappears. Thus, an abrupt and historically novel surfeit of food might cause us to overeat, become obese, and die young, almost certainly lowering our lifetime reproduction. Similarly, the introduction of effective, easy-to-use contraceptives allows us to indulge the pleasures of sex in ways that also almost certainly lower our lifetime reproduction. (Please note that I am not valuing success or failure in reproduction, indulgence in either sex or eating, or anyone's attitude toward any of these things—only considering their relationship to history and how that relationship might be exploited in efforts to understand humans.)

Tobacco, alcohol, drugs, innumerable products of technology, and even the results of sociological, psychological, biological, and other analyses of human sociality can also represent novelties obfuscating the relationship between proximate mechanisms and their historical functions. For the experimental scientist, whether biological or psychological, the most startling and significant realization is that essentially every experimental setup has the potential for being so novel in terms of the organism's evolutionary history that blinding confusion is generated.

Although the introduction of novel circumstances allows exploitation of the pleasure of sex, in terms of evolution such exploitation would lead eventually to a decreased pleasure in sex, as such, because sexual pleasure would be leading to behaviors no longer enhancing reproduction. Of course, any such evolutionary effects would appear so very slowly as to be of the most trivial significance in the modern, rapidly changing world.

Sex and food cause pleasure, then, pleasure being the label we have applied to sensations that tend to cause acts to be repeated. Pleasure and reproduction have evolved to be associated because repeating acts that lead to reproduction leads to further reproduction. Conversely, pain deters us from reproductively deleterious acts. To understand the explanatory or guiding significance of these thoughts about ultimate functions, it is useful to consider paradoxical situations. For example, enormous satisfaction may result from giving one's life for a brood of offspring if it is clearly the only way to save them: We lament the situation, yet we may appreciate the opportunity to be there to save our offspring. Conversely, eating could be sheer torture if it had to occur while one's offspring or other close relatives were known to be starving.

The proposition that organisms have evolved to be reproductive systems usually seems bizarre to anyone who deals principally in human activities, yet it is quite clear that we cannot avoid dealing with it. I think that our attitude toward this proposition is itself a profoundly important topic for investigation. For reasons still unclear to me, the evolution of human abilities and tendencies to be conscious and deliberate about *some* activities did not carry with it abilities or tendencies to spend our waking hours totally preoccupied with conscious and deliberate plotting of how to increase our personal reproductive success—at least not in those terms. Yet, despite our tendencies to deny concern with reproduction, anyone who takes a serious look at societal laws can scarcely fail to recognize that their underlying theme—from the Ten Commandments to the legal system of modern America—is the suppression of extremes of reproductive competitiveness by the individuals making up societies. The parade example is the uniquely human phenomenon of socially imposed monogamy. The acquisition of culture resulted in cumulatively heritable differences in resource control among individual humans leading to unparalleled degrees of difference in reproductive potential, especially among males, and even within small social groups. Yet men who are clearly capable of keeping several or many wives and successfully rearing their offspring are prevented by law from doing it, and this has apparently been true in every large, highly organized, highly unified society in history (for example, the industrialized or technological nations). Flaunting of this particular law, as Joseph Smith and his followers discovered, is one of the behaviors that may lead to death by lynching. Death penalties have historically been associated with what seem to me to be the most dramatic exploitations of others for the purpose of increased reproductive success—for example, through killing, rape, or treason (Alexander, in press).

Contrary to a widespread misimpression, the evolutionary or reproductive view of human behavior does not mean that we are forced to behave in any particular fashion in any particular circumstance; we are not subject to a genetic or ontogenetic determinism that somehow violates our own views of our potential for personal decisions or exercise of free will. Any modern human with knowledge of history and the power of self-reflection potentially can do essentially anything he wants to do with his life, including deliberate nonreproduction, or a life style that is consistently inconsistent with evolutionary history in essentially every regard (Alexander, in press). Nevertheless, the theory that all organisms have evolved to maximize the reproduction of their genes—even if they do not actually do so—is reasonable beyond doubt, consistent with every observation in biology, and overwhelmingly supported by biological facts gathered since Darwin. I can think of no valid reason for denying its applicability to the history of humans, as well as to that of every other organism (Alexander, 1975, 1977).

The question here is: How does this general idea relate to Lancaster's facts and arguments—especially when they seem to fall short of satisfactory conclusions? Is it of any use in evaluating the items she has so effectively brought to our attention?

Functions of Orgasms

We can begin with the function of orgasm. What is an orgasm good for? It gives pleasure—indeed it is often represented as a peak in human ability to experience intensity of pleasure. Why should an orgasm give intense pleasure? I venture that there is no *a priori* physiological reason why it should have to be so. I am confident that any organism could be taught to experience enormous pain and displeasure with orgasm.

The reproductive significance of a male's orgasm is obvious, even if male orgasms are frequently nonreproductive, and even if we do not understand all of the events associated with and leading up to every single situation in which males experience orgasms. Male orgasms release sperm, and when this happens during copulation, there is some likelihood that the sperm will find an egg and reproduction will result. Indeed, there is no other natural way for reproduction in humans to occur; and the one thing that we may safely assume about all of our ancestors is that they reproduced successfully.

Thus, we may speculate with reasonable confidence that the basis for male orgasms being pleasurable is that they have contributed to reproduction by releasing sperm in the proper places and at the proper times.

What about female orgasms? Lancaster raises this question but does not provide a very definite answer. At one point she suggests that "for some species" female orgasm may function as a preejaculatory trigger mechanism—in other words, that it may trigger or hasten ejaculation in the male. She does not take up the question of why this might be important, or why only in some species. Moreover, in another place she suggests that estrous females may choose mature males because the latter are more capable of stimulating them to orgasm.

I sympathize with Lancaster's apparent uncertainty, and have pondered this question for a long time without developing a satisfying answer. One unsatisfactory (or incomplete) answer, for either male or female orgasm, is that the pleasure of the orgasm is its own reward. While this is a perfectly adequate description of how a proximate mechanism works to cause repetition of an act favorable to reproduction, it tells us nothing about how the act is favorable to reproduction, therefore, why it should be pleasurable in the first place. Possibly, female orgasm somehow increases the likelihood of fertilization of the egg through contributing to the movement of the sperm; and, even more speculatively, a female orgasm may also communicate to a male that this likelihood is enhanced—thus, that the female's offspring of the near future have a certain likelihood of being his own. In this case, as in general, males obviously would not be required to be aware that they have received such information, only to behave as if they know. Obviously, this speculation about function introduces the question of deception as well as the problem of male confidence of paternity. Both, I believe, are central issues in understanding human sexuality and sociality.

Rather than females simply preferring males able to give them orgasms (which may imply that orgasms are their own reward and does not seem to lead us toward an explanation of their existence), perhaps females are more likely to have orgasms with males they prefer, and perhaps they prefer those males for reasons not yet apparent. Obviously, if this last were the case, males who could cause even "inadvertent" orgasms in females with whom they copulated could sometimes, or briefly, be favored on this account—illustrating again the complexity of the issues involved here.

One possible suggestion is that orgasm in the human female (and perhaps other primates as well) may function as an indicator to the male of the female's sexual satisfaction. Its apparent tendency, in humans at least, to mimic male orgasm, in the absence of a correlation with an event paralleling release of gametes, may suggest (1) that the correlation is instead with the pleasure or satisfaction of male orgasm to the male, and (2) that in humans the female orgasm is principally a communicative device that tends to reassure a male that the female is disinclined to seek sexual satisfaction with other males. If this interpretation is correct, female orgasm should (1) be characterized by obvious outward signs; (2) mimic male orgasms in regard to outward signs; (3) frequently involve deception, with females pretending to have orgasms when they do not; (4) occur most frequently (a) in deeply satisfying or long-term interactions with males committed to the female and her offspring, and (b) with dominant males or males with obviously superior ability to deliver parental benefits; and (5) occur least frequently in brief or casual encounters, and in copulation with a partner unsatisfactory in the above regards. All of these contingencies may correspond with orgasm in human females. All appear to be consistent with the information reported by Lancaster except for the suggestion that female primates achieve orgasms sooner if they have been deprived of sexual activity. The idea that female orgasms are principally communicative devices is obviously consistent with reports that female primates vocalize during orgasm and sometimes turn toward the male and exhibit characteristic facial contortions or lip-smacking. Moreover, the value of direct communication during sexual behavior may relate to the still-unexplained human tendency to copulate face-to-face, almost nonexistent in nonhuman mammals except in the great apes, where it apparently occurs less frequently than in humans.

We are forced to leave the function of the female orgasm at an unsatisfactory stage, but maybe I have made the point that it is potentially enlightening to seek the reproductive significance of female orgasms. The speculation that female orgasm is primarily communicative is consistent with the suggestion that increases in parental investment, in particular by males, were an important aspect of the evolutionary divergence of the human line from those of other primates (Alexander and Noonan, 1978).

Female (and Male) Preferences

Lancaster speaks of "personal preference" regarding sexual partners as if it frequently involves nothing more significant than individuality. She notes, however, that males prefer mature females, that immature females are considered "uninteresting," and that mature females rear more babies. She also points to maturity as the most important correlate of high status and to the significance of maternal lineage as a factor in mate selection. Similar observations have been made in studies of human populations. Chagnon (1978) finds that in Yanomama Indians both sexes prefer mates from high-ranking families, and that members of high-ranking families—whether men or women—reproduce more than members of low-ranking families. Dickeman (1978) reaches similar conclusions regarding Asian societies with caste systems.

Lancaster notes that some primate females prefer well-known males and "fully mature" males. She supposes that the principal mating advantage to females is that such males have proved they have the genetic makeup to survive to a mature age, therefore are likely to produce sons with similar abilities, so that the sons also will be more successful in reproduction. This is a definite possibility.

Lancaster also suggests that males in Old World primates probably never know who their offspring are. This would appear to be an overgeneralization, since gorilla males, hamadryas baboon males, gibbon males, and probably many others who monopolize or sequester females would have an excellent likelihood of being able to direct their paternal solicitude toward their own offspring. I think we must introduce into Lancaster's considerations on this topic the matter of parental investment by males. As soon as a male has something besides evidence of "good genes" to offer females, then females will profit from obtaining it. In the case of paternal care, one has to suppose that the female who is able to give her male a high confidence of paternity is considerably more likely to obtain his paternal care for her offspring than a female who is utterly promiscuous in his presence.

High confidence of paternity appears to be absent from multi-male social groups of all animals except monogamous birds, in which the male often is absolutely required to rear offspring, and in which males guard their females continuously during the period of egg-laying, the only time that fertilization can occur. Male parental care is clearly prominent in most societies of humans today and clearly not prominent in most multi-male societies of other primates. Katharine Noonan and I have argued (1978) that the increasing importance of male parental care may have been responsible for much of the divergence of the human line that caused us to become so distinctive from other primates. How did this change occur? Part of our scenario is quoted below:

> The human female has commonly been described as "continually sexually receptive" because she may willingly mate at any time during the menstrual cycle (James, 1971). Most other female mammals mate only during a brief oestrus period occurring around the ovulatory period. To refer to the human female's sexual behavior simply as "continuous receptivity," however, seems a gross oversimplification. First, this "receptivity" is unlike the relatively uninhibited receptivity of some oestrous female mammals. By comparison, the human female's behavior might best be described as a kind of selective or low-key receptivity, commonly tuned to a single male, or at least to one male at a time. From the point of view of males not bonded to a particular female, it might just as well be termed "continuous nonreceptivity." It is a truly remarkable attribute of

human females that their ovulation is often essentially impossible to detect, even, in some cases, through medical technology. . . .

In nonhuman primates the general period of ovulation always appears to be more or less dramatically signalled to males (even if only by pheromones or other means not obvious to human observers). All of the nonhuman primates in which females are known to show "pseudo-estrus" are group-living species, while the least obvious signs of ovulation seem to occur in monogamous species like gibbons, or polygynous species, like gorillas, which tend to live in single-male bands. . . .

We believe that two coincident circumstances can explain the evolution of concealment of ovulation: First, a social situation in which females of reproductive age are not completely inaccessible to males other than their mates or consorts (e.g., multi-male groups or defensible multi-female territories) and, second, a growing importance of parental care such that the value to a female of a male's prowess in monopolizing her at ovulation time would be overshadowed by the value of male prowess and willingness as a providing or protective parent. Gradual evolution of concealment of ovulation by females behaving so as to maximize their mate's confidence of paternity, hence likelihood of behaving paternally, would with each step toward concealment improve the female's ability to secure her mate's parental care. Because no male could tell when a female was ovulating, only a male who tended her more or less continuously could be sure of the paternity of her offspring. Occasional forced or clandestine matings outside the pair bond, in the absence of information about ovulation, would have a very low likelihood of resulting in pregnancy (Alexander and Noonan, 1978).

Lancaster suggests that in some primates the function of sexual swellings may be stimulation of the female's own "appetitive behavior." She discounts its significance as a stimulus to the male because "the most potent sexual stimulus to the male is an estrogen-dependent pheromone-like agent secreted in the vagina . . . neither redness nor swelling of the sexual skin is stimulating to the male without the presence of the olfactory cue."

Proximate mechanisms entail physiological and genetic expense. We are justified in expecting such expenses to be minimized by natural selection. Accordingly, it would be very difficult to explain the extreme sexual swelling and coloration in some primates solely by the effect on the bearer herself. We have no reason to believe that such evidently expensive changes are the only way an organism can cause itself to carry out effective reproductive behavior. Moreover, such an explanation leaves us with no way to account for the distribution of sexual swellings among primates.

I suggest this alternative: The sexual skin is a visual stimulus leading the male to investigate for the presence of the chemical indicating ovulation. This hypothesis suggests that the sexual skin is an aspect of female-female competition for attention of (the "best") males, hence leads to the prediction that sexual skin will be prominent only when multiple males are available. This prediction is realized since sexual swellings and bright sexual skin are absent in single-male species like gibbons and gorillas, and most prominent in multi-male troops as in chimpanzees, macaques, and baboons (Alexander and Noonan, 1978).

Male Dominance

Lancaster suggests that male "dominance" has been afforded too great a role in determining reproductive success. I agree that the whole subject needs careful review. One reason is that definitions of dominance have sometimes become essentially divorced from applicability to natural situations. Another is that many observations have occurred in clearly unusual situations, as in closely confined troops or in troops culled in ways that may have greatly altered the proportion and kinds of male-male interactions. A third reason is the significance of recognizing relationships among male dominance, female choice, and male parental care.

Nevertheless, I think Lancaster's arguments are somewhat vulnerable. For example, she notes that subordinates must copulate with estrous females out of sight of dominants and that subordinates are sometimes sexually incompetent in the presence of a dominant male. These and most of her other arguments indicate to me that dominance is indeed quite important. None of the arguments presented suggests that strategies alternative to attaining and maintaining dominance are anything but second best. The only reasonable hypothesis seems to be that in nonhuman primates living in multi-male bands all males strive toward dominance, and that they are diverted in this strategy toward alternatives because attainment of dominance is sufficiently unlikely that relatively low-return diversions such as sneakiness are sometimes profitable, or are profitable for particular males only. Hausfater's (1975) data, for example, tend to support what sexual differences in senescence patterns reveal on a much wider scale—namely, that males have evolved to play for higher stakes than have females, and are more likely to win big or lose completely. This is evidently true of humans, and of all polygynous species. Sex ratios as well as sex differences in parental behavior, time of maturation, and general behavior all support this interpretation (Williams, 1957, 1975; Hamilton, 1966; Alexander et al., 1978; see also Trivers, 1972).

Since "young, immature, and low status" females are in her own arguments poor bets in reproduction, and since copulation with "particular lineages of females" would lead to genetic inbreeding, I do not understand why Lancaster believes the fact that such females are neglected by mature males, hence "free to mate with any males," is contrary to a "priority-of-access" model of male sexual behavior (thus, a model relying on dominance).

Sex as an Integrative Mechanism

In connection with Lancaster's argument that sexuality was a prominent aspect of social interactions in our ancestors long before they had become human (with which I heartily agree), she suggests that sex is for things other than procreation and gives as an example "mechanisms of social attachment." In this context she also argues against the view that sex is a disruptive force in a society and for the view that it is an integrative force. Indeed, she implies that the rewards of sexual pleasure represent the bonds around which primate social groups are formed and maintained.

I would suggest a change in Lancaster's initial emphasis. Rather than sex being for things other than procreation, it appears that the ways in which sexual behavior actually leads (eventually) to procreation are more complex and indirect than had previously been supposed. One of these ways, for example, might be the promise or actuality of delivering sexual pleasure or unusual sexual pleasure; what we know of human behavior seems to support this view. Nevertheless, it is a more complex problem than we might think. Women whose beauty, intelligence, abilities to empathize, or other attributes seem to a great many men to promise extraordinary sexual pleasure may be able to cause such responses because the attributes in question simultaneously promise other things historically of much greater importance, such as success in child-bearing and nursing, faithfulness, or a lifetime of cooperativeness in mutually beneficial and satisfying activities. In this context it should not escape us that, in historical and biological terms, lifetimes are no more nor less than reproductive acts; indeed, there is no other way to explain their finiteness (Williams, 1957; Hamilton, 1966; Alexander, 1977).

Lancaster also implies that sexuality may actually be the cement of group formation and maintenance. I agree, in the sense that male and female have to come together to reproduce. But to use sexuality to explain all primate groupings would not easily explain why some primates group more than others, or why some are enormously more sexual than others. Moreover, it would represent a return to using proximate mechanisms to explain ultimate ones, rather than the other way around. Group living entails expenses to the individuals engaging in it: increased competition for all resources and increased likelihood of contracting diseases or acquiring parasites. If the physiological rewards of sexuality were wholly responsible for group living, then, during history, those deviants who were not so sexy as to feel compelled to engage in group living would not suffer these detriments to their reproduction, and sociality would have gradually diminished as a result of the superior reproduction of less sexy, less social, more reproductive deviants.

Thus, there are solid arguments that group living is forced by *extrinsic* pressures—most notably, predators and the value of group hunting for large or elusive prey (see Alexander, 1974; Hoogland and Sherman, 1976). Whenever group living occurs as a result of such forces, it leads to increased sexual competition, since mates are also resources. Under these conditions, sexual activity becomes more prominent, and this is why sexuality is very prominent in multi-male groups, such as savannah baboons, and not very prominent in primarily single-male polygynous groups such as gorillas, or monogamous pairs such as gibbons.

Humans are highly sexual, and this is but one of many indications that human history involved living in multi-male groups. If we are to explain unique human attributes in terms of their history, then we may as well resign ourselves to explaining how

93

they could have evolved in multi-male social groups. It is also quite evident that humans have been polygynous throughout most of their history, meaning that fewer males than females have generally contributed genetically to each generation, that some males have been more successful in reproduction than any females, and that sexual competition was more severe among males than among females (Alexander et al., 1978). All of these things are almost certainly true of every extant human society.

Thus, it seems clear that sexuality is both a disruptive and an integrative factor in sociality, depending largely on the composition of the group; it may integrate a pair, integrate male and female in a harem, but disrupt female-female interactions; but it cannot be the principal integrating factor in a multi-male primate group (Alexander, 1974).

Incest Avoidance

I find Lancaster's conclusions on incest difficult to grasp. This is not a very severe criticism, since so little is known of primate inbreeding and outbreeding, and so much confusion has existed in efforts to compare "incest" and marriage patterns in humans with breeding behavior in nonhuman primates.

It seems to me that ample data now indicate that nonhuman primates, like humans and the vast majority of sexual organisms, avoid sex with their closest relatives whenever they can, and especially sex likely to cause offspring. Thus, Lawick-Goodall (1968) found that adult female chimpanzees mate readily with most males in their groups, but resist their brothers violently. Adult males, moreover, do not mate with their mothers. Imanishi (1965) found no instances of mother-son matings in Japanese monkeys studied at Koshima, and Tokuda (1962) reported none in a captive group of rhesus and crab-eating macaques. Sade (1968) observed four mother-son matings in 363 copulations among rhesus monkeys on Cayo Santiago Island. Kaufmann (1965) reported only one instance of a male rhesus mounting his mother and another of a male copulating with his mother.

Missakian's (1973) data on rhesus monkeys may at first seem contradictory. In her extensive observations 5.4 percent of all mount series and copulations involved mother-son pairs, and mating was observed in 31 percent of 36 individual pairs of mothers and sons. She also saw matings in 12 percent of 42 individual pairs of brothers and sisters. Of 59 mother-son pairs, 21 (36 percent) were separated when sons permanently left their natal groups. Of these 21 males, 19 left between three and five years of age, evidently at or near the onset of their first breeding season. The remaining two left at eleven and ten years of age when they were the alpha and beta males, respectively. Both of the old males became solitary after their departure.

Except for a single dominant male who mated with his mother, however, all of Missakian's observations of mother-son matings involved young males from three to five years old who rarely or never mated with other females during that period. Of 30 males of that age who lacked mothers, only one mated with nonrelated females, and that when he was five years old. Similarly, all brother-sister matings involved males from three to five years old mating mostly with older sisters. Missakian's observations suggest that the young males involved in these "incestuous" matings lacked access to other females. She stated as well that they failed to form the usual consort relations with their mothers or sisters. Under more natural conditions a higher mortality of males, or differences in troop structure owing to a different sort of "culling" by natural predators, could reduce even these figures. Yet her data still seem to support the argument that close inbreeding is rare in rhesus monkeys even when sons remain in close proximity to their mothers, and brothers to their sisters. We do not know whether or not mother-son or brother-sister matings ever produce offspring.

These primate data call for some interpretation. First, how does one define incest avoidance, and how does one identify avoidance of close inbreeding? What percentage of all matings should be expected to occur between close relatives when all tendencies or mechanisms for avoiding such matings are absent? One cannot simply measure time spent in close proximity in determining opportunities for copulation, although this measurement may be useful in some cases.

In a polygynous one-male band a female (or male) may have no mating opportunities except with a close relative. A prepubertal or young-adult male in any primate group may spend little or no time near females other than his mother and sisters; but how can one tell by counting his matings with such relatives whether or not selection has tended to reduce their frequency?

If young males tend to leave their natal troops before achieving success in reproduction, and if dominant males tend to leave the troops in which they have sired more or all offspring at about the time their daughters mature (Boelkins and Wilson, 1972; Drickamer and Vessey, 1973; Packer, 1975), how does one know whether a history of deleterious inbreeding or some other factor such as sexual competition is principally involved? If indirect effects such as sexual competition incidentally bring about outbreeding, then selection cannot improve tendencies to avoid deleterious inbreeding because it never occurs. Failures to outbreed under altered conditions, when the situation incidentally effective in reducing outbreeding has been removed, cannot be used to support an argument that the animal involved is incapable of evolving an avoidance of outbreeding or would not benefit from outbreeding.

It seems to me that rather than incest avoidance being rare in nonhuman primates, in all those (few) species that have been adequately studied, some degree of avoidance of close inbreeding has been observed. How this relates to complex incest and marriage rules and patterns in humans, and the relationships of the various causal factors in the two cases, is another matter entirely.

References

Alexander, R. D. 1974. The evolution of social behavior. *Ann. Rev. Ecol. Syst.* 5:325–338.

———. 1975. The search for a general theory of behavior. *Behav. Sci.* 20:77–100.

———. 1977. Natural selection and the analysis of human sociality. In *Changing scenes in the natural sciences,* ed. C. E. Goulden. Philadelphia Academy of Natural Science, Special Publication no. 12.

———. In press. Natural selection and societal laws. In *Science and the foundation of ethics,* ed. T. Engelhardt and D. Callahan. Proceedings of two conferences at the Institute of Society, Ethics, and the Life Sciences, February and June 1977, Hastings-on-Hudson, New York.

Alexander, R. D.; Hoogland, J. L.; Howard, R.; Noonan, K. M.; and Sherman, P. W. 1978. Sexual dimorphisms and breedings systems in pinnipeds, ungulates, primates, and humans. In *Evolutionary biology and human social behavior*, ed. N. A. Chagnon and W. G. Irons. North Scituate, Mass.: Duxbury Press.

Alexander, R. D., and Noonan, K. M. 1978. Concealment of ovulation, parental care, and human social evolution. In *Evolutionary biology and human social behavior*, ed. N. A. Chagnon and W. G. Irons. North Scituate, Mass.: Duxbury Press.

Sexuality and Sociality

Boelkins, R. C., and Wilson, A. P. 1972. Intergroup social dynamics of the Cayo Santiago rhesus (*Macaca mulatta*) with special reference to changes in group membership by males. *Primates* 13:125–140.

Chagnon, N. A. 1978. Differential reproductive success, marriage, and genealogical relatedness among 3500 Yanomamo Indians. In *Evolutionary biology and human social behavior*, ed. N. A. Chagnon and W. G. Irons. North Scituate, Mass.: Duxbury Press.

Dickeman, M. 1978. The reproductive structure of stratified human societies: A preliminary model. In *Evolutionary biology and human social behavior*, ed. N. A. Chagnon and W. G. Irons. North Scituate, Mass.: Duxbury Press.

Drickamer, L. C., and Vessey, S. H. 1973. Group changing in free-ranging rhesus monkeys. *Primates* 14:359–368.

Hamilton, W. D. 1966. The moulding of senescence by natural selection. *J. Theoret. Biol.* 12:12–45.

Hausfater, G. 1975. Dominance and reproduction in baboons (*Papio cynocephalus*): A quantitative analysis. *Contrib. Primatol.* 7:1–150.

Hoogland, J. L., and Sherman, P. W. 1976. Advantages and disadvantages of bank swallow coloniality. *Ecol. Monogr.* 46:33–58.

Imanishi, K. 1965. The origin of the human family: A primatological approach. In *Japanese monkeys: A collection of translations*, ed. S. A. Altmann. (Published by S. A. Altmann, University of Chicago.)

James, W. H. 1971. The distribution of coitus within the human intermenstruum. *J. Biosocial Sci.* 3:159–171.

Kaufmann, J. H. 1965. A three-year study of mating behavior in a free-ranging band of rhesus monkeys. *Ecology* 46:500–512.

Lawick-Goodall, J. van. 1968. The behavior of free-living chimpanzees of the Gombe Stream reserve. *Anim. Behav. Monogr.* 1:161–311.

Missakian, E. A. 1973. Genealogical mating activity in free-ranging groups of rhesus monkeys (*Macaca mulatta*) on Cayo Santiago. *Behavior* 45:224–241.

Parker, C. 1975. Male transfer in olive baboons. *Nature* 255:219–220.

Sade, D. S. 1968. Inhibition of son-mother mating among free-ranging rhesus monkeys. *Sci. Psychoanal.* 12:18–37.

Tokuda, K. 1962. A study on the sexual behavior in the Japanese monkey group. *Primates* 3:1–40.

Trivers, R. L. 1972. Parental investment and sexual selection. In *Sexual selection and the descent of man*, ed. B. Campbell. Chicago: Aldine.

Williams, G. C. 1957. Pleitropy, natural selection, and the evolution of senescence. *Evolution* 11:398–411.

———. 1975. *Sex and evolution*. Princeton, N.J.: Princeton University Press.

Animal Models and Psychological Inference

Frank A. Beach

"When I use a word," Humpty Dumpty said, in a rather scornful tone, "it means just what I choose it to mean—neither more nor less."

"The question is," said Alice, "whether you *can* make words mean so many different things" (Lewis Carroll, *Alice Through the Looking-Glass*, Chapter 6).

Humptydumptyism is endemic during interdisciplinary discourse in which different kinds of specialists use the same words to mean quite different things. Attacks of this disease are difficult to diagnose, because those afflicted with it often are misled by what Quine has termed "the implicit assumption of a mutual understanding." The dangers are acute in a congregation of travelers from lands so distinct ecologically as sociology, anthropology, psychiatry, biology, and psychology. The antibodies of one population afford little protection against the viruses of another.

As a comparative psychologist I live in a border zone between biology and psychology, and am particularly sensitive to dangers inherent in using the same vocabulary to describe behavior of different species. For example, the word *sex* can and should mean the same thing in relation to all species that reproduce sexually; but *sexuality* and *gender* are terms applicable only to *Homo sapiens* (Beach, 1974). This is no mere semantic quibble. Language is more than a tool for describing the world. It is a means of *creating* the world.

A powerful semantic device is the metaphor, and one form of the metaphor currently popular in behavioral science is

The author's research mentioned in this article was supported by USPHS Grant 04000 from the National Institute of Mental Health.

the so-called animal model, which plays an increasingly important role in such diverse fields as sociobiology (Wilson, 1975) and psychiatry (McKinney, 1974).

Animal models for human behavior are seductively easy to fabricate. Many have been constructed without adequate empirical foundation, and in violation of the simplest rules for analogical reasoning in comparative science. I propose to illustrate the relevance and importance of such foundations and rules to the topic of this volume by analyzing one of the many comparisons that have been made between animal and human sexual experience—namely the phenomenon of female orgasm, which serves as a convenient example. The issues I shall raise are equally applicable to all interspecific comparisons of behavior. I believe they deserve first priority because "simple" comparisons between behavior of different species lie at the heart of evolutionary interpretations of human sexuality and, in fact, constitute the raw material of all sociobiological theories.

Constraints on Interspecific Comparisons

If building behavioral models is to amount to anything more than arm-chair theorizing, it must conform to two simple requirements: (1) *Intraspecific analysis must precede interspecific generalization.* Before we can make comparisons between two species we must possess a reasonably complete knowledge of the behavior of those species considered separately. (2) *Intraspecific analysis demands understanding of causes and consequences as well as external patterns of response.* To analyze behavior means not only to describe its formal properties, but also to discover the factors that evoke it, the mechanisms that mediate it, and the functions it serves.

How do these generalizations apply to behavioral models? The proposal that x shall serve as a model for z implies three things: (1) x is "understood" or has been "analyzed" as indicated above; (2) there are similarities between x and z; (3) application of the model will increase our understanding of z. To what extent are these implications realized in comparisons between "orgasm" in women and in nonhuman females? The example is unusual in that human behavior is represented as the model, and reactions of nonhuman species are the phenomena to be interpreted. Nevertheless, the basic issues involved are identical to those raised

99

by more common attempts to create animal models for human behavior.

We can best answer the question by examining separately (1) the overt responses involved, (2) the interpretation that has been placed upon them, and (3) the suggestions or assumptions made with respect to their functional significance.

Behavioral Manifestations

The most detailed descriptions of physiological or behavioral responses to sexual stimulation in human females have been provided by Kinsey, Pomeroy, Martin, and Gebhard (1953), and by Masters and Johnson (1966). These authorities are in close agreement in their answers to the first of our three questions, which is to say they list essentially the same physiological reactions as indicators of a woman's climactic response. However, there is disagreement regarding identification of these responses as "orgasm."

The position of Kinsey and his collaborators is as follows:

> The explosive discharge of neuromuscular tensions at the peak of sexual response is what we identify as orgasm. . . . There are . . . several advantages in restricting the concept of orgasm to the sudden and abrupt release itself, and it is in this sense that we have used the term (pp. 627–628).

Masters and Johnson propose a more inclusive definition:

> Physiologically [orgasm] is a brief episode of physical release from the vasocongestive and myotonic increment developed in response to sexual stimuli. Psychologically, it is subjective perception of a peak of physical reaction to sexual stimuli (p. 127).

Here, then, is an excellent example of the same word being used to mean two different things. For Masters and Johnson, human orgasm is a "psychophysiologic experience" or a "potpourri of psychophysiologic conditions and social influence." For Kinsey and his co-authors, it is only the reflexive contraction of smooth and striped muscles plus the neural impulses responsible for them.

With this degree of variance in definitions of human orgasm, how can we expect to identify an analogous event in other species? The customary procedure is to focus on physiological consequences of sexual stimulation. To examine the logic involved, let us therefore compare the physiological aspects of orgasm in human females with behavior that has been taken to indicate occurrence of orgasm in nonhuman primates.

The relevant evidence is summarized in Table 1, and resemblances are almost totally lacking except in the case of one experiment (Burton) that involved strapping a female rhesus to a metal frame and stimulating her vagina with a mechanical penis. Even in this case no "orgasm phase" as defined by Masters and Johnson could be identified, and the only "positive" results consisted of a few vaginal and anal contractions elicited from two females upon two or three occasions. Furthermore, the investigator expressed serious doubt that even these responses would be expected to occur in normal intercourse because of the brief duration of the male's insertions.

It would appear that, even if we restrict our comparison to overtly observable behavior, there is little basis for accepting a woman's orgastic response as a model for orgasm in female monkeys. But there are other dimensions to be considered.

Psychological Aspects of Orgasm

Masters and Johnson's insistence that the definition of orgasm must include an individual's perception of the crucial physiological reactions, and Kinsey's exclusion of this dimension of awareness, amounts to disagreement concerning the importance of cerebral events associated with sexual stimulation and its outcome. According to one interpretation, the sensations of orgasm are evoked by proprioceptive feedback to the brain from effectors involved in the peripheral events; and according to the other, the brain is not involved. Nothing could make this distinction clearer than the following quotation.

> When the human paraplegic receives genital or pelvic stimulation, he does not feel the stimulation or the consequent physiologic changes in those areas . . . and is not conscious of sexual satisfaction when he has coitus . . . even though he may come to erection and reach orgasm (Kinsey et al., p. 696).

In other words, after complete transection of the spinal cord, a human being may have orgasm without perceiving it, a conclusion that Kinsey further emphasizes by citing several authorities to the effect that the "true paraplegic" is unable to perceive

Table 1

Observable Reactions Associated with (Presumed) Orgasm

Human Female Reactions According to Masters and Johnson	Nonhuman Primate Female Reactions According to Various Observers
	Rhesus macaque
Contractions of outer two-thirds of vagina ("orgasmic platform"). Contractions of external rectal sphincter. Hyperextension including carpopedal spasm. Hyperventilation. Tachycardia. Maximal sex-flush. All of foregoing culminate in general release of vasocongestion and myotonia within a space of a few seconds.	During copulation female looks back at male, reaches back in "clutching reaction," smacks lips (Zumpe and Michael, 1970). Female mounting another female. In 5 of 3,837 episodes ($<.001\%$) mounting individual "appeared to reach a sexual climax [showing] small but obvious rhythmic contractions of thigh muscles and around the base of the tail" (Michael, Wilson, and Zumpe, 1974). Forcibly restrained female stimulated with artificial penis occasionally uttered "low pitched grunting sounds" and showed a few vaginal and anal contractions. Second female showed vaginal contractions plus "spasmodic arm reflex" on one occasion (Burton, 1971).
	Stumptail macaque
	During 14% of observed copulations female showed rhythmic expiration vocalization and "characteristic facial expression." When mounted on another female, the mounting female thrusts, shows body contractions and other reactions resembling those of male during his ejaculation (Chevalier-Skolnikoff, 1973).
	Chacma baboon
	During copulation female utters series of staccato grunts ("copulation call"). When male ceases thrusting, female "bounds away" (Saayman, 1970).

orgasm, and "for orgasm to be sensually appreciated the spinal connections with the brain must of course, be intact" (p. 697).

The concept of an "unfelt orgasm" that produces no "sexual satisfaction" may be logically defensible, but I am compelled to reject it on both intuitive and neurophysiological grounds. Sensory or perceptual appreciation of the neuromuscular events is an important, even vital feature in the personal experience of orgasm; and as acknowledged indirectly by Kinsey, this perception depends on brain function. Furthermore, inasmuch as "psychological" stimuli transmitted from the brain to spinal mechanisms are capable of either stimulating or inhibiting reflexes of the sex accessories, it seems inconsistent to ignore cerebral responses to stimuli returning from the same peripheral target organs.

Proximate Mechanisms, Rewards, and Evolution

The search for indications of orgasm in female animals rests on implicit assumptions regarding sexual satisfaction, even when the assumptions are not acknowledged by the searchers, and may be unrecognized by them. It is this lack of explicitness that forces Alexander, in his comments on Lancaster's paper, to complain of "a common deficiency in the [behavioral] analyses of biological and social scientists."

> The deficiency . . . is the failure to recognize or take into account that *proximate mechanisms* exist and are maintained because in the past . . . they have served the *ultimate function* of reproduction. By proximate mechanisms I mean things like pleasure and pain.

It could be argued that theories of animal orgasm are immediately relevant to the issue of proximate mechanisms. Such theories always rest on unexpressed assumptions that in animals, as in ourselves, orgasm is pleasant and rewarding. Orgasm is implicitly treated as a reinforcing consequence of sexual interaction, and the concept of reinforcement traditionally is invoked as one explanation for the recurrence of behavioral responses.

Saayman (1970) suggests that female baboons in estrus prefer to copulate with mature males *because* the latter are especially likely to stimulate the female's putative orgasm, which Saayman infers from her behavior. Here in a nutshell is material for a theory involving proximate mechanisms, individual learning, and sociobiological or evolutionary consequences!

In this volume Lancaster writes as follows.

One of the most significant generalizations to come from the new data is that, like humans, Old World monkeys and apes do not engage in sexual activity for the sole purpose of procreation.

Why, then, do they engage in such activity? This is a question of proximate mechanisms, and I suggest that the postulation of female orgasm represents one attempted answer. An entirely different issue, but one worth mentioning although it cannot be developed here, is the effect of sexual rewards on nonsexual activities. I have discussed this important feature of primate evolution elsewhere under the topic of "socialization of sex and sexualization of society" (Beach, 1974, 1977). One aspect of the matter is reflected in Lancaster's observation that "the stimulations and rewards of sexual behavior appear to be important mechanisms of social attachment in nonhuman primates."

Orgasm, Reinforcement, and Scientific Goals

A perfectly legitimate question is what difference it makes whether a female monkey does or does not have sexual orgasm, and as far as I can see it makes none whatsoever *unless* the occurrence of orgasm can be shown to exert a reliable effect upon subsequent behavior. If orgasm has reinforcing consequences that directly or indirectly increase the probability of reproduction, then it could make a very great difference indeed. But this way of asking the question restructures the entire issue and places it in a broader and scientifically more significant perspective. Furthermore, it opens the matter to experimental investigation.

Rather than seeking animal analogues for human orgasm (which is too poorly understood to serve as a useful model for anything), we might better attempt to identify the variables that reinforce the occurrence of sexual behavior. Perhaps a female rhesus in copulation with a male *does* have vaginal and uterine contractions that give rise to pleasant and rewarding sensations and thus reinforce her tendency to engage in similar behavior on subsequent occasions. The possibility is open to experimental test, but if that particular explanation is disproved, the basic question of proximate mechanisms remains and must be answered. It is conceivable that vaginal penetration rather than any climactic event is the essential basis for reinforcement, and this too can be experimentally verified or excluded.

My theory-hunch, or "thunch," is that there is no single source of reinforcement for a behavioral response so vital to perpetuation of the species. We shall probably discover that in animals, as in men and women, the occurrence of mating behavior normally depends upon a combination of reinforcing consequences, any one of which is dispensable as long as others remain.

However it turns out, the essential need is for explicit research rather than speculation about trivial questions. What we need to know is not whether baboons have orgasms, but why baboons (and human beings) copulate, and why they do so under conditions and in a manner that ensures perpetuation of their species. Answers to questions of this order may well contribute to an evolutionary interpretation of human sexuality.

Directions for New Research

Three major areas in which new research might be especially fruitful are (1) molecular analysis of sexual behavior, (2) comparative, physiological, and developmental study of feminine sexuality, and (3) formulation and testing of hypotheses relevant to the "new model" of evolution, which states that organisms have evolved to maximize the reproduction of their own genes.[1]

Molecular Analysis of Sexual Behavior

This category includes a number of subareas, one of which is study of stimulus control of sexual responses. The common assumption that mating behavior in animals depends on simple, unisensory cues, such as odor, is gradually giving way to concepts of multisensory patterns that are perceptually organized by the receiving organism. It is clear that for males and females of many species, sexual responsiveness embodies measurable degrees of preference for particular partners. Study of individual differences in sexual attractiveness for both sexes may lead to concepts of varying degrees of "compatibility" in different heterosexual pairs.

Translated into human terms, the issue of stimulus control is

1. These recommendations are based upon the author's discussions with Jane B. Lancaster and Richard D. Alexander.

directly related to the concept of "object choice" and therefore bears on problems of homosexuality as well as various paraphilias.

A second subcategory deals with effects of experience and learning in nonhuman species. Current evidence suggests that such effects are more likely to be exerted on the stimulus rather than the response aspects of sexual behavior. Enduring pair bonds between females and males may depend on close association in nonreproductive circumstances, and on absence or inhibition of responsiveness to "nonpartners." For some species "sexual imprinting" occurring during the equivalent of infancy or early childhood determines the nature and even the species of individual that will evoke sexual responses in adult life. The motor patterns of courtship and mating are unaffected by such early learning. This phenomenon may bear significant relations to human aberrations such as fetishism and exhibitionism (Beach, 1977).

The question of sexual reward or reinforcement is in need of exhaustive study, both because of its implications for "animal models" and because of its importance for understanding sexual behavior at the intraspecific level. We might even profit from examining the more fundamental question whether any concept of reinforcement is necessary to our behavioral analyses.

Finally, much research is needed on basic problems of neural and hormonal mediation of sexual and sex-related behavior in nonhuman species. Work in this area is proceeding apace, but a great deal remains to be accomplished.

Comparative and Longitudinal Studies of Female Sexuality

There is obvious need and opportunity for combined laboratory and field investigations of various problems relating to sexual responses of female primates. For example, physiological changes associated with mating can and must be described and measured under controlled conditions. Information provided by such study can then be utilized in more informative interpretation of field observations.

Currently available methods of measuring and manipulating hormone levels can be more broadly applied to females living in the natural environment.

Field work at the descriptive level is in need of increased emphasis and breadth. Greater attention to interspecific differences will prove especially illuminating and is badly needed as a safeguard against overgeneralizations purporting to describe behavior of "monkeys" or "apes" as homogenous groups.

In the area of human sexuality the question of male-female differences is in serious need of extensive analysis. There exists a widespread belief that certain psychological or behavioral sex differences are, or may be, traceable to biological differences between male and female, but most of the evidence comes from Western societies in which such differences are encouraged or enforced by social training.

Other societies exist that support quite different programs of sexual training. Some of these include explicit emphasis on recognition and expression of female sexuality. Female infants are regularly masturbated, the outer labia are stretched and pulled to increase their size, and young girls are taught dances that focus on pelvic movements simulating those used in copulation. It would be most important to learn if under such conditions females grow up to be sexually more assertive, active, and independent than females in Western countries. It is conceivable that many sexual dimorphisms common in our culture would be lacking in others with different concepts of child training.

A more specific issue pertaining to female sex functions, which calls for immediate attention, is the remarkable decrease in menarcheal age that has occurred in Western countries during the last century. The average age at first menstruation has dropped approximately four years (from seventeen to thirteen) between 1870–75 and 1970–75. The causes are complex and the consequences of major social import. In this country, for example, the incidence of pregnancy in twelve- and thirteen-year-old girls is rising. Reproductive precocity is not accompanied by earlier social maturity, and the resulting disparity creates serious problems for society and potentially crippling ones for the girl and her family.

Human Sexuality and Evolutionary Models[2]

Until recently the most widely accepted model of evolution hinged on the concept of group selection. According to this view, behavior of individuals evolved to preserve and perpetuate the genotype of the reproducing population.

The currently favored "new model" calls for a different

2. Comments by R. D. Alexander.

interpretation, which is that individuals behave in ways most likely to ensure the perpetuation of their own individual genotypes. In historical perspective what this model says is the following: We and our contemporaries tend to exhibit behavioral and nonbehavioral characteristics that in past generations contributed to preservation of the genes we have inherited from our ancestors. Various lines of research can be explored to test the validity of this new model as it applies to different aspects of human sexuality.

Evolution has commonly been viewed as the discipline that traces long-term changes through fossil remains and comparisons of related living forms. The more such studies focus on truly long-term changes, the less likely they are to unravel the causes of change because the environments of antiquity are inevitably so poorly known.

Another aspect of evolution, less well understood outside biology, is the use of what is known about the actual process of change, studied in living forms, to predict states of phenotypic attributes or combinations of attributes. A particularly well-studied example, relevant to this volume, is the ratio of males to females in a population.

There are similarities in sex ratios, not just across the animal kingdom, but across both the animal and plant kingdoms. Usually, they are about 1:1 in early adulthood. Even tiny shifts in sex ratio can affect sociality and sexuality. For example, one may contemplate the idea that whatever causes lie behind sex ratios might have produced one male for every ten females or vice versa. Under such conditions our sociality could scarcely have its current structure. But the sex ratio among humans also is generally about 1:1 in early adulthood. Only one explanation has been devised, and it works: An individual can maximize its reproduction in a sexual species, in which the two halves of genetic materials come from parents of the two different sexes, only by investing in the two sexes so as to produce a local sex ratio that will not cause any of its offspring to be devalued reproductively solely because of their sex (Fisher, 1958). This is what organisms appear to do, and it leads to strange predictions such as: If twice as much parental effort is required to rear a male as to rear a female then one expects a sex ratio at the end of parental care of 1:2 rather than 1:1; and things like this do happen. The major exceptions to a 1:1 investment are species in which all the females are inseminated by their brothers. Parents in those cases would be expected to invest only enough in males to assure insemination of all of their daughters. In such species the resulting sex ratio may be 1:20 or 1:45—even though the males in some cases are tiny, crippled, blind, short-lived things that do nothing but inseminate the female and then die (Hamilton, 1966).

Philosophically, the significant idea is that individuals evolve to maximize their reproduction. This seems counter-intuitive to human views of our own motivations. We all believe that humans do countless things besides reproduce. Part of this belief is derived from our ability to define *reproduction* as we see fit. Nevertheless, human sex ratios suggest that we too have evolved to maximize reproduction as individuals.

In almost all groups of the world's species, including all mammals, females invest more than males in rearing their offspring. Males work harder in competition for matings. Consequently, some males in all these species reproduce more than any female. Biologists refer to such species as polygnous, whether or not the males have harems. In polygnous species, *because sex-ratio selection produces about a 1:1 sex ratio in early adulthood,* the male's lifetime is a high-stakes, high-risk game compared with the female's (Williams, 1957; Hamilton, 1966; Alexander et al., 1978). In other words, because some males inseminate many females, other males do not reproduce at all.

Humans are polygnous in the sense that I have described and share many common characteristics with other polygnous species: In these species in which the sex ratios are about 1:1, males take longer to mature and senesce more rapidly; mortality is higher in males at essentially every age. In species that compete sexually on the ground, rather than in water or in the air, males are always bigger than females. Promising juvenile males get more help from their parents than do any females, while not-so-promising males are abandoned or killed either as fetuses or later; that is also true in humans to some extent. More males are conceived, but more die while still under parental care, even though males get more parental care than females. In mammals, males are carried longer during gestation and are larger at birth. Healthy and high-ranking parents produce male-biased broods, while low-ranking and less healthy parents do not, or in some cases produce female-biased broods. There is good evidence that in stratified human societies the same effect is brought about by sex-preferential infanticide (Dickeman, 1978).

Quotes from other papers in this volume show the connections between topics like sex-ratio selection and the goals of this conference. Luria, for example, indicates that in early or middle childhood the rigidity of sex-typing falls most heavily on the shoulders of boys. She points out that parents appear to be more worried about a boy's masculinity than about a girl's femininity; that boys are more likely to be ostracized as sissies than girls are as tomboys; that girls fight less than boys; and that "higher education and middle-class status are associated with more relaxed gender roles." All of these findings are consistent with what I have said about sex-ratio selection. In other words, *the basic aspects of sex and gender roles derive from the effects of sex-ratio selection upon our species.* Surely it is no triviality to realize this.

The consensus of authors in this volume seems to be that the reasons we are what we are and do what we do—like it or not—are mostly social. There are, of course, genetic differences between males and females, which lead to differences of appearance; but these appearances only initiate the social phenomena that cause the development, exaggeration, and diversification of gender-role differences. It seems that, historically, social contingencies have represented the most appropriate kinds of causes for achieving desired ends. How to succeed socially is the most difficult of all questions about how to succeed, because everybody else is also trying to succeed socially, and our individual goals necessarily conflict.

The sources of the effective social contingencies for the development of sex and gender roles also seem apparent in this volume. They are parents, peers, and ourselves. These are the sources of the social stimuli that put us in particular roles. An evolutionary biologist would suppose that these social influences work because parents want their offspring to succeed. But what constitutes "success" or "desired ends"? It is worth contemplating that, in terms of history, success may be defined in terms of the general theoretical approach that has developed in biology in the last ten years—namely, that attributes of organisms exist because they help those individual organisms maximize their reproduction.

This approach is a brand-new philosophy in biology. Previously we assumed that the attributes of organisms exist because they are good for perpetuating the species; but that explanation does not work. Sex ratios cannot be explained that way. Nor can senescence patterns, mating systems, sex differences and similarities, or sociality. We have thought that it is all a matter of personal satisfaction or pleasure or the acquisition of power or of influence; but those ideas will not work alone either. Beginning with things like sex ratios and considering others like patterns of senescence, social behavior, nepotism, and sexual competition, the hypothesis that individuals evolve to maximize their own reproduction, and not that of the species, *does* work (Alexander, 1977).

This discovery does not mean that we are bound to our history. We are the organisms who sit and contemplate these things. Then the contemplation itself becomes part of the environment, which means that in the end we can do almost anything we like. Perhaps this possibility is open to us only if we bring the significance of our evolutionary past into our consciousness through analysis of, and reflection on, the kinds of considerations raised here.

References

Animal Models and Psychological Inference

Beach, F. A. 1974. Human sexuality and evolution. In *Reproductive behavior,* ed. W. Montagna and W. A. Sadler. New York: Plenum Press.

————. 1977. Cross-species comparisons and the human heritage. In *Human sexuality in four perspectives,* ed. F. A. Beach. Baltimore: Johns Hopkins Press.

Burton, F. D. 1971. Sexual climax in female *Macaca mulatta.* In *Proceedings of the Third International Congress of Primatology,* vol. 3. Basel: S. Karger.

Chevalier-Skolnikoff, S. 1973. Male-female, female-female, and male-male sexual behavior in the stumptail monkey, with special attention to the female orgasm. *Arch. Sex. Behav.* 3:95–116.

Kinsey, A. C.; Pomeroy, W. B.; Martin, C. E.; and Gebhard, P. H. 1953. *Sexual behavior in the human female.* Philadelphia: W. B. Saunders.

McKinney, W. T., Jr. 1974. Animal models in psychiatry. *Perspect. in Biol. Med.* 17:529–541.

Masters, W. H., and Johnson, V. E. 1966. *Human sexual response.* Boston: Little, Brown.

Michael, R. P.; Wilson, M. I.; and Zumpe, D. 1974. The bisexual behavior of female rhesus monkeys. In *Sex differences in behavior,* ed. R. C. Friedman, R. M. Richart, and R. L. Vande Wiele. New York: Wiley & Sons.

Saayman, G. S. 1970. The menstrual cycle and sexual behaviour in a troop of free-ranging Chacma baboons (*Papio ursinus*). *Folia Primat.* 12:81–110.

Wilson, E. O. 1975. *Sociobiology: The new synthesis.* Cambridge: Harvard Press.

Zumpe, D., and Michael, R. P. 1970. Ovarian hormones and female sexual invitations in captive rhesus monkeys (*Macaca mulatta*). *Anim. Behav.* 18:293–301.

Human Sexuality and Evolutionary Models

Alexander, R. D. 1977. Natural selection and the analysis of human sociality. In *Changing scenes in natural sciences,* ed. C. E. Goulden. Philadelphia Academy of Natural Sciences, Special Publication no. 12.

Alexander, R. D.; Hoogland, J. L.; Howard, R. D.; Noonan, K. L.; and Sherman, P. W. 1978. Sexual dimorphisms and breeding systems in pinnipeds, ungulates, primates, and humans. In *Evolutionary theory and human social organization,* ed. N. A. Chagnon and W. G. Irons. North Scituate, Mass.: Duxbury Press.

Beach, F. A. 1977. Human Sexuality in Four Perspectives. Baltimore: Johns Hopkins Press.

Dickeman, M. 1978. The reproductive structure of stratified human societies: A preliminary model. In *Evolutionary theory and human social organization,* ed. N. A. Chagnon and W. G. Irons. North Scituate, Mass.: Duxbury Press.

Fisher, R. A. 1958. *The genetical theory of natural selection.* New York: Dover.

Hamilton, W. D. 1966. Extraordinary sex ratios. *Science* 154:477–488.

Williams, G. C. 1957. Pleiotropy, natural selection, and the evolution of senescence. *Evol.* 11:398–411.

Part II
Biological Perspectives

The evolutionary perspective, which represents the biological approach at the phylogenetic level, is supplemented in this section by the complementary biological approach at the onto-genetic level, where the primary focus is now on the individual, rather than the species.

Two of the contributors to this section, Richard Green and Anke Ehrhardt, are psychiatrists with special interest in the investigation of gender identity. Julian Davidson is a physiologist whose primary area of research is in the field of reproductive physiology and behavior. Green and Ehrhardt are clinical investigators who work mainly with human subjects; Davidson is an experimentalist who works with animals. The conceptual frames of references and the methodological approaches of these contributors provide interesting contrasts.

Richard Green introduces his contribution on the biological influences on sexual identity by an instructive historical overview. The primary focus of his approach is on the relationship between prenatal hormones and behavior. For this, he draws on evidence from experimental work with monkeys as well as "experiments of nature" whereby the human fetus is exposed to abnormal amounts of hormone, as exemplified by the adrenogenital syndrome. Another important study population consists of youngsters whose mothers, while pregnant, were given various estrogenic and progestational compounds. Green expands on this theme and deals with the broader implications of the relationship of hormones and sexual behavior, including homosexuality.

While Green's task is to focus on the biological determinants of sexual identity and behavior, he is well aware of the significance of nonbiological factors. His views on the importance of biological influences are quite circumspect as he refers to new respect "for the role that biological forces *may* play in *some* areas of psychosexual differentiation, at *some* times in development, and perhaps for *some* persons more than others."

In his response to Green's paper, Julian Davidson further refines the nature and role of biological determinants of sexual experiences, particularly in relation to gender identity. Davidson makes the important distinction between the "organizational" and "activational" influences of hormones and traces their effects through three levels of biological differentiation: anatomical, physiological, and brain mechanisms that are presumed to help establish gender identity and sexual behaviors.

Since current hypotheses on sexual differentiation of behavior are largely based on animal research, Davidson raises once again, as Frank Beach did in Part I, the problems in generalizing to humans from animal models and analogies. Davidson finds this process extremely problematic, and coming from an expert in the field of animal research, these concerns are particularly compelling.

Anke Ehrhardt's main focus is on an interactional model for the relationship of sex hormones and behavior. As to the relative strengths of the factors that shape gender identity, she finds that the effect of the fetal hormonal environment is not the decisive force. While by no means dismissing the importance of biological factors, Ehrhardt reiterates the common view of investigators in this field that gender identity seems to be mainly a result of rearing, given the limitations of animal models and the fragmentary evidence of human studies. With due caution Ehrhardt points out the tentative nature of these conclusions.

All three authors are in agreement about the need for further research and the profusion of worthwhile leads to pursue in the study of biological determinants of human sex-related behavior. A number of these research possibilities are outlined in the areas of prenatal hormones and behavior and the behavioral endocrinology of adult sexual behavior.

The contributions in this section highlight the significance of biological factors in sexual differentiation and behavior. They should also allay fears that those working in this field have a blind devotion to biological determinants to the exclusion of all else.—H. A. K.

114

Biological Influences on Sexual Identity

Richard Green

At the turn of the century biology reigned. The predominance of a female or male sex center in the brain was thought to determine dimorphic aspects of sexual behavior. Freud, in his early twentieth-century writings, borrowed heavily from Krafft-Ebing on the role of biology. He suggested that a constitutional over-endowment in the anal zone might predispose a male to homosexuality (Freud, 1905). And toward the end of his career, he relied on Steinach's theory of hormonal sexual rejuvenation by having his vas deferens tied so as to increase the output of male hormone (Benjamin, 1970).

There was no shortage of creative thinking. As recently as the 1930s, a theory of the genesis of male homosexuality was presented which may be termed the "Grecian short circuit." It was posited that the sensory nerves that generally bring impulses from the penis through the spinal column to pleasure centers in the brain had somehow been miswired so as to originate from the anus (Montazagga, 1932).

In his psychoanalytic study of a female homosexual, Freud suggested that psychoanalysis and metapsychology had gone as far as they could go in explaining the roots of homosexuality and must leave the remainder to biology (Freud, 1920). Regrettably, his words were not heeded by his successors, and the potential input of biology was lost in an avalanche of metapsychological theory and clinical reports. An exception to this monotonal chorus has been the work of Stoller, who has had the courage to suggest a biological force behind some aspects of male/female psychological differentiation and to press us to re-examine Freud's "bedrock" concept of bisexuality (Stoller, 1968, 1972).

115

Thus, the pendulum, which at the turn of the century rested two and a half standard deviations from the midline toward the biologic end of the arc, swung an equal distance toward the social end. During the most recent decade, it has begun to settle at midline. Let us hope this settling does not imply inertia, but rather a dynamic synthesis of what is of value at both ends of the grand arc.

Prenatal Hormones and Postnatal Behaviors

While the turn-of-the-century sexologists speculated about male and female sex centers in the brain, the concept was still little more than science fiction. The idea that areas of the brain might be constructed in such a way as to facilitate male- or female-type behaviors has reached the level of science fact only during the last fifteen years. The pioneering work of William Young and his colleagues (Young, Goy, Phoenix, 1964) demonstrated that just as androgenic (male) hormones differentiate the basically female genital structures in a male direction, the same potential for hormonal action exists within the brain. Regrettably, these findings are frequently overlooked by those who point only to postnatal socialization as affecting sex-typed behaviors. These "social scientists" would like to see the findings of Young and his co-workers erased from the passages of scientific history.

First with the guinea pig, then with the rhesus monkey, a compelling series of findings emerged that subsequently found support in the human primate. Pregnant rhesus monkeys were injected during the midrange of gestation with testosterone propionate (an androgenic hormone). Those fetuses that were female were then assessed after birth. Fortunately for those who would draw parallels between this laboratory experiment and human behavior, juvenile male and female rhesus monkeys show different behavioral patterns similar to the traditional differences shown by human boys and girls (Rosenblum, 1961). Juvenile male rhesus monkeys are more likely to show rough-and-tumble, chasing, and aggressive behaviors. The striking finding of Young and his co-workers was that young female monkeys exposed before birth to the injected androgen behaved more like young males. They have been popularly termed "tomboy" monkeys. Comparable amounts of androgen given to female rhesus monkeys shortly after birth did not produce the same effect. This

116

comparison suggests a prenatal critical period in the development of the central nervous system. However, it should also be noted that the genitalia of the "tomboy" females were virilized, and there may have been some influence on their behavior as a consequence of social feedback to abnormal-appearing female monkeys.

This experiment of the laboratory is complemented by an experiment of nature: the virilizing adrenogenital syndrome in the human female. Here, an inborn error of metabolism results in the female fetus producing an excessive amount of androgen. These persons are born with varying degrees of genital virilization. Endocrinological procedures developed during the last two decades make possible diagnosis of this syndrome in the newborn. Thus, in spite of ambiguous external genitalia, the infant can be correctly "sexed" and treated with cortisone with resultant suppression of adrenal androgen. The child, if karyotypically female, is assigned to female status, is raised as a girl, and undergoes genital reconstruction to appear anatomically normal (Money, 1968).

A series of studies has been conducted on the sexual identity of these females. An elegant design (Ehrhardt and Baker, 1974) compared these girls with their normal sisters (since the syndrome generally appears in one sibling only). The sisters exposed to high levels of prenatal androgen were found to be more inclined to rough-and-tumble play, more tomboyish, and less interested in doll play. Thus, the findings parallel those with the nonhuman primate. The genitalia of these girls were generally reconstructed by the end of the first year so that self-image and peer group relations were probably not affected by this variable. However, it is not possible to rule out differential parental reaction patterns to the siblings. They know that one child must continue to take cortisone to prevent revirilization and that at birth one child's genitalia were more male-appearing than the other's.

A recent study by Reinisch and Karow (1977) of children whose mothers received a variety of sex-typed hormones during gestation has pointed to subtle personality differences in children associated with such hormonal exposure.

Reinisch studied 26 males whose mothers received "pregnancy hormones" during gestation and 27 of their siblings from pregnancies in which no hormones were administered. She also studied 45 hormone-exposed females and 43 untreated female siblings. The 71 hormone-exposed subjects were in three groups: 16 who received primarily estrogen, 26 who received primarily progestin, and 29 who received large doses of both. Mean age of the subjects was 11 years. Children were given the Cattell personality tests, which assess comparable personality factors (usually 16) across childhood and adolescence.

The groups differed on four primary and two secondary factors. The progestin and estrogen groups were most different from each other, with the mixed group at an intermediate position. The progestin group was more independent, individualistic, self-assured, self-sufficient, and sensitive. The estrogen group was more group-oriented, group dependent, and phlegmatic, and less independent, sensitive, and self-assured.

Comparing the progestin group and their sibs, the progestin group was more independent, individualistic, self-assured, and self-sufficient. Comparing the estrogen group and their sibs, the estrogen group was less excitable, less individualistic, and less self-sufficient. The members of the mixed-hormone group, compared with their siblings, were more excitable and less sensitive.

Additional research with the human male, though less convincing, points to a similar phenomenon. Here we find some evidence that low levels of prenatal androgen may influence the developing male so that rough-and-tumble and aggressive play are less likely to manifest postnatally. In one study, 40 six- and sixteen-year-old males whose diabetic mothers had received estrogen and progesterone during pregnancy to prevent abortion were compared with males whose nondiabetic mothers received no hormone (Yalom, Green, and Fisk, 1973). The hormone-exposed males were found to be less rough-and-tumble, aggressive, and athletic. However, it is not possible to rule out the effect of the mothers' chronic illness on the psychosexual development of the child, although the minority of those males in the control group whose mothers were diabetic appeared more rough-and-tumble, athletic, and aggressive than the remainder of the controls.

More recently, Green, Kester, Finch, and Williams have studied 136 young adult males whose mothers, during pregnancy, had received diethylstilbestrol (DES), DES plus progesterone, progesterone, a progestin, or no hormone. These were all high-risk pregnancies with the hormones given to prevent abortion. The males were given a series of psychological tests that assess varying measures of masculinity and femininity, vocational interests, personality factors, and a field dependency measure, plus a research interview focusing on early childhood sex-typed behaviors and on adolescent and adult sexuality. There were 18 subjects who received diethylstilbestrol (DES) only, 24 who received DES and progesterone, 10 who received progesterone only, and 14 who received synthetic progesterone only. Each was pair-matched with a no-hormone control. The age range was eighteen to thirty. There was a wide range of drug dosage and duration of administration.

There were no differences on the Embedded Figures Test. DES, DES-plus-natural-progesterone, and synthetic progesterone groups tended to score higher than their controls on the femininity scale of the Bem Sex Role Inventory ($p < .10$). On the Strong Vocational Interest Test, the natural progesterone group was lower than its control on the Science scale ($p < .01$). On the Guilford-Zimmerman Temperament Survey, the natural progesterone group scored lower than its control on activity ($p < .01$). Synthetic progesterone subjects were more shy.

Synthetic progesterone subjects exposed in trimester 3 cross-dressed more often ($p < .01$). As for childhood peer group, synthetic progesterone subjects tended to have more female friends ($p < .1$). High dosages of natural progesterone were associated with more interest in rough-and-tumble play ($p < .05$) and synthetic hormone exposure was associated with less interest ($p < .05$). DES-plus-progesterone subjects participated less in sports ($p < .01$). With respect to adult sexual orientation, there were no group differences on homosexual vs. heterosexual fantasies or behaviors. The remainder of the data is undergoing detailed statistical analysis.

It is clear that the above findings do not provide a clear-cut personality and/or sexual profile of hormone-exposed vs. non-exposed young adult males. With the many scales and interview items used, considerable caution must be observed against over-interpreting differences "significant" at the 5 percent level.

Meyer-Bahlburg, Ehrhardt, and Grisanti (1977) studied 13 boys and 15 girls whose mothers received medroxyprogesterone acetate for more than one week sometime during the second to the eighth month of pregnancy. Controls were also high-risk pregnancies. Again, the range was wide for duration and dosage.

In interviews the male children showed no differences from controls on sex-typed toy preferences. However, the females were *less* often characterized as "tomboys."

In an earlier study by Ehrhardt and Money, most of the subjects considered "tomboys" whose mothers had received a progestational drug during pregnancy had received not progesterone but Norlutin, which is more virilizing. Also, no controls were utilized in that previous research (Ehrhardt and Money, 1967).

A composite of these recent studies does not offer a definitive conclusion as to the effect of prenatal exposure to sex-typed hormones on postnatal behaviors. Different methodologies have been used. Some findings are contradictory. Drugs and dosage are not constant. Subject age ranges and test instruments differ. It is remarkable considering the inconsistencies in these procedures (not originally designed as "experiments") that any personality differences are emerging. One is inclined to cite the old saying "With this much horseshit in the place, there must be a pony somewhere."

In a project currently under way in East Germany, Dorner and associates are studying prevention of homosexuality through a medical procedure based upon the effect of prenatal androgen on the central nervous system. They are drawing samples of amniotic fluid from pregnant females, determining the sex of the fetus by examination of the cellular nuclear material, and measuring the androgen level in the fluid. They are currently establishing norms for hormones associated with the presence of a male fetus. The next phase anticipated in the research might be to administer testosterone to those women with a male fetus whose assay levels are below normal (Dorner, 1976).

The theory behind this procedure is that deficient levels of androgen fail to organize the central nervous system in a male direction and that male-directed organization is necessary for an opposite-sex sexual partner preference. This procedure has been criticized on several grounds: First, there is no direct evidence that a prenatal period exists during which androgen deficiency organizes the primate central nervous system to respond to male sexual partners, especially when hormone levels have been sufficient for male differentiation of the genitalia. Further, there is a poor relation between amniotic fluid levels of androgen and levels in the fetal plasma (and thus those levels reaching the developing central nervous system—Goy and Gold-foot, 1976). Finally, one cannot ignore the question of the ethics of this intrepid effort to prevent an erotic preference that many regard as an alternative sexual life style.

Neonatal and Year-One Sex Differences

Aside from the appearance of the genitalia, are there any physiologic differences between newborn males and females? Apparently there are, although attempting to synthesize these into a coherent pattern of psychosexual development requires greater ingenuity than the designs employed to discover the differences. One finding that has been replicated (a rather unusual occurrence in this field) is the "prone head reaction" (Bell and Darling, 1965). Newborn males placed on their abdomens are more likely to raise their heads from the horizontal position than are females. This tendency is believed to be due to greater gross muscle development in the male, probably as a result of higher levels of prenatal androgen. However, while there may be an *inter*sex difference that reaches statistical significance, there is still a considerable *intra*sex difference. More important, the age at which a biological sex difference in muscle strength and/or coordination becomes socially significant for a given individual remains to be clarified. While anyone who has looked at Olympic records could not deny that males, as a population, are stronger than females, the more important question is, at what age does such a sex difference become developmentally meaningful?

Autonomy of the infant from the mother at the beginning of the second half of the first year appears to discriminate males and females. Females appear to be held more by their mothers at five or six months of age, and when male and female infants are placed on the floor next to their mothers at twelve months, males are more likely to crawl away (Goldberg and Lewis, 1969). This earlier autonomy of the male is paralleled by a finding in our close relative, the squirrel monkey, in which young males also wander farther from their mothers, in spite of their mothers' attempts to retrieve them (Rosenblum, 1974).

A controversial study suggested that twelve-month-old males and females respond differently when access to toys is frustrated. They were also found to manifest a different play style with toys (Goldberg and Lewis, 1969). In this experiment, a transparent barrier, extending the length of the room, was placed between the child and the toys. Male infants were more likely to crawl toward the end of the barrier, ostensibly trying to get around it and gain access to the toys. Female infants were more likely to sit where placed and cry. Given the toys, males were more likely to toss them about, while females tended to gather them. These findings were not replicated in a subsequent study (Maccoby and Jacklin, 1974).

Lewis has now published two even more provocative findings that have been neither confirmed nor disconfirmed. They point to the capacity of twelve- to eighteen-month-old infants to discriminate same- from other-sex children. Photographs were taken of infant males and females, and all sex clues except facial features were removed. The pictures were then shown to adult judges, who were unable to state the sex of the child correctly. However, when the pictures were shown to the infants, they spent longer periods focusing on pictures of their own sex (Lewis and Weinraub, 1974). In the second study, four children, two males and two females, were placed in the corners of a rectangular enclosure, and one child at a time was permitted to crawl toward one of the other three (Lewis, 1976). Although the odds of crawling to an opposite-sex child were two to one, more often the child crawled toward a same-sex infant. These studies suggest that as early as one year children are able to distinguish between male and female.

Why should this capacity be present in the infant and absent in the adult? One can, with some exertion, mobilize an evolutionary argument. This same-sex, nonsame-sex recognition may be an initial factor that enters into the first component of sexual identity: core-morphologic identity. Sexual identity is here defined as encompassing (1) core-morphologic identity—an individual's earliest self-awareness of being anatomically male or female, or belonging to one of two categories of human beings; (2) gender-role behavior—those dimorphic patterns that discriminate males and females in a given culture at a given time; and (3) sexual orientation—an erotic and romantic preference for persons of the same, other, or either sex (Green, 1974).

Persons whose core-morphologic identity is contrary to their anatomy are best exemplified by transsexuals (Benjamin, 1966; Green and Money, 1969). These people want sex-change surgery.

Core-morphologic identity is significantly correlated with gender-role behavior and sexual orientation. And persons who manifest significant degrees of cross-gender behavior during childhood appear more likely to mature into homosexually oriented adults (Saghir and Robins, 1973). Both transsexuals and homosexuals are less likely to reproduce. Thus, it would be advantageous to the survival of the species for infants to label themselves correctly as male or female so that the development of sexual identity will proceed in a manner that maximizes the potential for species reproduction.

Other sex differences in infants have been reported. Newborn females have a preference for sweet. This preference is demonstrated by adding sweetener to a formula that results in female infants increasing their intake to a greater degree than males (Nisbett and Gurwitz, 1970). For whatever it is worth, the capacity for discriminating sweet exists into adulthood with female adults showing a lower threshold for detecting sugar in a solution (Panborn, 1959). Of even vaguer implication is the fact that newborn males will show a cardiac sign of attention (slowing of heart rate) when listening to an interrupted tone, whereas females show this sign while listening to modern jazz (Kagan and Lewis, 1965). As the findings become more esoteric, the implications become more obscure. Foundations might offer a prize for the best synthesis of this last finding into either a theory of psychosexual development or the origins of musical genius.

Twin Studies

Studies of monozygotic twins have always intrigued behavioral scientists because they seem to provide a reasonable chance to hold genetic factors constant. Postnatal experiences of twins are studied as though they were ideal independent variables. A few twin studies have been reported in the investigation of sexual identity. The first concerns a set of male monozygotic twins, one of whom experienced loss of his penis because of circumcision trauma at six months of age. At eighteen months of age this twin was reassigned to female status after considerable parental counseling. Nearly a decade later, a report now suggests that the children are maturing as a typical brother and sister pair (Money and Ehrhardt, 1972). It is still too early to know the sexual orientation

123

of the twins. Will the chromosomally male child who was prenatally exposed to typical levels of male hormone, but reared as a female, become a lesbian?

Two other twin reports describe monozygotic sets, one male pair and one female pair, with the co-twins discordant for sexual identity. With both sets it was possible to identify patterns of socialization that appeared to set the co-twins on different developmental tracks.

Matched pairs of hermaphrodites offer the closest analogy to twin studies (Money and Ehrhardt, 1972). For example, two persons born with the virilizing female adrenogenital syndrome, delivered by different obstetricians prior to the development of sophisticated diagnostic procedures, are assigned to discordant sex roles. No one should be especially surprised that the child assigned to female status develops a female identity and heterosexual orientation, since chromosomal and gonadal sex are female. Of some surprise, however, is the finding that the chromosomal and gonadal female assigned to male status develops a male identity, masculine gender-role behavior, and a sexual orientation toward females. It should be stressed that the former group of females, in spite of heavy pre- and postnatal exposure to androgen, does not appear to have a higher incidence of either transsexualism or homosexuality. However, critics point out that the anatomically intersexed, as evidenced by their genital ambiguity, have not been exposed to typical levels of sex steroids prenatally, and thus their central nervous systems may be comparably intersexed. Possibly they are more "plastic" and more amenable to environmental manipulation with respect to the establishment of sexual identity (Diamond, 1965; Zuger, 1970). Because of this objection, there is considerable interest in the monozygotic twin pairs who develop discordant sexual identities.

In experiments of *nurture* where prenatal androgen and genetic contributions are held as close as possible in research with the human being, socialization factors appear to predominate in psychosexual ontogeny. However, the numbers are small and the findings can only be suggestive.

Early Sexual Behaviors

Autoerotic behavior is the earliest manifestation of genital sexuality and remains one of the behaviors with enduring sex differences. While several other indices of sexuality manifested by males and females have converged during recent decades, including age of initial coitus, number of sexual partners, and responsivity to visual and narrative erotic materials, the rates of masturbation have remained discrepant. Although many more females report masturbating today than twenty years ago, the frequency with which they masturbate remains considerably lower than for males (Schmidt and Sigusch, 1972). Why should this be the case?

Some preliminary reports of children in their first year suggest little or no sex differences in the frequency of autoerotic play (Galenson, 1975). When and why does this sex difference appear? Is it a social learning phenomenon, with girls taught that their genitalia are "dirty" and that "nice girls don't do such things"? Or is there an overriding biologic factor? Anthropologists report no societies in which the frequency of masturbation is acknowledged to be higher for females (Davenport, 1976). And sex differences in masturbation exist at the nonhuman primate level. Separating a young rhesus monkey from its mother and raising it with a surrogate mother will induce high rates of masturbation in the male, but not in the female (Goy and Goldfoot, 1976). Is it possible that the presence of the larger male genital, more available for contact with objects, animate or inanimate, leads to higher rates of self-stimulation through an operant conditioning sequence? Could it be that for some biological reason, it is easier for males to achieve sexual climax, and therefore the extent of pleasurable feedback is greater and more frequent?

Hormones and Sexual Behavior

The role of hormones in the regulation of human sexual behavior has long intrigued researchers. Well over a decade ago it was observed that women with breast cancer who were given testosterone in an effort to retard metastatic spread showed an increased sex drive (Waxenberg et al., 1959). Elegant research on the rhesus monkey (Herbert, 1970) has demonstrated that adrenal androgens are necessary for the female to show sexual interest in the male. If one removes the adrenal cortex and replaces cortisone (nonandrogenic, but necessary for electrolyte balance, stress response, and so on), the female will show no sexual behavior. Testosterone restores sexual behavior. The role of adrenal testosterone in the aging human female was brought into sharper focus in recent work. Postmenopausal females who were given human chorionic gonadotropin (HCG) showed no increase in secretion

125

of ovarian hormones, which include testosterone (Persky and Lief, 1976). However, they did show an increase in testosterone when given adrenocorticotropic hormone (ACTH), which stimulates the adrenal cortex. And female-to-male transsexuals given testosterone injections to induce male secondary sex characteristics typically report an increase in sex drive. However, the degree to which this increase is due to the ensuing clitoral hypertrophy or central nervous system effects is unknown.

It has long been thought that testosterone levels are responsible for the degree of sex drive in the human male. There are, however, too many contradictory findings for this simple explanation. Consider first the studies of males with varicoceles and significantly lowered testosterone levels (Raboch and Starka, 1973): There is no significant decrease in their level of sexual activity. Consider the complex finding in another study of male sexual activity and the relation to testosterone (Kraemer et al., 1976): For individual subjects, higher levels of testosterone were found on days during which the men were sexually active. However, the elevation appeared to be a consequence of the activity, rather than an antecedent. And between subjects, a *negative* correlation was found between hormone level and orgasmic frequency.

Does testosterone rejuvenate potency in aging males? In spite of testosterone's venerable reputation, no double-blind studies have been conducted. Typically, a clinician gives an injection of "male potency hormone" to a patient complaining of difficulties with erection, who then reports increased sex drive. Consider also those males whose sexual behavior has resulted in confrontations with the law and who have been given "anti-libido" drugs. These are typically rapists or pedophiliacs who are given Provera® or cyproterone acetate. These drugs may act by reducing testosterone levels or blocking the action of testosterone. The subjects report diminished sexual drive. However, these persons have never been treated in a double-blind study. Rather, a drug described to the subject as reducing sexual drive is given to persons highly motivated to report diminution of sexual behaviors that have caused them legal difficulty (Laschett, 1973; Money, 1976). Consider, finally, the puzzling research with the non-human primate. Castrated male rhesus monkeys show widely disparate levels of sexual behavior (Phoenix et al., 1973). In some animals, sexuality disappears almost immediately, whereas in others it continues (although somewhat diminished) for years. It is unlikely that the rhesus monkeys whose sexuality disappeared almost immediately were those suffering from castration fear.

Since a wide range exists for the "normal" level of plasma testosterone, threshold levels may be critical. Perhaps some individuals operate at one edge of that limit. When the testosterone level drops appreciably via testicular atrophy or surgical castration, the individual with a lower threshold for eliciting sexual behavior may have enough remaining testosterone, of either testicular or adrenal origin, to continue sexual behavior.

Homosexuality

The last five years have witnessed a resurgence of interest in levels of sex steroids in homosexual males and females. Earlier studies, using gross measures of endocrine secretion, failed to discriminate heterosexuals and homosexuals. Now more sophisticated assay procedures permit measurement of several hormones with exquisite sensitivity. The consequence has been an array of conflicting reports. Some studies have found homosexual males to have lower testosterone levels than heterosexual males (Kolodny et al., 1971), and others have found no difference (Pillard et al., 1974). One study found homosexual males to have higher estradiol levels (Doerr et al., 1973).

Lesbianism is rarely studied clinically and even less often endocrinologically. To date it appears that some four lesbians have been scrutinized. Three had higher testosterone and lower estradiol levels than a control group (Loraine et al., 1970).

Since we know that levels of testosterone during adulthood have no demonstrable bearing on the *direction* of sexuality—although they may affect intensity—it is hard to appreciate the significance of finding lower testosterone levels or elevated estradiol levels among homosexual males, unless one speculates that these altered levels existed prenatally. In that case it could be argued that the nervous system was organized in a female direction, or at least not organized in a male direction.

One provocative investigation has attempted to look at central nervous system mechanisms by studying the hypothalamic-pituitary axis with respect to patterns of sex hormone secretion. Heterosexual males, homosexual males, and heterosexual females were compared. In the typical male and female, a different response pattern exists with respect to levels of luteinizing hormone (LH) after the person receives an intravenous injection of estrogen.

127

In the typical male, there is a drop in LH with a return to baseline, but no rebound. In the female, the drop is followed by a rebound above baseline. A sample of homosexual males showed the female response. The interpretation given was that the central nervous system of the male homosexuals had not differentiated in the male direction (Dorner et al., 1975). This provocative study has not been replicated. Clearly, it is more directed at basic mechanisms than at assessing plasma testosterone levels.

Another finding that hints at a basic mechanism, but defies explanation, has been replicated twice (Margolese and Janiger, 1973; Evans, 1972). This is the altered 24-hour urine ratio of androsterone and etiocholanolone (two stereoisomeric metabolites of testosterone) derived from the adrenal and testes. The ratio appears to discriminate some persons of diverse sexual orientation. However, in the first report (Margolese, 1970) a few depressed and/or diabetic heterosexual males showed the pattern found in the homosexual healthy subjects, thus raising the question of specificity. Also a variety of other factors, including stress, may affect the ratio of these metabolites. This urine metabolite finding is haunting because it has been replicated, and suggests the possibility of altered metabolic pathways of testosterone. If true, such pathways could reflect on a more basic physiologic level of influencing central nervous system organization.

Finally, let us not neglect the heroic neurosurgical approach being conducted in West Germany for treating "sex offenders." These latter include 80 males who are repetitive pedophiliacs, rapists, exhibitionists, or "excessive masturbators." They are being treated with stereotaxic psychosexual surgery, a procedure that entails destruction of the ventromedial nucleus of the hypothalamus in the nondominant hemisphere. According to the neurosurgeons, the patients typically report some degree of reduction in sexual drive and primarily a *redirection* of sexuality toward "more appropriate" objects and situations. Testosterone levels are not affected (Muller, 1976). No dramatic side effects on personality have been reported as a concomitant of the procedure, except for one patient who died of pneumonia (with a presumably dramatic effect on personality).

Debate rages over at least two facets of this project. First, there is little evidence from nonhuman laboratory studies suggesting that a unilateral lesion in this brain area should dramatically affect *level* of sexuality and less evidence that it would affect *direction* of sexuality. Next, there is the major ethical issue of whether the individuals undergoing this treatment are being coerced. Typically, these sex offenders are already in prison or about to be incarcerated. Further, it is not clear whether the procedure is having a specific effect on sexual "centers" or yielding clinically reported results via suggestion or patient falsification of behavioral reports. These patients are told that the procedure will reduce aberrant sex drive and redirect it to appropriate legal outlets. One might say that they are highly motivated to report normal sexuality. Social and behavioral scientists have called for a moratorium on these procedures pending independent evaluation of the psychosexual and general psychologic status of those who have undergone surgery.

One cannot but be awed by the Herculean leaps from animal to human research currently under way by the intrepid researchers on both sides of the Berlin Wall.

The Pendulum at Midarc

For some it may be unsettling to leave this discussion of research findings and possible interpretations with less than a clearly defined picture of biological influences on sexual identity. I consider such an unsettled feeling to be healthy for science. Too much of "scientific" history in this area has seen this over-determined, complex phenomenon from an "either/or" perspective, a narrow view that has not advanced the state of knowledge. Phenomena have been prematurely written off as purely biologically determined, or purely socially determined. At times, findings have been burdened by political implications or interpreted in such a way as to preclude alternative hypotheses. And yet a new respect has derived from the research cited here— respect for the role that biological forces *may* play in *some* areas of psychosexual differentiation, at *some* times in development, and perhaps for *some* persons more than others.

To me, the wisest answer in response to a "simple" question such as "What causes homosexuality?" is "We don't know." This is not to say we know *nothing*, but that we have evidence available from a wide range of strategies pointing to a multi-determined phenomenon. These influences include the biological as well as the nonbiological. Both interact in a dynamic system.

129

We can give wise, partial answers that reflect the state of the science, but reductionism will not advance this field, and simple answers to complex questions will not enlighten. Disregard for findings contrary to one's viewpoint is not science. Premature closure disserves a field moving forward with increasing speed and vigor into the arena of scientific respectability.

Researchers will doubtlessly continue to grind up the brains of hamsters, slip electrodes into areas of monkey brains, and poke and probe the orifices of humans, perhaps even making new orifices, in an effort to get at those vital juices and reverberating circuits. Meanwhile, people keep on copulating, largely unmindful of all these important variables that contribute to their ecstasy.

The healthiest position we can take on the role of biological influences on sexual identity is one that stays within the metaphor of a dynamic pendulum at midarc between the prenatal programmists and the postnatal socialists. From this dynamic, *nonstatic* position, researchers can move forward, incorporating all components of the multi-determined nature of human sexuality in the dynamic interface between biologic and social systems.

References

Bell, R., and Darling, J. 1965. The prone head reaction in the human newborn. *Child Dev.* 36:943-949.

Benjamin, H. 1966. *The transsexual phenomenon.* New York: Julian Press.

———. 1970. Reminiscences. *J. Sex Res.* 6:3-9.

Davenport, G. 1976. Paper read at meeting of International Academy of Sex Research, August 1976, Hamburg, West Germany.

Diamond, M. 1965. A critical evaluation of the ontogeny of human sexual behavior. *Quart. Rev. Biol.* 40:147-175.

Doerr, P.; Kochett, H.; Vogt, H.; Pirke, K.; and Dittmar, F. 1973. Plasma testosterone, estradiol and semen analysis in male homosexuals. *Arch. Gen. Psychiatry* 29:829-833.

Dorner, G. 1976. Paper read at meeting of International Congress of Sexology, October 28-31, 1976, Montreal, Canada.

Dorner, G.; Rhode, W.; Stahl, F.; Krell, L.; and Masius, W. 1975. A neuroendocrine predisposition for homosexuality in men. *Arch. Sex. Behav.* 4:1-8.

Ehrhardt, A., and Baker, S. 1974. Fetal androgens, human central nervous system differentiation and behavior sex differences. In *Sex differences in behavior,* ed. R. Friedman, R. Richart, and R. Vande Wiele. New York: John Wiley.

Ehrhardt, A.; Evers, K.; and Money, J. 1968. Influence of androgen in women with late-treated andrenogenital syndrome. *Johns Hopkins Med. J.* 123:115–122.

Ehrhardt, A.; Grisanti, G.; and Meyer-Bahlburg, H. In press. Prenatal exposure to medroxyprogesterone acetate in girls. *Psychoneuroendocrin.*

Ehrhardt, A., and Money, J. 1967. Progestin-induced hermaphroditism: A study of 10 girls. *J. Sex Res.* 3:83–100.

Evans, R. 1972. Physical and biochemical characteristics of homosexual men. *J. Consult. Clin. Psychol.* 39:140–147.

Freud, S. 1953. Three essays on the theory of sexuality (originally published in 1905). In *Standard edition of the complete psychological works of Sigmund Freud,* vol. 7. London: Hogarth.

_____. 1955. The psychogenesis of a case of homosexuality in a woman (originally published in 1920). In *Standard edition of the complete psychological works of Sigmund Freud,* vol. 18. London: Hogarth.

Galenson, E. 1975. Paper read at annual meeting of the Society for the Scientific Study of Sex, October 1975, New York.

Goldberg, S., and Lewis, M. 1969. Play behavior in the year-old infant: Early sex differences. *Child Dev.* 40:21–31.

Goy, R., and Goldfoot, D. 1976. Neuroendocrinology: Animal models and problems of human sexuality. In *New directions in sex research,* ed. E. Rubinstein, R. Green, and E. Brecher. New York: Plenum.

Green, R. 1974. *Sexual identity conflict in children and adults.* New York: Basic Books.

Green, R.; Kester, P.; Finch, S.; and Williams, K. In press. DES, DES plus progesterone, progestin: Effects on psychosexual development in human males.

Green, R., and Money, J., eds. 1969. *Transsexualism and sex reassignment.* Baltimore: Johns Hopkins Press.

Herbert, J. 1970. Hormones and reproductive behavior in rhesus and talapoin monkeys. *J. Reprod. Fertil. Suppl.* 11:119–140.

Kagan, J., and Lewis, M. 1965. Studies of attention in the human infant. *Merrill-Palmer Quart.* 11:95–127.

Kolodny, R.; Masters, W.; Hendryx, J.; and Toro, G. 1971. Plasma testosterone and semen analysis in male homosexuals. *N. Engl. J. Med.* 285:1170–1174.

Kraemer, H.; Becker, H.; Brodie, H.; Doering, C.; Moos, R.; and Hamburg, D. 1976. Orgasmic frequency and plasma testosterone levels in normal human males. *Arch. Sex. Behav.* 5:125–132.

Krafft-Ebing, R. von. 1933. *Psychopathia sexualis.* Brooklyn: Physicians and Surgeons.

Laschett, U. 1973. Antiandrogen in the treatment of sex offenders. In *Contemporary sexual behavior,* ed. J. Zubin and J. Money. Baltimore: Johns Hopkins Press.

Lewis, M. 1976. Early sex differences in the human: Studies of socio-emotional development. In *New directions in sex research*, ed. E. Rubinstein, R. Green, and E. Brecher. New York: Plenum.

Lewis, M., and Weinraub, S. 1974. Sex of parent x sex of child. In *Sex differences in behavior*, ed. R. Friedman, R. Richart, and R. Vande Wiele. New York: Wiley-Interscience.

Loraine, J.; Ismail, A.; Adamopoulus, A.; and Dove, G. 1970. Endocrine function in male and female homosexuals. *Brit. Med. J.* 4:406–408.

Maccoby, E., and Jacklin, C. 1974. *The psychology of sex differences*. Stanford: Stanford University Press.

Margolese, M. S. 1970. Homosexuality: A new endocrine correlate. *Horm. Behav.* 1:151–155.

Margolese, M. S., and Janiger, O. 1973. Androsterone-etiocholanolone ratios in male homosexuals. *Br. Med. J.* 2:207–210.

Meyer-Bahlburg, H.; Grisanti, G.; and Ehrhardt, A. In press. Prenatal effects of sex hormones on human male behavior: Medroxyprogesterone acetate. *Psychoneuroendocrin.*

Money, J. 1968. *Sex errors of the body*. Baltimore: Johns Hopkins Press.

—————. 1976. Issues and attitudes in research and treatment of variant forms of human sexual behavior. Paper read at Conference on Ethics, Reproductive Biology Research Foundation, January 22–23, 1976, St. Louis.

Money, J., and Ehrhardt, A. 1972. *Man and woman, boy and girl*. Baltimore: Johns Hopkins Press.

Montazagga, P. 1932. *Anthropological studies of sexual relations of mankind*. New York: Anthropological Press.

Muller, O. 1976. Paper read at meeting of International Academy of Sex Research, August 1–3, 1976, Hamburg, West Germany.

Nisbett, R., and Gurwitz, S. 1970. Weight, sex and eating behavior of human newborns. *J. Comp. Physiol. Psychol.* 73:245–253.

Panborn, R. 1959. Influence of hunger on sweetness preferences and taste thresholds. *Am. J. Clin. Nutrition* 7:280–287.

Persky, H., and Lief, H. 1976. Paper read at International Congress of Sexology. October 28–31, 1976, Montreal, Canada.

Phoenix, D.; Slob, A.; and Goy, R. 1973. Effects of castration and replacement therapy on the sexual behavior of adult male rhesus. *J. Comp. Physiol. Psychol.* 84:472–481.

Pillard, R.; Rose, R.; and Sherwood, M. 1974. Plasma testosterone levels in homosexual men. *Arch. Sex. Behav.* 3:453–458.

Raboch, J., and Starka, L. 1973. Reported coital activity of men and levels of plasma testosterone. *Arch. Sex. Behav.* 2:309–315.

Reinisch, J., and Karow, W. 1977. Prenatal exposure to synthetic progestins and estrogens: Effects on human development. *Arch. Sex. Behav.* 6:257-288.

Rosenblum, L. 1961. The development of social behavior in the rhesus monkey. University of Wisconsin Libraries, Madison.

_____. 1974. Sex differences, environmental complexity and mother-infant relations. *Arch. Sex. Behav.* 3:117-128.

Saghir, M., and Robins, E. 1973. *Male and female homosexuality.* Baltimore: Williams and Wilkins.

Schmidt, G., and Sigusch, V. 1972. Changes in sexual behavior among young males and females between 1960-1970. *Arch. Sex. Behav.* 2: 27-45.

Stoller, R. 1968. *Sex and gender.* New York: Science House.

_____. 1972. The "bedrock" of masculinity and femininity: Bisexuality. *Arch. Gen. Psychiat.* 26:207-212.

_____. 1975. *The transsexual experiment.* London: Hogarth.

Waxenberg, S.; Drellich, M.; and Sutherland, A. 1959. The role of hormones in human behavior. *J. Clin. Endocrinol.* 19:193-202.

Yalom, I.; Green, R.; and Fisk, N. 1973. Prenatal exposure to female hormones: Effect on psychosexual development in boys. *Arch. Gen. Psychiat.* 28:554-561.

Young, W.; Goy, R.; and Phoenix, C. 1964. Hormones and sexual behavior. *Science* 143:212-218.

Zuger, B. 1970. Gender role differentiation: A critical review of the evidence from hermaphroditism. *Psychosom. Med.* 32:449-463.

Biological Determinants of Sex: Their Scope and Limitations

Julian M. Davidson

Given the diversity of professional allegiances and scientific ideologies represented in this book, it seems appropriate to begin by stating my own bias. First, as a student of reproductive physiology and behavior, I am guided in the animal laboratory by purely behavioristic concepts. Despite the decline of Skinnerian psychology, this position causes me no trouble with colleagues, journals, or granting agencies. It appears that the behavioristic-mechanistic paradigm is the only presently available, convenient strategy for studying the biological determinants of animal behavior—but I hesitate to apply it to people. Indeed, I believe that to carry this approach over to the attempt to understand human sexuality is to attend to the shell of behavior while avoiding the kernel of conscious experience. So I tell myself that this volume deals with what makes female humans *feel* female (and sexy) and males feel male (and sexy), and not just with what makes them *act* accordingly.

This position (which I think we all hold privately if not publicly) is not easily incorporated into a discussion on "biological determinants of behavior." The very use of that expression implies that the "mental" conditions relating to sexual identity and behavior are determined by such entities as genes, molecules, cells, and all the other known paraphernalia of the biophysical universe. But there should be no mistake that this is a statement of faith, not of fact. That faith is the embodiment of the materialistic-deterministic assumptions of our scientific culture, and regard-

Thanks go to Dr. Gary Gray for reading and commenting on the manuscript.

less of our present and/or future failures to demonstrate explicitly the mechanisms of psychophysical determinism, that faith is likely to endure, if only because it is a doctrine that cannot be disproved. That is to say we can't actually demonstrate that a given mental state is *not* determined by physiological events until we know everything there is to know about human physiology. Since I do not believe that we have many real answers yet regarding the biological determinants of human sexuality, my goal will be limited to trying to clarify the issues. In this discussion I attempt to evaluate evidence regarding the physical determinants of sexual behavior and experience, particularly as it relates to gender identity, but do not attempt to deal with nonsexual behavior or experience, except *en passant*.

The Neuroendocrinology of Sexual Differentiation

The dominant and universally accepted theory of the biology of sex differentiation is that maleness is imposed on a basic, potentially female pattern by the action of testicular hormone(s) at critical periods in development. This principle has been applied successfully to three levels of differentiation that have a bearing on sex and gender. A clear concept of the separateness of these processes is helpful in the analysis of the biology of sexual differentiation.

The first level is that of *anatomy*. The sexes are differentiated in genital, gonadal, and secondary sexual structures, anatomical features important or essential for reproduction and sexual behavior. The mechanism of this process of anatomical differentiation has been well studied in both animals and humans. It depends on multiple exposures of embryonic *anlagen* (precursors) to testicular hormone(s), first during critical periods in early development and later in the pubertal and (to a lesser extent) the adult phase. The term *organizational* is applied to the process of hormonal determination at critical periods in early development, and *activational* to the later stimulation of pubertal development and the maintenance in adulthood of sexually differentiated structures. In the absence of masculinizing influences from the testes, only female structures develop, which respond later to the activational influences of ovarian hormones.

The second level of biological differentiation is that of sexual *physiology*. Here the same principle of organization by perinatal androgen and later activation by male or female hormones is applied to function rather than structure. First, there are complex neuroendocrine mechanisms that determine the different reproductive patterns of males and females. A clear example of this is cyclic ovulation, the capacity for which is obliterated by perinatal androgen in several laboratory species. As a result of this early androgenic action, a constant level of pituitary-gonadal function suitable for spermatogenesis is assured, rather than the basic female pattern of cyclic pituitary function and resulting ovulatory cycles of reproductive readiness. It is usually assumed that this effect involves a permanent alteration of brain mechanisms controlling the pituitary. The induction of acyclicity by early androgen is best established in rodent species and has not yet been shown to operate in primates (Goy and Resko, 1972; Knobil, 1974).

A second group of physiological functions is in all species dependent on the presence or absence of organizational and activational androgen. These are the genital functions involved in sexual behavior: erection and ejaculation in the male, and presumably also the vascular, secretory, and muscular changes affecting the female genitalia during the sexual response. Paradoxically, though the early differentiation of the female genitalia depends on the absence of testicular hormone, androgen may promote sexuality in females during adulthood. As Richard Green points out, the latter influence may be limited to clitoral stimulation. The common view that adrenal androgen is necessary for sexual function in the normal human female is based on inadequate evidence.

The importance of these two levels of sexual differentiation for establishing and maintaining human gender identity is perfectly obvious. The perception of *anatomical* differentiation by self and others is surely the primary basis for gender identity. Second, there is the capacity of the male genital to erect, intromit, and ejaculate and of the female sexual apparatus to be penetrated and pass through the transformations of the sexual response as well as to menstruate and bear children. These capacities reinforce the gender role in sexual behavior and by extension presumably also in other areas of social behavior.

There is, however, a third and much more problematic level at which perinatal androgen is said to control sexual identity and behavior. It is believed that there are brain mechanisms which are necessary to establish gender identity and various sexually differentiated behaviors. Thus, perinatal androgen, apart from differentiating reproductive structure and function, is supposed to act on a specific brain area(s) to make us feel as well as act in masculine or feminine ways. Unlike our ideas on the first two levels, this concept depends largely on animal data, with the notable exception of the work of Money, Ehrhardt, and their colleagues (Money and Ehrhardt, 1972). Green, like most authors in this area, invokes the results from animal research in support of the data on humans. Unlike Green, others engage in wholesale undiscriminating extrapolation of the animal data to homosexuality, transsexualism, and other problems of human sexuality. Thus, it is important to ask just what is the nature of the animal evidence, before proceeding to consider its relevance to humans.

It has been repeatedly demonstrated in rats, guinea pigs, mice, hamsters, dogs, and rhesus monkeys that exposure of the fetal or neonatal female to high levels of androgen, and perinatal castration or antiandrogen treatment of the male, have permanent effects on the future behavior of these animals (see Bermant and Davidson, 1974). Basically these treatments increase the probability that sexual and certain other sexually dimorphic behavior patterns appropriate to the *opposite* sex will be manifested in preference to the homologous sex-related behavior. The kinds of behavior most studied have been male coital patterns; lordosis and other responses indicating sexual receptivity in the normal female; and maternal, aggressive, and some other emotional and social behaviors.

Though the behavioral findings are well established, it is not yet possible to pinpoint an area of brain that responds to androgen by inducing masculinization of behavior, despite several serious experimental attempts (for example, Nadler, 1968). There is considerable indirect evidence, however, that the medial preoptic area may be involved. Destruction of this area virtually eliminates male sexual behavior in adult rats, dogs, cats, and rhesus monkeys (see Hart, 1974; Slimp et al., in press). Studies on the intracerebral implantation of androgen provide strong evidence that this area is a major location of the activational effects of testosterone on male sexual behavior in rats (Johnston and Davidson, 1972). Some small sex differences in neuronal connections have been located in this region (Raisman and Field, 1973; Greenough et al., in press) and very recent data indicate that there may be a difference in gross size of the medial preoptic nucleus area of male and female rats (Gorski et al., 1977). It functions in the neural control of ovulation and, presumably via coupling to the neighboring suprachiasmatic nucleus, plays a role in the reproductive cycles of laboratory rodents. Though all this information is quite suggestive, nevertheless little *direct* evidence is available that the differentiating action of perinatal androgen on behavior is exerted at this or any other specific brain location. Yet the permanent behavioral effects of perinatal androgen at specific critical periods in development seem to demand explanation in terms of direct cerebral action.

Application to Humans

What is the evidence that this hypothesis of sexual differentiation of behavior may apply to humans? There are in my view at least three major arguments that make this analogy extremely problematic, at least as regards differentiation of sexual behavior (as opposed to sex-dimorphic nonsexual behavior).

Limitations of Animal Models. First, consider the disparities between the phenomena of animal behavior and human sexuality. Animal behaviorists do not investigate the feelings of their experimental subjects and, strangely enough, have seldom looked at physiological responses *during* sexual activity—the two dimensions that have been emphasized in studies on human sexuality. The animal behaviorist generally investigates the effects of neural, endocrine, or environmental variables on overt motor activities associated with the female's role in attracting the male and in being receptive to his coital attempts; and with the male's role in insemination, which often involves complex behavior patterns.

Although mammalian sexual behavior should never be considered a machinelike stimulus-response affair, in animals (particularly *non*primates) the reflex component is clearly much greater than in humans. The major expression of female sexual receptivity (lordosis) in the most studied laboratory species has the properties of a spinal reflex, although there are also more active, "proceptive" behaviors having the function of attracting the male. In male animals, although sexual behavior is often intricate and complex, there is again a strong reflex component.

Thus, normal male rats restrained in a supine position with retraction of the prepuce will show a series of genital reflexes resembling the events occurring during normal mating and having the approximate frequency of the bouts of mounting and intromission behavior. In both male and female rats there is a patterning of responses in mating behavior that seems to follow an inborn rhythm rather than being determined by circumstances of particular mating situations (Sachs et al., 1973). One can also pace mating behavior by fairly nonspecific electrical stimulation of the brain or periphery (Sachs and Barfield, 1974).

Models developed from observations of relatively stereotyped motor responses in animals cannot be frivolously applied to the manifestations of human consciousness that underlie the establishment of gender identity, role, and orientation and of sexuality in general. The goal of human sexuality (procreation aside) is not the completion of certain motor responses, but rather the achievement of a sense of sexual satisfaction, certainly a complex intrapsychic process.

A particularly striking example of failure to appreciate the change in context involved in animal-human extrapolation is Dorner's claim that deprivation of perinatal androgen produces homosexuality. The contention of this investigator that he has observed, in neonatally castrated male rats, behavior analogous to human male homosexuality is not acceptable. It is not based on the rats' preference to engage in sexual activity with the same-sexed partners, but rather on performance of behavior patterns associated with the opposite sex. Thus, to Green's objections regarding Dorner's suggestions for the future "treatment" of incipient homosexuality, I would add the inappropriateness of the animal model on which his human research is based.

In addition, the studies on LH response to estrogen in homosexuals, to which Green refers, are hard to reconcile with the animal evidence. As mentioned above, there is still no reason to believe that the brain-pituitary mechanisms subserving gonadotropin regulation are sexually differentiated *in the primate*. If so, it is hard to see why a differential gonadotropin response to estrogen should be interpreted in terms of defective brain masculinization.

The Uncertain Role of Primate Data. Second, the infrahuman primates are cast in the role of intermediaries between animals and humans. This role could be particularly important in the present case, since the data on humans collected to date have not shown any significant effects of early androgen on sexual behavior. Unfortunately, however, the relevant primate evidence is far from conclusive.

Adult males of all mammalian species seem to require concurrent ("activational") exposure to androgen in order to bring out the expression of the appropriate sexual behavior previously "organized" by perinatal androgen exposure. Neither the adrenogenital-syndrome females of Money and co-workers nor the pseudohermaphroditic monkeys of Goy and Phoenix in Beaverton have been studied extensively after exposure to androgen in adulthood. The few published data (Eaton et al., 1973) suggest that masculinization of adult sex behavior in rhesus is not as complete as in the lower species. The early untreated adrenogenital human subjects of Ehrhardt and her co-workers (1968) were exposed to endogenous androgen in adulthood. However, since these women were reared with altered genitalia, they were subject to a profound masculinizing influence on behavior irrespective of any cerebral effect of early androgen.

Furthermore, to date the evidence for the influence of early androgen in primates is based only on androgenization of *females*. It remains to be demonstrated that demasculinization follows removal of androgen in early development of the *male*. The information on men with androgen insensitivity syndrome does not of course help here, because of the overwhelming confounding influence of their female anatomical phenotype. The principle of hormonal masculinization will not be established until the "second half" of these experiments is done on primates.

The evolutionary change in hormonal dependence of the female provides another set of considerations that must bear on our judgment of the possible relevance of primate evidence on sexual differentiation to human sexuality. The hypothesis of perinatal action on the brain in determining future patterns of sexual behavior is far stronger in regard to the suppression of female behavior patterns than to the activation of male patterns. In fact, the case has been argued that the action of perinatal androgen on *male* sex behavior is limited to the "organization" of the male phallus, possession of which leads to the acquisition of masculine behavior patterns involving mounting, intromission, and ejaculation (Beach, 1971). This case may have been overstated, but if the *major* cerebral effect is on expression of female behavior patterns, it should be noted that these patterns are strictly dependent on ovarian estrogen and/or progesterone in subhuman species. When deprived of the ovaries, female mammals of all known subprimate species become asexual to all intents and purposes, and this is true to a lesser extent of subhuman primates. The action of perinatal androgen is perceived as changing the thresholds of behavioral responsiveness to these hormones (see Davidson and Levine, 1972).

A woman's sexuality is not dependent in any important way on ovarian hormones. It would thus be far-fetched to expect those biological mechanisms that determine the pattern of hormone-dependent behaviors in animals to apply to the endocrinologically emancipated human female. But what about the Beaverton monkeys? The demonstration by this group (Goy and Resko, 1972) that prenatal testosterone results in the male pattern of mounting behavior manifested by the prepuberal "pseudohermaphroditic" female rhesus is generally regarded as confirming the subprimate work on sexual behavior differentiation and therefore providing a "link" to the human species. It does not. All that has been documented to date has to do with increasing male behavior; the suppression of specifically female responses has not been demonstrated. Actually, the observations of malelike mounting could be the result of these females seeking stimulation for their hypertrophied phalluses. This suggestion derives support from the demonstration that testosterone can induce increases in clitoral rubbing during mounting in normal adult females (Goy and Resko, 1972). Thus, the rhesus data may serve only to support the hypothesis that acute masculinization of peripheral genital structures, rather than central behavior mechanisms, underlies the organizational action of perinatal androgen on sexual behavior. There are counter arguments to this view, however. It must be admitted that the typically male pattern of mounting in the pseudohermaphrodites, which can involve or approximate intromission behavior, suggests a cerebral effect, though it does not prove its existence. The same can be said of new work on the behavioral effectiveness of prenatal dihydrotestosterone, which masculinizes the genitals less than testosterone.[1]

Recently Goy and Goldfoot (1975) have presented a modified

1. R. W. Goy, personal communication, 1977.

view of the hypothesis of hormonal differentiation of sexual behavior to incorporate the fact that early androgen does not seem to defeminize the rhesus even when it masculinizes her. They suggest that the effect of early androgen in primates is to produce a bisexual situation in which male responses coexist with such female ones as "presenting" behavior. This could be interpreted as a lack of a *central* organizational effect of androgen on behavioral mechanisms. There is no reason why the masculinization of the genitals should suppress presenting, and, in fact, normal male rhesus do show a high frequency of this behavior.

Parenthetically, it is unfortunate that almost the whole burden of conducting these tedious long-term experiments on sexual differentiation in primates should have fallen on the shoulders of one group of investigators (albeit an excellent one). Many questions remain regarding the primate situation and can be answered only by enlisting the interest of more laboratories in this work.

Questionable "Sex Differences." The final argument relates to the tautologic, but often neglected proposition that one can speak of sexual differentiation only when the functions under study really are sexually dimorphic to begin with. In fact, careful examination shows that the sexual behavior of male and female humans is not that different, except for the obvious anatomical constraints and clearly culturally determined factors.

Both Kinsey (1953) and Masters and Johnson (1966) have pointed out that the physiologic similarities in genital and particularly extra-genital autonomic and somatic effects far outweigh the differences in sexual response between the sexes. We do not know of any sex differences in the neuromuscular components of sexual activity. Furthermore, psychophysiologic differences previously thought to be immutable seem to have been overstated, or to be diminishing with the passage of time. It appears, for instance, that the capacity for multiple orgasms is not limited to women.[2] According to Robbins and Jensen (1977), some males can have multiple climaxes without refractory periods. Each of these manifests various physiological indices of orgasm but not ejaculation, which is limited to the final orgasm. Of course this phenomenon does seem rare, at least in our culture. In general, however, the subjective, experiential aspect of orgasm does not

2. B. Campbell, personal communication, 1976.

appear to show any consistent sex difference, as judged by the analysis of verbal reports (Vance and Wagner, 1976).

The sex difference in susceptibility to visual erotic material (Kinsey, 1953) is no longer found in recent studies (Schmidt and Sigusch, 1973), and the difference in rate of masturbation is declining, though not disappearing, as pointed out by Green. Are we to explain these apparent changes within a couple of decades, along with others in dress and employment patterns, as resulting from changes in the fetal hormonal environment or the structure of neural networks?

In summary, the three sets of considerations presented all lead to one conclusion: that extrapolation of existing findings on hormonal differentiation of animal sexual behavior to problems of human sexuality is a highly questionable undertaking. It should be reiterated that this discussion relates to sexual behavior; it is not applicable to the differentiation of nonsexual behaviors such as those related to aggression and sexually dimorphic play patterns in monkeys. One comment is apropos, however, with regard to Green's recent research on the feminization of personality traits of boys following prenatal exposure to estrogenic and progestational hormones. I know of no animal model for this effect. All the experimental work to date indicates *masculinization* of behavior, regardless of whether testicular or ovarian hormones were used. In fact, a currently popular hypothesis proposes that the "organizational" effects of early androgen are mediated by conversion to estrogen in brain cells (Hart, 1977).

Activational Effects of Androgen

The apparent weakness of analogies between human and animal species regarding the differentiation of sexual behavior by early androgen does not necessarily apply to the activational effects of androgen on male sexual responses in adulthood. Certainly sexuality in men is not to be equated with male rat mating patterns. Nevertheless, the presence of adequate testosterone in the blood of the male seems to be of vital importance for maintenance of male sexual arousal and potency in both men and rats, and in fact, in all mammalian (and many submammalian) species that have been studied.

How then are we to understand the apparent lack of relationship between blood testosterone levels and sex drive, to which

Green refers? I think he is on the right track in pointing to the wide normal range in circulating testosterone levels and in suggesting that some men may have much higher titers than they "need." Nevertheless, I doubt that the required concentration is so low that adrenal androgen can suffice to maintain normal sexual behavior after castration. This operation eliminates almost all of the circulating testosterone, leaving mostly androgens that are biologically less potent.

Removal of the testes seems to have basically similar effects on sex behavior in all mammalian species, with differences only of detail. There is a rapid postoperative decline in the probability that copulatory behavior will occur within any population of castrates, though great individual variation in the rate of decline is encountered. Some castrated men, monkeys, dogs, and cats may retain sexual capacities for years (see Bermant and Davidson, 1974; Hart, 1974), though there is little if any data to show that such retained behavior is "normal." In shorter-lived species such as the rat, an occasional animal will continue to mate up to about six months after castration (that is, about one-fifth of the life span), though mating patterns are disrupted and mating frequency decreases. We do not know what is responsible for this retention of behavior in men and animals. It does not seem to be dependent on adrenal androgen, since adrenalectomy has not been shown to affect the postcastration decline, at least in subprimate species. I believe there is a certain minimal amount of circulating androgen necessary for normal male sexual behavior and that this amount is definitely greater than the castrate level and considerably less than that usually found in normal healthy individuals.

We have attempted to correlate all available measures of sexual behavior with testosterone levels determined by repeated blood sampling on a group of 70 male rats, and have found no correlations. The animals were then castrated and received subcutaneous implants of constant release (Silastic) capsules containing testosterone. These capsules produced stable androgen levels, which were monitored regularly for several months. The circulating level required to maintain normal male sexual behavior was well below the range found in normal rats (Damassa et al., 1977).

Thus, there is marked redundancy in the amount of testosterone available for male sexual behavior. This explains the lack of a positive correlation between circulating levels and behavior in our rat study, in a small study on guinea pigs (Harding and Feder, 1976), and in the Raboch and Starka (1973) and the Kraemer et al. (1976) reports on men. The negative interindividual correlation found in the last-mentioned study is indeed difficult to explain ānd could well be spurious. In a recent investigation on 101 men (Brown et al., in press) no correlations were found. The suggestion mentioned by Green that testosterone may increase following coitus has been investigated in a variety of animal species with results that are inconsistent, depending on the species (see Davidson, 1977). In humans, despite the suggestive evidence in the Kraemer study and two other entertaining reports, each with an N of 1 (*Nature,* 1970; Fox et al., 1972), neither we (Davidson and Trupin, 1975) nor other laboratories (Stearns et al., 1973) have been able to find consistent effects in men.

When Green points to the lack of double-blind studies on the effects of androgen, he is merely highlighting the sorry state of human sexual psychoendocrinology. In the absence of reliable studies with adequate endocrinologic and psychologic expertise and proper controls, casual observation poses as data and speculation as well-based conclusions. This criticism certainly applies to the recent European research on antiandrogen discussed by Green. While cyproterone seems to be effective in treating "sexual offenders," the claim that it acts as a specific inhibitor of brain mechanisms subserving sexual behavior (Laschet, 1973) is unjustified. There is still a very real possibility that it acts by suppression of normal testosterone secretion (because of its progestational antigonadotropin activity), thus producing a functional castration.

Then there are the proposals of Dörner to treat with testosterone pregnant women with low amniotic fluid levels of androgen, and the production of hypothalamic lesions by Roeder and his colleagues—treatments intended to prevent and "treat" homosexuality respectively. These projects are reminiscent of the past excesses of psychosurgery in that neither is based on adequate scientific rationale; nor has there been careful evaluation of the results of the lesions.

Although there are many difficulties in the performance of adequate research on the biological basis of human sexuality, one cannot justify the premature adoption of biological treatments for sexual problems, particularly in light of recent successes with behavioral-psychological approaches. For me, this conclusion derives not only from the poor quantity and quality of the existing research on human sexual psychobiology, but also from my theoretical position. Despite the problems of psychophysical determinism, I believe that one can continue to look for biological determinants while avoiding the absurdities of mechanistic explanations of human sexuality. This balance may be achieved by simply remembering that the biological factors in sexuality are not to be viewed as absolute determinants, but rather as constraints that have a given statistical probability of producing effects on consciousness and behavior. It is important to recognize the extent to which these constraints can be transcended.[3]

Everybody knows that a mouse cannot make love with an elephant. But I believe there are mice who have dreamed of making love to elephants, and perhaps some who "make" it. Indeed, I am not sure this fantasy is any harder to accept than the fact that a biologically "normal" human male or female can successfully change sexes. The fact of transsexualism, like the elephantine dreams of my fictional mouse, may simply be an extreme example of the transcendence of biological determination. Other candidates for this designation are fantasy-induced orgasms—the transcendence of genital determination; copulation in male castrates—the transcendence of hormonal determination; and the sexual achievements of paraplegics—the transcendence of neural determination. On the other side of the coin, there is the whole host of psychogenic sexual disabilities wherein a seemingly normal sexual "apparatus" coexists with anorgasmia, impotence, vaginismus, dyspareunia, gender dysphoria, and so on.

Now the traditional counter-argument to the above is that transsexuals and overachieving mice are not really biologically the same as other members of the population—they only appear to be the same. But until the biological origins of transsexuality

3. I make no claim to know what "it" is that does the transcending. You can call it free will or God, if you please. More simply you can say that biological variables known to constrain behavior are constituents of a larger system (the behaving individual), whose emergent properties are different from those of its constituent parts. The term "transcend" was chosen for its dramatic properties, but without any intention of invoking supernatural forces.

or the interspecific sexual ambitions of mice are actually revealed, the doctrine of covert biological origins for apparently "cognitive" phenomena should be recognized as a matter of faith. While scientific experimentation should and will continue to be motivated by that faith, in the meantime we may consider biological factors in human sexuality as constraints that can be transcended within limits to be determined empirically. These limits must always be regarded as being potentially expandable. Only in this way, I think, can we maintain a truly humanistic approach to human sexuality without relinquishing or ignoring biology.

References

Anonymous. Effects of sexual activity on beard growth in man. 1970. *Nature (London)* 226:869–870.

Beach, F. A. 1971. Hormonal factors controlling the differentiation, development and display of copulatory behavior in the ramstergig and related species. In *Biopsychology of development,* ed. L. Aronson and E. Tobach. New York: Academic Press.

Bermant, G., and Davidson, J. M. 1974. *Biological bases of sexual behavior.* New York: Harper and Row.

Brown, W. A.; Monti, P.; and Corriveau, D. In press. Serum testosterone and sexual activity and interest in men. *Arch. Sex. Behav.*

Damassa, D. A.; Smith, E. R.; and Davidson, J. M. 1977. The relationship between circulating testosterone levels and sexual behavior. *Horm. Behav.* 8:275–286.

Davidson, J. M. 1977. Neurohormonal bases of male sexual behavior. In *International review of physiology,* vol. 13, ed. R. O. Greep. Baltimore: University Park Press.

Davidson, J. M., and Levine, S. 1972. Endocrine regulation of behavior. *Ann. Rev. Physiol.* 34:375–408.

Davidson, J. M., and Trupin, S. 1975. Neural mediation of steroid-induced sexual behavior in rats. In *Sexual behavior: Pharmacology and biochemistry,* ed. M. Sandler and G. L. Gassa. New York: Raven Press.

Eaton, G. G.; Goy, R. W.; and Phoenix, C. H. 1973. Effects of testosterone treatment in adulthood on sexual behavior of female pseudohermaphroditic rhesus monkeys. *Nature New Biol.* 242:119–120.

Ehrhardt, A.; Evers, K.; and Money, J. 1968. Influence of androgen and some aspects of sexually dimorphic behavior in women with the late-treated andrenogenital syndrome. *Johns Hopkins Med. J.* 123:115–122.

Fox, C. A.; Ismail, A. A. A.; Love, D. M.; Kirkham, K. E.; and Loraine, J. A. 1972. Studies on the relationship between plasma testosterone levels and human sexual activity. *J. Endocrinol.* 52:51–58.

Gorski, R. A.; Shryne, J.; Gordon, J.; and Christensen, L. 1977. Evidence for a morphological sex difference within the medial preoptic area (MPOA) of the rat. *Anat. Rec.* 187:591.

Goy, R. W., and Goldfoot, D. A. 1975. Neuroendocrinology: Animal models and problems of human sexuality. *Arch. Sex. Behav.* 4:405–420.

Goy, R. W., and Resko, J. A. 1972. Gonadal hormones and behavior of normal and pseudohermaphroditic female primates. *Recent Prog. Horm. Res.* 28:707–733.

Greenough, W. T.; Carter, C. S.; Steerman, C.; and DeVoogd, T. J. In press. Sex differences in dendritic patterns in hamster preoptic area. *Brain Res.*

Harding, C. F., and Feder, H. H. 1976. Relation between individual differences in sexual behavior and plasma testosterone levels in the guinea pig. *Endocrinology* 98:1198–1205.

Hart, B. L. 1974. Gonadal androgen and sociosexual behavior of male mammals: A comparative analysis. *Psychol. Bull.* 81:383–400.

————. 1977. Neonatal dihydrotestosterone and estrogen stimulation: Effects on sexual behavior of male rats. *Horm. Behav.* 8:193–200.

Johnston, P., and Davidson, J. M. 1972. Intracerebral androgens and sexual behavior in the male rat. *Horm. Behav.* 3:345–357.

Kinsey, A. C.; Pomeroy, W. B.; Martin, C. E.; and Gebhard, P. H. 1953. Sexual behavior in the human female. Philadelphia: Saunders.

Knobil, E. 1974. Maturation of the neuroendocrine control of gonadotropin secretion in the rhesus monkey. *Proc. Int. Colloq. Sex. Endocrinol. Prenatal Period. Inserm.* 32:205–218.

Kraemer, H. C.; Becker, H. B.; Brodie, H. K. H.; Doering, C. H.; Moos, R. H.; and Hamburg, D. A. 1976. Orgasmic frequency and plasma testosterone levels in normal human males. *Arch. Sex. Behav.* 5:125–132.

Laschet, U. 1973. Antiandrogen in the treatment of sex offenders; Mode of action and therapeutic outcome. In *Contemporary sexual behavior: Critical issues in the 1970s,* ed. J. Zugin and J. Money. Baltimore: Johns Hopkins Press.

Masters, W. H., and Johnson, V. E. 1966. *Human sexual response.* Boston: Little, Brown.

Money, J., and Ehrhardt, A. A. 1972. *Man and woman, boy and girl.* Baltimore: Johns Hopkins Press.

Nadler, R. D. 1968. Masculinization of female rats by intracranial implantation of androgen in infancy. *J. Comp. Physiol. Psychol.* 66:157–167.

Raboch, J., and Starka, L. 1973. Reported coital activity of men and levels of plasma testosterone. *Arch. Sex. Behav.* 2:309–315.

Raisman, G., and Field, P. M. 1973. Sexual dimorphism in the neuropil

of the preoptic area of the rat and its dependence on neonatal androgen. *Brain Res.* 54:1-29.

Robbins, M. B., and Jensen, G. D. 1977. Multiple orgasm in males.
In *Progress in sexology*, ed. R. Gemme and C. C. Wheeler. New York:
Plenum Press.

Sachs, B. D., and Barfield, R. J. 1974. Copulatory behavior of male rats
given intermittent electric shocks; Theoretical implications. *J. Comp.
Physiol. Psychol.* 86:607-615.

Sachs, B. D.; Pollak, E. I.; Krieger, M. S.; and Barfield, R. J. 1973.
Sexual behavior; Normal male patterning in androgenized female rats.
Science 181:770-772.

Schmidt, G., and Sigusch, V. 1973. Women's sexual arousal. In *Contemporary sexual behavior: Critical issues in the 1970s,* ed. J. Zubin
and J. Money. Baltimore: Johns Hopkins Press.

Slimp, J. C.; Hart, B. C.; and Goy, R. W. In press. Heterosexual, auto-
sexual and social behavior of adult male rhesus monkeys with medial
preoptic-anterior hypothalamic lesions. *Brain Res.*

Stearns, E. L.; Winter, J. S. D.; and Faiman, C. 1973. Effects of coitus
on gonadotropin, prolactin and sex steroid levels in man. *J. Clin.
Endocrinol. Metab.* 37:687-691.

Vance, E. B., and Wagner, N. N. 1976. Written descriptions of orgasm:
A study of sex differences. *Arch. Sex. Behav.* 5:87-98.

The Interactional Model of
Sex Hormones and Behavior

Anke A. Ehrhardt

Discussions on biological determinants of sex-related behavior suffer from the use of ambiguous terms, as do similar discussions among other specialists. The confusion stems in part from the fact that scientists from different disciplines use the terms *gender* and *sex* in different ways. There is good reason to separate *gender* from *sex* in order to have a term that is not restricted to sexuality in the sense of eroticism, but rather includes all behaviors that may have something to do with being a girl or a boy, a woman or a man (Money, Hampson, and Hampson, 1955). However, it is difficult to use the same terms consistently, especially if one describes behavior across species in a comparative perspective.

As Beach (1974) has pointed out, *gender* and *sexuality* should be restricted to human behavior. This limitation presents no problem if one refers to *gender identity* as the basic identification with one sex or the other, since it describes a specifically human phenomenon implying a state of consciousness not evident in subhuman species. However, *gender role behavior*, as a term that includes all those behavior aspects in which males and females differ in our culture, is useless if one wants to compare human behavior with the behavior of other primates; therefore, I as well as many of my colleagues resort to *sex-dimorphic* or *sex-related* behavior in that context. These terms, of course, lose the broader connotation of *gender role*.

A third term is *sexual orientation*, widely accepted and frequently used as defining homosexual, heterosexual, and bisexual

Dr. Ehrhardt's research is in part supported by a grant (#B-243) from the Spencer Foundation. The author is grateful to Virginia Ann Huson for her invaluable technical assistance in the preparation of this paper.

150

partner choice in human beings. One could argue that *sexual* in this context is also a rather narrow term, since love, erotic attraction, and affectionate bonding clearly are not restricted to the choice of a partner for sexual activities, although this aspect usually is a vital component.

The terms *gender identity, gender role* behavior, *sex-dimorphic,* or *sex-related* behavior, and *sexual orientation* as defined above will be used consistently in this paper, although the other two authors on biological determinants of sexual behavior have their own variations of these terms. One wonders, of course, if even colleagues in a relatively narrow field do not find the same words useful in describing the same phenomena, how scientists from several disciplines can be expected to adopt certain words for general use. To take this a step further, how can we ever be amazed at the degree of misunderstanding and confusion in the general population about sex differences in behavior of people, about sexual life-styles, phenomena like transsexualism, and their various etiologic roots, if scientists do not introduce a consistent, generally-accepted nomenclature of terms? Let us hope this goal will be achieved one day.

From the discussion of biological determinants of sex-related behavior, two central themes emerge: One concerns the question of prenatal hormone effects on behavior; the other refers to adult behavioral endocrinology and the relationship between hormone levels and various aspects of sexuality.

Prenatal Hormones and Developmental Aspects of Behavior

In spite of the many limitations of animal models, and the fragmentary evidence of human studies, some tentative conclusions can be drawn. Gender identity as a strictly human phenomenon seems not to be shaped and influenced in any decisive way by the hormonal environment to which the fetus is exposed in utero. The evidence of human hermaphrodites born with discrepancies between some determinants of their biologic sex, including abnormalities of their prenatal hormone levels, is clearcut: gender identity typically follows the sex of rearing and seems, therefore, to depend largely on a process of learning (Money and Ehrhardt, 1972).

Of particular interest is the example of matched hermaphrodites (Money, 1970). In this case, two people are born with the same genetic sex, same gonadal sex, same presumed prenatal hormonal environment, and same degree of ambiguity of the external sex organs. One child, however, may be assigned to the female sex and the other to the male sex, depending on different medical opinions at different times and at different institutions. The rule has been that gender identity agrees with the particular sex of assignment, provided that parental doubts are resolved and surgical corrections and postnatal hormonal therapy are in agreement with the assigned sex, so that the physical appearance of such a child is usually unambiguously female or male.

Once gender identity has been firmly established, it cannot be reversed easily, as we have learned, in particular, from those persons who unexpectedly virilized or feminized at puberty with secondary sex characteristics in contrast to their sex of assignment (Ehrhardt, 1978). If a person is raised as a girl but suddenly develops a low voice, beard growth, and a clitoris that enlarges to phallic size, her gender identity typically remains female, although the physical changes are very disturbing to her and need to be corrected without delay.

While we have learned very little about gender identity formation from the study of the various abnormalities of prenatal hormone levels, investigations of their possible relationship to gender role behavior have been more fruitful. There is little to add to Green's review of the results of studies using clinical groups who were exposed to abnormally high levels of prenatal androgen or estrogen and progesterone. We have some evidence that such characteristics as high-level expenditure level in play and sports and a lowered interest in various forms of parentalism in childhood may be influenced by high prenatal androgen levels (Ehrhardt, 1975). What estrogen and progesterone may do in terms of predisposing a girl or a boy to certain behavior characteristics is less clear. Some studies suggest that these hormones may work in the opposite direction to androgens in females; for example, maternal intake of progesterone (Zussman, Zussman, and Dalton, 1975) or medroxyprogesterone acetate (Ehrhardt, Grisanti, and Meyer-Bahlburg, 1977) during pregnancy was found to be correlated with a significantly lowered frequency of long-term tomboyism in the experimental groups compared with control groups. In boys, however, the results are not consistent in various studies (for example, Zussman, Zussman, and Dalton, 1975; Meyer-Bahlburg, Grisanti, and Ehrhardt, 1977). Clearly, many intervening variables, such as adequate experimental and comparison group selection or maternal characteristics and similar factors, will have to be better controlled for in future studies.

To pursue careful and sophisticated research in the area of prenatal hormones and their possible effects on postnatal behavior is sometimes an overwhelming task. The complexities of retroactively assessing hormone levels and pregnancy conditions, of measuring the behavior of a child and the environmental rearing conditions cannot be overestimated. It is easily understandable why some researchers suggest giving up on the whole area of prenatal hormones rather than attempting to gain the beginnings of insight into a discrete behavior involving a complicated process of interaction between possible effects of hormone conditions on the developing central nervous system and social-environmental forces. The recommendation to ignore any hormonal factor that may influence behavior comes particularly from sociologists and social psychologists who are understandably concerned about the political misuse of evidence that one may draw from such research. Even a carefully formulated tentative conclusion can all too easily be misquoted as the basis for sex-discriminatory beliefs, and scientific evidence can be exploited for one prejudicial belief system or the other. Neither objection is in itself enough reason to terminate all investigations, but the scientist must be particularly careful with formulations of conclusions and theoretical speculations of results that may potentially induce sensationalism and abuse.

The dilemma of interpreting the effects of prenatal hormones on gender-role behavior stems to a large extent from the confusion around the interactional model. Clearly, we have no evidence that prenatal hormones predetermine in a rigid way any behavior characteristics of an individual. At best they may predispose a person to a certain temperament set that can express itself in various ways depending on the specific environmental influences to which a child is exposed. For instance, if prenatal androgens are related to a predisposition to a higher physical energy level, it will depend largely on cultural expectations, parental reinforcements, physical condition of the child, specific peer environment, the particular school setting, and so on, whether the expressed behavior characteristic becomes active outdoor play, athletic skills, or a tendency to be a withdrawn loner with occasional temper tantrums. Along the same lines, if one postulates that boys and girls differ in predisposition to high energy expenditure because of their different prenatal androgen levels, it does not follow at all that automatically only boys can do certain things which girls cannot. There may conceivably be a mild constitutional differential in predisposition, which typically meets a social-environmental reinforcement system that widens the gap between the sexes dramatically by programming for rigid male and female role division. If, on the other hand, a society had an interest in minimizing sex differences in behavior and would rather prepare members of both sexes for all activities and all social roles in an equal way, one could take the opposite approach and apply the concept of compensatory training (Rossi, 1977). This would include particular reinforcement in physically energetic activities for females. It also would suggest more intense education and training in parentalism for males, since the response to infants may be sex-dimorphic in terms of a relatively higher threshold in males.

Clearly, our knowledge of the intricate interplay of prenatal hormones and behavior is very fragmentary at this point and will become modified and more multi-faceted with better techniques in hormone measurements and behavior assessments.

Behavioral Endocrinology of Adult Behavior

Davidson largely focuses his discussion on the interplay between sexual behavior and sex hormones and points out how limited our knowledge is in this area. My discussion will deal specifically with the research on sex hormones in homosexuality and highlight some points of Green's review in this regard.

During the recent upswing of endocrine research on homosexuality starting in the 1970s, a great many attempts have been made to compare homosexuals and heterosexuals on the basis of various sex hormone levels. The measurement of testosterone has been particularly popular. Presently, there are at least fourteen studies in the literature reporting testosterone values in male homosexuals. The results are highly inconsistent but, according to Meyer-Bahlburg's (1977) comprehensive review, one can draw two general conclusions:

1. The vast majority of male homosexuals have testosterone levels within the normal male range.
2. There is no uniform trend. Differences between homosexual and heterosexual males vary capriciously. Some authors

have reported lower testosterone in homosexuals, some have found elevated testosterone, and most studies have reported no difference.

The heterogeneity of findings is due partly to many design errors in the reported investigations. Studies often lack sophisticated hormone assay methodology and suffer from faulty sample selection and crude behavior assessment. The picture is similar regarding the reports on other endocrine measurements in homosexual men and women.

At this point, one should consider whether this specific approach of behavioral endocrinology toward the etiology of homosexuality is not erroneous altogether. While it is true that we do not know the causes of a preferential hetero-, homo-, or bisexual partner choice, it seems highly unlikely that we will find the answers in differences of adult hormone levels among the various groups. To make this approach a promising avenue for research, one should have some evidence that homosexuality is increased among samples of patients with gross hormonal abnormalities. Follow-up studies of such patient groups do not yet substantiate this theory (Meyer-Bahlburg, 1978). Furthermore, if adult hormone levels were related to sexual orientation, it should be possible to influence hetero-, homo-, and bi-sexuality by exogenously administered hormones—an approach that has been unsuccessfully tried at various times by medical and behavioral scientists.

Some scientists argue that the crucial factor cannot be adult hormone levels, but rather differences in prenatal hormones at a critical time of brain development. However, although our data base is still limited, we have some evidence from the follow-up studies on patients with known fetal hormone abnormalities and know now that sexual orientation is not dictated by prenatal history, but seems rather decisively influenced by the individual's postnatal learning experiences.

The final answer to the question of whether there is an increased frequency in homosexuality or bisexuality associated with specific hormone conditions before birth has to wait until we have more long-term, carefully designed studies on such patients. On the basis of two studies on young women with the early-treated syndrome of congenital adrenal hyperplasia, it seems that most of them are heterosexual. There is a question of whether bisexuality may be somewhat increased among them. However, both

155

studies are still lacking in adequate control group comparisons (Ehrhardt and Baker, 1976; Money and Schwartz, 1977).

If prenatal hormone levels should turn out to be correlated with adult sexual orientation, they clearly would be only *one* factor contributing to a predisposition toward a specific sexual orientation. As outlined before, the model has to be viewed as an interactional process of different constitutional and social-environmental factors, rather than as a rigid inborn cause of a specific behavior trait. However, at the present time we do not even know whether prenatal hormones have any influence on sexual orientation at all. It may depend entirely on an individual's life experiences and the cultural norms of a particular social environment whether he or she develops a predominantly or exclusively heterosexual or homosexual, or a bisexual, orientation.

Of course, behavioral endocrinology is not the only area of research that has contributed very little to our knowledge of the etiology of sexual orientation. The study of specific environmental conditions has been equally disappointing.

One wonders whether the general approach toward finding the roots for homosexuality has not been wrong and doomed to fail from the start. To put people into one category simply on the basis of their sexual life-style and to ignore the many individual differences between such people may very well be a naive assumption of a unifying principle that may prove to be of little relevance. It seems that we are badly lacking a representative description of the various forms of hetero-, homo-, and bi-sexuality. Our knowledge is usually limited to standard forms of any of these sexual preferences, rather than based on the characteristics of the many different clinical, and especially nonclinical, versions and facets of people's life styles with a particular sexual orientation.

Directions for New Research

If society as a whole, and especially the funding agencies, will support this type of research, the next decade should provide stimulating and relevant new findings on the various interactional patterns of hormones and behavior in the field of psychosexual differentiation. Our recommendations, which follow, point to research areas with particular promise.[1]

1. These recommendations are based upon the author's discussions with Richard Green and Julian M. Davidson.

Prenatal Hormones and Behavior

As soon as the technology is perfected to measure maternal and fetal hormones without any negative side-effects, normative studies on the various types of sex hormones among females and males would be of great interest and could provide standards for sex differences. With amniocentesis and determination of the sex of the fetus already possible procedures, the goal is not far-fetched. Once norms of prenatal sex hormones for females and males have been established, a next step might be to determine extreme groups of, for example, high and low testosterone values among groups of same-sex and opposite-sex fetuses and subsequently to compare postnatal behavior development. A research design of the type described by Eleanor Maccoby during this conference for detailed longitudinal studies on children from birth on, comparing this behavior with their prenatal, neonatal, and postnatal hormone profiles, may render intriguing results.

Apart from research on normal children, there are still many abnormal conditions that have not been studied. On the basis of animal experimental work, it has been suggested, for instance, that barbiturates and antibiotics may have an antiandrogenizing effect on fetal development (Gorski, 1971). Many women take sleeping pills and antibiotics during pregnancy without knowing whether their babies may be affected physically or psychologically by these drugs.

Children born with spontaneous abnormalities of their fetal development continue to be of great interest. They help us not only to obtain principles for optimal clinical management, but also to gain more insight into the effects of extreme prenatal hormone levels on behavior, which may aid in formulating relevant hypotheses for normal sexual differentiation.

In the area of prenatal hormonal effects on the developing central nervous system and, thus, on behavior, we are still in need of better animal models. The observations on subhuman primates exposed to high levels of prenatal androgens are limited to very few animals and to one research group carrying out the investigations. Although the studies carried out by Goy and Phoenix and their colleagues have been excellent, one would wish for additional projects with different conditions and behavior assessments. For instance, it would still be extremely interesting to follow a group of prenatally androgenized female monkeys born with masculinized genitalia after they have been neonatally surgically feminized. With this procedure, we would be able to eliminate the possible effect of the appearance of the masculinized genitalia on the perceptions of the mother, the peers, and the hermaphroditic monkey herself.

We also lack data yet on genetic male monkeys who have been deprived of prenatal androgens. This research study might be possible with the use of cyproterone acetate, an antiandrogen widely applied in lower species and used for the treatment of human sexual disorders. Other antiandrogens also are available.

During a time when neurosurgery is being performed on sex offenders, one clearly would like careful studies on brain effects of such interventions on subhuman primates. While the approach of stereotactic procedures to eliminate criminal sexual behavior is clearly based on very insufficient knowledge and, therefore, regarded as an unfortunate development in the treatment of sexual disturbances, one should at least try to explore the various ramifications of this type of neurosurgery on lower species.

Behavioral Endocrinology and Human Sexual Behavior

The field of endocrinology is progressing very rapidly and can be expected to come up soon with reliable norms for hormonal changes during critical life phases, such as adolescence, menstruation, menopause, and old age. However, we need interdisciplinary work to collect data on behavior in correlation and interaction with hormone levels. For instance, the whole area of the menstrual cycle and sexuality in women has only recently begun to be explored with appropriate methodology (McCauley and Ehrhardt, 1976).

The notion that androgen is a libido-enhancing hormone for both sexes is based on a very few inconclusive studies and should be substantiated by better hormone and behavior assessments. The approach would be to study different levels of androgens and their relationship to sexuality both in normal women and in abnormal conditions such as the Stein-Leventhal syndrome, which suddenly exposes women to high levels of androgen from their polycystic ovaries. Many women and men are being treated with agents that suppress androgens, such as cortisone for rheumatoid disease. Their sex lives should be assessed before and after treatment.

We would like to see a double-blind study on cyproterone acetate (antiandrogen) and the effects on sexual behavior. Presently, the evidence is based strictly on clinical studies without adequate control-group comparisons (Laschet and Laschet, 1969).

People with clearly atypical behavior patterns, such as transsexuals, have not been sufficiently studied endocrinologically, and such studies may give us new insights.

Parenting Behavior of Atypical Adults

Presently, child custody claims by heterosexuals against homosexuals or transsexuals are based on no evidence that heterosexuals are better parents. In spite of the lack of data, the courts usually decide for the heterosexual parent, even if the other parent with the less typical sexual life style might be the better caregiver to the child. We urgently need good behavior data on the various types of parent-child interactions. This research should include parents with atypical behavior patterns and/or children who have an unusual development of gender-role behavior, such as effeminacy in boys or gender identity confusion in girls.

References

Beach, F. A. 1974. Human sexuality and evolution. In *Reproductive behavior*, ed. W. Montagna and W. A. Sadler. New York: Plenum.

Ehrhardt, A. A. 1975. Prenatal hormone exposure and psychosexual differentiation. In *Topics in psychoendocrinology*, ed. E. J. Sachar. New York: Grune and Stratton.

———. 1978. Psychosexual adjustment in adolescence in patients with congenital abnormalities of their sex organs. In *Proceedings of the 7th birth defects institute symposium on genetic mechanisms of sexual development*. New York: Academic Press.

Ehrhardt, A. A., and Baker, S. W. 1976. Prenatal androgen exposure and adolescent behavior. Paper read at the International Congress of Sexology, October 28–31, 1976, Montreal.

Ehrhardt, A. A.; Grisanti, G. C.; and Meyer-Bahlburg, H. F. L. 1977. Prenatal exposure to medroxyprogesterone acetate (MPA) in girls. *Psychoneuroendocrinology* 2:391–398.

Gorski, R. A. 1971. Gonadal hormones and the perinatal development of neuroendocrine function. In *Frontiers in neuroendocrinology*, ed. L. Martini and W. F. Ganong. New York: Oxford University Press.

Laschet, U., and Laschet, L. 1968. Die Behandlung der pathologisch gesteigerten und abartigen Sexualität des Mannes mit dem Anti-androgen Cyproteron-acetat. In *Das Testosterone: Die Struma*. Berlin: Springer.

McCauley, E. A., and Ehrhardt, A. A. 1976. Female sexual response: Hormonal and behavioral interactions. In *Primary care*, vol. 3. Philadelphia: Saunders.

Meyer-Bahlburg, H. F. L. 1977. Sex hormones and male homosexuality in comparative perspective. *Arch. Sex. Behav.* 6:297–325.

_____. 1978. Homosexual orientation in women and men: A hormonal basis? In *Proceedings of the conference on bio-psychological factors influencing sex-role related behaviors,* ed. J. E. Parsons. Washington, D.C.: Hemisphere.

Meyer-Bahlburg, H. F. L.; Grisanti, G. C.; and Ehrhardt, A. A. 1977. Prenatal effects of sex hormones on human male behavior: Medroxy-progesterone acetate (MPA). *Psychoneuroendocrinology* 2:383–390.

Money, J. 1970. Matched pairs of hermaphrodites: Behavioral biology of sexual differentiation from chromosomes to gender identity. *Eng. Sci.* 33:34–39.

Money, J., and Ehrhardt, A. A. 1972. *Man and woman, boy and girl: The differentiation and dimorphism of gender identity from conception to maturity.* Baltimore: Johns Hopkins Press.

Money, J.; Hampson, J. G.; and Hampson, J. L. 1955. Hermaphroditism: Recommendations concerning assignment of sex, change of sex, and psychologic management. *Johns Hopkins Bull.* 97:284–300.

Money, J., and Schwartz, M. 1977. Dating, romantic and nonromantic friendships, and sexuality in 17 early-treated adrenogenital females, aged 16–25. In *Congenital adrenal hyperplasia,* ed. P. A. Lee, L. P. Plotnick, A. A. Kowarski, and C. J. Migeon. Baltimore: University Park Press.

Rossi, A. S. 1977. A biosocial perspective on parenting. *Daedalus* 106: 1–33.

Zussman, J. U.; Zussman, P. P.; and Dalton, K. 1975. *Postpubertal effects of prenatal administration of progesterone.* Paper read at meeting of the Society for Research in Child Development, April 1975, Denver.

Part III
Psychological Perspectives

Significant as the contributions of other perspectives may be, there can be little doubt about the central importance of developmental psychology to our understanding of gender identity and related issues. Traditionally, psychologists have paid far less attention to sexuality than to other aspects of development. Yet this relative neglect gradually has been replaced by more focused concern in recent years, especially in the broader study of sex differences.

The contributors to Part III, all developmental psychologists, bring an impressive mastery of the field to bear on the issues at hand. Zella Luria's major contribution is a comprehensive discussion of the psychosocial determinants of gender identity, role, and orientation. Just as the contributions to the biological determinants of sexual identity made due allowance for the interplay of psychological variables, Luria and her colleagues show ample awareness and appreciation of the role of biological factors. The first part of Luria's paper, in fact, draws on the same basic literature cited by the authors of the preceding section. She further expands on the theme of the influence of the child's sex in the reactions whereby adults reinforce the youngster's gender of assignment. Luria concludes with a consideration of the relation of gender identity and gender role to sexual orientation.

In her response to Luria's exposition, Eleanor Maccoby is in fundamental agreement with the primacy of social ascription in defining gender identity. But she reiterates the well-taken concern that much of the research underlying this conclusion is based on work with individuals whose prenatal hormonal conditions were ambiguous. Maccoby also reexamines the critical-period hypothesis for the establishment of gender identity and considers the implications of recent evidence that seems to cast doubt on the view that gender identity is irrevocably fixed during the first two to three years of life.

In the third contribution of this section, Robert Sears integrates the information brought together by Luria and Maccoby into sets of hypotheses concerning the development of sex-typing and sexual object choice. In the area of cognitive development, Sears singles out the relationship of the labeling process to sex-typing and the distinctions made between masculine and feminine. He then considers the implications of sex-typing for sexual object choice, which defines the person's sexual orientation. Fundamental to these considerations are the effects of child rearing and early experiences (a field of study that has been enriched by Sears' own distinguished contributions over several decades of work).

Of particular importance are the directions for new research suggested by Sears in collaboration with Luria and Maccoby. These recommendations are aimed mainly at enrichment of knowledge about sex-typing and sexual behavior: in particular, discovering the developmental relationships between them and identifying the influence of antecedent experiences in subsequent behaviors. More knowledge of the kind Sears asks for would cast light on the very roots of human sexual development.
—H. A. K.

Psychosocial Determinants of Gender Identity, Role, and Orientation

Zella Luria

In our culture, a gender identity carries with it considerable baggage. We are taught that each gender identity carries an appropriate set of emotional, social, vocational, motivational, and sexual behaviors. These are lessons well taught, well enforced, and often over-learned. Anyone who denies the difficulty of the struggles of people trying to be "new men" or "new women" has not been observing very closely. This chapter explores some relationships among gender identity, gender role, and sexual orientation.

We have much to learn about ourselves from examining the psychology of insults. We are offended most by challenges to the concepts of self we value most. Very young children do not often tell us directly of their sources of personal pride but we can learn about them nonetheless—by examining what statements offend them: Perhaps the prime insult is to suggest to a young girl that she's really a boy, or to a young boy that he's really a girl. People not only learn their gender identities at a very young age, but they also defend them and by inference cherish them. They hold their gender values for the rest of their lives. People may want some of the apparent advantages of the opposite gender, but they rarely wish to *be* what they are not. They defend what they are. Even

This paper was immensely aided by the critical eye and the fine editorial hand of my colleague, Dr. Mitchel D. Rose. The paper has profited from the suggestions of Drs. Jeffrey Z. Rubin and Brenda Steinberg. The author was supported in part by Training Grant #5-T01-MH-12672, awarded to Tufts University.

163

in cases of confused or mislabeled gender identities, people look for one of the two genders to adopt and defend. No one is ever committed to ambiguity.

I should like first to review recent clinical evidence that may cast some light on the psychosocial determinants of gender identity within the first three years of life. Next I shall turn to gender role and adult sexual orientation. Finally, I shall discuss the exceptional cases, the transsexuals.

Money and Ehrhardt (1972) use a definition of gender identity that includes three components: (1) the early private sense of gender, or *core gender identity*; (2) the *gender role* of public behaviors, or expression of gender; and (3) *sexual orientation,* or private (and perhaps public) expression of the gender of the object of sexual arousal. For my purposes, I have chosen to deal separately with the three components. A private sense of gender, including the label attached to one's gender by self and significant others, exists throughout the life cycle. I shall refer to the gender identity developed in early childhood as *core* gender identity and to the gender identity of postpubescence as *adult* gender identity.

My reason for adopting 'a definition at variance with Money and Ehrhardt's for gender identity is that there are so few problems of core gender identity in comparison with the number of variants in gender roles and sexual orientation. Separating the three elements allows us to give attention to each separately.

The Evidence of a Critical Period

The many biological stages in the creation of a human male or female are only now beginning to be known. The first step is the chromosomal determination: 46XX as female and 46XY as male. Until the sixth week of gestation XX and XY fetuses appear identical. Genetic instructions on the Y thereafter direct testicular development. The second step in sex differentiation is directed by the testes, which produce fetal hormones. These hormones direct the further morphological masculinization of the XY fetus. The absence of testicular hormones results in female differentiation. Ovarian development in the XX fetus becomes manifest in the twelfth week of embryonal development. The ovaries, unlike the testes, play no role in the early differentiation of the internal and external genital structures. The rule is: In the absence of testicular hormones, differentiation is female; in the presence of testicular hormones, differentiation is male.

For testicular hormones to be effective, however, the organs to be sexually differentiated must be capable of recognizing and responding to these hormones. The gene that controls the development of receptor sites for one of the testicular hormones is on the X chromosome. Normally, the gene is present in both males and females. The presence of androgen and the receptor sites for androgen in the precursor structures of the internal and external genitalia determine that the internal and external genitalia will be male. Either the absence of androgen or the absence of receptor sites for androgen will feminize the external genitalia and will fail to differentiate fully the male internal genitalia, even in an XY fetus.

In lower mammals, androgen at critical periods affects the central nervous system via the hypothalamus so that cycling at puberty is suppressed. It is tempting, when regularities are noted in lower mammals, such as the rat, the hamster, and the guinea pig, to apply them to primates. Frank Beach calls this "generalizing from the 'ramstergig.'" Human as well as nonhuman primates that are prenatally androgenized are indeed affected by the hormone, but not in the same way as the ramstergig: The onset of cycling at puberty is delayed but never irreversibly suppressed.

The main reason for this short detour into genetics and embryology is to heighten awareness of how many biological choice-points exist between chromosomal makeup and the newborn's sexual morphology. There is room for the genetic "computer tape" to be programmed incorrectly in a number of places. There is also room for variability in the read-out, so that the same gene may have variable expression. The timing of read-out introduces wide variation. While the simple delivery-room definitions of a boy as a baby with a penis, testes, and scrotum, and of a girl as a baby with a clitoris and vagina usually work well, these definitions also mask complexity. Each of the many genetic and biochemical steps involves genetic programming *for a range* of phenotypes, or final outcomes. What we come to identify as male and as female are, in fact, two overlapping biological ranges. It should not surprise us, then, that male and female behavioral ranges also show such overlap. Furthermore, it should not surprise us that behavioral ranges are wide within both sexes. Overlapping behavioral ranges occur while reproductive characteristics remain safely nonoverlapping for the two sexes.

The concept of overlapping behavioral ranges for males and females is widely accepted in all cultures. Human societies do not sex-type *all* abilities and *all* personality characteristics, even though certain divisions of labor are widespread by gender (D'Andrade, 1966). Every society to date seems to choose *some* dimensions of ability and/or personality along which to sex-type. That tradition makes the task of studying sex-typing in one's own culture more difficult. Clinical cases that provide violations of sex-typing expectancies sometimes startle us enough to loosen our cultural blinders.

Core Gender Identity and Gender Role

Our psychosocial interpretations of sexually dimorphic fetal development follow upon the simple act of labeling the gender of the newborn. Once the child's gender is decided, the course of rearing the child is generally consistent with the gender label. The evidence is clear that we see children from birth on as markedly different once we label them boy or girl.

Some recent studies suggest that labeling serves to preselect how we view babies, even our own. When primiparous parents were asked to rate their babies on day one, they already saw their daughters as *soft, fine-featured,* and *little* and their sons as *hard, large-featured, big,* and *less inattentive* than girls. While boys, on average, are born slightly larger and heavier than girls, in this sample average birth size and weight were alike. Although both parents stereotype their babies on the basis of the minimal information of the sex of their newborns, fathers are significantly more extreme than mothers in the extent of their stereotyping (Rubin, Provenzano, and Luria, 1974). The finding that males stereotype more than females with respect to sex roles is confirmed repeatedly in the literature.

As a culture, we share belief systems of the physical and personality characteristics to be expected of children, even babies, as a function of gender. We "know" greater size, strength, and potential for doing harm are masculine; and lesser size, weak-

166

ness, and harmlessness are feminine. And we apply this knowledge even when it is not demonstrably true. When college students were shown an anonymous eighteenth-century painting of two babies, labeled Georg and Regula Rohn, and asked to identify which was the girl and which the boy, their agreement was close to 90 percent. The cues they used to reach their decisions were minimal, but stereotyped and widely shared (Luria and Rubin, in press). No one in the study knew which baby in the painting was the girl and which was the boy, but students were very reliable in their guesses. Unfortunately, in gender stereotyping, we often confuse high reliability for validity.

In the everyday world as well as in the world of psychological research, people require information on a baby's gender in order to interact comfortably with the baby or its parents. In an attempt to find out what people "see" when a baby is not gender-identified, graduate students were asked to play with Baby X, who was labeled *boy* for one group, *girl* for another group, and just *X* for a third group. Subjects in the latter situation were extremely uncomfortable and solved their problem by making a decision on gender, based on ascribed strength and softness. Women played *more* with the unlabeled than the labeled baby. Men did the reverse. But the male or female label did not elicit different behavior from the adults (Seavey, Katz, and Zalk, 1975). When mothers were used as subjects in a study in which the same baby was labeled sometimes as male and sometimes as female, sex-typed toys were used congruently with the labels (Will, Self, and Datan, 1974). But people's behavior and labeling are not always congruent. When different gender labels are attached to the same baby in a videotaped sequence, results vary. In one study a child fussing after a jack-in-the-box popped open was called "frustrated" when labeled as a girl, and "angry" when labeled as a boy (Condry and Condry, 1976). In another study, men judged girls more favorably and women judged boys more favorably (Gurwitz and Dodge, 1975).

Nature has provided us with some curious—luckily rare—test cases for studying the power of psychosocial interpretation of gender. These cases typically involve either some ambiguity in the external genitalia or some lack of correspondence between external genitals and chromosomal makeup. The work of John Money and his colleagues at Johns Hopkins—especially John and Joan

Hampson and Anke Ehrhardt—has led to a formulation that stresses the psychosocial determination of core gender identity. The psychosocial process is set in motion by the gender labeling or assignment of a child (as male, female, or ambivalent) and the corresponding rearing of the child (as male, female, or ambivalent).

The Johns Hopkins group has provided two classes of cases as evidence for the critical role of the early psychosocial determinants of core gender identity: (1) cases matched biologically but assigned and reared differentially, and (2) cases reassigned to the opposite gender before and after a presumed critical period for development of a sense of core gender identity.

Matched Cases. In the first category of cases were children karyotyped 46XX with masculinized external genitalia. Because of a genetic disorder, these children had been androgenized in utero while the external genitals were being differentiated. Before cortisone was used to treat the disorder, some of these children were assigned and reared as males and others as females—even when the degree of genital masculinization was similar. The children's perceptions of their own gender were typically concordant with the gender of assignment and rearing.

As a test of the power of psychosocial determinants of gender identity, androgenized children of 46XX karyotype with virilized external genitalia are analogous to partially androgenized children of 46XY karyotype with incompletely virilized external genitalia. Androgen insensitivity, whether total or partial, appears in highly variable phenotypes, even within a single pedigree (Wilson et al., 1974).

Money and Ogunro (1974) have reported on ten cases of partial androgen insensitivity in patients with 46XY chromosomal make-up. Although the genitalia of these patients are described as "more female-looking than male," they were assigned and reared in two cases as girls and in eight cases as boys. Among the latter eight, three had been reassigned from girl to boy before two years of age; the remaining five had been assigned from birth as boys and raised as such. The two cases assigned and reared as girls were not chromosomally diagnosed until adolescence and adulthood, respectively. Among the eight boys, phallic surgery had been considered or accomplished in seven. Only three have erectile phalluses adequate for shallow intromission in coitus. Nonetheless, when assessing their gender identity, one female-assigned and the eight male-assigned patients all expressed satisfaction with their gender. Only one woman was ambivalent, obsessed with fears of discovery of her secret by a sexual partner. However, she did not wish reassignment as a male. Two of her three affected sibs had reassigned themselves as males in adulthood while she was young—no mean source of confusion. Six of the seven adult males are married or planning marriage. All ten patients dress appropriately for their assigned genders: two as females, eight as males. Evidently the core gender identity of the androgenized 46XX cases and the under-androgenized 46XYs reflects the gender of assignment and rearing.

So far the matched cases have been discussed only in terms of how well the assigned gender "takes" for the child—whether the child accepts the gender label as its own. Perhaps a harder test would be to ask how the child functions in the gender role assigned. To consider this issue, we shift to another set of matched cases.

The most famous example of matched cases followed by differential assignment and rearing is Money's report of identical twin boys, one reared as male, the other as female, from the age of 17 months (Money, 1975). At 7 months the twins were circumcised, and an operating error on one of the twins led to necrosis and sloughing off of the penis. Reassignment to female gender was recommended by a Johns Hopkins team that studied the case. When the boys were 17 months old the parents agreed to the medical recommendations, and the penectomized child's name, clothing, and hairstyle were changed. At 21 months, the first feminizing genital surgery was performed. Meanwhile, psychologists and physicians at Johns Hopkins gave family members full support, guidance, and knowledge about previous experience in cases of sex reassignment.

The parents' behavior *became* different for the two children after the reassignment. The mother found her son's urinating in the yard amusing; similar behavior by the daughter was considered immodest, not what "nice little girls do." By age four, the little girl preferred dresses to slacks and took pride in her long hair. The mother described the girl at four-and-one-half as neat and concerned about her appearance, while the brother was unconcerned even about being dirty.

169

Before reassignment and surgery, the boy who was later re-assigned had been the dominant twin, the "leader." As a girl at age three, this same child was described as "bossy."[1] Her twin brother was already protective toward her in situations of danger or threat.

The children's toys and activities had been encouraged along gender-differentiated lines. And the encouragement "took." The girl's tomboyishness—common in androgenized females and not rare in nonandrogenized females—was discouraged. The girl got dolls and other girl toys; the boy got cars, tools, and other boy toys. The mother's educational aspirations for both twins remains high and egalitarian; but she feels the fulfillment of her aspirations is more important for her son. Money describes these two children as uneventfully achieving their different gender roles, despite their genetic identity as twin boys.

The importance of this case should not be underestimated. It shows twins matched not only for prenatal hormones, but also for postnatal infant hormones since sex differences in testosterone are found until seven months of age, but not thereafter until pubertal changes begin (Forest et al., 1973).

Females with the adrenogenital syndrome, who have been treated early with exogenous cortisone and surgical feminization, can be studied to learn how a one-stage fetal androgenization affects the way the girl takes on her gender role. But for the partially androgenized male, the disorder creates an effect that continues throughout life—not just at one stage. The defect affects fetal development, pubertal development, and adult appearance. As adults, these men continue to appear young for their age.

How do fetally androgenized females play their childhood gender roles? And how do partially androgenized males play their childhood gender roles? The answer is that they play them within the socially accepted limits of those roles, but with some important differences from their normal counterparts.

First, there appears to be a consistent effect of androgen on vigorous play in childhood. The androgenized girls tend to be tomboys, more frequently involved in sports than control girls are. Among the eight partially androgenized boys, only two were involved in rough-and-tumble sports with other boys, and these

1. Anke A. Ehrhardt, personal communication, 1970.

170

two drifted away from sports when, at puberty, breasts developed and masculine musculature failed to develop. Neither the androgenized females nor the partially androgenized males (and XY females) pick fights. They may be assertive but they are not aggressive, nor are they much concerned with dominance.

Tomboys play the feminine role differently from other girls. They prefer pants to skirts in order to play active games, and they play less—if at all—with dolls than do their control counterparts. But they are accepted by peers of their own sex; moreover, tomboyism is sufficiently common among young girls that a tomboy can find tomboy friends. Aside from the lower than expected frequency of sports involvement and the lesser concern with dominance shown by the partially androgenized boys, they too seem to be able to find an acceptable place among their peers. They are not described as loners, nor as "sissies."

What does all this add up to with respect to childhood gender roles? It appears that childhood gender roles—unlike core gender identities—can be cut to many sizes. A girl may possess and a boy may lack some of the characteristics considered masculine, but so long as the same-sex peers do not isolate the child, enough gender role acquisition and performance occurs to support the transition to adult gender roles and to normal adult gender identity. There is greater latitude for girls being masculine, however, than for boys being feminine. Fathers do not tolerate well any behaviors by sons that might be considered feminine. Aberle and Naegele (1952) reported fathers' nervous concern about even preschool-aged sons learning to behave in ways maladaptive for the work world. Crying from frustration or from physical pain at age three or four already is disapproved by fathers, though not by mothers.

Negative sanctions on feminine behavior for boys are exercised especially by the peer group. Boys who are judged to be "sissies" tend to be isolated by other boys. And by about second grade, girls are less willing than earlier to provide friendly refuge for the isolated boy.

These descriptions of childhood gender roles come from clinical practice for the most part. Good observational and experimental studies on peer group interaction are surely in order now that we can capture some of the interactions on videotape. Recent work on toddler play groups is already beginning to suggest why,

171

in the second year at least, some children interact and are interacted with more than others (L. Lee, cited in Mueller and Vandell, 1978).

Clinical Sex Reassignment. Clinical work made developmental psychology more aware of the importance of early core gender identity as the first step in the development of later gender role. Psychologists may still argue about how children take on gender roles (Mischel, 1966; Kohlberg, 1966), but everyone accepts—in some form—the conception clinicians have given us of core gender identity.

Perhaps the best summary statement of clinical experience with sex reassignment of children with congenital sexual anomalies is the following:

> Comparisons based on 105 pseudohermaphrodites demonstrated that the sex of assignment and rearing is consistently and conspicuously a more reliable prognosticator of a hermaphrodite's gender role and orientation than is the chromosomal sex, the gonadal sex, the hormonal sex, the accessory internal reproductive morphology, or the ambiguous morphology of the external genitalia. There were only 5 among the 105 patients whose gender role and orientation was ambiguous and deviant from the sex of assignment and rearing.
>
> . . . Further supportive evidence concerning the importance, psychologically, of the sex of assignment and rearing is provided by cases of reassignment of sex by edict. Among our cases there were 14 patients who underwent a reassignment of sex after the early neonatal weeks. Of these 14, there were 9 below the age of 2 years 3 months at the time of the change; with 3 exceptions, they appeared subsequently to have negotiated the change without even mild signs of psychologic nonhealthiness. By contrast, only one of the five children older than 2 years 3 months at the time of reassignment of sex could possibly be rated as psychologically healthy. One infers that once a person's gender role begins to get well established, an attempt at its reversal is an extreme psychologic hazard.
>
> . . . Nonetheless, a small group of five patients whose sexual outlook diverged somewhat from that of the sex to which they had been assigned prevents a "simple-minded" view of environmental determinism. Rather, it appears that a person's gender role and orientation becomes established, beginning at a very early age, as that person becomes acquainted with and deciphers a continuous multiplicity of signs that point in the

direction of his being a boy, or her being a girl. These signs range all the way from nouns and pronouns differentiating gender to modes of behavior, hair cut, dress, and personal adornment that are differentiated according to sex. The most emphatic sign of all is, of course, the appearance of the genital organs. . . . The salient variable in the establishment of a person's gender role and orientation is neither hereditary nor environmental, in any purist sense of those terms, but is his own decipherment and interpretation of a plurality of signs, some of which may be considered hereditary or constitutional, others environmental (Money, Hampson, and Hampson, 1957).

The outstanding contributions of the Johns Hopkins group of clinical psychologists and psychiatrists in teasing apart the effect of hormones, prenatal development, later labeling, and psychosocial development on gender identity has led to the proposal of a critical period in gender identity, between about 18 months and 27 to 36 months, probably coincident with the burgeoning of language development. Clinical management of gender reassignment becomes progressively and steeply more difficult with increasing distance from the critical period. It has even been said that the process becomes virtually impossible in a sexually mature, fully gender-identified person. This leads us into the issue of transsexualism, which we will discuss later. While further clinical work has led Money and Ehrhardt to designate three years as the upper limit on this critical period, the essential argument cited above still is said to hold for management of sex reassignment. Late cases of sex reassignment appear in the literature, but they usually require far more extensive and radical psychiatric and environmental manipulation (Lev-Ran, 1974).

The issues raised by the need for intervention before age three, suggest that we could profitably study the nature of children's understanding of sex and gender before three.

Early Conceptions of Gender

Perhaps it is the very *simplicity* of early gender identity that helps the child to learn about gender within the first two to three years. The concept of gender *role* with its variety of behavioral dimensions is of enormous complexity by comparison. Gender is at first only a label, albeit a label of high value. But what do two-year-olds know about gender, their own and other people's? How do children use and understand gender labels? The clinical data

173

discussed above force our attention to labeling and the behavior that follows from early labeling. Only recently have we begun to find some answers.

The reason for the long delay is not hard to fathom. Even that veritable powerhouse of early experimental psychology, Walter Hunter, reported that the two-year-old human was not a good experimental subject. Two-year-old children do not respond consistently to questions. Sometimes only their parents know what they mean. They refuse to stay put. They lose interest fast. They are plainly unreliable. That does *not* mean they are incompetent, that they lack knowledge. It means *we* have had less competence than we need to tap reliably into *their* competence.

Children from 18 months to 36 months provide the outer age ranges for the study of the first steps in the acquisition of gender identity, judging by the *clinical* data on the impact of gender reassignment. What should we be asking children of those ages in order to clarify the process of acquisition of gender identity and gender role?

We might ask: When do children know the name for their own gender? And how and when do they learn about other people's gender? And do they use their labeling of gender to choose activities? If so, how do they do it? When and how do children finally learn that genitals alone are the critical criteria for gender? And how does gender *naming* tie into the gender-role definitions characteristic of the child's culture? How does the child come to share gender stereotypes? Money and the Hampsons early noted the importance of nouns and pronouns for gender "modes of behavior, haircut, dress, and personal adornment [and] of course, the appearance of the genital organs" for gender identity. To understand *why* it is clinically difficult to reassign children past age three to a new gender, obviously answers to these questions would be needed.

Some significant studies have addressed these questions. Many of these studies have been done by UCLA psychologists who, perhaps because of their own clinical work on identifying children at risk for adult gender disorders, have seen the gaps in our knowledge of what children know about gender. One study (Thompson, 1975) focused on what children know of their own and others' gender at 24, 30, and 36 months. Instead of requiring elaborate verbal responses and explanations, the tests required

174

for the most part only verbal comprehension, sorting, and preference choices. Since children understand more than they can verbalize spontaneously, this research strategy enables the young child to demonstrate competence without interference from limited capacity for verbal expression.

Thompson found that the order of acquisition of gender labels went from labeling others to labeling one's self. The 24-month-old children could identify even nonstereotypic pictures when given noun labels such as boy/girl, man/woman, man/lady, father/mother, and mommy/daddy. They sorted clothing and common sex-typed articles beyond chance into a boy box and a girl box. But they did not yet correctly apply gender labels to their own photographs.

By 30 months, children added to—as well as improved on—the 24-month-old's repertoire. They could sort pictures of themselves into appropriate noun and pronoun gender categories, and identify their likenesses to dolls of their own gender. Moreover, when two identical objects were described, one as "good," the other as "bad," the 30-month-old chose the "good" one, which the 24-month-old did not. Like the 24-month-old, the 30-month-old did not yet show a preference for the choice between two identical objects when one was labeled "for boys" and the other "for girls." The gender label was not as yet clearly operating on choices, but by 36 months, it was.

Thus, we may conclude that by 24 months children have effectively begun sex-sorting the outside world of people and objects. They then extend it to themselves at 30 months, and by 36 months use gender labels to guide their choices. The process probably becomes more refined as well as deeper throughout childhood. The power of sex-sorting before 24 months may not be negligible, however. Fein and associates (1975) have demonstrated that 20-month-old boys and girls, when tested in their homes by examiners who are familiar to them, *already* show more free play with toys typed for their own sex; that pattern is also true for toy ownership, although more girls own boy toys than boys own girl toys. Only one of the twenty-four children studied had a "favorite" toy that was not sex-appropriate. That the boys' preference for sex-appropriate toys is not simple is indicated by seven of the eleven boys' behavior with a doll: They stepped on it, pulled its hair, or threw it. Fein and associates consider parental attitudes underlying toy ownership as, "It's okay if my daughter plays with both hammers and bracelets, just so long as my son doesn't play with a doll." Preferences for familiar toys may require neither labels nor gender identity, but so strong a reaction to a doll suggests that important learning occurs for boys by 20 months. Since the greater hostile reaction occurred *only* to the doll, the boys' behavior cannot be interpreted as generalized aggression.

Just as one sees early sex-typing of toy preferences, so does one see—where children can choose—same-sex playmate choice at age two (Koch, 1944; Maccoby and Jacklin, 1974). Thompson's 1975 paper is the first indication that 24-month-olds can discriminate fairly reliably—though not with 100 percent accuracy—the gender of other persons. On the other hand, since children are not certain of their own gender until 30 months, if they choose same-sex playmates *before* consistent self-gender label acquisition, one would be forced to conclude the selection was based on some same-sex compatibility or perceived similarity that transcends their own gender *label* acquisition. It is a question worth posing.

No one but Thompson, to my knowledge, has studied children *so young* as to their self and other gender knowledge. Dependence on imitation of models and verbal performance as indicators of gender *knowledge* has tended toward underestimation of what children know. Thompson's methods give us a basis for characterizing a specific child's knowledge and potentially relating the state of that knowledge to his or her sex-role behaviors.

Kohlberg's cognitive theory of gender-role acquisition predicts that children will most reliably sex-type and most reliably attend to same-sex models only *after* they have achieved gender constancy at about age five or six. Gender constancy is defined as knowledge that a male (or female) may change in extraneous attributes (hair length, clothing, name, and so on), but so long as the criterional attribute—the genitals—remains, gender stays constant. Maccoby and Jacklin (1974) have pointed out that many sex-role preferences exist well before such gender constancy can be demonstrated.

Interviewers assessing gender constancy typically ask children "Are you going to be a mommy or a daddy?"—and then, opposite to their choice—"Could you be a mommy/daddy if you wanted to be?" The child is then encouraged to explain his or her answers. It now appears that, when one poses these questions (without requiring explanation) to four-, five-, and six-year-olds, one does not get the orderly year-by-year change required of a developmental trend in response to the second question, although virtually all the children know correctly whether they will be mothers or fathers (Thompson and Bentler, 1973). According to these results, we would have to say that four-year-olds already have gender constancy. That does not mean children know that genitals are the criteria for gender at age four. Children below five or six use hair, clothes, and body build as cues to the gender of others (Conn, 1940; Katcher, 1955; Levin, Balistrieri, and Schukit, 1972; Thompson and Bentler, 1971). But by seven, virtually all children use genitals as the sole reliable criterion for judging a doll's gender, regardless of variations in hair length and body build (Thompson and Bentler, 1971). This does not mean younger children aren't interested in genitals. They surely are (Elias and Gebhard, 1969). But, since nongenital cues are available and do the job well, only in the artificial conditions of a laboratory experiment with a self-conscious 2 x 2 x 2 factorial design does one see that young children *ignore* genitals to use more familiar cues.

All of these data mean that the child does have an orderly system for judging gender of others at 24 months, and for himself or herself at 30 months. The system is not perfect, but it works. Psycholinguists have taught us that children generate quite imperfect rules, as demonstrated by a sentence like "The mouses are in their houses." Similarly, two-year-old children will generate rules about gender and gender roles, aided, very likely, by the convenience of gender being binary. Phonetic development occurs in steps of binary discrimination as does much semantic development, including adjective opposites.

If the evidence from rule acquisition in language is the proper analogy for the acquisition of sex-role knowledge, then we may expect children to overregularize, at least to begin with. If boys most often do something and girls most often do something else (usually seen as opposite!), the rule induced is likely to be of the order, "All boys do *x* while all girls do *y*." The peer group is likely to function in the same binary way to begin with. What boys or

177

girls *could* do is not likely to be discriminated by young children from what they *are* doing. In fact, behavior may well have to be radically different from expectation for children and parents to recognize the violation of sex-role expectations. Stereotypes do not invite disconfirmation.

The literature on gender-role development has been critically reviewed by Maccoby and Jacklin (see especially their chapters 8 and 9, 1974). The evidence they summarize shows that by nursery school age, both boys and girls already are sex-typed for toy and activity preferences, that is, they show the role behavior considered appropriate for their gender; but boys from four on are increasingly more sex-typed than girls. Girls are freer to do boy things as preschoolers than boys are to do girl things. Before children ever get to grade school, they show preferences for play-mates of their own sex. Girls play in smaller groups than boys do. And they show less rough-and-tumble play than boys do. Girls in their smaller groups fight less than boys do in their larger groups. And girls seem to use adults more as resources in accomplishing tasks than boys do (Maccoby, 1976).

The early social segregation by gender means early differences are likely to be increased over time. And, in fact, this increase is found to occur. The question of how these differences become established is an important subject of debate among psychologists. Neither of the varieties of explanations of how sex-typing occurs—by modeling with differential rewards and punishments to self and to model (Mischel, 1966), or by cognitive self-socialization (Kohlberg, 1966)—is fully congruent with the evidence summarized in Maccoby and Jacklin. No one believes now that sex-typing is determined simply by parental rewards of wanted (sex-appropriate) and parental punishments of unwanted (sex-inappropriate) behavior. It is clear that children learn from a variety of sources within and outside of their families how their culture expects them to be boys or girls. They surely watch other people and then practice what they have seen. It is also possible that children attend selectively to information about their own gender, although the evidence for this in young children is questionable. One study of preschoolers found some evidence for selective looking at same-sex models by boys who had gender constancy, but not by girls (Slaby and Frey, 1975). Janice Bryan and I have been unsuccessful at finding any evidence of selective same-sex looking in five- to six-year-olds (or for that matter in nine- to ten-year-olds) using an elegant electroencephalographic measure of attention (Bryan and Luria, 1978).

Nonetheless, the activities of groups of boys *are* different from those of groups—or more likely pairs—of girls at all ages. Some of that difference (as in rough-and-tumble play) may be androgen-mediated. But not all of the difference is so rooted. Regardless of what the origins of the differences are, the social opportunities to learn what boys or girls do, think, and want require exposure to peers as well as peer interaction. What Gagnon and Simon (1973) call the "sexual scripts" for an adult sexual life are—like much of sex-typing—mostly learned in the peer group.

Gender Identity, Gender Role, and Sexual Orientation

The testimony of some transsexuals that they have always felt themselves to be the gender opposite to their apparent sex has inevitably raised this question: Just what is the relation of early gender identity to later sexual orientation? And to adult gender identity?

There are relatively few data to tie sexual orientation to early gender *identity*. Male homosexuals almost universally feel they are men, and female homosexuals virtually all feel they are women; and as children they were assigned and felt like boys and girls, respectively. From the Kinsey data on number of sexual partners, Gagnon and Simon (1973) have documented that lesbians resemble other females more than they resemble males; and male homosexuals, in turn, resemble other males more than they resemble females. Later work also bears this out (Saghir and Robins, 1973).

Homosexuality is only sporadic among hermaphrodites and pseudohermaphrodites (Money, 1970). The one exception that has been reported is the high rate of bisexuality in a group of ten sexually experienced women with still uncorrected manifestations of adrenogenital syndrome (Money and Ehrhardt, 1972). There was, however, no evidence of confusion of gender identity in the ten markedly virilized women. After cortisone treatment and diminished androgenization, these women marry, bear, and rear children in normal marriages. In 1970 Money concluded, "There

179

is far and away more male homosexuality among organists, hair-dressers, actors, interior decorators, or antique dealers than among patients with any given endocrine diagnosis" (p. 434).

In their study of adult homosexuals and unmarried adult het-erosexual controls, Saghir and Robins (1973) do not find evidence for confusion of early core gender *identity* in the early school years, but they do find gender *role* disturbances. Two-thirds of Saghir and Robins' sample of homosexuals say they avoided doing what most children of their gender were doing. Two out of three adult male homosexuals describe themselves in childhood as effeminate or "sissy," as compared with only 3 percent of the male heterosexuals. A similar two-thirds of adult female homo-sexuals describe themselves in childhood as tomboyish, as did 16 percent of the female heterosexuals. The social difference is great, however. "Sissy" boys usually end up isolated from other boys, while tomboys are not socially isolated. We cannot, however conclude that in our society homosexuality is always foreshad-owed by the "sissy" or the tomboy history, since one-third of the homosexuals studied lacked such histories. The social isolation of the "sissies," however, hurts them in childhood; that finding gives some warrant for early intervention with effeminate boys, but similar intervention with tomboys would be absurd since their base rate is so high while the base rate for female homosexuality is relatively low. The rare girls who believe they *are* boys repre-sent quite a different problem (see Green, 1974). Nonetheless, tomboyishness and later cross-gender preferences by girls should serve to remind us that girls, who are given wide role latitude in childhood as compared with boys, nonetheless have reliably *lower* rates of obligative homosexuality than do males.

There must, however, be an additional caution. Before con-cluding that the retrospective account of childhood given by re-spondents recruited via the gay movement—such as Saghir and Robins' sample—accurately describes childhood, we must be aware that part of the socialization process by the gay movement is aimed at strengthening the gay person's feeling that s/he has always been different. This may well be true. But we should be cautious about accepting that before we have some independent proof.

Part of the reason for my suspicion of retrospective self-descriptions comes as a result of the recent work on bisexual women by Blumstein and Schwartz (1976). Whether bisexual women consider themselves homosexual, bisexual, or just libertarian seems to depend not on actual sexual behavior but on ideological justifications for their sexual behaviors, and on the social world of which they are a part.

Blumstein and Schwartz document multiple life-history routes for the bisexual sample they interviewed. Some women have a long, stable, heterosexual marriage followed by a long, stable, homosexual liaison, after which some return to long-term heterosexual relations. Whether such women consider themselves bisexual, heterosexual, or homosexual is more likely to be a function of which relationship is current and of social factors outside of their sexual lives, that is, whether their social contacts are with the gay community, the women's movement, and so on. Nonetheless, some women—despite virtually equal sexual contact with male and female partners—feel themselves to be homosexual, because the emotional commitment to their women partners is far greater than it is to their men partners.

Another pattern Blumstein and Schwartz found was that of self-identified bisexual women who have concurrent and/or successive partners of either sex. One bisexual woman expressed the feeling it was "sexist" to discriminate against a gender in one's choice of sexual partner! Still other patterns exist of entry and exit from both homosexual and heterosexual relationships. The age patterns, marital patterns, libertarian patterns are of great variety and varying self-description. It seems reasonable to me to be cautious in characterizing this sexual pattern only in terms of sexual *orientation*, when so many nonsexual social choices seem to be involved (see Lipman-Blumen, 1975). Given the distribution of economic resources, heterosexual marriage offers women the possibility of upward mobility. The gay world offers males the same possibility.

American women in the recent generation start their sociosexual lives earlier than previous generations. They also have high expectations of gratification. Whether or not they use contraception and abortion, they know contraception and abortion are there and, if I may resort to biblical language, they "know" more partners than their mothers and grandmothers did. So sexualized a generation of women will be even less celibate than earlier generations of women after divorce and separation, especially when high rates of divorce develop close bonding among women. I think I would predict that the greater visibility of the homosexual choice plus the diminishing male-to-female ratio with age will lead a sexualized younger generation of women into more frequent *late* (after 35) choices of homosexuality than earlier generations have made. If homosexual choice is dependent—as Saghir and Robins as well as Money and Ehrhardt suggest—on preadolescent and adolescent homosexual fantasy, as cognitive rehearsal for homosexual behavior, then my prediction would be disconfirmed. But if we assimilate higher rates of late adult homosexual choice in women to our conception of situational homosexuality or to "underlying homosexuality," we will cheat ourselves of important information on what sexual choice means in social context.

Early Gender Identity and Transsexualism

The classical description of transsexualism was altogether reasonable: The disorder was early reversed gender identity, which led to sexual attraction to members of the same sex with fantasy of *being* the opposite gender. The female was "entombed" (as Jan Morris described it) in the male body (or vice versa) and seriously depressed about the desperate situation. That model can be dubbed the iatrogenic description of transsexualism. Fisk (1973) suggests that the desire to get by psychiatrists—since most sex-change requests are not accepted for surgery—led to the wide dissemination and adoption of a "required" history. More recently, among nonpsychotics presenting themselves for sex change, three routes appear: the homosexual, transvestite, and asexual. The homosexual route is often—but not always—taken by effeminate homosexuals. The transvestite route is generally taken by a heterosexual whose cross-dressing has disrupted a marriage. Transvestites report degrees of homosexual experience that vary from frequent to absent (Feinbloom, 1976; Mehl, 1973; Meyer, 1973). The asexual route may be taken when *any* sexual contact is felt to be anomalous. The asexual's experience may be neither really hetero- nor homosexual, but lacking or very low in gratification.

A similar breakdown has been reported by Bentler and Prince (1975) in a follow-up study of forty-two male-to-female transsexuals after surgery. The self-descriptions by post-surgery male-to-female transsexuals of their presurgical histories in response to a questionnaire could be divided into three groups: hetero-sexual, homosexual, and asexual.

How is one to find common psychosocial determinants for an adult gender dysphoria when the routes are so different? The asexual subgroup may well be searching for a sexual identity, since whatever they had didn't work well for them. Within this subgroup are some men who, clinicians believe, truly have early reversed gender identity, and that early core reversal has pre-vented them from attempting sexual interaction of any kind because their bodies contradict their most deeply felt gender feelings. Fisk (1973) and Meyer (1973) suggest the other two subgroups—the effeminate homosexual and the heterosexual transvestite—have hit on a new identity that assuages a strong conscience unable to accept a homosexual self.

Current estimates approach a 1:1 ratio of males and females requesting sexual reassignment (Pauly, 1974). Earlier estimates of greater numbers of male transsexuals were more congruent with biological error in fetal masculinization. Now we will have to seek complementary errors in female fetal development if bio-logical determinants are to be considered as central determinants of transsexualism. We cannot rule out the possibility that such errors exist, but there is no good evidence yet.

The female-to-male transsexual shares much of her early his-tory with female homosexuals: the tomboyism, the stability of romantic and (homo-)sexual relationships, the high incidence (57 percent) of heterosexual dating, and heterosexual intercourse (48 percent), the latter two with little emotional satisfaction. More than a third of female transsexuals seek surgery to legalize a *de facto* marriage. After surgery 46 percent live in a stable hetero-sexual liaison with a very feminine, heterosexual woman. These transsexual husbands form relationships that are even more stable than those of homosexual women (Pauly, 1974). The fe-male transsexual—unlike the homosexual woman—cannot ac-cept a homosexual self. Also, unlike the homosexual woman, the tomboy-to-be-transsexual is horrified by the pubertal changes in her body. Her breasts are an affront to her sense of self.

The female transsexual has been less studied than the male transsexual, although she seems to be a better, more businesslike

183

patient to the surgeon. As more female transsexuals request surgery, perhaps we shall see an expansion in the number of psychosocial and psychosexual routes to sex change, just as we saw them among male transsexuals.

Studies of Effeminate Boys

There are suggestions in the literature that some effeminate boys seen by clinicians showed consistently feminine behavior very early in life, despite repeated and steady parental disapproval (Zuger, 1970). If this is the case, then purely psychosocial explanations of the origins of early cross-gender behavior are likely to run into difficulties.

Green (1976) has summarized data on sixty effeminate boys compared with fifty control boys. The controls came from families matched for the boy's age, the family's sibling sequence, educational level of the father, marital status of the family, and ethnicity. The two groups differed predictably on interest in sports, interest in rough-and-tumble play, cross-dressing, peer-group relations, doll play, gender of the persons to whom the boy related best, attentiveness to mother's clothing, wish to grow up to be like mother, interest in play-acting, readiness to play female in playing house, parental preference, and wish to be a girl.

The direction of all these significant differences, of course, fits the effeminate pattern that brought the child to clinical attention. The effeminate boys liked sports and rough-and-tumble play much less than did the control boys; and they liked feminine dressing, doll play, play with older or peer females, play acting, and playing female roles more than did the control boys. The effeminate group boy was more likely to be a loner or rejected by other boys, to be interested in the mother's clothes, to wish to be like the mother, and to wish to be a girl. The only differences that appeared between the groups that fell outside the range of sex-typing were two: Effeminate boys were more likely to have been separated from their fathers before age five and to have been hospitalized for medical reasons.

Although 90 percent of the effeminate boys were first evaluated clinically after the fifth birthday, 84 percent were reported as having already started cross-dressing by then. By the third birthday almost half had begun cross-dressing. The largest rate of reported increase—a jump of 32 percent—in incidence of cross-dressing among these boys occurs during the year between the second and third birthdays, just when Thompson localizes self-gender labeling and identification of sex-typed objects and clothing.

Bentler (1976) has proposed a developmental theory that includes thirty-two steps in the acquisition of gender roles; he hypothesizes that these thirty-two steps differ in systematic ways among the three classes of men requesting sex-change operations: the effeminate homosexual, the heterosexual transvestite, and the asexual transsexual. Table 1 is taken from Bentler's paper. All three subcategories have in common the critical absence of a male peer reference group with whom the male gender role for childhood and, later, for adolescence could be practiced. The isolation results in a self-concept as different from other boys. Ultimately, it leads to elaboration of the fantasy of self as feminine.

Bentler's theory does not cover most male homosexuals nor any female homosexuals. Except for item 17 (emphasis on intellectual success), the first twenty items on Bentler's list describe *defective* developmental circumstances from childhood to prepuberty. These pile up faster and earlier for the asexual transsexual, a bit more slowly for the effeminate homosexual, and more slowly still for the heterosexual transvestite. Clinical programs of intervention are aimed at reinforcing male role behaviors, interests, and same-sex friendship (undoing steps 9, 10, and 11). Clinicians literally teach masculine skills—interpersonal as well as sports—to help feminine boys to interact with male peers. If the theory is correct, then new learning should throw the switch so the child's course is on a normal track. Integration into a male peer group appears to be the crux for such a change (Bates et al., 1973, 1975; Bentler, 1968). The fact that such social intervention may work to turn effeminate boys around can in no way be considered proof that the source of the original predisposition to effeminacy is under full social control. That would be like arguing that since aspirin cures headaches, the cause of headaches is the lack of aspirin.

Delayed Gender Reassignment

An apparent exception to the rule of early gender reassignment has been reported in the Dominican Republic. A Cornell Medical

Table 1
Development of Feminine Sex-Role in Males: A Theory

Possible Developmental Basis of:	Homo-sexuality	Trans-sexualism	Trans-vestism
1. Prenatal feminization of the brain	x	x	
2. Low activity and energy level		x	
3. Inborn temperament to fussiness and unresponsiveness	x	x	x
4. Nonoptimal stimulation during infancy		x	x
5. Rigid identification with anatomical correlates of sex roles (body type, hair)		x	
6. Presence of a weak and non-nurturant father	x	x	x
7. Training in impulse control, harm-avoidance, and behavioral inhibition		x	x
8. Learning of negative attitudes toward sexual organs		x	
9. Reinforcement of feminine role behaviors and attitudes by a significant other or peer	x	x	x
10. Absence of consistent, effective rewards for sex-role stereotyped behaviors and interests	x	x	x
11. Emphasis on independence, with absence of same-sex affiliative behavior	x	x	x
12. Unresolved Oedipal complex	x	x	
13. Becoming unresponsive to social influence by same-sex peers and parents	x	x	x
14. Development of a self-concept as different from boys	x	x	x
15. Lack of disclosure of self-concept to significant others	x	x	x
16. Homosexual sex play	x		
17. Emphasis on intellectual success			x
18. Rejection by boy and girl playmates	x	x	x
19. Rejection of sex-role stereotyped attitudes with acceptance of the behaviors		x	x
20. Learning not to look at females as sex objects	x	x	x
21. Development of rewarding masturbation patterns	x		x
22. Anxiety reduction associated with orgasm while cross-dressing			x

Possible Developmental Basis of:	Homo-sexuality	Trans-sexualism	Trans-vestism
23. Orgasm with fantasies focusing on homosexual behavior	x		
24. Perceived difficulties in dealing with heterosexual dating patterns	x	x	x
25. Rejection of homosexual self-concept and experiences			x
26. Elaboration of feminine self in fantasy and behavior	x	x	x
27. Perceived difficulties with masculine work roles		x	
28. Use of marriage to bolster the masculine sense of self			x
29. Elaboration of homosexual self-concept and behavior	x		
30. Finding marriage stressful and unsuccessful in eliminating feminine gender behavior			x
31. Greater enjoyment of masturbation than heterosexual sex			x
32. Elaboration of feminine self-concept	x	x	x

From Bentler, 1976.

School team found an isolated village where, by genetic drift, an autosomal recessive gene had established itself. The mutant gene cannot make 5-alpha reductase, the enzyme that converts testosterone to dihydrotestosterone. The biochemistry of this disorder is now clear, thanks to a Dallas medical team (Walsh et al., 1974). In utero, dihydrotestosterone normally virilizes the external genitalia in XY fetuses.

Twenty-three Dominican children were born looking like girls, but at puberty testes descended and their voices deepened. The hypospadiac "clitoris-phallus" (in fact, a short hypospadiac phallus) enlarged and could ejaculate live sperm. Masculinization of musculature also developed. Testosterone at puberty could accomplish the virilizing tasks performed by dihydrotestosterone in utero. All of these cases were, of course, chromosomally male.

The Cornell physicians report that these "girls" readily adopted a masculine gender identity at puberty (Imperato-McGinley et al., 1974). Current reports are too spare to show the outcome of this late reassignment of gender. Descriptions of seven of the men

187

(considered typical of the group) range from one who is very withdrawn and living alone to another who is not only married but also has a mistress. The Dominican Republic cases appear to violate the Money, Hampson, and Hampson rule to avoid late gender reassignment.

Anthropologists now working in the village hope to clarify the gender shift further.[2] The study of these sex-reassigned men is important for leads on what conditions might allow late intervention and management. Perhaps we will learn what aspects of their gender identity and gender role kept the choice open, or what aspects of the culture of the Dominican village allowed new role assumption.

Rigidity of Sex-Typing

Reviews like this one easily fall into a scientific tone that makes one's concern with issues like sex-typing seem cold and even sterile to lay readers. Therefore, I should like to end by urging more attention to work on conditions that discourage rigidity of sex-typing. (And I am fully aware that this is a value statement.)

The literature suggests that in early and middle childhood the rigidity of sex-typing falls most heavily on the shoulders of boys. It may, in fact, contribute to making fathers rigid stereotypers of their sons and daughters. We know that environments vary in degrees of sex-typing and that higher education and middle-class status are associated with more relaxed gender role requirements (Kohn, 1959). Rigidity of definitions of masculinity may well increase the likelihood of men making self-attributions of homosexuality when they find themselves deviating from narrow role definitions.

We are a far cry today from the early anthropological visions of the hunter-gatherer society, and so attempts to justify—or value—current gender roles because they come from that past have a hollow ring. We are a species with the plasticity needed to live in highly diverse habitats, with highly diverse adaptations. It is indisputable that adaptations to roles within the family will change. Life cycle changes *that have already occurred* underscore the necessity of change for women. On the average, women are having fewer children and are living longer than ever before. The time left after the last child's entry into first grade (or even the

2. D. Federman, personal communication, 1975.

end of high school) leaves today's women many more productive years than women born in the nineteenth century ever had. Neugarten (1972) has estimated that at age thirty-two, the average 1966 woman's last child was in first grade and she still had forty-six years to live. It is, therefore, not surprising that women have been entering the labor force at increasing rates since 1960 (Luria, 1974; Livi-Bacci, 1976).

A relaxation of rigid roles could well include shared male and female attention to child rearing, as well as shared male and female attention to breadwinning. I do not believe that wider ranges for roles can be legislated, although greater work opportunities for women as well as child-care work leaves for both men and women can be. Support systems for families that do not fit our sex-typed conceptions are definitely in order (Bronfenbrenner, 1975).

We have a genuine concern with understanding the nature of sex differences and the methods by which gender roles are assumed. We should not allow our concern about these issues to be construed as justification for the position that the way we find gender roles to be now is the way gender roles *must* be in the future.

References

Aberle, D. F., and Naegele, K. D. 1952. Middle class fathers' occupational role and attitudes toward children. *Am. J. Orthopsychiatry* 22: 366–378.

Bates, J. E.; Bentler, P. M.; and Thompson, S. K. 1973. Measurement of deviant gender development in boys. *Child Dev.* 44:591–598.

Bates, J. E.; Skilbeck, W. M.; Smith, K. U. R.; and Bentler, P. M. 1975. Intervention with families of gender-disturbed boys. *Am. J. Orthopsychiatry* 45:150–157.

Bentler, P. M. 1968. A note on the treatment of adolescent sex problems. *J. Child Psychol. Psychiatry Allied Discip.* 9:125–129.

———. 1976. A typology of transsexualism: Gender identity theory and data. *Arch. Sex. Behav.* 5:567–584.

Bentler, P. M., and Prince, V. 1975. Distinctions and diagnosis in sexual and genderal dysphoria. In *Current research in human sexuality*. Paper read at regional meeting of the Society for the Scientific Study of Sex, June 1–3, 1973, Las Vegas, Nev.

Blumstein, P. W., and Schwartz, P. 1976. Bisexuality in women. *Arch. Sex. Behav.* 5:171–181.

Bronfenbrenner, U. 1975. Reality and research in the ecology of human development. *Proc. Am. Philos. Soc.* 119:439–469.

Bryan, J. W., and Luria, Z. 1978. Sex-role learning: A test of the selective attention hypothesis. *Child Dev.* 49:13–23.

Condry, J., and Condry, S. 1976. The development of sex differences: A study of the eye of the beholder. *Child Dev.* 47:812–819.

Conn, J. H. 1940. Children's reactions to the discovery of genital differences. *Am. J. Orthopsychiatry* 10:747–755.

D'Andrade, R. G. 1966. Sex differences and cultural institutions. In *The development of sex differences,* ed. E. Maccoby. Stanford: Stanford University Press.

Ehrhardt, A. A.; Evers, K.; and Money, J. 1968. Influence of androgen and some aspects of sexually dimorphic behavior in women with the late-treated adrenogenital syndrome. *Johns Hopkins Med. J.* 123: 115–122.

Elias, J., and Gebhard, P. 1969. Sexuality and sexual learning in childhood. *Phi Delta Kappan* 50:401–405.

Fein, G.; Johnson, D.; Kosson, N.; Stark, L.; and Wasserman, L. 1975. Sex stereotypes and preferences in the toy choices of 20-month-old boys and girls. *Dev. Psychol.* 11:527–528.

Feinbloom, D. H. 1976. *Transvestites and transsexuals: Mixed views.* New York: Delacarte Press/Seymour Laurence.

Fisk, N. 1973. Gender dysphoria syndrome (The how, what, and why of a disease). In *Proceedings of the second interdisciplinary symposium on gender dysphoria syndrome,* ed. D. R. Laub and P. Gandy. Stanford: Stanford University Press.

Forest, M.; Saltz, J. M.; and Bertrand, J. 1973. Assessment of gonadal function in childhood. *Paediatrician* 2:102–128.

Gagnon, J. H., and Simon, W. 1973. *Sexual conduct: The social sources of human sexuality.* Chicago: Aldine.

Green, R. 1974. *Sexual identity conflict in children and adults.* New York: Basic Books.

————. 1976. One-hundred ten feminine and masculine boys: Behavioral contrasts and demographic similarities. *Arch. Sex. Behav.* 5: 425–446.

Gurwitz, S. B., and Dodge, K. A. 1975. Adults' evaluations of a child as a function of sex of adult and sex of child. *J. Pers. Social Psychol.* 32:822–828.

Imperato-McGinley, J.; Guerrero, L.; Gautier, T.; and Peterson, R. E. 1974. Steroid 5 α-reductase deficiency in man: An inherited form of male pseudohermaphroditism. *Science* 186:1213–1216.

Katcher, A. 1955. The discrimination of sex differences by young children. *J. Genet. Psychol.* 87:131–143.

Kinsey, A. C.; Pomeroy, W. B.; Martin, C. E.; and Gebhard, P. H. 1953. *Sexual behavior in the human female.* Philadelphia and London: Saunders.

Koch, H. L. 1944. A study of some factors conditioning the social distance between the sexes. *J. Social Psychol.* 20:79–107.

Kohlberg, L. 1966. A cognitive-developmental analysis of children's sex-role concepts and attitudes. In *The development of sex differences*, ed. E. Maccoby and C. Jacklin. Stanford: Stanford University Press.

Kohn, M. L. 1959. Social class and parental values. *Amer. J. Sociol.* 44: 337–351.

Levin, S. M.; Balistrieri, J.; and Schukit, M. 1972. The development of sexual discrimination in children. *J. Child Psychol. Psychiatry Allied Discip.* 13:47–53.

Lev-Ran, A. 1974. Gender role differentiation in hermaphrodites. *Arch. Sex. Behav.* 3:391–424.

Lipman-Blumen, J. 1975. Changing sex roles in American culture: Future directions for research. *Arch. Sex. Behav.* 4:433–446.

Livi-Bacci, M. 1976. Demographic changes and women's life cycle: Notes on the problem. Paper presented at the conference on "Le Fait Feminin." Centre Royaumont pour une Science de l'Homme, Sept. 3–5, 1976, Paris.

Luria, Z. 1974. Recent women college graduates: A study of rising expectations. *Am. J. Orthopsychiatry* 44:312–326.

Luria, Z., and Rubin, J. Z. In press. The neonate's gender and the eye of the beholder. *Sci. Am.*

Maccoby, E. E. 1976. The psychology of the sexes: Implications for adult roles. Paper read at conference on "Le Fait Feminin." Centre Royaumont pour une Science de l'Homme, Sept. 3–5, 1976, Paris.

Maccoby, E. E., and Jacklin, C. N., eds. 1974. *The psychology of sex differences.* Stanford: Stanford University Press.

Mehl, M. C. 1973. Transsexualism: A perspective. In *Proceedings of the second interdisciplinary symposium on gender dysphoria syndrome*, ed. D. R. Laub and P. Gandy. Stanford: Stanford University Press.

Meyer, J. K. 1973. Some thoughts on nosology and motivation among "transsexuals." In *Proceedings of the second interdisciplinary symposium on gender dysphoria syndrome*, ed. D. R. Laub and P. Gandy. Stanford: Stanford University Press.

Mischel, W. 1966. A social-learning view of sex differences in behavior. In *The development of sex differences*, ed. E. E. Maccoby. Stanford: Stanford University Press.

Money, J. 1970. Sexual dimorphism and homosexual gender identity. *Psychol. Bull.* 74:425–440.

————. 1975. Ablatio penis: Normal male infant sex-reassigned as a girl. *Arch. Sex. Behav.* 4:65–72.

Money, J., and Ehrhardt, A. A. 1972. *Man and woman, boy and girl.* Baltimore: Johns Hopkins Press.

Money, J.; Hampson, J. G.; and Hampson, J. L. 1957. Imprinting and the establishment of gender role. *Arch. Neurol. Psychiatry* 77:333–336.

Money, J., and Ogunro, C. 1974. Behavioral sexology: Ten cases of genetic male intersexuality with impaired prenatal and pubertal androgenization. *Arch. Sex. Behav.* 3:181–205.

Morris, J. 1974. *Conundrum.* New York: Harcourt Brace Jovanovich.

Mueller, E., and Vandell, D. 1978. Infant-infant interaction. In *Handbook of infant development,* ed. J. Osofsky. New York: Wiley.

Neugarten, B. 1972. Education and the life cycle. *School Rev.* 80:209–218.

Pauly, I. 1969a. Adult manifestations of male transsexualism. In *Transsexualism and sex reassignment,* ed. R. Green and J. Money. Baltimore: Johns Hopkins Press.

———. 1969b. Adult manifestations of female transsexualism. In *Transsexualism and sex reassignment,* ed. R. Green and J. Money. Baltimore: Johns Hopkins Press.

Pauly, I. B. 1974. Female transsexualism: Part I and part II. *Arch. Sex. Behav.* 3:487–526.

Prince, V., and Bentler, P. M. 1972. Survey of 504 cases of transvestism. *Psychol. Rep.* 31:903–917.

Rubin, J. Z.; Provenzano, F.; and Luria, Z. 1974. The eye of the beholder: Parents' view of sex of newborns. *Am. J. Orthopsychiatry* 44:512–519.

Saghir, M., and Robins, E. 1973. *Male and female homosexuality.* Baltimore: Williams and Wilkins.

Seavey, C. A.; Katz, P. A.; and Zalk, S. R. 1975. Baby X: The effects of gender labels on adult responses to infants. *Sex Roles* 2:103–110.

Simon, W., and Gagnon, J. H. 1969. On psychosexual development. In *Handbook of socialization theory and research,* ed. D. A. Goslin. Chicago: Rand McNally.

Slaby, R. G., and Frey, K. S. 1975. Development of gender constancy and selective attention to same-sex models. *Child Dev.* 46:849–856.

Thompson, S. K. 1975. Gender labels and early sex role development. *Child Dev.* 46:339–347.

Thompson, S. K., and Bentler, P. M. 1971. The priority of cues in sex discrimination by children and adults. *Dev. Psychol.* 5:181–185.

———. 1973. A developmental study of gender constancy and parent preference. *Arch. Sex. Behav.* 2:379–385.

Walsh, P. C.; Madden, J. D.; Harrod, M. J.; Goldstein, J. L.; MacDonald, P. C.; and Wilson, J. D. 1974. Familial incomplete male pseudohermaphroditism, type 2: Decreased dihydrotestosterone formation in pseudovaginal perineoscrotal hypospadias. *New Eng. J. Med.* 290: 944–949.

Will, J. A.; Self, P.; and Datan, N. 1974. Maternal behavior and sex of infant. Paper read at American Psychological Association meeting, Aug 30–Sept. 3, 1974, New Orleans, La.

Wilson, J. D.; Harrod, M. J.; and Goldstein, J. L. 1974. Familial incomplete male pseudohermaphroditism, type 1: Evidence for androgen resistance and variable clinical manifestations in a family with the Reifenstein syndrome. *New Engl. J. Med.* 290:1097–1103.

Wilson, W. C. 1975. The distribution of selected sexual attitudes and behaviors among the adult population of the United States. *J. Sex. Res.* 11:46–64.

Zuger, B. 1970. The role of familial factors in persistent effeminate behavior in boys. *Am. J. Psychiatry* 126:151–154.

Gender Identity and
Sex-Role Adoption

Eleanor E. Maccoby

Zella Luria's excellent contribution to this volume begins by distinguishing three aspects of sexual identity: gender identity, role, and orientation. Her definition of gender identity is clear, and she examines the evidence for the twin propositions (defended most strongly by Money and his colleagues [1972]) that gender identity is a product of social ascription, and that there is a critical period for its formation, following which gender assignment is not reversible without great damage to the individual.

Luria discusses in detail findings from studies of two kinds of hermaphrodites: genetic females virilized by the presence of excess androgens during fetal development, and genetic males who are feminized (or more precisely, fail to be masculinized) in utero because of the insensitivity of relevant target tissues to the androgens produced by the male fetus. The great majority of such cases have adopted, without obvious signs of conflict, the gender identity to which they were assigned at birth, and this acceptance is the strongest evidence we have for the power of social definition in the development of gender identity. Additional evidence is offered to show that adults' reactions to children are strongly affected by their knowledge of a child's sex, so that adults create a consistent climate supporting the assigned gender.

I agree with Luria's assessment of the evidence of the power of social ascription, with certain reservations. We should remember that the conclusion is based largely on hermaphrodites, for whom the prenatal situation was abnormal. If gender identity in normal individuals depended to some degree on prenatal hormonal sensitization, hermaphrodites would be in an intermediate state with respect to some or all of these predisposing factors. They might therefore be more malleable to social assignment than children whose prenatal environments predisposed them more definitely to the characteristics of one sex or the other.

The Critical Period Hypothesis

The evidence for a critical period in the formation of gender identity seems more problematical. In the Money files there are only five documented cases in which adults have attempted to change a child's gender assignment after the age of two years three months; in four of these cases serious problems of adjustment resulted. These cases are contrasted with nine for whom gender reassignment occurred before the age of two years three months, and for whom there were no documented problems of gender identity encountered during subsequent development. Compelling though these cases are (and their study is a remarkable achievement considering how difficult such cases are to locate and follow up), it is necessary to emphasize that this is a very thin data base for documenting the age boundary of a critical period with any accuracy.

And there is counter evidence from the twenty-four cases in the Dominican Republic reported by Imperato-McGinley and associates (1974). Of course, much more information is needed about these cases. Most important, we need to know whether they were recognized in early childhood as ambiguous or unusual in sexual identity; if so, the adults of the society may have suspended some of the usual definitional pressures that confirm a child's initial assignment, so that it was possible for the children to switch assigned sex at puberty without serious disruption. Nevertheless, this report indicates that if a society can assign one gender identity to a child at birth, it can assign another at a considerably later date. Presumably the success of the reassignment would depend upon how consistent members of the society were in accepting and acting upon the reassignment. Perhaps it is not children who have critical periods with respect to gender assignments, but societies; that is, after a given age, too many people know a child, and their memories are too long to permit them to change the nature of their supportive behavior.

Even more serious questions about the existence and boundaries of a critical period for the formation of gender identity are posed by transsexuals. A growing number of individuals insist that they wish to be surgically transformed into the opposite sex, denying the identities in which they have been assigned and reared. The only way to reconcile such cases with the view that gender identity is developed very early and is subsequently irreversible is to argue that the initial gender assignment never "took" with these individuals, and that they had cross-sex identities from earliest childhood. And, indeed, Luria presents evidence that many effeminate boys showed preferences for female clothing before the age of three. Still, she also shows that there are a number of routes to transsexualism, only one of which appears to be the failure of initial gender assignment. Another route involves a boy who is reared as a boy and appears to accept this identity, but develops a strong sexual orientation toward males. His anxiety over homosexuality is so strong, however, that he would rather be transformed into a female, so that he can have a normal heterosexual relationship with a male, than live as a homosexual. There are parallel cases for individuals who are genetic females raised concordantly as girls.

What these cases appear to show is that it takes very strong motivation to overcome early gender assignment, but if this motivation exists, the initial assignment is not irreversible. We need to know more about the psychological state of individuals who have undergone changes in gender identity in adolescence or adulthood—what elements of their earlier identities remain, and how these residuals may be incorporated into the new identity. The evidence on this point seems very thin.

One of the reasons why Luria leans strongly toward accepting the critical period hypothesis is that she sees it as consistent with the data on the development of the child's gender self-concept— the ability to label self and others accurately with respect to membership in gender categories. She cites Thompson's work (1975), tracing what children know about gender labels at 24, 30, and 36 months, and showing that children as young as 24 months can sort pictures accurately according to the labels man/woman, boy/girl, mommy/daddy, and so on. At 30 months, they have developed appropriate *self*-labeling as boy/girl or he/she, and have begun to recognize some similarity (in terms of gender labels, at least) between themselves and other children of the same sex. We now are able to shift some of the responsibility for determining the boundaries of a critical period from the adult socializing agents to the child: Once *the child* has identified his/her own sex, he/she will presumably begin preferring sex-appropriate playmates, toys, and activities. (One can recognize Kohlberg's theory here.)

I agree that the acquisition of gender labels and gender concepts is a crucial process in the formation of gender identity, and I believe that Luria has added greatly to the depth of the discussion about critical periods by bringing this kind of data to bear upon it. But again, I believe that the boundaries of the "critical period" are fuzzier than would be indicated by Luria's account of the development of self-labeling, and that there is evidence to suggest a more gradual acquisition of gender labeling extending considerably beyond the 30-month watershed. At 30 months, a little boy may be able to label himself as a boy, and he may be able to distinguish men from women reliably; but he may not realize that boys and men belong in the same category—that they are both males. Perhaps more important, he may have little or no understanding that he will inevitably grow up to be a man.

Just when a child usually achieves "gender constancy" is still in doubt. Emmerich (in press) continues to find it occurring later than the four-year level that Luria specifies. Clearly it is not until the "we males" or "we females" category becomes stable, and sometimes later than this point, that children begin to imitate same-sex models preferentially. It seems likely, then, that between the ages of three and six a child's gender-identity concepts are still malleable in some respects. More specifically, it might be very hard to convince a little boy of this age that he really is a little girl; but it might be fairly easy to convince him that he could *become* a woman. It is possible, then, that unusual life conditions at this age could predispose a child to later shifts in identity. I feel we must suspend belief a little longer concerning how critical the critical period is, and whether there are several critical developmental milestones, rather than one, in the formation of gender identity.

Sex Differences and Gender Roles

Luria uses the term *gender role* to designate the "public behaviors that express gender." Thus, her usage is very close to the meaning

197

that others have given to the terms *sex-typed behavior* or *masculine* and *feminine behavior.*[1] If the sexes characteristically differ in a certain aspect of behavior, does this necessarily imply that there is a corresponding difference in sex roles, to which the two classes of incumbents are adapting themselves? It is arguable that this is so, but I think not. A striking example is the sex difference in performance on visual-spatial problems. Members of social groups do not usually have explicit expectations that a man will do well on an Embedded Figures Test while a woman will not. Furthermore, a man is not labeled unmasculine if his spatial ability is poor, nor is he subjected to social pressure to shape up to a masculine ideal in this respect. I would argue that spatial ability is not therefore part of the male role. Nor is a woman's greater acuity in detecting certain odors. Nor, probably, is a boy's tendency to play in a large group and a girl's to play with one or two chums. All these characteristics are sex-typed, however, in the sense that they are sex-differentiated.

Characteristics that are sex-differentiated can become part of sex roles. Using spatial ability as an example, it may be that there are some derivative occupations for which spatial ability is required that initially became male because of their linkage to spatial ability. Because of the social expectations that have grown up around such jobs, a woman might be criticized as "unfeminine" if she wanted to enter these occupations. The occupations, then, would have become part of sex roles, but spatial ability would not.

It is an important empirical issue to determine which sex differences are sex-role linked and which are not. The important thing about sex roles is that they are prescriptive. Once one has been labeled as an incumbent of the position "man" or "woman," there are things that others believe one *should* or *should not* do. There are large areas of behavior, however, which are sex-role

1. I agree with Katchadourian's comments in this volume that there are some useful distinctions to be made among these terms. He notes that in the Maccoby-Jacklin book, *The Psychology of Sex Differences* (1974), the term *sex role* does not appear in the index, although there is a chapter on sex-typing. The omission is deliberate. I prefer to reserve the term *sex role* for the sociological definition: a set of expectations held by others for the incumbent of a position. Our book did not attempt to deal directly with sex roles in this sense. We focused upon sex differences.

free, although the sexes may differ in their modal performance in some components of these areas. (Dare I use the phrase "sex-role-free ego space"?)

We must ask whether it is possible for people to recognize that the sexes differ on the average with respect to a certain attribute, without making this attribute part of sex *role* as narrowly defined. This is partly a conceptual, partly an empirical issue. We found in an early study (Rothbart and Maccoby, 1966), for example, that parents of preschool children agree that boys are more likely than girls to be rough and noisy in their play. When asked whether they thought it was important (or desirable) for boys to be rough and noisy, they thought, on the contrary, that it would be better for them to be less so. Their socialization goals seemed to be very similar for the two sexes in this respect, and one could infer that boys were *not* being pressured by their parents to conform to this aspect of "boyish" behavior. Therefore being rough and noisy is not, strictly speaking, part of the male role as defined by adults. But if parents had been asked which of two boys was more masculine, one who was rough and noisy or one who was gentle and quiet, chances are the parents would have said that the rough, noisy child was more masculine. The attributes that enter into the meaning of "masculine" or "feminine," then, include some (but probably not all) of the attributes in which the sexes are believed to differ. And not all behaviors labeled "masculine" or "feminine" are inherent in the male and female roles.

We should be aware that "perceptions" of differences, or beliefs about differences, may or may not be accurate. It is widely believed, for example, that boys are typically more active than girls. Although we do not have a clear picture yet of the conditions under which a sex difference in activity level emerges, the statement in its simplest form is not consistent with the existing evidence. But so long as it is *believed* to be true, a highly active child is thought to be more masculine than a quiet one.

Several distinctions have been made so far:

1. There are some attributes with respect to which the sexes *differ* in the average frequency, intensity, or topography of the behavior, or in the circumstances under which the behavior occurs. The existence of the difference may or may not be generally recognized.
2. There are *perceived* sex differences—and the perceptions may

or may not be accurate—which contribute to the stereotyped concept of what is typically male or typically female behavior.
3. Role prescriptions are applied to a subset of the behaviors included under perceived sex differences. A member of a given sex is considered more likely to have a certain attribute, and it is felt that he/she *ought to have* this attribute; this is the definition of *gender role* in its strictest sense.

We could argue about whether any of the sex differences that are part of the cultural beliefs (stereotypes) about "typically male" or "typically female" behavior are totally free of social pressures for the individual to adopt the behaviors thought to be typical of his/her own sex. I believe there *are* such behaviors. At least we could probably agree that behaviors perceived as sex-differentiated vary greatly in the degree to which they are subject to the pressures of role prescription.

Even if we agree that behavior perceived to be more common in one sex than the other need not be *prescribed,* we nevertheless would expect that there must be consequences of the perceptions. If a girl is rough and noisy, her behavior will be more noticed because it is defined as unusual. Parents may take a more accepting (or resigned!) attitude toward undesired behavior that is considered typical of the child's sex because they may feel there is little they can do to change it. But not all behavior that is different from what is thought to be typical of a child's sex is attention-getting or subjected to negative parental pressure. The quiet, mannerly, scholarly boy does not make his parents uncomfortable. Although they might also be pleased with him if he were more athletic, he is conforming to some aspects of their socialization goals, and is well within the range of what is acceptable and "normal." If he adopts distinctively feminine mannerisms, clothing, and tastes, however, such choices produce strong anxiety in his parents. A combination that is very likely to draw negative attention from socialization agents is behavior that is both incompatible with parents' values and perceived as atypical for the child's sex.

We ought to maintain distinctions between sex differences, sex stereotypes, and prescriptive sex roles, instead of blurring these distinctions by the use of a single term such as *gender role.* The point of maintaining the distinctions is simply this: The young child has certain tasks to achieve in the process of becoming socialized. The child must establish a gender identity, but this achievement usually comes very early and is accomplished with little conflict. The more difficult task is adopting a coherent set of interests, values, and behaviors that come to define the self. The child's "self" must fall within the range of what is considered appropriate for its sex or great conflict will be engendered. Social definitions of what is sex-appropriate are in many respects quite loose, and there are many facets of human functioning to which they hardly apply. Of course, the areas in which sex-role prescriptions are applied are the ones on which students of sex-role socialization and deviance need to concentrate their attention.

Asymmetry in Role Definitions

One of the most interesting aspects of data on social pressures to conform to gender-role stereotypes is that boys seem to be subjected to considerably stronger pressures of this kind than girls. Furthermore, the pressure directed toward boys is of a negative kind: It is deemed especially important for them *not* to behave in feminine ways. Boys have considerably more latitude with respect to how fully they must conform to the positive masculine image.

It is important to consider who defines gender role and how this definition changes with age. I suspect that adults have a different definition of how a boy aged (say) six to ten ought to behave than do his age mates. Fathers are probably more likely than mothers to demand "toughness" from their sons, but the pressure from fathers is probably mild compared with that emanating from a boy's peers (boys of the same age or especially those slightly older). At several points in Luria's paper we see evidence of the power of peers in the development of masculine behavior in boys. Interestingly, there seems to be less peer pressure for a girl to be feminine. There is a further asymmetry between the sexes in role definitions: The most feminine things a little girl can do, and the activities specifically forbidden to boys, are to play with dolls and dress up in adult women's clothes with adult make-up and jewelry. These activities have obvious kinship to adult female roles. But the boys' activities that are seen as most typically masculine (rough-and-tumble play, fighting, certain boys' group games) are much less related to adult male roles.

So far, I believe we do not have a good explanation for the asymmetries between the two sexes in the process of acquiring sex-appropriate behaviors. Many of us have continued to be profoundly dissatisfied with the Freudian view that boys must overcome an initial feminine identification, and therefore need more socialization pressure not to be feminine. The problem with this view is simply that there is no evidence that young boys *do* identify with their mothers more than with their fathers. Is the male role more difficult in some sense? Or is the sexual object choice more malleable among males? There must be some explanation of the asymmetries, and the problem is worthy of greater attention than it has received in recent theorizing.

Luria's primary point about the development of what she calls sex-role behaviors is that great variation is possible in the way these roles can be played out by individuals of either sex without disturbing core gender identity. She might have added that there is considerable variation among societies as to the definition of masculinity and femininity, and that human beings have proved themselves capable of adapting themselves smoothly to a surprising variety of definitions. Levine, in this volume, points to a highly instructive example: that the various elements of "machismo," which we take to be highly related to the definition of masculinity in most of the societies we know (although more strongly so in Latin cultures), do not appear as a concept of masculinity in certain African societies. It startles us to think of a social group in which sexual performance in men is not seen as linked to muscular physique, strength, or "toughness," and where the most desirable male mate is middle-aged, paunchy, and prosperous. The main point here is that individuals can vary widely, both between cultures and within cultures, in the way they act out their gender roles without in any way disturbing their underlying gender identity.

The Motivation to Conform

Luria points out that core gender identity, in the vast majority of cases, is formed early and remains stable throughout life, while the individual goes through a number of developmental vicissitudes with respect to the nature of his/her concepts about what kind of behavior is sex-appropriate, and the degree to which he/she conforms to these changing definitions.

With all this I fully agree. But it is not clear why some individuals go beyond the range of the permissible variations and adopt behavior that is strongly at variance with their gender identity and extreme enough that they are labeled as deviants. It seems probable that the problem does not lie primarily in errors in the development of sex-role concepts, although there is some evidence that effeminate boys do not monitor their own behavior adequately. For example, some do not realize they are using effeminate gestures.

However, deviants, moderate conformers, and hyper-conformers must all be quite fully aware of what the usual sex-typical patterns are, unless they are retardates. The problem must be a motivational one, and one would expect to find the key in one or several patterns of disturbance in early interpersonal relationships, so that the individual was deflected from the wish, need, or ability to follow the usual course of development. Putting this formulation in its strongest form, it is as though a boy said to himself: "I know what it is to act in a boy-like way. I know that my parents want me to act this way (or at least enough to get by). My schoolmates expect it—in fact, they will tease me and leave me out of their activities if I don't. But just the same, I don't *want* to act this way. (Or feel I *can't*? Or I'm *afraid* to?)" The first question, of course, is how close this formulation comes to an accurate statement of the situation for any substantial portion of sex-role–deviant children. I do not find in Luria's chapter an adequate explanation of how a child might arrive at this state, and I suspect it is not the chapter that is at fault, but the existing state of our knowledge.

References

Emmerich, W.; Goldman, K. S.; Kirsh, B.; and Sharabany, R. In press. Evidence for a transitional phase in the development of gender constancy. *Child Dev.*

Imperato-McGinley, J.; Guerrero, L.; Gautier, T.; and Peterson, R. E. 1974. Steroid 5 α-reductase deficiency in man: An inherited form of male pseudohermaphroditism. *Science* 186:1213–1243.

Maccoby, E. E., and Jacklin, C. 1974. *The psychology of sex differences.* Stanford: Stanford University Press.

Money, J., and Ehrhardt, A. A. 1972. *Man and woman, boy and girl.* Baltimore: Johns Hopkins Press.

Rothbart, M., and Maccoby, E. E. 1966. Parents' differential reactions to sons and daughters. *Psychol.* 4:237–243.

Thompson, S. K. 1975. Gender labels and early sex-role development. *Child Dev.* 46:339–347.

Sex-Typing, Object Choice, and Child Rearing

Robert R. Sears

The information brought together by Luria and reviewed by Maccoby serves as a basis for developing three strings of hypotheses concerning causal relations in the development of sex-typing and of object choice for sexual behavior. These strings lead naturally to the formulation of clusters of research problems focused upon sex-typed behaviors, response to arousal, and the developmental relationship between these two domains. Available data are scarce in support of all three sets, and theoretical inference is more evident than empirical evidence.

Cognitive Development

Developmental changes in cognitive capacities have as much significance for the development of sex-typing and sex behavior as for any other area that requires learning, discrimination, and labeling. Whatever influence genetic preprogramming may have on sex-typed behavior and ultimately on object choice, the conditions under which behavioral maturation occurs are in large part the determiners of the observed quality of such behavior.

The crucial evidence cited for this assertion is the work of Money and Ehrhardt (1972) on the matter of sex-role assignment in early childhood. Between 24 and 36 months there appears to be a critical period during which the gender identity of the child must be established. Attempts to reassign the child thereafter create substantial distress and are often ineffectual. Prior to age two, the chief problem of reassignment is experienced by the parents, rather than the child. Identifying a child's gender is a labeling process, and it may be that sex-typing can be understood only when the significance of this labeling is understood.

Sex-typing is the process by which a child develops those behaviors that differentially characterize males and females in their behavior repertoires (R. Sears, 1965). What constitutes masculine and feminine behavior varies at different ages, in different societies, and during different historical times. Whether there are any universal characteristics of behavior that have been considered masculine or feminine in all societies at all times is so far unknown. For the present, diversity seems more evident than universality. Furthermore, within any one population sample there is variability in the extent to which a particular behavior actually occurs in one sex as contrasted with the other. Even highly sex-typed occupations such as engineering or child care have some very able cross-sex practitioners. Even in the most conservative middle-class American society, styles change sporadically to permit at least some men to wear gaudy colors. Behaviors that are commonly considered sex-typed simply occur with significantly greater frequency in one sex than in the other. If the totality of all sex-typed behaviors could be counted, and if a sample of individuals could be examined as to the proportion of that total each displayed, there would be a substantial overlap between the two sex populations.

Despite this relativity, *masculine* and *feminine* are labels stereotypically applied to persons, rather than to behaviors. Gender is conceived as dichotomous, just as individual behaviors are coded into binary classes. It is this binary coding, or labeling, that seems to play such an important part in the development of sex-typed behavior.

Binary coding is a characteristic of early cognitive processing. *Hot* and *cold, good* and *bad, up* and *down* exemplify the earliest discriminations of the child. Gender is simply another example. Binary coding may provide a poor reflection of nature, but it is efficient for the limited processing capabilities of the two- to three-year-old. *Hot* and *cold* soon change to a discriminative dimension of temperature, and by five or six years most children have expanded the dichotomous classification to not less than a four-level discrimination including *warm* and *cool*. More adjectives are then added. In nontechnical social discourse, most people make use of six to ten points on the temperature scale. *Black* and *white* gradually become the extremes of the dimension with greys in it. There has been some research on this aspect of cognitive development during the first few years of life, but the

205

findings have not been applied to gender role and are not applicable without considerable further research. The temperature events that come to the senses of the growing child from nature are not as polarized as are the gender events. Male and female are different not only by stereotype but by anatomical fact and physiological function.

The binary coding of *masculine* and *feminine* seems to begin about as early as language expression begins. It has begun by 24 months, though attribution of gender to the self (by using a photograph of the child) does not appear to develop until about 30 months. By 36 months the self-labeling is prominent, and the growth of binary coding about objects and about other people's behavior continues rapidly thereafter. By age seven a whole host of events appear to be sex-typed, and to have combined into a stereotype of what is appropriate for a person of each sex to do. In contrast to other early binary codings, such as temperature or even ethical absolutes, sex-typing is not converted into a comparable discriminative dimension, either for items of behavior or for individuals.

To understand the process of sex-typing as applied to both behaviors and people, and to discover the ways in which sex-typed behaviors cluster together in the behavior repertoire of the person, it will be necessary to know what discriminations are being made at various ages from two years on, to discover what children know about gender differences at each stage of development, to learn what cognitive processes normally occur in the period of shift from binary to more dimensional coding, and to determine the environmental conditions that influence these processes.

In this latter connection, we must suppose not only that reinforcements of particular discriminations are relevant, but also that expectations on the part of society serve a directing function as well as a reinforcing one. We must ask how much of sex-typed behavior is truly internalized and the product of internal instigation and how much of it is elicited by a constant bombardment of stereotypic expectations from the rest of society. The cross–sex-appropriate behavior of the transsexual appears to be a critical instance of such expectation induction.

Finally, with respect to the role of cognitive development, there is a problem concerning the fate of self-labeling. At certain points in their lives, people appear to label themselves as tough or tender, as masculine or feminine, or as homosexual, bisexual, or heterosexual. The point in development at which such decisions are made varies enormously, both among persons and with respect to the different decisions. There is little hard evidence on the matter, but children of six to seven years often have begun to label themselves quite definitely with some of the characterological adjectives without using labels that represent what adults mean by the more abstract terms *masculine* and *feminine*. The object choice labels of homo- and heterosexuality come even later, usually after pubescence, but there are great individual differences as to when this choice occurs, in some during adolescence and in others as late as midlife.

Such self-labeling tends to close the doors toward certain future directions of development and to leave others more clearly open. The opening and closing of doors may occur as a means of reducing dissonance in a situation in which the person feels great ambiguity about his or her "real" character. On the other hand, self-labeling may result from some kind of final psychological shift into a particular category such as homosexual or heterosexual. In any case, self-labeling as to gender, or as to certain specific gender qualities, may well be an important determinant not only of sex-typed characteristics but of actual homo- or heterosexual object choice in sex behavior. Perhaps both homosexual and heterosexual behavior and character are ultimately the consequence of self-labeling. Clearly more needs to be known about the self-labeling process itself as well as its outcomes.

Sex-Typing and Object Choice

From a procreative standpoint, the choice of a male or female object for sexual behavior is a function of the sex of the subject. Since the procreative difference between the sexes is an important determinant of the *fact* (not necessarily the specific behavior content) of sex-typing, one might expect an intimate relationship between sex-typing and object choice. What influence do other aspects of sex-typing have on actual sex behavior itself? The term *sex behavior* is meant to include all the various types of response to sexual arousal, not only the homosexual or heterosexual choice of object toward whom the response is made. As with sex-typing, there have been scattered and incomplete reports of the development of object preferences through the first twenty years of life, but the data are far from systematic, nor is there adequate longitudinal study of the same individuals (Hamilton, 1929; Kinsey et al., 1948, 1953). Such study is essential if the sequence of development of sexual activity is to be understood and if we are to discover the influence of sex-typing of nonsexual activity on sexual behavior itself.

Developmental studies of parent preference have shown that three- to five-year-old children of both sexes tend to show a little more warmth and fondness toward the mother than toward the father in American nuclear-family settings. Evidence that this early preference on the part of boys may be linked with actual sexual arousal, as in the classical Oedipus theory, is by no means lacking in the clinical literature, but the extent to which such a linkage characterizes the broad spectrum of normal child development has not been well examined (R. Sears, 1943).

Observational studies and retrospective reports suggest that there may be rather extensive exploratory sex play with peers of both sexes from age five to adolescence. Freud's notion of a latency period during which the libido was relatively quiescent was an exaggeration. There is good evidence of a clear separation of the sexes, increasing toward the immediate prepubescent period, with boys choosing other boys to play with and girls choosing other girls (Campbell, 1939). For the transition period—say ten to fourteen for girls and twelve to sixteen for boys—there are a number of pathways of development. Nonsystematic observations have shown that homosexual play is common among boys during the early part of that transition and then decreases as the boys approach full adolescent responsiveness. Overt sexual activity appears to be less common in girls than in boys, with respect to both autoerotic stimulation and sex play with others (Kinsey et al., 1948, 1953). By the time a cohort reaches late adolescence, at the end of the teens and in the early twenties, most individuals have made an object choice for their sexual activity, and of course in the very large majority the choice is heterosexual. There remains a substantial number, though a small percentage, who make homosexual object choices.

At this developmental point the binary coding comes into play again. There is a strong tendency on the part of society to label individuals as homosexual or heterosexual. A growing number of unsystematic reports cast doubt on the validity of any such binary coding. Many lesbian women have been described who only by a rather arbitrary labeling can be identified as homosexual. Some have married, had children, and in middle life left their male partners and paired off with female partners. Other cases are known in which there is a shifting back and forth or a true bisexuality that eventuates in dual object choices. Manifestly there are many styles of ultimate resolution of the object choice problem, different pathways chosen to reach a state of settlement in maturity.

Sex behavior is similar to sex-typing in two respects: There is a stereotypic binary coding of male and female object choice, and there is little discrimination by labeling of radically different kinds of social behavior by which object choices are exhibited. Two contrasting instances can be used as an example of non-discrimination: one is a stable living arrangement with partial or full sexual interaction with the partner; the other is the choice of a purely sexual partner without cohabitation or any other involvement. The choices made in these two connections are not necessarily correlated, according to common observation, and yet either one or the other may be used as the basis for attaching a label of homosexual or heterosexual to the person involved.

Just as sex-typing is displayed in many aspects of behavior, so there are multiple behaviors that occur in connection with sexual arousal. Many of these behaviors involve object choice as well as choice of expression or style. In the absence of longitudinal study of the development of forms of sexual behavior and object choice, it is impossible to determine the relationship of specifically sexual actions to all the various kinds of sex-typed learnings that go on during the same period. What needs untangling is the relationship between the effects of social reinforcement of sex-typing in all the nonsexual behaviors, and the influence of experiences that are directly sexual and involve sexual arousal.

A few scattered studies have given hints of a relationship between the two domains. One study has shown that adult homosexuals show high retrospective recall of having been deviant in early childhood as tomboyish girls or effeminate boys. Still another has shown that adult lesbians have no recollection of fantasies of being a boy, while transsexual women do have such recollections. Transsexuals also recalled finding their bodily changes highly aversive at puberty, while the lesbian women did not remember any particular reaction to the changes. These scattered findings suggest that the gender of the chosen object can be quite independent of other aspects of the sex-typing process.

Effects of Early Experience

The above discussion has been directed largely to the cognitive processes involved in the development of sex-typing and sex behavior, and to the influence of one set of behavior characteristics on another. Consideration must be given also to child rearing and other experiences that make use of the cognitive processes and serve as causal events in sex development. We turn, therefore, to a self-consciously antecedent-consequent, or causal, approach to these kinds of behavior.

There is a substantial amount of information on the child-rearing experiences that are conducive to the development of such various types of behavior as aggression (Feshbach, 1970), dependency (Maccoby and Masters, 1970), and achievement motivation (LeVine, 1970). There are very few data relating early experience to sex-typed behavior after the preschool years and almost none relating to various forms of sexual behavior or object choice (cf. Mischel, 1970). The theoretical orientation of two to three decades ago, when much of the study of child-rearing influences began, proved to be too simplistic to provide a full understanding of the developmental sequence as it occurred in a social context (cf. R. Sears, Maccoby, and Levin, 1957). The theory was essentially a *tabula rasa* conception of the effects of parental behavior on the child. Parents were the providers of the reinforcement contingencies that established various types of child behavior by operation of the laws of learning. In effect, the causal relationship was conceived as the unidirectional influence of parents on children.

In recent years, recognition has been given to the effect of a parallel causal sequence that derives from the child's own spontaneous development and the effects of the child's previous learnings on later behavior. Thus, to take an example from the sex-typing process, a girl who develops tomboyish activities in her preschool years can continue to play with boys and receive peer-group rewards up to age ten or eleven, regardless of whether her tomboyishness was the product of some genetic bias or specific conditions of learning in the family setting. Similarly, it makes no

difference whether the effeminate boy developed his characteristics from one source or the other, or a combination of both,
because he is isolated by both boys and girls from about age six
on. The effects of isolation for the boy, or the more prolonged
masculine peer-group association for the girl, can serve as antecedent events that create new consequences for the child's social
and sexual development.

During the last decade, another and more precise causal chain
has been recognized: the influence of the child on the parent as
a determiner of what the parent will do in reverse behavior toward
the child. This relationship is the classical dyadic tangle, long
recognized in other contexts but only recently subjected to detailed analysis in connection with early childhood development.
For example, a simple comparison of the effects of high or low
intensity in a mother's responses to her child suggests that an
intense mother produces an active child. But there is evidence
that more active children tend to produce more intensive responses from their mothers. Concurrent measures of mother
intensity and child activity level cannot be considered independent measures of the effects of intensity on the child's behavior,
because the activity levels of high- and low-intense mothers' children already differ.

Another finding, though in relation to other than sexual behavior, is a difference in direction of correlations between mother
and child behavior for the two sexes; that is, a given kind of
parental treatment appears to have one effect on boys and another effect on girls. Furthermore, there is evidence that what
appears to be similar behavior on the part of father and mother
has opposite effects on sons and daughters (R. Sears, Rau, and
Alpert, 1965). So far these data are minimal and there has been
little replication of the findings. There are several hypotheses
that deserve investigation: (1) The sexes may respond differently
to a given kind of treatment. Basic temperamental differences
may influence the threshold at which a given kind of parental
behavior is effective in producing a particular kind of response
in the child. Or there may be differences in the child's perception
of the two parents with respect to such variables as power, em-
pathy, or follow-through, with the result that the parents' influences will differ. It was from this congeries of differential

211

perceptions of the parents that Freud drew his conception of the different outcomes of the Oedipal complex. (2) The apparently similar behavior of parents toward boys and girls may actually be subtly dissimilar. Parental expectancies of compliance or rebellion, sometimes based on actualities of previous experience, may introduce subtle differences in the treatment given the two sexes.

Notwithstanding the complexities of this dyadic (or triadic) tangle, the causal factors in the development of sex-typing and sex behavior must be unraveled. The discovery of child-rearing antecedents for aggressive feelings gives hope that there can be some comparable discovery of causal relationships in the development of sexual behavior. Severe early punishment of aggression has been shown to produce a reduction in antisocial aggressive feelings by late prepubescence (R. Sears, 1961). It would be important to discover whether early nonpermissiveness and suppression of sexual behavior has similar long-lasting effects, especially into adulthood.

Still another source of influence entering into the causal sequence concerns the social setting in which the child rearing is performed. Even if we disregard the influence of the specific child's temperament on parental behavior, there are still major differences in the settings in which children grow up. There has been considerable study of the effect of father absence on various aspects of children's behavior, mainly aggression. Young boys whose fathers were absent during World War II showed a significant reduction in fantasied aggression (P. Sears, 1951). More recently there has been a study of the effects of father absence on girls' behavior and a comparison of the effects of absence of father by death or divorce (Hetherington, 1972). One study has shown substantial effects of father absence on certain aspects of daughters' development; specifically, daughters of divorced mothers tend to be precocious in their heterosexual interests, while daughters of widowed mothers are inhibited in their relations with the opposite sex. As yet we have little information on the reasons for these differences. Do mothers, on the average, behave differently toward their children when there is no father present? Similar questions can be raised with respect to the number of children in a family and the size of the living space.

In summary, then, the rather halting progress of antecedent-consequent studies of the effects of child rearing have been promising. In any case, sex-typing and sexual behavior have been subjected to very little investigation, although the former has been more fully studied than the latter. Future research will undoubtedly take into account at least four general causal chains: (1) the direct effects of parental practices on children's behavior; (2) the initial temperamental or constitutional characteristics of the child; (3) the effects of the child in determining parental behavior toward the child; and (4) social settings as determining the similarities and differences among parents and the way in which they perform their child-rearing functions.

Directions for New Research

We have noted a significant discontinuity between two aspects of sexual development, sex-typed characteristics and sexual behavior. The former refers to those attributes that appear significantly more in the behavior of one sex than the other, and the latter to behaviors associated with sexual arousal, which may be noted in human beings either by verbal report or by physiological indices. Sex behavior and sex-typing have a common adjective, but there is little propositional cross-referencing between the data sets that describe them. There are many kinds of sex-typed behaviors and there are many varieties of response to arousal, but what connection there may be between these two domains—and how they influence one another—is largely unknown. The reason for this separation is that the data for both domains are very sparse.

Our recommendations for high priority in research are directed toward enriching these two bodies of data, discovering the developmental relationship between them, and tracing the influence of preceding experiences on later behaviors.[1] Where data are available for these three areas of investigation, there is considerable unevenness in their amount and precision. Generally, the age range from two to twenty years is least well served by present knowledge. The substantial contributions of the Johns Hopkins group have shown the importance of early experiences and developmental pathways. In the field of sex-typing, there is a substantially greater body of knowledge about the ages three to five

1. These recommendations are based upon the author's discussions with Zella Luria and Eleanor Maccoby.

years than any other part of the first two decades of life. As far as sex-typing and sex behavior both are concerned, the period from six to sixteen is virtually a terra incognita. There are great uncharted areas in the decades following age twenty also; the full life-cycle should not be ignored, but because of the great importance of the early period as a determinant of lifetime sexual adjustment, the highest priority should be given to research on the first two decades.

Research on these problems will be difficult. Both sex-typing and sex behavior are sensitive areas of great social and political concern. Sex-typing implies sex differences. Among the more militant members of the women's liberation movement, the mention of such differences calls to mind sex discrimination and all the inequities associated with sex-role stereotypes. Justifiable resentment against these real evils generalizes to the scientific study of the associated phenomenon of sex-typing.

Sex behavior and object choice are areas intimately related to the goals of the gay liberation movement. The understandable efforts of the homosexual community to gain respect and acceptance for that particular style of object choice makes the search for causes of homosexuality suspect to such persons. It is open to the interpretation that researchers view homosexuality as changeworthy behavior and, intentionally or not, are undermining the efforts to gain acceptance and nondiscrimination.

In fact, social prejudices and discrimination cannot be swept under the rug of ignorance in the hope that they will just go away. The best way of attacking such evils is by gaining solid information about the phenomena associated with them. The anguish of the subordinated woman and the rejected homosexual are problems of massive importance to our society. At whatever cost, they must be attacked openly and forthrightly at the scientific level of causal understanding as well as at the level of activist social reform.

Sex-typing

There are many pathways to maturity. What is needed is a full-scale natural history of the ways in which the two sexes grow up to be alike or different. So far no one has charted the several dimensions of sex-typed behavior that can vary during the course of development. Although gender identity is established early and almost always remains unchanged throughout life, the strength of the conviction that one is and always will be basically male or female may vary with steps in the life cycle. Preferences for such things as games, self-decoration, sexual companions, and interests change greatly, but their normal course is poorly understood. Body images and gestural and postural qualities are also relevant. In the early adolescent period, vocational and recreational interests become important. Among the major motivational systems, aggression, achievement, and affiliation are areas of considerable difference between the sexes. A natural history of development along all these dimensions is essential in order that we may learn how they vary in their relationship to one another through the life cycle, and how much connectedness there may be in their patterned combinations.

A major problem that runs through all developmental research is that of the changing characteristics of behavior as the child grows older. For example, the form of outward-directed aggression in the two-year-old is quite different from that in the five-year-old, and the aggression of the adolescent bears little resemblance to either. We are accustomed to assuming that aggression is nevertheless a continuous motivational system throughout life and that as aging occurs there are progressive changes in style, intensity, and various other attributes of the aggressive expression. The same principle holds true for sex-typed behavior. An occupational interest in fire fighting or aviation at age eight commonly gives way to other masculine occupational interests and aspirations in late adolescence. In girls, the rise and decline of interest in horses has often been noted.

To discover the sequence in these rising and falling behaviors through the first two decades of life will require longitudinal research. Only by following individual children through this time period will it be possible to discover the different manifestations of sex-typed behavior that are either equivalent at different ages or at least developed sequentially. Since there are very broad individual differences in the rate at which all kinds of behavior potentialities develop, chronological age is an exceedingly rough —in early adolescence almost useless—index with which to correlate development. For this reason, cross-sectional studies of children, listing the frequency with which various types of behavior occur at different ages, are of relatively little value except as a gross source of information about population samples. Longitudinal analysis of individual cases permits a discovery of what kinds of behavior follow what other kinds of behavior and are precursors to still others.

There are many pathways that children can follow in reaching maturity. The majority of these lead to recognizable sex-typing of the young adult, but the criteria society uses for judging what is masculine or feminine are quite broad, and it would be a mistake to suppose that there is some final platonic ideal personality structure that is or should be reached. Recent emphasis on the development of the androgynous personality highlights the recognition of this fact. The various dimensions of behavior or motivation that are susceptible to sex-typing are quite evidently somewhat independent of one another. In a male, for example, a consistently high level of aggression through adolescence is not necessarily associated with a high masculinity of occupational interest. But just how independent these dimensions are, and to what extent experiential modification of one can influence the other sex-typed characteristics of the personality, are simply unknown.

Clinical observation makes it very evident that different pathways to maturity are associated with different degrees of anguish. Those that represent a significant degree of deviance from the norm often have the most severe discomfort for the developing person. The present state of our knowledge does not permit us to recognize which deviations are likely to have severe consequences for satisfactory sex-typing and sexual adjustment in adulthood and which ones are passing phases that have little future implication. A significant example of this problem is tomboyishness in girls and effeminacy in boys. Depending on the criteria used for identifying a girl as a tomboy, from 10 to 50 percent of girls in our own society can be so labeled. Retrospective judgments by young women tend to reach the upper limit. Currently we know little or nothing about which identifying tomboy behaviors indicate a long-term dedication to a masculine sex-typing and which ones are simply temporary preferences that will fade out in late adolescence.

It is evident that extreme cases of cross-sex-typing lead to adult personality outcomes that are distinctively deviant within the population as a whole. To the extent that such deviances cause anguish, their causes deserve discovery. It would be good to be able to recognize them early and to provide the opportunity for personality modification before a particular developmental pathway becomes a source of pain and social disablement.

Sex Behavior

Information about the effects of sexual arousal in the first two decades of life is about as sparse as that about sex-typing. For the first five years of life, there is no body of data parallel to that which has been collected on the sex-typed behavior of preschool-age children. What is known is largely inferential or is based on retrospective reports of adults who have undergone some kind of deep therapy. The free-associative recall of neurotic adults is a poor substitute for direct longitudinal study of normal children. Such recall may have validity, but the nature of the therapeutic process is designed to reactivate memories that have had conflictual and ambivalent affect attached to them. What is seriously needed now is a natural history of the normal development of sexual behavior during the first two decades of life.

Again, longitudinal study is indicated. The same sequence of changing forms of overt behavior occurs with respect to sexual behavior and response to arousal as occurs in sex-typing. Masturbation is commonly observed in children as early as age two, but we know virtually nothing about the sequence of development of this activity. Mutual sex play has often been observed as early as age three, and among boys at least, it is a common form of play during the years from six to adolescence. The relation of one kind of sexual behavior to another is largely a mystery today. Neither the sequential changes in forms of behavior nor the influence of the behavior at one time on the feelings and behavior at later times is known. In spite of meticulous research on adult sexuality, there has been no comparable effort to discover the pathways of development during the earlier years.

One of the major characteristics of sexual development is its severe isolation from adult influence. Even in today's superficially liberated environment, most sex education appears to occur in the peer group, not in an open relationship with supportive adults. Aside from the sheer lack of information that the young child and preadolescent suffers, the hiatus between adult and child cultures provides a fertile field for children's development of myths and anxieties that are not susceptible to external correction.

217

Relations of Sex-typing to Sex Behavior

One clear connection between sex-typing and sex behavior is the process of object choice. Differential responsiveness to children of the same or opposite sex has been observed in children as young as two years of age. By ten years the preferential choice of same-sexed companions is sufficiently intensive and common that it has become a part of the sex-typing process. Again, however, there is great variability in the extent to which this choice is accepted with comfort or discomfort. Ordinarily there is a shift to opposite-sex choices for overt sex behavior after pubescence. The period from ten to fourteen in girls and ten to sixteen in boys is one of considerable fluctuation, however, and since this is the period when a start is being made on overt physical responses to sexual arousal, object choices tend to be characterized as homosexual or heterosexual. Without careful longitudinal study of children who vary in their path toward maturity, it is impossible to untangle the relationship between what appears to be sex-typed behavior in the prepubescent period and overt sex behavior through object choice in the postpubescent period.

Effeminacy in boys at pubescence, and tomboyishness in girls, are often linked in popular thought with the development of homosexuality of object choice. Recently there has been substantial effort to use behavior modification methods with effeminate boys on the supposition that postural, gestural, and other indicators of feminine sex-typing are precursors of homosexual object choice. There is some question about the validity of this assumption. However, there is little doubt that such sex-typed characteristics produce indecision or hostility on the part of other males toward the effeminate boy, and hence the effort to modify the external indicators may be justified. On the other hand, little is known of the relation between sex-typing and object choices that are made in adolescence and adulthood. The whole sequence of events from role assignment at age two to object choice made in adolescence is of crucial importance, and every effort should be made to study the sequence among children who are following different sex-typing pathways. Clinical interest has been focused, naturally, on the most deviant cases, and there is very little information about the less anguishing pathways to maturity.

Effects of Early Experience

Emphasis has been placed here on a natural history approach to both sex-typing and sex behavior. While such information has obvious value in its own right, it is also the essential basis for study of the effects of early experience on sexual feeling and conduct as these develop through adolescence into adulthood. Again it is clear that longitudinal research is the essential element for the study of these effects. Whatever may be the inherent genetic sources of continuity of development along a particular pathway, and whether these are expressed through neurological, chemical, or cognitive processes, there is ample evidence to show that experiences which the growing child has in relations with other individuals and with social institutions are important determinants of both sex-typing and behavioral reactions to sexual arousal.

A major influence appears to come from the parents during the first two years of a child's life. Child-rearing attitudes and practice with respect to sex-typing and sex behavior vary considerably. There is sufficient evidence with respect to the development of aggression, dependency, and achievement motivation to lead us to suppose that sex-typing and sex behavior also are influenced by such events. There has been virtually no research on the effects of parental attitudes toward sex behavior on the sequence of development even in later childhood, let alone in adolescence or adulthood. Longitudinal study of children whose experiences vary widely through the normal to the extremely deviant in these respects needs to be performed.

Ideally such studies should begin soon after a child's birth and be continued for a quarter-century. The well-known difficulties of maintaining a longitudinal study for that period of time make it urgent that the general field of sexuality be introduced to other on-going longitudinal studies already in existence. A number of these deserve consideration. Both the Berkeley studies (Jones et al., 1971) and the Fels research (Kagan and Moss, 1962) have extensive data banks on early childhood experience in the family and continuing measures of parental treatment. In these studies the subjects are now in midlife and a current retrospective investigation would throw considerable light on the relationship between early child-rearing experiences and adult behavior. An equally promising body of data exists in the *Patterns of Child Rearing* sample (R. Sears, Maccoby, and Levin, 1976). The nearly 400 cases of individuals whose socialization experiences were systematically measured when they were five years old provide a potentially valuable resource for the study of early experience as a precursor to adult sexuality as measurable at age thirty.

While we consider longitudinal study an essential method for these various problems, we recognize their difficulty and expense. A quarter-century is a long time to wait for definitive answers to urgent questions. Capitalizing on earlier studies can be valuable, but the form of longitudinal researches begun a quarter- to a half-century ago is not necessarily the most efficient. For new investigations there should be consideration of both short-term overlapping longitudinal studies and replication on time-separated age cohorts. Times change as well as people, and the more basic causal relationships can be best isolated by repetitions of sequential analyses with same-aged groups spaced a few years apart.

A second major area for investigation is the influence of peers. While there has been a long history in psychology of the study of friendships and feelings about peers, there has been very little investigation of the influence of peer groups on personality development. The so-called peer culture has been widely recognized by sociologists and anthropologists, and of course the work on gangs in the field of delinquency presents a significant approach to the study of such factors. Again, sex has been largely left out of studies that represent an approach to peer influences, even though, as noted earlier, the peer group is often the chief source of sex education.

Finally, there are social institutions that have an impact on the child's development. In the absence of the natural history of the development of sex-typing and sex behavior, it is difficult to analyze the institutional structure of a society with respect to its causal influence on development. The differential rate of development of boys and girls, particularly through the early adolescent period, suggests the importance of looking at school arrangements, which may place special stress on one sex or the other at different times. For both sexes, there is a changing self-concept and body image during the transition period. While some attention has been given to the effects of this age discrepancy in pubescence with respect to achievement motivation, only clinical study has been made of the effects on sexual feelings and choices. By its very nature, clinical study is limited largely to youngsters who are most deviant from the norm, and hence we have little information about the effects of various social institutions on the child who does not deviate sufficiently to get into a clinical setting.

The importance of these various antecedents cannot be overestimated. Whatever may be the genetic routes of variation in development, the environmentally produced events are the ones most easily controllable. Both parent education and sex education, through schools or with the aid of older peers, are channels that could be influenced by some solid knowledge in the behavioral realms we have discussed here.

Some pathways to maturity cause more anguish than others. To the extent that these pathways are chosen because of particular parental attitudes, or peer group experiences, or social institutional influences, to that extent they could be modified for children of the future. It may well be that some types of development—some of the pathways—are genetically determined and not subject to modification through experience. So be it. Many others apparently are chosen because of a particular nexus of events. It is for the purpose of blocking off the more anguishing pathways that we give high priority to the areas of investigation recommended here.

References

Campbell, E. H. 1939. The social-sex development of children. *Genet. Psychol. Monogr.* 21, no. 4.

Feshbach, S. 1970. Aggression. In *Carmichael's manual of child psychology,* vol. 2, ed. P. Mussen. New York: Wiley.

Hamilton, G. V. 1929. *A research in marriage.* New York: A. and C. Boni.

Hetherington, E. M. 1972. Effects of father absence on personality development in adolescent daughters. *Dev. Psychol.* 7:313–326.

Jones, M. C.; Bayley, N.; Macfarlane, J. W.; and Honzik, M. P. 1971. *The course of human development.* Waltham, Mass.: Xerox College Publishing.

Kagan, J., and Moss, H. A. 1962. *Birth to maturity.* New York: Wiley.

Kinsey, A. C.; Pomeroy, W. B.; and Martin, C. E. 1948. *Sexual behavior in the human male.* Philadelphia: Saunders.

Kinsey, A. C.; Pomeroy, W. B.; Martin, C. E.; and Gebhard, P. H. 1953. *Sexual behavior in the human female.* Philadelphia: Saunders.

LeVine, R. A. 1970. Cross-cultural study in child psychology. In *Carmichael's manual of child psychology*, vol. 2, ed. P. Mussen. New York: Wiley.

Maccoby, E. E., and Masters, J. C. 1970. Attachment and dependency. In *Carmichael's manual of child psychology*, vol. 2, ed. P. Mussen. New York: Wiley.

Mischel, W. 1970. Sex-typing and socialization. In *Carmichael's manual of child psychology*, vol. 2, ed. P. Mussen. New York: Wiley.

Money, J., and Ehrhardt, A. A. 1972. *Man and woman, boy and girl.* Baltimore: Johns Hopkins Press.

Sears, P. S. 1951. Doll play aggression in normal young children: Influence of sex, age, sibling status, father's absence. *Psychol. Monogr.* 65, no. 6.

Sears, R. R. 1943. *Survey of objective studies of psychoanalytic concepts.* New York: Social Science Research Council, Bulletin 51.

————. 1961. Relation of early socialization experiences to aggression in middle childhood. *J. Abnorm. Soc. Psychol.* 63:466–492.

————. 1965. Development of gender role. In *Sex and behavior,* ed. F. A. Beach. New York: Wiley.

Sears, R. R.; Maccoby, E. E.; and Levin, H. 1976. *Patterns of child rearing.* Stanford: Stanford University Press.

Sears, R. R.; Rau, L.; and Alpert, R. 1965. *Identification and child rearing.* Stanford: Stanford University Press.

Part IV
Sociological Perspectives

Whatever the biological and psychological roots of gender identity and sexual behavior may be, their expressions always unfold and can only make sense in social contexts. Although this context is clearly the domain of sociologists, they have rarely focused on sexuality as an object of study. Among the notable exceptions is John Gagnon, the author of the first contribution to Part IV.

Gagnon attempts to look beyond mere differences between men and women in sexual conduct, and to focus on the ways in which observed differences and commonalities come about, their stability, and the manner in which they are maintained. He takes exception to the "developmental and/or biological tilt" that he sees in most theoretical explanations of the acquisition of gender and sex differences, and offers an alternative perspective whereby the relationships between gender role and sexual conduct may be viewed as manifestations of different social-learning histories in varying cultural contexts. Thus, compared with most developmental psychologists, Gagnon sees the development process as less fixed, more discontinuous and environmentally conditioned. A corollary is that differences between male and female, such as in responses to erotic materials, are accepted not as fixed but as subject to historical change. The sociological perspective as articulated by Gagnon thus views gender and sexual behavior as far more malleable than a more biological or traditionally developmental view would presume.

The second installment in this part is an independent contribution, rather than a response. Jean Lipman-Blumen, a sociologist, and Harold Leavitt, an expert on organizational behavior, have developed an achievement typology and apply it to the understanding of sexual behavior. They identify common linkages between sexuality and achievement and show the relationship of both to distinctive gender stereotypes.

In the final contribution to this part, Lee Rainwater reiterates the sociological view on the variability and openness in gender roles and sexual behavior and skepticism at presumed uniformities in gender and sexual development based on biological and psychological determinants. Rainwater goes on to show manifestations of variability in sex-related behavior, in gender role, and in the different meanings of sexual behavior to the individual and others.

In suggesting new directions for research, Rainwater draws on the recommendations of the other authors in this part and of sociologists William Simon and Patricia Miller, who were participants in the conference discussions. Their recommendations flow mainly from the central theme of variability and change in gender and sexual behavior. The greatest research need, they believe, is for social accounting whereby through periodic surveys descriptive information would be obtained on sexual behavior and its relationships to changes in life style, family situations, and other aspects of social roles and institutions. These sociologists see the need also for a better understanding of the meaning of sexuality in people's lives at different nodal points in the life cycle, and they call for broader historical and cross-cultural studies to supplement our understanding of our current culture.
—H. A. K.

The Interaction of Gender Roles and Sexual Conduct

John H. Gagnon

The choice of a particular theoretical or explanatory perspective and its application in a systematic fashion is a significant decision in all areas of scientific inquiry. Our theoretical preferences contain some of the decision rules by which we decide what are the "facts," what significance the "facts" might have, and their interrelationships. Theories guide our scientific conduct, for they instruct us about what to notice and what to ignore, what is important and what is trivial.

The thoughtful choice of a theoretical perspective is particularly important in the study of sexuality. This is in part the result of the peculiar importance of sexuality both collectively and individually in Western cultures. Even though social life, which includes the study of social life, has been secularized, sexuality still manages to retain for many people its exemplary status as the observable margin between the sacred and the profane.[1] As a result of the problematic status of sexuality, both in the lives of individuals (including scientists) and in the collective life of the society, those who make sexuality a matter of professional concern often find it necessary to justify and defend their interests. As a result, theories that have been brought to bear on

1. "Whatever the force of certain arguments of a biological or philosophical nature [that masturbation is common or a part of normal sexual development], which have sometimes been used by theologians, in fact both the magisterium of the Church—in the course of a constant tradition—and the moral sense of the faithful have declared without hesitation that masturbation is an intrinsically and seriously disordered act." From the *Vatican Declaration on Sexual Ethics*, December 29, 1975, quoted in Gagnon, 1977.

sexuality have, more often than not, contained more than a little ideology—often involving attempts to use sexuality to defend or oppose what is the contemporary and established social and cultural order (Gagnon, 1975).[2]

Even with the surge of popular media interest and representations of sexuality over the last three decades, with a special acceleration in the last ten years, constraints on sex research have been only modestly relaxed.[3] As a result, knowledge about human sexuality remains scanty and much sexual research is lacking in methodological sophistication. Given this absence of a robust body of data, the choice of theories or interpretative frameworks becomes even more critical. As we attempt to sketch in the larger outlines of the landscape of sexuality, often by leaping from one isolated and often inadequate study to another, it is our theories that guide our speculations. Further, as we try to decide what research we might do next, again it is more often our theories than our data that guide us.

These problems of the relations between theories and ideologies and between theories and data are particularly confounded when the discussion of sexual conduct includes consideration of gender roles and performances. This confusion, in part, is due to the fact that what appear to be scientific discussions of gender role differences have substantial ideological components as well, components that have serious consequences in the politics of both science and society. Often what we approve of in sexuality is based on what we approve of in gender role conduct and vice versa. A second source of difficulty is that our conceptions of both sexual conduct and gender role conduct (in terms of their

2. This use of the sexual to symbolize other social purposes exactly reverses the Freudian symbolic dicta—for instance, that politics substitutes for sexuality, or political ideologies are symbolic of sexual conflict. A glance at life or literature will equally often show the opposite—for instance, the use by D. H. Lawrence of sexual themes and conflicts to symbolize political and class conflicts of a more fundamental sort. Disapproved sexuality has often been used in the twentieth century to attack or criticize conventional *nonsexual* values and institutions.

3. The decision by the Dean of Students at Harvard University in 1976 to prohibit a study of sexual arousal that involved direct measures of penile tumescence of undergraduate subjects is a recent example of such constraints.

origins, their development, their maintenance, their appropriateness and, let us not forget, their morality) have been steadily changing over the last half-century. This cultural dynamic makes it very difficult to judge whether it is the same *we* who are talking about the same phenomena, that is, whether *we* have changed, whether the phenomena themselves have changed, or both.

As a result of these sociocultural changes, within and outside of science, what appeared to be one of the most consistent and obvious findings in sex research, namely, that women and men differ over a wide range of sexual conduct, now appears to have a far more problematic cast. At one time this male/female difference had the same status in sex research that social class has in sociology; if one could find no other differences to report from a study, one could always find one there.

The sexual revolutionaries of the turn of the century (whom Paul Robinson has recently and accurately labeled "sexual enthusiasts") confirmed what the sexual folklore of the times recorded: that women and men differed in their sexuality (Robinson, 1976). From the clinical impressions of psychoanalysts to the survey researches that began in the United States in the 1920s to the work of Kinsey and even after, it was the differences between men and women that caught the researchers' attention. While *different* differences were thought to be important, it was the differences that were systematically noted. Even the work of Masters and Johnson, which has focused on the commonalities between men and women in their physiological responses to sexual stimuli, still leaves substantial room for variation at the psychological and the social levels (Masters and Johnson, 1966).

The contemporary issue, however, is not merely whether differences in sexual conduct between women and men are observable —differences in incidences, frequencies, feelings, preferences, stimuli have all been recorded. What is more at issue now is the relation between differences and commonalities in gender role conduct and sexual conduct—the ways in which differences and commonalities come about, the degree of fixity or reversibility they have in the lives of individuals or cultures, and the ways in which they are maintained.

In general, most theories or explanations of the acquisition and maintenance of gender and sexual differences between women and men possess a developmental and/or biological tilt. This

227

tilt became prominent when Freud grounded the source of such differences in the observable genital anatomy (with underlying hypothesized "chemical" differences). Out of these biological origins would emerge what we would now call gender identity, roles and performances, *and* sexual conduct, all further shaped, modified, and fixed as they passed through the furnace and forge of family life. What were thought to be models of healthy adulthood found in central Europe in the middle of the nineteenth century thus became the concrete cultural goals of normal gender-sexual development in the West. Heterosexuality and reproduction remained the goals of gender-sexual development as well as the basis for judging the social and psychological normality of individuals.

The search for a noncultural template for plotting the course of gender and sexual development (and judging their cultural normality) remains a pivotal, if not always explicit, concern in much of our research (Lunde, 1975; Tiger and Fox, 1971). Even Kinsey, with his emphasis on the variability of sexuality as a species characteristic, often treated maleness and femaleness as close to fixed biological essences (Kinsey, 1953, pp. 642–689). This approach was in startling contrast to his politically quite liberated (and I believe scientifically incorrect) treatment of heterosexuality and homosexuality, which he viewed as two ends of a biological continuum of sexual potential (Kinsey, 1948, pp. 610–666). This latent (and often not so latent) vision of man and woman as members of separate sexual species—or more recently as possessors of distinct internalized gender-learning histories that determine their patterns of sexual conduct—does not do justice to either the cultural or the individual variability involved in the acquisition, maintenance, and interaction of gender roles and sexual conduct.

There is an alternative perspective through which the complex relationship between gender roles and sexual conduct may be examined and emphasized. It is possible to view these domains not as outcomes of fixed developmental sequences (either biological or psychosocial), but as examples of different social-learning histories in different cultural contexts. This view focuses on the role of current learning contexts as the source of much of current conduct that might otherwise be viewed as the result of internalized predispositions. A second dimension of such an environmentally weighted social learning model would also predict a greater capacity for change in gender roles and sexual conduct under naturalistic circumstances.

Gender Roles and Sexual Conduct

Until the middle 1960s the most common model for the acquisition of gender roles and sexuality assumed that the matrix for both was laid down early in life and nearly contemporaneously. Even when the traditional Freudian view of the gender and sex dimorphism between women and men as features of early childhood was rejected, it seemed reasonable to assume that the male/female differentiations of such conduct began early in life and were closely linked (Money and Erhardt, 1972).

More recently it has been suggested by a number of researchers that this relationship, at least in Western cultures, could be better viewed as both more sequential and more discontinuous in character (Simon and Gagnon, 1969). Thus, the manifestation of sexual conduct in adolescence is seen as dependent on, but not exclusively determined by, preexistence of gender-role dimorphism. It was generally agreed that early in life male and female children acquired gender identities and then cumulated gender-specific roles and performances. However, it was not until adolescence that most young persons became sexual actors. Since the dominant culture does not overtly encourage sexual conduct among youth until their late teens (though local cultural supports and covert learning systems may exist considerably earlier), most young persons have a well-developed sense of "boyness" and "girlness," "manness" and "womanness" prior to the acquisition of sexual conduct.

As a result of the cultural emphasis on relatively sharp differences in gender identities and roles earlier in life, when sexual conduct (both as plans for conduct and actual activity) begins to be practiced, young people commonly proceed using the previously acquired self-labels and cognitive materials associated with the boy-girl/man-woman distinctions. The acquisition of sexual conduct is then based in part on coding sexual conduct in terms of previously learned gender categories influenced by the adolescent environment, which itself is coded in dimorphic terms. In adolescence there begins what might be called a second stage of woman/man dimorphism in this culture.

In many ways this reconceptualization of the relationship, or at least the priority in sequencing, between the acquisition of gender roles and the later acquisition of sexual conduct is reasonably satisfactory. It is particularly useful in organizing our perspective on the movement of young adolescents into the gender-separate homosocial worlds of early adolescence—homosocial worlds that contain the primary interpersonal sources of sexual learning. It should be pointed out that gender segregation still remains relatively strong during this period regardless of "unisex" predictions. Thus, the transition into these separate worlds and the sexual patterns that they support appears relatively quick and unproblematic for most children (Gagnon, 1971). The existence of previously internalized gender-role differences would make the recognition and the acceptance of different patterns of early sexual conduct quite reasonable.

However, it is important to recognize that even this view tends to overdetermine the strength of early differences between females and males. Regardless of the verbal fixity of the gender self-label sentence at age three or four—"I am a boy" or "I am a girl"—this label in fact has very little cultural content. It is only because *later* learning environments are coded girl/boy in specific kinds of ways that the child acquires further sense of differences. It is not that the child has been cognitively reorganized, but rather that the child has acquired a volitional self-label that is frequently referred to by others and makes the next cultural materials labeled boy/girl easier to assimilate. This apparent ease of learning is clearly a consequence of the environmental labeling of arbitrary connections within a culture. If the occupational structure and the world of sexuality were *not* coded in terms of male/female, then the original self-label as boy/girl would be irrelevant to those domains of conduct.

Even when young children can adequately (however tested by the psychologist or parent) distinguish between boys and girls and men and women in what appear to be culturally appropriate ways, it is not entirely clear that they know that boys belong to the category *men* or girls to the category *women* or that they all belong to some larger set of categories *male* and *female*. As

230

children accumulate materials that we judge to be culturally appropriate to their gender, we are often not at all sure what connections they are making between these external performances internally. The ability to perform a culturally appropriate task adequately and a commitment to that task as self-appropriate are far different phenomena, as any introspective person can tell. Thus, even though children may have a number of quite discrete gender performances labeled, identified, and performable, new gender performances (such as different sexual patterns in adolescence) do not have obvious or natural connection for children unless they are continuously and emphatically labeled as appropriate to them at the time of acquisition.

In addition, more recent reviews of the literature on the strength and directional potential of psychological differences between the genders suggest that they are fewer in number and less powerful in determining future conduct than we have commonly believed (Maccoby and Jacklin, 1974). Instead of strong differences between the genders on a wide range of attributes, recent studies have found primarily a great deal of inter- and intragender variability. Those differences that remain are not easily related to different gender patterns of acquisition and practice of sexual conduct. Even in cases where the mean differences between the genders are substantial (such as measures of aggressivity or spatial skills), it is difficult to assess their interaction with the differential acquisition or content of sexual conduct.

This recognition that there are few psychological differences may be surprising because in the past there was a tendency to "overfind" differences or not to notice studies that found no differences, that is, a cultural prejudice in favor of gender differences. At the same time, however, any cursory observation of the world around us would reveal that there is a striking division of activities and statuses in society between men and women and commonly between girls and boys as well. Why are these differences not reflected in the cultural circumstances of psychological experiments?

Unlike the majority of circumstances in which gender differences are part of the responses demanded by the environment, the psychological experiment is often one of the few circumstances in society in which differences between females and males are not demanded (or are randomized). It may well be that in order to sustain cultural differences between women and men, we are required to create redundant environmental demands that constantly reiterate gender differences. In this sense the psychological experiment is not the way to discover the differential weight to be given to different gender-linked factors—and therefore a guide to what is "really" different and what is not (and as a result a guide to political and social change as well). Instead, the experiment is an environment that is relatively gender neutral and that results in similarities between male and female subjects.

The issue is that gender identity, roles, and performances do not become constants but in fact remain quite variable and relatively incoherent. A model of development that emphasizes the sequential unfolding of fixed attributes, stage following stage, tends to obscure the range of gender and sexual conduct variation around the stereotypical averages (naive and scientific). The interaction of intragender differences with patterns of acquisition and performance of sexual conduct is rarely examined and understood. Since most of developmental theory remains linear in emphasis, what comes before in the organism's history is primarily determinative of that which comes after. Such theory depends on the constant taking into the individual of programs or dispositions to act that are relatively irreversible. The aging of the organism is seen as involving increasing response fixity and decreasing adaptive flexibility. Thus male/female differences in sexual conduct are viewed both as necessary outgrowths of prior gender experience and as nearly irreversible characterological or personality components. Such versions of development view the difficulty of behavior change as an individual attribute, rather than examining the set of continuing environmental contingencies that maintain and change a wide range of both conventional gender roles and sexual conduct.

The alternative perspective on development offered in this paper emphasizes its incoherent, discontinuous, and improvisational character at the individual and collective levels and diverges substantially from conventional psychological models. Most psychological models are based on linkages between what are categorized as similar molar events observed over time and assigning the majority of causative weight to the earlier. Development then becomes a string of connected similar molar events; thus, earlier defined and measured intellective or gender factors shape similar but later events in a "variance-accounted-for" framework. In contrast, my perspective emphasizes what might be called the relatively memory-less character of human development—as persons acquire new labels and reorganize their cognitive maps of the world, the past, even the recent past, loses its power to organize their future. A move into a significant cultural category may wash away the different pathways to it—thus, the child who ends up being defined as a tomboy or as a sissy, no matter how she or he came to that definition, ends up with a common cultural outcome. The past, in these cases, is less important than the demand characteristics of that common labeling experience and is thus less important in terms of predicting future conduct. Also, since the new category offers new justifications for past, present, and future conduct, the individual's memories of the past are reconstructed. Movement into the sexual aspects of adolescence, into membership in the gay community, or into heterosexual marriage are all boundary transitions in which commonalities for the future may be predicted more from the new social group membership than from the ways in which the membership was acquired.[4]

Masturbation and Adolescent Gender Roles

The differential gender rates of acquisition (in terms of incidences and timing) of masturbation among young men and women and the different patterns that exist among those who masturbate (in terms of frequencies and fantasies) are only weakly a function of the gender-role histories of young people. At the present time the basic Kinsey findings are still supported: (1) a larger proportion of young men masturbate than do young women; (2) young men begin earlier than do young women; (3) men peak rapidly in incidence in the middle teens, while women continue to discover masturbation into their later years; (4) the males who masturbate do so on the average at much higher rates than do females

4. The extraordinarily low correlations found in the developmental research, even the most molar, suggest that only very short-run effects between events should be expected over time. When the correlations are high, they are commonly a function of individual reconstructions of the past to fit with current conditions—the correlations are between verbal constructs all presented in a common context.

all the way into young adulthood; and finally (5) the fantasies of young men are more concrete representations of conventional and deviant sexuality than those of young women (Kinsey, 1948, 1953; Gagnon, Simon, and Berger, 1970; Clifford, 1975).

These differences in masturbation by males in contrast to females are very difficult to interpret if we try to locate some direct connection to prior gender-role learning. None of the differences between ten- and eleven-year-old males and females, even differences that may extend back further in development, are predictive of a difference of this type and power. What seems more likely is a sequence of events depending primarily on entry into a pre-existing gender-segregated adolescent culture. Merely being a boy or a girl at age ten and eleven is often enough to qualify most children for these alternative worlds.

The covert learning system for young boys, which provides information, misinformation, occasions of mutual nudity and comparison of genitals as well as possibilities of shared and instructed sexual practice, does not exist for most young women. It is not that there is some set of previously acquired attributes that make masturbation more accessible to young males (though they may exist for some young people), but rather that the homosocial environments for young males and females contain opportunities to learn different patterns of masturbatory conduct. However, there is a proportion of young men who do not masturbate (between 10 and 15 percent) and a substantial proportion of females who do (about 40 percent by the senior year of college). Further, there are a few young women who masturbate at rates that are quite similar to those of the males who have high rates. Thus, there are sufficient deviant cases to suggest that we should look in detail at the environments for both females and males to examine the sources of overlapping patterns of conduct.

The fact that the environment makes masturbation more easily acquired by males has gender-role consequences. A commitment to masturbation now creates an opportunity for new dimensions of difference between young men and women and may contribute substantially to changes in the content of gender roles. Frequent masturbation increases the probability that males will have a strong genital focus in sexuality, that they will have reinforced their fantasies with orgasm, that they will have had sex in certain stereotypical ways that may influence their sexual conduct with young women (Gagnon, 1974). In contrast, many of the responses that young women have to heterosexuality may be conditioned on the relative absence of a self-selected and autonomous sexuality that characterizes at least some of masturbation. In this way masturbation influences the content of gender roles by feeding back into and changing the content of the original differences. Indeed, the new differences between young women and young men in the sexual arena may well be some of the most powerful sources for the maintenance of old and creation of new gender-role differences.

This suggested relative discontinuity from and independence of masturbatory conduct from prior gender-role training may provide us with an exemplary lesson about the dangers of explaining present conduct through appeals to "commonalities" with the past. For instance, if masturbation patterns of this "male" type had been environmentally accessible to females, then we would have seen a quite different set of explanations of the interactions between gender "predispositions" and sexual conduct. It is likely that researchers would then find that there was in female gender development a particular set of factors that made females more likely to masturbate. Perhaps the "female" traits of passivity, dependency, and submission would have been used to explain the passive, solitary, unsocial practice of self-masturbation. The point is that *what is, is not what has to be.* Because environments are sequentially coded does not mean that persons are previously internally programmed.

Homosexuality and Gender Roles

The study of the "real" reasons people become homosexual or do homosexual acts is probably a fruitless enterprise, though it has occupied most of the attention of those who have studied homosexuality (Simon and Gagnon, 1967a, 1967b). Data have been obsessively searched to prove that there is a unique set of pathways or sequence of experiences (type of family, type of peer group, type of school experiences, first homosexual experience, and so on) that will produce a homosexual. But the meaning of being homosexual is not merely an accumulation from the past; it comes from the environments that await the child, environments where childhood labels and experiences are unrelated to the sexual preferences adults may want to make.[5] The "meaning" of sexuality is continually evolving as people get older; an act at age fifteen is different from the same act at age twenty; a deep emotional crush at age fourteen is fundamentally different from a love affair at age forty.

The basis for most theories of becoming homosexual is that something has gone wrong with the process of gender-identity formation—that the connection has broken down between the development of manhood and a preference for women in the case of male homosexuality, and womanhood and a preference for men in the case of female homosexuality (Bieber et al., 1962). The underlying argument is expressed primitively by saying that male homosexuals are basically effeminate men and female homosexuals are masculine women.

The importance that contemporary nuclear family patterns may have for the development of homosexuality (and heterosexuality) at the present time (it is unclear what role the family may have played in the development of homosexuality, say in Classical Greece) is to offer patterns of role differentiation. The contemporary family strongly emphasizes gender-role dimorphism by providing as primary role models an opposite-sex couple (usually heterosexual) with different tasks assigned to the different genders.

All children learn or observe these patterns in the home or in other areas of society, and become either comfortable or uncomfortable with these models of what the future may hold. However, it is not clear that the "sissy" or the "tomboy" is in fact reacting solely to this family constellation. The boy who is weak, timid,

---

5. My colleague William Simon once suggested to me that "there are more reasons to be deviant than there are ways to be deviant (or conventional)." He pointed out the case of a heterosexual man who had a powerful interest in sadism, but was unable to find many sexual partners. Because masochism appears to be more common among male homosexuals than among female heterosexuals, the man began to go to gay bars seeking masochists. He was capable of substituting the gender of the sexual object if his primary interest in inflicting pain was satisfied. His conduct in a gay bar would have given the impression of a "gay" male, and indeed for purposes of finding sexual partners he "played the role."

and fearful may in fact be physically less apt or legitimately afraid of getting hurt. The tomboy may be highly rewarded by the peer group for her performances during much of her childhood.

What may be important developmentally is not whether children possess a particular set of stigmas or abilities or inabilities, only whether they feel some sense of alienation from the conventional gender roles offered by parents, peers, teachers, or television. Thus, there is no particular pattern of parent-child relations that will produce a "homosexual"; there are only many children more or less comfortable with the usual gender-role expectations. A lack of comfort, or alienation, can have different outcomes, depending on other aspects of the environment, present and future. Two examples: A small, physically weak boy is rejected by and rejects his aggressive working-class peer group. In school he may find opportunities to be upwardly mobile, go to college, and become successful, while his classmates are still hanging around the corner tavern. In the same circumstances, the sense of alienation may influence the boy's preference for sexual partners. A girl who is a tomboy, and who is disvalued in a gender-stereotyped society because of her interests in "boy" things, may become interested in homosexuality; or, in a society where female athletics are highly rewarded, she could become famous and the object of considerable heterosexual attention. In both of these examples there are expressions of values—between heterosexuality and homosexuality, between upward mobility and working-class life styles, between fame and obscurity.

The family constellation of role models prepares the child not so much for "homosexuality" as for a wide range of responses, the contents of which are to be specified in the arena of adolescence. "Poorly adjusted" children may find many opportunities as well as problems, depending on the resources that become available to them as they move from period to period in their lives. Socialization patterns may produce discomfort; whether this discomfort is a potential for becoming different from what is expected (indeed most people do not realize this potential) is not as important as whether that "different" is defined as good or bad.

Young people uncomfortable with conventional gender-role expectations often find themselves also uncomfortable with the heterosociality and heterosexuality of adolescent social life. Only

237

for a few of the most popular does youth culture approximate its television versions; and most young people, those moving into heterosexual and those moving into homosexual preferences, find the period only sometimes pleasurable and joyous. However, the period is usually more comfortable for those who are moving or drifting into a heterosexual pattern. Even if they are heterosocially inept, it is possible to be carried by the general tide into a minimum heterosexual adaptation.

A further reason it is easier to realize a potential heterosexuality is that a commitment to the opposite sex does not have to be thought about the same way a commitment to the same sex does. It is possible to go through the public rituals of heterosexuality and heterosociality without much conscious effort; the same rituals do not exist for the young people who have an alternative sense of what they want emotionally and physically. This period appears to be particularly chaotic for adolescents with same-sex interests because there are no affirming public markers about what they are feeling and thinking.

The experience of being different, of being invisible or too visible, is profoundly demoralizing for many young people (Brown, 1976). All around them others appear to be "turning out right" (no matter how unhappy those others may be in fact). Indeed, many similar feelings are shared by young people who drift into heterosexuality later. The worries that these young people have about their masculinity or femininity during this period are often connected with believing the cultural myth that there is a necessary connection between gender-role conformity and sexual conformity.

Some homosexuals say that they knew they were homosexual when they were five or six years old. It is unclear what this means—it may mean only that they felt different at that time; it may mean that they are more comfortable locating their "homosexuality" very early in life; it probably tells us something about how they relate now, and little about their pasts. What is likely is that most people who develop a same-sex object choice do so during adolescence, in a sequence of events that involves recognition that they are "different" and that they might label themselves as "homosexual" or "gay" or "lesbian"; the beginnings of association with others who label themselves in the same way;

beginning to have sex with others of the same sex; and finally at some point informing significant others (homosexual and heterosexual) of their preferences. The sequence of these events has no "natural" order; some people think it first, other people do it first, still other people are told it by others first (Dank, 1971).

The adolescent period can be quite different for males than for females who have emerging homosexual commitments. Here the influence of adolescent expectations about sexuality is quite important. Many young women move into strong emotional relationships with other young women without physical sexual commitments at all; some have sexual experiences without knowing what to call the experiences; a few connect both the physical experience and the emotional commitment to a person of the same sex. These patterns of emotional and sexual self-identification also occur among males, as does sexuality without self-identification—however, males more often have a physical introduction, females an emotional one. As with heterosexual young women, the early period of development for young women who are developing a homosexual commitment is less physically focused than for most young men. Young women also move into overt homosexual experience at later ages, and many may marry before making a final commitment to homosexuality at some later point in life (Simon and Gagnon, 1967a, 1967b).

The interplay between sexuality and gender roles and the complexity of the relation between them is displayed as young persons find the homosexual community or the "gay" subculture. Historically, roles in the gay subculture were aligned along strongly differentiated gender lines. Particularly the male homosexual community, but also the female, tended to be modeled on heterosexual male/female stereotypes. Often this characteristic of the subculture was confused with the preferences of the members of that subculture. This confusion existed on the part of observers of the gay subculture (including most researchers) as well as many members of the community. In the same way that the subculture of the Marine Corps is more macho than most individual marines, so the gay community is more strongly divided along butch-fem lines than are individual homosexuals. This public characteristic of the community has two effects: first, it offers the persons just coming into the community a set of roles that are more exaggerated or differentiated than are actually needed; second, it continues a tradition that is less and less fully adequate to the needs of its members.

As we have noted, many young people who are beginning to adopt an alternative sex-object preference feel very uneasy. Since the cultural stereotype of the gay male is effeminate and of the lesbian is masculine, it is hard to shake these imposed conceptions. At the same time, the young person is not receiving those nonsexual reinforcements of gender-role identity that are the automatic rewards of those who are heterosocial. Nonsexual association between men and women probably contributes more to gender-role comfort than does sexual association—if young people are cut off from these social supports, there can be an uneasiness about the stability of their gender-role identity. The exaggerated roles offered by the gay community are accepted with rather more passion than reflection by many young people, some of whom find for the first time a sense of connection between gender and sexuality (Gagnon and Simon, 1973).

What the homosexual case offers us is a more acute sense of the dynamics of the interaction between sexual conduct and gender roles throughout the life cycle, an interaction that is constantly being shaped by cultural environments. Because homosexuality is a "deviant" case, we are constantly alert to these interactions, of the tension between sex and gender; however, these same tensions exist for heterosexuals as well. Again gender is not a fixed category, nor is sexual conduct.

Sexual Response in Women and Men

In addition to evidence that the relationship between gender roles and sexual conduct is environmentally conditioned and relatively discontinuous and changing over the life cycle, there is a growing body of evidence that what were thought to be fixed relations between maleness and femaleness and sexual conduct have changed historically. One example indicates that changing learning conditions in the society affect gender differences in sexual responsiveness to erotic stimuli of various kinds.

For instance, previously observed differences in men and women in their responsiveness to erotic materials have not been replicated in more recent survey and experimental studies. Kinsey in his researches in the late 1940s and early 1950s found (as did

240

other survey researchers) that fewer women than men reported being aroused by erotic materials (Kinsey et al., 1953, pp. 642–689). It was not a measure of differential intensity of arousal, but a measure of incidence. As the most plausible explanation of the difference in erotic response, Kinsey chose a difference in conditionability of men and women based on inferred differences in the central nervous system. An environmental explanation of this gender difference of response to visual erotica is that most women in the 1940s seldom saw such materials, that the materials were largely prepared for men (that is, they did not connect with women's sexual scripts, though romantic movies did), and finally that women had learned to talk about these materials in a negative manner. The differences between men and women then could partly rest on the fact that (1) some women who saw the materials did not define them as sexually arousing (and there is no reason why they should have), and (2) some women did find them arousing, but did not want to say so.

More recent studies of visual arousal, conducted in the 1960s and 1970s, suggest that the differences between men and women are less than in earlier studies (Victor, 1977). More men in these studies were aroused by seeing pictures of naked women, than women were aroused by pictures of naked men, including men with erections. However, when offered pictures of sexual activity (petting or coitus) or a film showing extended sexual activity (petting through coitus), both men and women registered quite similar responses (erection in men, vaginal lubrication in women). Blood flow changes in the genitalia of a significant sort were found in both men and women when they were exposed to erotic materials either on film or auditorily—and about the same proportions report a similar degree of arousal on verbal scales.

A similar gender difference in erotic response that seems to be changing is the previous "finding" that males seem relatively unresponsive to generalized body touching in sexual activity and have a greater genital focus for pleasure, while women are more responsive over the entire body, have orgasm more easily from nongenital contacts, and are less focused on the genitalia for arousal and orgasm. Much of the reporting of these differences is anecdotal and comes from therapeutic and clinical sources, but seems to be expressive of real differences in responsiveness between women and men.

241

In the past the lack of genital focus on the part of women was seen as one possible source of lack of orgasm, and many clinicians looked for ways to increase women's focus on their genitals—at one time the vagina, now the clitoris. More recently, however, the male focus on the genitals has become defined as a lack as well—a lack that might be producing both premature ejaculation and in some cases impotence when the capacity for erection becomes part of a performance demand. The sensate focus exercises are techniques to increase the range of male sexual response—to increase the sensitivity to general tactile stimuli (Masters and Johnson, 1970). At the present time there is considerable interest in the male nipple and breast as a newly defined erogenous zone.

Changing Contexts of Gender and Sexuality

The last seventy years has been not only the envelope in time that contains the bulk of research on human sexuality, but also a period in which the content and meaning of both sexual conduct and gender roles have changed as well. Research in sexual conduct and into gender-role differences, as well as the politicalization of both of these aspects of human conduct (by sexual enthusiasts as well as persons in the woman's movement), have changed not only the scientific perception of the phenomenon, but the experiences of the lay public as well. In modern societies what begins as the arcane knowledge of the scientific community quickly becomes part of the vulgate—the mass media quickly invade the quiet of science (and scientists invade the media) and promulgate whatever they choose.

Thus, as erotic materials have become more available (in part because scientists say that they are not harmful), the learning environments of men and women become more similar. The stimuli that arouse men become more accessible to women and are defined as part of their repertoire of deserved responses. In the same fashion there is an increased commonality of experience with the body as a source of erotic experiment. Masturbation was one of the reasons for the genital focus of men in sexual response; in contrast women less often had a strongly focused genital commitment. As masturbation grows more common, there will be an increase in genital focus among women, particularly those who enter therapy. For instance, there are now available a number of books for women that offer masturbation as a central component in sex therapy for preorgasmic women (Heiman, LoPiccolo, and

LoPiccolo, 1976). There is additional opportunity for younger women to learn about masturbation, through different channels than males, but channels that may result in similar sexual outcomes. At the same time there is pressure for men to reduce their commitment to the penis and assume a more sensate or sensual response to sexuality. While the majority of these innovations are occurring among adults, there is an increased likelihood that they will be promoted both as sex education and as covert information among the young.

As the homosexual community becomes increasingly politicized (in the sense of creating a collective image and individual conceptions as a sexual minority rather than as a class of perverts), there will be changes in the relation between gender roles and sexuality. Advanced sections of the gay community recognize that there is no fixed relation between masculinity and femininity and sexual object choice; as this discovery is generally accepted, there will be less need to imitate the content of heterosexual models. With the establishment of gay outposts in adolescence (at least in large urban centers), and as the information explosion about homosexuality grows, fewer persons will need to grow up estranged from one dimension of their lives because they have a minority preference in another.

The relation between gender roles and sexual conduct is a function of specific historical-cultural conditions, not the acting out of either a developmental or a biological program. Our dilemma is that we have taken the processes of a single set of historical examples (the United States and Western Europe for a century) and have assumed that they have universal validity. In this sense most of sex and gender research is antihistorical and anticultural. It is often insisted that men and women and sexual conduct are not only the same in similar places, but that all combinations of gender and sexual activity also have transhistorical meanings. The patterns of gender role and erotic development that we observe in Western European societies and their descendants are only a few of the potential designs available for humans.[6]

6. Ann Hollander has pointed out that clothing fashions of the 1950s are now viewed as unnatural, usually because they involved the use of metal-supported bodices, pantie-girdles, and the like. Fashions seem to have a very short "half-life" of naturalness. It would be very useful to have a sense of how long a sexual or gender practice has to be around

Further, there is evidence that even after having experienced the conventional divergent processes of gender and sexual development, there can be a remarkable convergence in female/male patterns of sexual conduct later in life. What appeared to Kinsey less than three decades ago as an inviolable difference in nervous systems turns out to be merely a difference in environmental contingencies. The convergence of patterns between men and women in various areas, and the use of learning programs in sex therapy, suggest the importance of viewing sex and gender through not only a social learning perspective, but also one that gives particular weight to the continuing environmental factors for either the maintenance of conduct or its change.

The theories that one uses provide the meanings for the evidence one examines. An environmental social learning model not only affects specific interpretations of specific information, but has a more significant set of consequences. Sexuality can be viewed not as a special domain of conduct with special theories, special researchers, special curricula, but rather more mundanely, as part of conventional social life. I am not suggesting that this change in gender roles and sexual conduct will be more *natural* in the sense that it conforms more closely to what human beings need in some evolutionary, developmental, or functional sense. All human environments are *artificial* and all modes of arranging gender roles and sexual conduct are arbitrary. Our current preferences seem to be moving us in the direction of a culture that will treat sexuality as a far less special form of conduct and in which greater equality will exist between men and women, boys and girls. As a result, both our theories and our facts about gender and sexuality will change as well.

References

Bieber, I. et al. 1962. *Homosexuality: A psychoanalytic study.* New York: Basic Books.

Brown, H. 1976. *Familiar faces, hidden lives.* New York: Harcourt Brace Jovanovich.

Clifford, R. 1975. *Female masturbation in developmental and clinical application.* Ph.D. dissertation, Department of Psychology, State University of New York—Stony Brook.

Dank, B. M. 1971. Coming out in the gay world. *Psychiatry* 34:3–21.

---

or approved before it assumes the status of the (or what are understood to be) biological or developmental phenomena.

Gagnon, J. H. 1971. The creation of the sexual in early adolescence. In *Twelve to sixteen: Early adolescence*, ed. J. Kagan and R. Coles. New York: Norton.

———. 1974. Scripts and the coordination of sexual conduct. In *1973 Nebraska symposium on motivation*, ed. J. K. Cole and R. Deinstbier. Lincoln: University of Nebraska Press.

———. 1975. Sex research and social change. *Arch. Sex. Behav.* 4: 111–141.

———. 1977. *Human sexualities.* Glenview, Ill.: Scott Foresman.

Gagnon, J. H., and Simon, W. 1973. *Sexual conduct: The social sources of human sexuality.* Chicago: Aldine.

Gagnon, J. H.; Simon, W.; and Berger, A. J. 1970. Some aspects of adjustment in early and later adolescence. In *The psychopathology of adolescence*, ed. J. Zubin and A. M. Freedman. Lincoln: University of Nebraska Press.

Heiman, J.; LoPiccolo, L.; and LoPiccolo, J. 1976. *Becoming orgasmic: A sexual growth program for women.* Englewood Cliffs, N.J.: Prentice-Hall.

Kinsey, A. C.; Pomeroy, W. R.; and Martin, C. E. 1948. *Sexual behavior in the human male.* Philadelphia: Saunders.

Kinsey, A. C.; Pomeroy, W. R.; Martin, C. E.; and Gebhard, P. H. 1953. *Sexual behavior in the human female.* Philadelphia: Saunders.

Lunde, D. T. 1975. Sex hormones, mood and behavior. In *Sexuality and psychoanalysis*, ed. E. T. Adelson. New York: Bruner Mazel.

Maccoby, E., and Jacklin, C. 1974. *The psychology of sex differences.* Stanford: Stanford University Press.

Masters, W., and Johnson, V. 1966. *Human sexual response.* Boston: Little, Brown.

———. 1970. *Human sexual inadequacy.* Boston: Little, Brown.

Money, J., and Ehrhardt, A. 1972. *Man and woman, boy and girl.* Baltimore: Johns Hopkins Press.

Robinson, P. 1976. *The modernization of sex.* New York: Harper and Row.

Simon, W., and Gagnon, J. H. 1967a. Homosexuality: The formulation of a sociological perspective. *J. Health Hum. Behav.* 8:177–185.

———. 1967b. Femininity in the lesbian community. *Social Probl.* 15: 212–221.

———. 1969. On psychosexual development. In *Handbook of socialization theory and research*, ed. D. A. Goslin. Chicago: Rand McNally.

Tiger, L., and Fox, R. 1971. *The imperial animal.* New York: Holt, Rinehart and Winston.

Victor, J. L. 1977. The social psychology of sexual arousal. In *Studies in symbolic interaction*, ed. N. Denzin. New York: J. A. L. Press.

Sexual Behavior as an Expression of Achievement Orientation

Jean Lipman-Blumen and Harold J. Leavitt

Conceptual frameworks, as Gagnon suggests, tend to predetermine at least two phenomena in the conduct of scientific inquiries: (1) the facts considered relevant, and (2) the possible interpretations of those facts. Gagnon quite appropriately suggests that sexual behavior must be understood in conjunction with the social codes established for sex roles. His paper outlines a process through which youngsters, by age three or four, are made aware of the self-labels "girl" and "boy." Later, Gagnon argues, a secondary, but pervasive, dimorphism is superimposed on sexual behavior by the social codes that prescribe and proscribe sex roles.

We should like to approach the same issues by offering a related perspective, drawn from a different conceptual domain. In applying that perspective to some of the same issues Gagnon raises, perhaps we can draw a complementary picture. The framework we are suggesting is a typology of achievement orientation, emanating from an interest in the presumably differing achievement patterns of women and men (Lipman-Blumen and Leavitt, 1976).

A Typology of Achievement Orientations

The relevance of an achievement typology to an understanding of sexual behavior rests, we propose, on at least two bases: (1) sexuality often is experienced, perceived, and expressed as an achievement, and vice versa;[1] and (2) both achievement and

1. The very language with which sexual behavior is described (e.g., "sexual conquests," "sexual exploits," "achieving an orgasm," "making her/him," "on the make," "achieving an erection," and—from an earlier

sexual behavior tend to be linked not only to one another, but also to rather distinctive gender stereotypes.

In a general way, we may distinguish at least two major types of achievement behavior, each of which probably encompasses a broad band of subtypes. The first we have called *direct achievement*. Here, an individual takes the initiative, actively and personally seeking to meet his/her achievement needs by acting directly upon the environment. The second type we have labeled *vicarious* or *relational achievement*, in which an individual indirectly or vicariously meets her/his achievement needs through relationships with other individuals with whom s/he usually identifies.

Vicarious achievers place primary emphasis upon relationships and secondary importance upon tasks or accomplishments. Direct achievers, by contrast, are primarily task- or accomplishment-oriented, and secondarily relationship-oriented. Vicarious achievement behavior involves using or facilitating the success of others, while direct behavior tends to focus upon confronting and shaping one's own environment.

The social codes for female and male sex roles often tend to channel women, both within the family and in the wider occupational context, into vicarious achievement roles, and men into direct achievement patterns. Elsewhere (Lipman-Blumen, 1973; Lipman-Blumen and Leavitt, 1976), we have described a "sexual brownie point" system that serves as a mechanism for keeping sex-role stereotypes securely in place. This achievement-sexuality scoring system allows points for masculinity and femininity when "correct" sex-role choices are made. As Figure 1 suggests, males who select direct achievement roles, such as airline pilot, receive a plus point for achievement and another plus for sexuality. By contrast, males entering vicarious achievement roles, like nursing, receive two minus points. They are seen neither as very masculine nor as very achieving.

---

period—"winning her hand") reflects achievement imagery. Conversely, the descriptions of achievement behavior often involve both positive and negative sexual references (e.g., "s/he is a fuck-up," "get fucked over," "get screwed," "s/he is a comer," "s/he has balls," "s/he is hot," "s/he is turned on to her/his work," "balls to the wall"). Power, often associated with specific types of achievement, is an acknowledged aphrodisiac, even beyond the city limits of Washington, D.C.

Gender of Role Occupant

ACHIEVEMENT ORIENTATION OF ROLE	Female		Male	
	SCORING DIMENSIONS		SCORING DIMENSIONS	
	Sexuality	Achievement	Sexuality	Achievement
Direct Achievement Role	−	+	+	+
Vicarious Achievement Role	+	−	−	−

From Lipman-Bluman, J., and Leavitt, H. J., 1976. Vicarious and direct achievement patterns in adulthood. *The Counseling Psychologist* 6:27.

Fig. 1. Sexuality-Achievement Scoring Mechanism

Sub-types of Vicarious and Direct Orientations

Vicarious and direct achievement orientations each subsume at least three identifiable types: altruistic vicarious, contributing vicarious, instrumental vicarious; instrumental direct, competitive direct, and intrinsic direct (see Figure 2). In what follows, we shall attempt to describe each type and to indicate its expression in sexual terms.

An *altruistic vicarious* orientation involves the "tendency to take satisfaction and pleasure from someone else's activities, qualities, and/or accomplishments as if they were one's own" and the ability to "derive pleasure simply from having a relationship with a direct achiever." "The relationship is primary; it is an end in itself" (Lipman-Blumen and Leavitt, 1976, p. 26). The selfless wife who conceives her role simply as being perpetually available to nurture "the great man" is a stereotypical illustration.

When we translate the altruistic vicarious achievement orientation into sexual terms, a primary example is the nonorgasmic partner who finds satisfaction simply by engaging in a relationship with a partner who achieves orgasmic release. Another

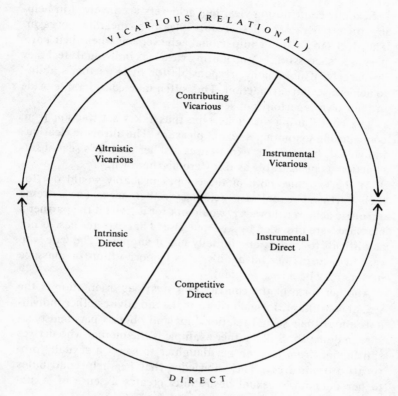

Fig. 2. Achievement (Sexual) Orientations

example is the "macho" father who takes pleasure in his son's sexual encounters.

The *contributing vicarious* achiever is characterized by enabling or facilitating behavior and attitudes toward the direct achiever. The contributing individual, like the altruistic one, takes pleasure in the characteristics and successes of the other individual as if they were his/her own. But in the case of the contributing person, the pleasure is derived primarily from the belief that s/he has contributed in some measure to the success of the direct achiever, if only by maintaining the relationship (Lipman-Blumen and Leavitt, 1976, p. 26).

Sexually contributing vicarious achievers are involved in helping their partners achieve sexual pleasure, including orgasm. They feel satisfaction and personal achievement when their partners are "successful." Contributing vicarious individuals feel they are largely, if not wholly, responsible for their partner's ability to achieve sexual satisfaction. They often take considerable pride in their own repertoires of sexual skills.

The contributing vicarious type thus takes satisfaction from contributing to another's sexual pleasure. The altruistic vicarious individual, by contrast, experiences his/her partner's sexual satisfaction as pleasurably as if it were his/her own.

At the extreme, both of these types probably would opt for their partners' sexual satisfaction over their own. The extreme altruistic achiever, however, would opt for it, even if the partner's pleasure were provided by someone else. That extreme case is not as difficult to find as one initially might suppose. The wife who casually accepts her husband's visits to porno films or massage parlors may be a case in point.

Another form of the contributing vicarious orientation is the sexual consultant, formal or informal, who advises other individuals about their sexual relationships and obtains personal pleasure in doing so. Still another example is the mother who derives satisfaction from helping her daughter to select a sexually provocative prom dress. The knowledge that her help contributes to her daughter's sexual desirability creates a sense of sexual achievement for the mother.

The *instrumental vicarious* achiever tends to use relationships as a means to other achievements. Such achievements may include security, status, money, and even other relationships. In the extreme instrumental vicarious case, there is no requirement of identification with the other person, nor even a dependency on the other person's satisfaction. The only requirement is that the relationship between the two serve as a conduit to the vicarious achiever's satisfaction. The instrumentally vicarious person may manipulate the relationship in order to achieve other ends, including those that the vicarious individual may feel unsuited to attempt on his/her own. The employee who marries the boss's daughter primarily for economic gain exemplifies this type, as does the stereotypical courtesan.

In the sexual realm, the instrumental vicarious individual tends to use the relationship to establish a secure source of sexual gratification. The relationship as a means to sex is more important than the relationship *per se*. The traditional masculine ploy of telling her he loves her simply to entice her to the bedroom falls within this instrumental vicarious category.

We have described the *instrumental direct* achiever as an individual who uses his/her "own achievements as a generalized means for achieving other goals, including power, status, and more success. The instrumental direct achiever uses whatever talents and success s/he has to meet her/his other needs. In a sense, this individual uses her/his direct achievement skills as a medium through which s/he can acquire relationships to people" (Lipman-Blumen and Leavitt, 1976, p. 28).

Transferring this achievement type to the sexual realm is not difficult. It is epitomized by the person who uses sex to secure or prolong a relationship. Such instrumental direct behavior often occurs when casual sexual encounters are initiated with the fanciful hope that they will lead to "meaningful" relationships.

A common variation of instrumental direct behavior is the use of other achievements, particularly power, to gain sexual (and other) relationships.[2]

The *competitive direct* achiever's most salient feature is his/her need to outdo a competitor. The competitive direct achiever often casts relationships in competitive terms and enjoys accomplishments only when they are better than another's. "The excitement of achievement is enhanced specifically by the fact that the success is accomplished within a competitive setting, proving that the individual is not only succeeding, but succeeding more than anyone else," or more than the specially selected competitor (Lipman-Blumen and Leavitt, 1976, p. 28).

Competitive direct individuals enjoy the sexual encounter most when they have outdone a competitor. The person who prefers sexual partners who must be won away from other relationships exemplifies this type. Competitive direct individuals often need to feel that their sexual prowess outshines all other lovers their

2. Henry Kissinger acknowledged this phenomenon when he said, "Without an office, you have no power, and I love power because it attracts women" (*Washington Post*, January 7, 1977).

partners may have known. The need to be "best," to prove their sexual superiority, often prompts them to select as sexual "targets" only those partners whose seduction represents a difficult test (and adds a special piquancy).

A variation on the competitive direct theme is the individual who expresses competitiveness toward another by trying to seduce the other's partner. The wife who becomes the object of her husband's colleague's sexual advances may be the pawn in the diffuse professional competition between the two men. Sexual competitiveness also may show up *within* the sexual relationship itself. (A: "I'll get you to bed no matter what." B: "No way.")

The *intrinsic direct* achiever derives satisfaction from the achievement or activity *per se*. This person is more task- than relationship-oriented and judges his/her performance against a certain standard of excellence, much like McClelland's (1953) high N achievement individual and Maslow's (1954) "self-actualizer." The intrinsic nature of the accomplishment is what attracts and satisfies the intrinsic direct type. People who use the intrinsic direct mode may also show altruistic vicarious patterns since they are capable of intrinsically valuing a relationship as well as a direct accomplishment. Unlike the competitive direct person, the intrinsic individual competes only against some impersonal standard, not against someone else.

When the intrinsic direct profile is transposed into the sexual realm, sexual activity becomes a pleasurable and satisfying end in itself. Sexual fulfillment is the goal. The relationship is merely the medium through which sexual activity occurs, just as the laboratory is the context within which the intrinsic direct scientist's work is pursued.

The sexually intrinsic direct individual probably is interested in the myriad aspects of sexuality. S/he finds the development and growth of sexuality a satisfying activity in and of itself. The sexual intrinsic direct type probably applies the same single-mindedness to sexual activity that the intrinsic direct achiever brings to the nonsexual domain. S/he may spend considerable time planning and conducting ever more "interesting" or "satisfying" sexual encounters.

Salience, Flexibility, Range, and Intensity

Our typology does not assume uniform or linear human development. All we assume is that persons who early on achieve more or less easy and full satisfaction from relationships will tend to prefer and practice relational or vicarious means to get what they want in life. And people who, in early life, find less positive reinforcement through relationships and more from direct action upon their environment will tend to prefer and practice direct achievement strategies.

We suggest that individuals thus develop a salient achievement orientation involving one or more segments in our circle diagram but that other orientations are available to them *situationally* and/or *simultaneously*. Some examples might clarify further what we mean. A person who is a competitive direct achiever in an occupational situation often will transform her/his achievement orientation to an altruistic or contributing vicarious type within the family context.

In sexual terms, the same individual can be "competitive direct" in seeking a sexual partner for him/herself, but can be "altruistic" or "contributing vicarious" with respect to the sexual experiences of the same-sex child. Thus, *situational* activation refers to the mobilization and use of diverse achievement orientations by the same individual in different settings, at different times, under different conditions, with different individuals.

In addition, diverse orientations may be mobilized *simultaneously* (at the same time, in one setting, with one individual, and so on). For example, the individual who just "loves sex" and values highly his/her own sexual satisfaction *simultaneously* can take pleasure from contributing to the sexual arousal and satisfaction of his/her partner and also enjoy his/her partner's achieving sexual satisfaction through autoeroticism.

We posit considerable individual variation in the salience, range, flexibility, and intensity of achievement (sexual) orientations. For example, some individuals probably encompass a wider arc on the achievement (sexual) orientations "circle" than others. In addition, differences are likely among individuals in the intensity they bring to any of the six sexual orientations. We believe it would be possible to develop individual sexual orientation profiles that take into account the salience, range, flexibility, and intensity of the six orientations. Some measure of enrichment of sexual life (somewhat analogous to the "balanced personality") presumably could be derived from such a strategy. An alternative to "traditional" sex therapy might focus upon developing different saliencies, ranges, flexibilities, and intensities between two partners.

Relation to Sex Roles

Until recently, stereotypically defined sex roles tended to lock women into vicarious and men into direct achievement patterns. Our circle diagram suggests, however, that there is a point at which vicarious (relational) and direct achievement patterns probably meet. With continuing social change in this area, we expect to see increased movement across previously sex-linked barriers.

When we think about sexual behavior, the stereotypes of the passive, altruistic, or long-suffering female and the aggressive, self-interested, and eager male come to mind. Available data do not permit adequate assessment of new currents in gender-bound sexual behavior; however, some recent evidence (Hite, 1976) suggests that males and females do not fall neatly on their respective halves of the sexual orientations circle. More specifically, we expect there still may be more women than men in the altruistic and contributing vicarious segments, and more men than women in the competitive direct one. The intrinsic direct segment, however, probably is shared almost equally by both sexes. To complicate matters, more males than females traditionally have approached sex from a vicarious instrumental position, while more females than males have used the instrumental direct approach. Thus, we think more men than women have used relationships to "get sex," and more females than males have used sex to "get relationships."[3] As a result, there is no neat, compartmentalized (and stereotyped) division of sexual orientations according to gender roles.

We might speculate on why private sexual behavior is less gender-bound than other achievement behaviors. We acknowledge that there is a general historical belief in the sexual "passiv-

3. We are treating sex and relationships as two conceptually distinct entities, in contradistinction to the usual assumption that sexual interaction necessarily involves a relationship. Prostitution demonstrates that sex and relationships are separable.

ity" of the female and "aggressivity" of the male. However, the taboos against explicit discussion of the details of sexuality have prevented the development of highly specified private sexual behavior codes, thus, allowing greater diversity in private sexual behavior of individuals. This diversity stands in marked contrast to the specificity of nonsexual gender-role socialization, which has straightjacketed the more public and observable modes of behavior.

The social codes for male and female behavior, which left an historical imprint on sexual patterns, were not totally effective. As Gagnon suggests, there always were some females who masturbated and some who acknowledged arousal by erotic or pornographic materials. And, undoubtedly, those who violated the general codes of "passive female" and "aggressive male" commonly were thought (and perhaps thought themselves) deviant. As feminist criticism weakens sex-role stereotypes in the more public behavioral modes, sexual behavior, practiced beyond public scrutiny, can expand even more readily across gender-bound boundaries. But sexual behavior, in turn, influences sex-role stereotypes.

The fact that sexual orientations are less locked-in to rigid gender-role proscriptions is a hopeful and healthy sign. It suggests that in our more "instinctive" behavior there is greater likelihood of breaking through the artificial, gender-bound codes described by Gagnon. Perhaps some beneficial "fall-out" will occur from our growing ability to discuss openly the details of sexual behavior. The recognition that sexual behavior is growing even less encumbered by sex-role stereotypes may spread to other behavioral domains. Eventually, we may even expect behavior that meets the needs of the situation, place, and person—behavior unfettered by traditional sex-role stereotypes.

The conceptual scheme presented here derives from work in achievement behavior. This is merely a preliminary attempt to apply a somewhat different conceptual framework in order to evoke alternative or supplementary interpretations of "facts" we collect under the rubric of "sexual behavior."

A fruitful paradigm, however, not only answers some old questions; it also raises new ones. For example, what can we expect as more women become predominantly intrinsic direct achievers, sexually and nonsexually? How will that change mesh with the achievement and sexual orientations of males with whom they interact? How will changing male and female achievement orientations influence sexual orientations, and vice versa? Will changing gender-role codes drive the changes in sexual behavior and achievement behavior, or will sexual and achievement behavior change the outlines of gender roles? Which way shall we draw the causal arrows? These and other questions in the sexual behavior/achievement behavior/gender roles matrix remain to be answered. We hope that the typology presented here raises useful questions and the promise of some answers.

References

Hite, Shere. 1976. *The Hite report: A nationwide study of female sexuality.* New York: Macmillan.

Lipman-Blumen, Jean. 1973. The vicarious achievement ethic and non-traditional roles for women. Paper read at the Eastern Sociological Association annual meeting, New York, April 1973.

Lipman-Blumen, Jean, and Leavitt, Harold J. 1976. Vicarious and direct achievement patterns in adulthood. *Counseling Psychologist* 6:26–32.

Maslow, Abraham. 1954. *Motivation and personality.* New York: Harper.

McClelland, D. C.; Atkinson, R. A.; and Lowell, E. L. 1953. *The achievement motive.* New York: Appleton-Century-Crofts.

Sociological Perspectives on Sex and Its Psychosocial Derivatives

Lee Rainwater

Sociologists are interested in the multiple ways that sex and its psychosocial derivatives affect and are affected by social structures and institutions and the various social roles men, women, boys, and girls play in modern society. Gender role and sexual goals and behavior are both vital interests held by the society's members and also important factors for understanding other kinds of interests and for understanding issues of policy and social control in societies. Although the history of scholarly attention to sexual behavior has tended to be extremely narrow in focus on sex as such, the sociologist tries to make connections between sex and other aspects of life, perceiving, for example, politics in the bedroom and sexuality in the situation room.

The papers presented at the conference by Gagnon, Simon and Miller,[1] and Lipman-Blumen and Leavitt make these complex interrelations amply clear. They also stress another theme. The sociological perspective on sex and its psychosocial derivatives serves to highlight issues of variability and openness in gender role and sex behavior and in the relationships between these and other aspects of social life. This variability can be observed within particular individuals' life cycles and among persons who can be assumed to have the same gender identity. The sociological perspective is specifically skeptical concerning some of the so-called uniformities of gender and sexual development putatively based on biological and developmental psychological factors. In what

1. Since the Simon and Miller paper does not appear in this volume, inquiries regarding its availability should be directed to Patricia Y. Miller or William Simon.

follows I propose to emphasize what seem to me to be the most important issues raised by the papers presented at the conference.

Variance in Sex-Related Behavior

Sociologists interested in sexual behavior are concerned to show that the variance in sex-related behavior is not so tightly associated with gender roles as we tend to assume on commonsense grounds. Much of the discussion of gender role development and psychosocial development of sexuality implies that the developmental models account for essentially all of the variance in the relevant behavior. In fact, however, research tends to focus on differences in means between, say, boys and girls or younger and older ages and to reify those average differences as laws. The sociologist, instead, is likely to raise the question of how much of the variance in particular behaviors of interest is linked to gender or to developmental stages—100 percent? 75 percent? 25 percent? 5 percent? Variability is not simply an academic issue but has important implications for the well-being of members of society. To the extent that ideas concerning "normal" gender roles and development have credence, individuals whose behavior deviates from those standards may pay a price for their deviation.

Three principal types of variation are cited in this volume: one having to do with biography, one with gender as a predictor of behavior, and one concerning the connection between sexual behavior and its personal relevance.

Variation in a Life History

Gagnon stresses the openness of adaptations in an individual's sexual biography. A life-history approach to sexual biographies suggests not that stages follow in an orderly sequence, one upon another, or that sexual behavior shows a great deal of stability, but rather that individuals prove to be highly responsive to their immediate environments, and that if those environments are disparate from one life stage to another, then sexual identity and behavior are likely to change. Individual biographies reflect complex interweavings of sameness and change and cannot be understood through a primary focus on intrapsychic processes without attention to the immediate and powerful influences of the social worlds through which individuals move.

258

Because most research on sexual behavior covers only very short spans in individual lives, and because it focuses so much on establishing average differences between groups rather than on the question of explaining the variance of behavior, it is very difficult to know how much consistency there is in individuals' sexual biographies; but unsystematic sampling of the sexual biographical data available from various sources demonstrates that consistency is not nearly so high as is suggested by most of the literature on sexual development.

The Gender-neutral Role

The second sense in which putatively sex-related behavior shows a high degree of variability has to do with gender role. Here the most general way of phrasing the issue is to ask, for a range of human behaviors, how much and in what ways those behaviors are linked to gender. How salient is gender for various kinds of behavior? Such discussion often seems to assume that gender is highly salient, but the nature of that salience is not always obvious. While it is true that much behavior is gender-coded in the same way that much of the environment is, that coding may or may not be an adequate predictor of behavior.

It may be useful to distinguish the extent to which behavior is gender-linked in terms of its gross characteristics, in terms of its more detailed characteristics, and in terms of the style with which the particular behavior is carried out.

There was a time, for example, when washing dinner dishes in families was strongly linked to gender roles. That link is not as strong today. It might be that males and females wash dishes in a somewhat different way so that although the statement "I washed the dishes tonight" could not be predicted very well from knowing the gender of an individual, an observation that an individual washed dishes with care, not chipping any and drying them carefully, might be predicted by knowing the gender—but probably not very accurately. Or, there may be something intrinsically masculine or feminine about the style with which the dishes were washed. The gender coding of style, however, should not obscure the gender neutrality of the activity. It is likely that a great deal of human behavior is in a sense gender-neutral, and that in modern times increasingly larger proportions of individual behavior repertories are not gender-linked.

Yet individuals in modern society continue to know their gender as certainly as in the past. Thus, the connection between specifically gender-linked role behavior and relatively gender-neutral role behavior becomes an important subject for study. Related to this issue is the issue of variability within the overall rubrics of male and female genders—that is, the question of particular ways of being male or female. One of the reasons that gender is not highly predictive of behavior is that societies develop different recipes for being of one or the other sex. There is much evidence that the most masculine and feminine of identities are parodies, not ideals. The world is populated by a large number of different male and female types equally persuaded of their essential maleness and femaleness and each readily recognizable by others as valid representatives of their particular gender.

Unfortunately, most research on the development of gender role tends to oversimplify this range of types. We might get further in understanding so-called deviant gender identities—effeminate males and masculine women—by trying to identify what is true of those identities that is not true of any of the "proper" masculine and feminine identities.

It would be useful to look upon both gender and sexuality as particular resources individuals draw upon in constructing their own sense of identity. It is likely that each individual's use of cultural and biological gender resources and sexual resources is idiosyncratic, both in terms of what is selected out of all that biology and culture make available, and in terms of the particular ways that such selections are combined with other identity materials. As Simon and Miller emphasized in their presentation, this highly idiosyncratic construction produces each individual's particular version of gender identity, role scripting, and role performance. Any meaningful understanding of human sexual development requires an appreciation of the complexities, subtleties, and dynamics of these constructions.

While much research has emphasized the ways in which parent-child relations instruct children concerning their gender identities, within families children often find the greatest degree of acceptance, and perhaps encouragement, for the development of relatively gender-free aspects of their repertories. Similarly, school, for all its "sexism," in some of its functioning systematically downplays the importance of gender identity by emphasizing a variety of achievements for which gender is explicitly defined as irrelevant. Indeed, the struggle against sexism in the schools is specifically designed to expand the already existing gender-free area.

The Meaning of Behavior

The third way in which the sociological perspective emphasizes variability of sex and its psychosocial derivatives has to do with the connection between behavior and its meaning to the individual (and to others). Particular kinds of gender-role and sexual behavior can have different meanings to different persons who appear to do the same thing. Research that focuses very narrowly on behavior in the Kinsey tradition and does not inquire into meaning can distort the human experiences that it purports to describe. Inevitably, one makes assumptions about meaning from the description of behavior; but there is no correspondence between behavior and meaning.

Once the issue of meaning is introduced to the study of sexual behavior, the variability of sexuality is even more striking. Simon and Miller emphasized in their presentation, and the discussion further illustrated, that much analysis of sexual behavior is cased in a framework in which erotic components are underplayed. Yet we know that the rich intrapsychic processes associated with sexual behavior are built around complex sets of erotic meanings. The individual's sexual biography is to be understood as unfolding over time. Erotic scenarios are constructed from the cultural resources available and the situational possibilities of any given time. Research abstracts particular behavioral components from this richly textured cultural-social-psychological process. In the process of that abstraction, understanding of the human behavior involved may be obliterated.

Abstraction of issues and gender and sex from the individual's other role relationships and the institutions in which those roles are acted out often vitiates the effort to understand sexuality. Issues of gender and sex are, of course, intimately related to issues of the family as an institution in society and of family relationships. Even in modern times sexual behavior is closely monitored in terms of its implications for family roles and appropriate behavior on the part of children, spouses, and others.

The impact of family and sex on each other is perhaps not as

261

great as in the past because of development in contraception technology, but it is still considerable. Intertwined sexual, marital, and parental aspirations continue to loom large in Americans' conceptions of how one achieves self-fulfillment and a gratifying life. It is unlikely that in the thinking of the individual members of society these three aspects are highly segregated, yet in much of the social science literature they are.

The connections between the worlds of sex and work are not as pervasive as those of gender and work. An historic change has taken place in the past quarter-century in the sexual division of labor so that the old dichotomy between male provider and female homemaker is no longer maintained. In the United States a minority of all households contain a father who is a breadwinner and a stay-at-home homemaker-mother. Changes in the relationships among individuals, family, and work have had and will continue to have important effects on the content of gender identity and very likely on sexual behavior.

The issue of gender stereotypes and gender identity in connection with women's participation in the labor market has received a great deal of attention of late. Much less is known, however, about the interrelations of sexuality and work roles. There is good reason to believe that the changing division of labor should have important effects on the gender and sexual socialization of children. Those connections, however, are not likely to be established, as opposed to hypothesized, so long as research in human sexual development is so narrowly defined that it does not incorporate a focus on other aspects of the socialization of children and the role relationships of adult men and women.

Directions for New Research

Directions for future research follow from the themes of the change and variability in gender and sex behavior, the importance of the erotic in understanding the psychosocial significance of sexual behavior, and the interrelation of sexual aspects of life to other roles and institutions.[2]

The greatest research need is for social accounting. Most of the discussion of changing sex roles and behavior in the United States proceeds on the basis of sketchy, almost nonexistent, evidence.

2. These recommendations are based on discussions with John Gagnon, Jean Lipman-Blumen, Patricia Y. Miller, and William Simon.

Researchers and others will often be misled in trying to understand these issues so long as systematic social surveys dealing with sexual experience are not done on a regular basis—say, every five years. There is an instructive parallel in the periodic surveys dealing with fertility and contraceptive behavior and expectations. These surveys allow a precise charting in changes in family-size planning and in contraceptive behavior. Similar surveys should be carried out on the subject of sexual experience and aspiration. The goal of the surveys would be, first of all, to provide descriptive information concerning sexual behavior. The data concerning sex should then be systematically related to information concerning individuals' changes in the life cycle and their family situations, and similarly, should be related to individuals' positions in the stratification system and in the labor market.

Ideally, such a survey of sexual experience should be carried out cross-nationally in other industrial countries because many of the changes taking place in sex and family roles are taking place in a number of different countries, and a much better understanding of trends could be achieved from a comparative study.

Such a major survey should have the highest priority. Second-best alternatives would involve much scaled-down sets of measures, which could be added on to other kinds of surveys. Many important questions concerning sexual experience could be answered on a basis of as few as a dozen questions in a survey that also involved the collection of relevant family and socioeconomic information.

If such data should become available to investigators from both the survey report and computer tapes, it would be possible to provide much more accurate information to researchers with more specialized interests as a context for their work, and much better guidance for public policy related to those issues than is now available.

The analysis of this kind of survey data should focus on understanding the complex of interrelations throughout the life cycle of the sex, family, and work roles of males and females. In order to deepen the understanding that can come from survey research, however, it is also necessary to design research that relies on more qualitative methods.

Here the focus should be on understanding sexual behavior and the erotic in the lives of individuals at different points in the life cycle. The interest is not in easily countable behavior, but rather in the meaning of sexuality in people's lives.

One strategy for this kind of research would involve studies at particular points of transition in the life cycle—say, the ages of ten to fourteen, eighteen to twenty-two, the immediate post-parental years, and so on.

Traditional interviewing methods—either structured or unstructured—would probably be inadequate for such studies because the subjective aspects of sexual experience are subject to a high degree of conventionalizing both in memory and in the telling. Methods should be developed to avoid this kind of bias. The use of diaries and repeated interviews would be one way of developing a more accurate picture of the role of sexuality in individuals' life histories. A number of small-scale exploratory surveys might be carried out by different investigators.

There is also need for systematic historical studies of issues related to gender and sex roles. There is a great deal of interest these days in the "new social history," and in that sense, the time is ripe for work along this line. Much of what we think about sex and its psychosocial derivatives involves various assumptions about what has been true in the past and how things have changed. The new social history, however, has time and again struck down conventional wisdom about how things used to be. It would be well to expose our everyday assumptions in this area also to the systematic investigation of historical research.

Finally, there is need for research that examines the interrelations among public policy, gender, and sex roles. There have been studies, and there should be more, concerning law and sexual behavior. Interrelated changes in the area of sex and family behavior have important implications for developing new public policies. It is important that systematic attention be paid to the extent to which old and new policies play a constructive or destructive role in individuals' pursuits of self-fulfillment and personal well-being. The wide range of relevant policies embraces schooling and job training, earnings, fringe benefits, taxation, child care, and social insurance and public transfers.

Part V
Anthropological Perspectives

It is fitting that this volume, which began with cross-species comparisons, should end with cross-cultural comparisons. As the evolutionary approach attempts to clarify our phylogenetic background, the anthropological approach helps us to understand our culture in relation to other cultures. We turn to anthropologists to find out how expressions of gender and sexual behavior are shaped by cultural contexts.

All three contributors to this section are anthropologists. Judith Shapiro's contribution is a comprehensive review of the more recent anthropological literature dealing with issues like the position of women in the hierarchical power structure, sex-linked social roles, cultural definitions of maleness and femaleness, and differential allocation of knowledge between men and women. The focus is on the relationship between the sexes, but not on their sexual relationships. Shapiro has emphasized the importance of looking at patterns of sexual differentiation as meaningful systems, with interpretation considered as important a goal as explanation.

Compared with the other behavioral sciences, anthropology has had a large share of distinguished women investigators and leaders. In addition, Shapiro points out that there has been a recent impetus for more focused anthropological research on women by women to correct what is felt to be an androcentric bias within the discipline. Shapiro thus reiterates for anthropology what was expressed earlier by Jane Lancaster about primate research: In both cases newer approaches show females —nonhuman primate and human—in a different light.

Robert LeVine views Shapiro's contribution and the literature it surveys as characteristic of recent ethnographic writing, which ignores the erotic side of life. Alternatively, ethnographers have merely described some facets of sexual behavior with no attempt at further theoretical analysis. The net effect is the "absence in contemporary anthropology of a coherent theoretical framework in which to collect and analyse cross-cultural data regarding human sexual behavior."

LeVine offers an approach that examines the varieties of cross-cultural meanings given to sexual conduct as well as to gender, and focuses on how these meanings and adult patterns of behavior are acquired by children. LeVine's perspective is thus developmental and predicated on the existence of trans-culturally valid universal principles governing the unfolding of the life cycle. It is cross-cultural research that makes possible the elucidating of these governing principles. LeVine also illustrates how anthropological research (in this case his work with the Gusii children of Kenya) can act as a control for testing the validity of concepts like the critical-period hypothesis discussed by Luria.

Beatrice Whiting also is dubious about how directly Shapiro's sources contribute to our learning about sexuality. Yet she sees the relevance of the work of this new generation of anthropologists to our understanding of the changing roles of men and women during the life span and the significance of new detailed information on concepts of the nature of men and women and their relationship to each other.

Whiting's own perspective is more compatible with LeVine's in its commitment to detailed cross-cultural comparison and prediction. Of particular relevance to the theme of this volume is her work with John Whiting on cross-sex identity.

In their discussion of new directions for research, Whiting, LeVine, and Shapiro point out the problems attendant upon doing research in sexuality in cross-cultural settings. A similar complication exists nearer home when the sexual life of various ethnic minorities is to be studied. We probably know less about these components of our own culture than we know about more remote people. Yet such research has proven particularly difficult, and the lack of representation is sadly apparent in this volume, even though some attempt was made to include an ethnic minority viewpoint, and Chester Pierce added that perspective to our conference discussion.

As LeVine concludes the anthropologists' collective comments, "Scientific research on human sexual behavior remains a neglected and vulnerable enterprise. . . ." It does indeed. But we hope the active involvement of individuals of the caliber of contributors to this volume will help to bring about changes long overdue.—H. A. K.

Cross-Cultural Perspectives on Sexual Differentiation

Judith Shapiro

The feminist movement of the 1960s and 1970s provided a new impetus for studies of sex differences, and the body of literature from recent work of social and cultural anthropologists shows this influence in a number of ways. First of all, the research focus is on women; the social and cultural dimensions of maleness are often dealt with implicitly rather than explicitly. Moreover, much of the recent cross-cultural research is not only about women, but by women, and in some sense, for women. Women anthropologists have been concerned with correcting what they feel has been an androcentric bias in their discipline, and many have also sought to make their research relevant to contemporary social problems. Their work shows a preoccupation with such themes as power, status, and inequality. Some studies underline the degree of power that women exercise; others attempt to come to grips with dominance and subordination in relationships between the sexes. Attempts are made to arrive at an understanding of the general status of women in particular societies and to compare societies in this regard.

The studies I shall discuss have been ordered into four categories: (1) economic and ecological approaches to the cross-cultural investigation of sexual differentiation; (2) analyses of the relationship between sex differences and social roles; (3) studies of the cultural definition of maleness and femaleness, in which sex is approached as a symbolic system; (4) communications perspectives that deal with the differential allocation of knowledge between men and women.

The term *sexual differentiation* is used here to refer to what might more carefully be termed *gender differentiation*. The terms *sex* and *gender*, when used contrastively, serve to distinguish biological differences between males and females from patterns of social, cultural, and psychological differentiation that bear some relationship to such biological differences. In practice, the term *sex* is commonly used to cover both of these concepts and I use it this way myself, reserving the narrower definition for passages that address the relationship between biological differences and gender attributes.

Materialist Approaches to Sexual Differentiation

A number of recent studies have as their major purpose an attempt to discover and explain cross-cultural differences and similarities in the activity patterns and social positions of men and women. They focus on those aspects of social life that appear most amenable to objective description and comparative treatment and see in economic roles the key to the relationship between the sexes in society. This relationship is stated in terms of the degree of male dominance in particular societies, or, conversely, in terms of the degree of "status" that women enjoy.

Two of the more comprehensive efforts in this direction are *Female of the Species* by M. Kay Martin and Barbara Voorhies, and *Women and Men: An Anthropologist's View* by Ernestine Friedl. Both studies propose a causal chain from ecological adaptation and technology, to the sexual division of labor, to the differential allocation of power between the sexes and the general status of men and women in society. They take as their point of departure a classification of societies into the major subsistence types recognized by cultural evolutionist theory: hunting and gathering (or foraging), horticultural, agricultural, pastoral, and industrial. Friedl concentrates on the first two types, while Martin and Voorhies include all of them within their comparative enterprise. There is some difference in the way the respective authors deal with economic roles. Martin and Voorhies place primary emphasis on participation in productive activities, although they realize that it is also important to consider the degree to which members of each sex exercise control over the products of their own labor. Friedl focuses more sharply on patterns of exchange. In her view, the degree of male dominance in a society varies inversely with women's participation in extradomestic exchange, that is, the allocation of goods outside of the restricted household sphere.

Both books show that there is significant variation in the economic roles of the sexes within such broadly defined subsistence adaptations as foraging and horticulture, and thus contribute to dispelling the familiar stereotypes that have developed in this regard. One such influential and persistent stereotype that has gone by the boards in recent years is the man-the-hunter and woman-the-economic-dependent view of human social organization before the advent of food production. It is now more widely recognized that women's gathering and, in a few cases, hunting activities play a central role in the subsistence of foraging peoples; this, in turn, has led to a reappraisal of evolutionary reconstructions. That this recognition of women's economic role in hunting and gathering societies was so long in coming has been attributed to ethnocentrism and male bias in anthropology (see also Slocum, 1975; Gough, 1975).

Friedl proposes a typology of foraging groups, based on the following patterns of division of labor by sex: (1) men and women collect plants separately; male hunting is minimal; (2) men and women work together in communal task forces to acquire a sufficient segment of subsistence; (3) women gather more than half the food supply; men's hunting accounts for 20 to 40 percent of subsistence; (4) men's hunting provides almost all food; women process all food and skins. Male dominance is concluded to be greatest among peoples of type 4. According to Friedl, societies of this type give men the greatest advantage in distributive activities because of the male monopoly over hunting and the high prestige accorded to game as a scarce or irregularly available resource. Societies of type 2 are, in her view, those most characterized by equality between the sexes.

Friedl's analysis of variation among horticultural societies involves similar considerations. She contrasts groups in which men raise only prestige crops while women raise staple crops, with groups in which both sexes raise staple crops and prestige crops are absent. Martin and Voorhies also emphasize the importance of the distinction between subsistence and prestige spheres of the economy in their treatment of horticultural systems. They connect the development of the prestige sector with the increasing productivity of the system and propose a correlation between productivity and the economic subordination of women. They see this subordination as a function of women's involvement in activities relating to the domestic economy and men's monopoly of activities

271

associated with wider economic institutions. As Martin and Voorhies put it, "In those situations where women are confined to strictly domestic economic activities, we begin to see the development of the basic male-female role dichotomy characteristic of more complex societies. Namely, the exclusion of women from major economic-event systems outside the household signals their increasing isolation from central roles in other societal institutions as well" (p. 240).

The advent of intensive agriculture completes the process of subordination, according to Martin and Voorhies. They claim that intensive cultivation based on a plow and irrigation technology is associated with a highly consistent pattern of division of labor, in which productive work outside the home is carried out largely by men. In agricultural systems, they say, "women dropped out of the main stream of production for the first time in the history of cultural evolution"; they claim, furthermore, that "[the] conceptual distinction of domestic and extradomestic labor, or what we call the inside-outside dichotomy, had the effect of isolating the sexes from one another, and women from public life" (p. 290). It should be pointed out that their discussion of agricultural societies is concentrated heavily on Europe and the Middle East, which raises Galton's problem concerning the independence of cases advanced to support a hypothesis. (For a more complete discussion of Martin and Voorhies, see Shapiro, 1975.)

The relationship between developments within horticultural systems and the socioeconomic evolution of sex roles has been addressed also by C. S. Lancaster, in a comparative analysis of sub-Saharan societies (Lancaster, 1976). Like Friedl and Martin and Voorhies, Lancaster stresses the distinction between subsistence activities and prestige economics and relates social dominance to dominance in the latter sphere. He also insists on the importance of distinguishing among horticultural systems in terms of their productivity, connecting intensified production to population pressure and competition over resources. Another point addressed by Lancaster, and by Martin and Voorhies as well, is the relationship between descent rules and the productivity of horticultural systems. Both studies find that intensified production correlates with patriliny, while systems with matrilineal descent tend to be found at the lower end of the scale.

Based on his understanding of variation within the class of horticultural systems, Lancaster develops a critique of the entire relationship between subsistence activities and political economy. In his view, there is no necessary connection between the two in societies whose subsistence centers around foraging or simple horticulture. Male dominance may be a common pattern in such societies, but Lancaster does not see it as a necessary one; he believes, on the contrary, that there is considerable latitude with regard to the sociopolitical roles of men and women. It is only with the development of more intensive horticulture, commonly characterized as "incipient agriculture," that subsistence can be analyzed in terms of political economy and that direct connections can be sought between the respective roles of the sexes in subsistence and the power relations that obtain between them.

The arguments presented by Lancaster and by Martin and Voorhies place the material conditions for a general pattern of male dominance at a relatively recent point in human history— not quite so recent as claimed by Marxist theorists who associate the division between public and private domains with capitalism, but recent in contrast to evolutionist reconstructions that relate male dominance to the importance of hunting during the early stages of human social life.[1] Lancaster's argument, in addition, draws attention to a problem implicit in the studies of Friedl and of Martin and Voorhies, namely, the limited usefulness of traditional subsistence-based categories for understanding patterns of sex role differentiation. The cultural evolutionist typology does, to be sure, provide a convenient ordering device for cross-cultural data, but if the goal is both to identify significant variations in the sexes' respective involvement in the economy and to interpret these variations in political terms, then a more sophisticated approach to the analysis of economic systems is necessary.

1. Some anthropologists have attributed patterns of economically based male dominance in certain Third World areas to the impact of colonialism and involvement in capitalist economic systems (Boserup, 1970; Bossen, 1975; S. Brown, 1975; Rubbo, 1975; Remy, 1975). See also Murphy and Murphy, 1974 for an analysis of how the participation of a South American Indian group in the regional economy of Brazil has led to a greater economic dependence of wives upon their husbands, and LeVine, 1966, for a comparative study of the effects of socioeconomic change on the respective roles of the sexes in East and West Africa.

Anthropologists engaged in the cross-cultural study of men's and women's economic roles have had to consider how these roles are affected by the reproductive division of labor. Judith Brown (1970b) has shown that women tend to be involved in the kinds of productive activities that can be combined with child care; she claims that women's contribution to production is greatest when activities of this sort are central to subsistence. Lancaster makes a similar point in his discussion of the economic preconditions for male dominance. Sanday (1974), who argues that women's greater involvement in reproductive activities puts men in a strategic position to obtain control over resources, has sought to discover factors that mitigate this situation. The relationship between women's reproductive and economic roles has been examined from the other side by Nerlove (1974) and by Friedl, who point out that reproductive patterns can be affected by women's economic activities. Talmon's (1965, 1972) research on the Israeli kibbutz presents one of the more detailed analyses of the interaction between women's reproductive roles and the demands of a particular socioeconomic system. (For a discussion of Talmon's and other attempts to explain sex-role differentiation in the kibbutz, see Shapiro, 1976c.)

The Meaning of Status

In materialist or economic theories of sex role differentiation, reference is commonly made to the *status* of each sex in society. The term *status* is not, however, used in a clear and consistent manner in the literature. In some cases, differences in economic roles are themselves taken as markers of differential status; the position of women is thus said to be strong insofar as they play a central role in production or exercise authority over the allocation of resources. Other studies involve some separate notion of status, which is said to be correlated with subsistence or economic roles. Actually, what one generally encounters is a shuttling back and forth between the two approaches within a single work. It is also common to find status treated as a dependent variable without explicit definition.

Sanday (1974) has attempted to operationalize the concept of status, listing the following four components, which she feels can be studied objectively within the tradition of large-scale cross-cultural survey research: (1) female material control, defined as the ability to allocate things beyond the domestic unit; (2) demand for female produce—again, beyond the family unit; (3) female political participation; (4) female solidarity groups devoted to female political or economic interests (p. 192).[2] Other kinds of considerations are, however, evident in many attempts to evaluate women's status cross-culturally. These have to do, on the one hand, with the respective value accorded to the sexes in different cultures, and on the other hand, with how "well off" women in various societies feel themselves to be. The problem is that such matters cannot be handled satisfactorily with the analytic tools and methodological strategies characteristic of large-scale cross-cultural survey research.

There have as yet been no successful attempts to correlate the structuring of economic roles with cultural conceptions of maleness and femaleness. We encounter in the literature statements like the observation by Martin and Voorhies that in agricultural societies "an elaborate mythology concerning the natural inferiority of women takes shape" (p. 277); such mythologies are, however, by no means limited to societies based on this form of subsistence activity. An examination of women's subjective experience of their lives would involve extensive psychological research, which anthropologists working within materialist paradigms have tended to neglect.

Because there is no explicit and agreed-upon standard for comparing the general status of the sexes in different societies, interpretations tend to be ad hoc and the same society may be evaluated in different ways by different authors. The Eskimo, for example, are seen by Friedl as presenting a clear case of male dominance (a stage 4 foraging society, as defined above), while Jean Briggs, an ethnographer who has done field work with them, emphasizes the balance and complementarity between the sexes (Briggs, 1974). The Bemba of Central Africa, whom Friedl focuses on to illustrate the kind of horticultural society in which the status of women is high, are elsewhere contrasted with the Iroquois, in order to show that the position of Bemba women leaves much to be desired when compared with that of their

2. This analysis of female status is a further development of earlier work, in which Sanday proposed a correlation between high female status and a balanced contribution of the two sexes to subsistence (Sanday, 1973).

North American counterparts (Brown, 1970a). Martin and Voorhies conclude that the status of women in matrilineal societies is
almost universally high, but Alice Schlegel (1972) has attempted
to identify and account for what she regards as significant variations in authority patterns and female autonomy in societies
with matrilineal descent.

Judgments of the respective status of the sexes in other societies
are likely to be skewed by the current concerns and goals of wom-
en anthropologists and, more generally, by our own culturally
derived views of what makes for social superiority and inferiority.
Sacks (1976) has claimed that the application of concepts of inequality to patterns of sexual differentiation may be inappropriate
for pre-state societies. She charges her fellow anthropologists
with what she calls "state bias" in conceiving of social differences between men and women in hierarchial terms; "separate
but equal" may be an ideological mystification in the context of
our own social order, but it need not be in other kinds of societies.
Friedl, in her comparative discussion of foraging societies, connects high female status with a minimal sexual division of labor;
is such a connection theoretically motivated, or is it the result of
a tendency to view parity between the sexes in only one mode?
While the dichotomy Sacks draws between state and pre-state
societies does not suffice to cut the Gordian knot of comparing
the statuses of the sexes cross-culturally, her general point is
well taken.

Attempts to arrive at generalizations about sex roles through
a study of economic activities commonly converge around a distinction between the domestic economy and wider socioeconomic
institutions, often phrased in terms of the opposition between
"private" and "public" spheres. Universals in sex-role differentiation are connected with women's greater involvement in the
domestic economy; variation has to do with the degree to which
the public/private dichotomy obtains in particular socioeconomic
systems, and in the extent of the sexes' respective involvement
in the two domains. *Status,* in turn, generally means status in
the public domain, a point that is made explicit in Sanday's
definition. What is needed, however, is a more definitive theory
of relations of dependence and determination between the domestic economy and wider socioeconomic institutions.

In sum, a satisfactory economic approach to sexual differentiation would require fuller economic description and analysis than is generally found in anthropological writings on sex roles. It is also important to be careful about the conclusions one draws from analyses of the economic dimension of male-female relationships, to see more precisely just how far economic approaches can take us toward an understanding of such things as cultural concepts of sex differentiation, power relations in daily life, and the self-conceptions of men and women.

Sex and Social Roles

In the preceding section, the terms *status* and *role* are used to designate, respectively, general position in society, commonly viewed along a continuum from high to low, and the part played by an individual or group of individuals in an economic system. In this section, however, *status* and *role* are generally defined within the sociological tradition: *status* is used to indicate a recognized position within a given social order; *role* refers to the pattern of social action associated with a particular status, considered in terms of both normative expectations and typical behavior.

One way to approach the relationship between sex and social roles is to determine which roles are differentially allocated according to sex and to contrast the properties of such sex-linked social roles. One might focus on particular complementary statuses, like husband and wife, or on comparable but sexually differentiated statuses, like father and mother. Comparisons may also be made among the different roles an individual plays. Studies of this type, which are common in the sociological literature on sex roles, include those that contrast occupational roles with family roles, often focusing on the issue of role conflict. At a more general level, the social patterning of sex differences may be viewed in terms of contrasts between the characteristic role repertoires of men and women.

Another side of the subject concerns the nature of the relationship between sex and social roles, that is, how sex serves as a principle of recruitment to social statuses and how it influences the performance of social roles. One might consider as a limiting case the concept of a status that bears a natural relationship to

277

biological differences in terms of both recruitment and role performance, a "sex role" in the strictest sense of the term. Some have viewed the mother role in this light, maintaining that women are suited for motherhood not only because of their reproductive capacities, but also by virtue of genetically determined behavioral propensities toward nurturance, altruism, and other qualities appropriate to a caretaking role. For others, the natural basis for a relationship between sex and parental roles is primarily a matter of the practical consequences of pregnancy and lactation; the actual performance of caretaking roles, in terms of nurturance and other such qualities, is not believed to be genetically determined. It is this kind of practical connection that Brown (1970b) is exploring in her cross-cultural study of sexual differentiation in work roles. A different approach is necessary to account for the fact that certain roles are sexually stereotyped, but not associated with the same sex in all cultures. Here it is the very principle of sexual differentiation that is at issue, rather than some intrinsic connection between the nature of the role and the sex of the person who performs it.

The relationship between sex and recruitment to social roles may take many forms. In our own society, the statuses of father, priest, and surgeon are all related to sex, but each in a different way: father in terms of our biological definition of kinship statuses; priest in terms of our religious ideology, and surgeon in terms of diverse factors such as length and intensity of training. And each status is affected by our beliefs about the sex-linked temperamental and characterological prerequisites for occupational roles. Since we are interested not only in discovering patterns of association between roles and the sex of their incumbents, but also in understanding how such associations are ordered, thought about, and rationalized in different societies, a study of sex roles leads into a study of cultural conceptions of sexual differentiation. The distinction between sex and gender is important in this context, since socially relevant differences between men and women are not simple and direct consequences of biological differences between males and females. Moreover, gender identity is not always a matter of ascription based on sex; gender roles thus need not be restricted to members of one sex.

Since anthropological analyses of social roles have thus far been most heavily concentrated in the field of kinship studies, and since sexual differentiation is basic in the structuring of kin statuses (though not, as we shall see, invariably so), kinship studies constitute an important contribution to the comparative sociology of sex, or gender, roles. One comparative strategy is to view particular complementary kin statuses, for example, that of husband and wife, in cross-cultural perspective.[3] These statuses can be studied with respect to the explicit rights and duties that inhere in them, including those delineated in legal codes where these are present, and also in terms of the less formal norms and expectations and the typical behavior patterns associated with the relationship.

Jural approaches to kin statuses are best represented in the British social anthropological tradition that developed in the context of research on African tribal societies. Studies of the jural dimensions of the husband-wife relationship in African societies raise interesting issues for comparative research. For example, a distinction is commonly made between a husband's rights over the domestic and sexual services of his wife (rights *in uxorem*) and his rights over her reproductive capacities (rights *in genetricem*); the bridewealth given in payment by the husband's kin to the wife's kin guarantees above all rights of the latter type, that is, it enables the husband to filiate his wife's offspring to his own kin group. Kathleen Gough, in her restudy of E. E. Evans-Pritchard's classic account of the Nilotic Nuer (Evans-Pritchard, 1940), considers how systems of this type permit wives a certain latitude in how they arrange their lives. A woman may be able to live with a man other than her husband and even bear children by him, as long as these children are given over to their legal father. There may be provisions for the man she is living with to offer compensation to her husband for depriving him of the woman's services *in uxorem*. Some women may even succeed in thwarting their husbands' attempts to obtain the children to whom they are legally entitled (Gough, 1971).

The question of jural inequality between husbands and wives has also been addressed in the Africanist literature. In a summary statement, A. R. Radcliffe-Brown (1950) suggested that whereas

3. The term *kinship* is used in different ways and at various levels of generality in the anthropological literature. I am here using it in the widest sense, to include relationships of affinity (i.e., those based on marriage) as well as relations of consanguinity.

the rights men exercise over wives, and over other female relatives as well, can be characterized as both personal rights and property rights (rights *in personam* and *in rem*), the rights of wives over husbands, and women over men more generally, fall almost exclusively into the category of rights *in personam*; that is, men do not constitute for women something that is controlled over and against the possible claims of others, as women do for men.

The relationship between husband and wife in any society depends on a number of factors. Particularly important is the system of property or rank within which the marriage is contracted. A wife's position may be strong if she brings valued property into a union or if she marries down in the social hierarchy in a system that does not cause her to be declassed as a result (see Friedl, 1967; Silverman, 1967; Albert, 1963; D. Jacobson, 1974). Relative age is another factor, especially in societies with a strong gerontocratic bias; among Australian Aborigines, a considerable age difference between spouses contributes to the dominance of husbands over wives (see, for example, Warner, 1937 and Hart and Pilling, 1961). The sexual division of labor must also be considered. The sexual stereotyping of tasks involved in food production and meal preparation contributes to a wife's power if she can express anger toward her husband by refusing to feed him. On the other hand, the lack of a sharply defined and exclusive sphere of female control in subsistence activities can contribute to the weakness of a wife's position vis à vis her husband (Shapiro, 1971, 1976b).

The cross-cultural comparison of particular kin statuses must be supplemented by a consideration of the wider status repertoires of which they are a part. If the goal is to understand patterns of authority between men and women, attention should be given to the full range of relationships in which they participate. As Jane Goodale has pointed out in her reanalysis of an Australian Aborigine society previously described in terms of male dominance and female subordination, things look somewhat different when it is remembered that one man's wife is another man's mother-in-law (Goodale, 1971). The point is stated concisely in the following characterization of a woman's kin roles among the Bamileke in Africa: "In so far as she is a descendant of an ancestress, [she] is respected and even feared by her maternal kin; but in her role as daughter she is handed over, exchanged, or given away by her father without consideration for anything but his own interests, and in her role as wife she is kept under strict discipline by her husband" (J. Hurault, paraphrased in Paulme, 1963, p. 14). A recurrent theme in studies of women's kin statuses is that women experience the greatest degree of male domination in the context of their role as wives (see, for example, Strathern, 1972 and Dole, 1974).

Since the roles an individual plays are diverse and sometimes conflicting, it is of interest to see if judgments can be made about the relative salience of the different statuses held by the same person. Strathern (1972), in her study of the conflicting kinship roles of women in a New Guinea society, says that women are thought of primarily as wives, that is, their affinal status is more salient than their membership in the descent group into which they were born; moreover, their conjugal duties receive more cultural emphasis than their maternal ones. In other societies, particularly those with matrilineal descent, a woman's status as descent group member may outweigh relationships established by marriage. The salience of the mother role is well documented for societies in such areas as Africa and the Far East. Perhaps because of the influence of the Africanist tradition in social anthropology, women have tended to be viewed first and foremost as mothers in all societies, but it is important to keep in mind that there is significant variation in the degree of cultural emphasis and prestige associated with motherhood and in the part it plays in a man's attitude toward his wife.

Investigations into the relative salience of different social relationships have shown a concern with the weighting of same-sex, as opposed to cross-sex, social bonds. A special focus on relationships among women can be seen in part as a reaction to ethnological writings that stress the social importance of male bonding and propose a genetic explanation for it (Tiger, 1969; Tiger and Fox, 1971). In some societies, ties between kinswomen are the central bonds in domestic group organization (see, for example, Lamphere, 1974, on the Navaho, and Murphy and Murphy, 1974, on the Mundurucú Indians of South America). The degree of social separation between the sexes is sometimes such that relationships between women are far more important in the course of daily life than relationships women have with men, a fact that must enter into the evaluation of whatever cultural patterns of male dominance may be found in these societies (Murphy and Murphy, 1974; Fallers and Fallers, 1976). The importance of female bonds has been emphasized in many studies of West African societies, where women's associations are extensive both in membership and in territorial range (see, for example, Leis, 1974, and Hoffer, 1974).

Social roles can be studied from a diachronic as well as a synchronic perspective, that is, in terms of how roles succeed one another as well as in terms of the roles an individual plays concurrently. This approach permits us to compare and contrast the typical transitions that men and women experience in their respective social careers. The extensive social anthropological literature on the developmental cycle of domestic groups (see Goody, 1958, for a collection of papers on this theme) provides a focus on changing familial roles. Lamphere (1974), noting the male orientation of many such studies, has taken a similar developmental perspective toward the kin roles of women. The changing domestic status of women in societies with patrilineal descent and virilocal residence has been documented in many different ethnographic contexts; a common picture is one in which a woman moves from a position of subordination to one of domestic authority. In some cases, this authority is achieved through a strengthening of her relationship to her husband; often, it is a question of the influence she wields over her sons and daughters-in-law.

The social transition that has received the greatest amount of attention is the one commonly occurring during adolescence in which an individual is initiated into the familial and work roles that will characterize his or her life as an adult. Such transitions are often marked by elaborate rites of passage. Young (1965) provides a review of the literature on initiation rites and develops a theory to explain variation in the degree of elaboration of initiation rites in different societies, as well as differences between male and female initiation.[4] Initiation ceremonies are a rich source of information on the way gender identity is viewed in particular cultures, since they generally involve explicit tutoring

4. See also Whiting, Kluckhohn, and Anthony, 1958, and J. Brown, 1963. For a classic description of a girl's initiation rite, see Richards' (1956) account of the *chisungu* ceremony among the Bemba of central Africa.

in the qualities and behavior associated with maleness and femaleness.

Key transitions in the social careers of individuals are frequently traumatic, and are thus spoken of as "life crises." Rites of passage are said to serve an important psychological function both for individuals undergoing a transition and for others who will be affected by the change; it has, in fact, been claimed that the painfulness of many social transitions in our own society is due in part to the absence of rituals for dealing with them. Adolescence has received much attention as a time of crisis in American society. A comparative perspective on the causes of adolescent crisis is presented in Schlegel's (1973) study of Hopi girls. Other transitions that have been recognized as life crises in American society are the experience of women at menopause or when the last child has left home, and the experience of men at retirement. The traumatic nature of such transitions is indicative of the centrality of the mother role for women and the occupational role for men, and also of the ways in which motherhood and work are defined in our society. The relationship between life crises and changing social roles is analyzed in Silverman's (1967) study of women in a community in central Italy. Silverman explores variation between women of different social classes and also offers some general observations on contrasts between the two groups of Italian women and their American counterparts.

The kinship statuses we have been discussing so far might be thought to involve a clear principle of recruitment based on sex. Indeed, in the normal course of events, females become wives and mothers, while males become husbands and fathers—however these roles are defined in a particular society. But there are exceptions, even to this general rule, which raise interesting questions about the relationships between sex, gender, and social role.

In a number of African societies, a woman can acquire a wife of her own through the payment of bridewealth and also, in some cases, can become the legal father of her wife's children (Krige, 1974). The female husband either arranges lovers for her wife or permits her to choose them herself; these men do not, however, have legal rights over the offspring. This option generally depends upon a woman's ability to acquire wealth. It serves as a political strategy in societies where leadership positions are open to women. Among the Nuer, it was a social career available to barren women, though it is not clear that only barren women could take wives (Gough, 1971; Krige, 1974). The institution itself must be understood in terms of such principles as the centrality of the kinship system in defining an individual's place in society (if a woman is to transform her status, that transformation is likely to occur within the kinship domain); a definition of marriage based on transactions in wealth rather than sexual intercourse; the importance of a woman's status as a member of a descent group and the possibility that this status can override her sex as criterion for recruitment to kinship roles (a woman may obtain the right to filiate children to her own patrilineage and in this respect stand in a relation of equivalence to her brothers).

An interesting comparative case is found in Aswad's (1967) study of the roles of noblewomen in a Middle Eastern society. Here widows may take over the social roles of their deceased husbands, and sisters may stand in for their brothers. When a woman does either of these things, she is described as becoming "like a man" (p. 145); she may not marry or, if a widow, remarry. Her situation differs from those African cases in which a woman can maintain her roles as wife and mother while acquiring the additional statuses of husband and father. Krige (1974, 19–20) discusses such a pattern among the Lovedu. She also notes that many cases of woman-marriage among the Lovedu are a matter of a woman's right to the domestic services of a girl from her brother's house, based on the fact that her bridewealth was used to pay for her brother's wife. In the usual course of events, this service comes in the form of a daughter-in-law, a brother's daughter who marries the woman's son; where this is not possible, the woman can take her brother's daughter as her own wife or as a wife for her daughter (Krige 1974, 17–18, 24–25).

That one person may step into another's place in the context of domestic group organization, that a person may, in fact, have to do so in order to keep the domestic group functioning, is a sufficiently widespread phenomenon to cause us to reexamine any overly rigid interpretation of the sex-linked nature of kinship roles. What is of interest in the African and Middle Eastern cases is that women are moving into statuses that we usually think of as being associated with men, not only implicitly but explicitly as well. We are thus tempted to describe the situation by saying that women in these societies can become sociologically male.

An Africanist, in the course of an informal discussion, remarked that in Africa "men are so important that you have to turn women into them." A better way of putting it is to say that normal sex-role boundaries can be crossed insofar as the relationship between sex and status is determined by sociological rather than biological factors.

It is important to keep in mind that a woman's ability to transform her kin and domestic group status is often a function of her position in a system of rank or stratification. The place of sex as a determining factor in an individual's role set must be weighed against other principles of social differentiation—age, rank, class, caste, descent group membership, relationship to the supernatural, to name just a few—to see which take priority in which social contexts. The possibilities for role segregation, an important element in some of the African cases, must also be considered. In our own society, role segregation seems to constitute something of a cultural problem. The phrase "playing a role" is used to indicate disapproval; role-playing is commonly associated with artificiality, with fragmentation of the self. If one's gender is felt to be a central dimension of one's identity as a person, it is not clear that there are any social roles or situational contexts in which gender is totally irrelevant. Considerations of this sort may help us to understand how women have assumed positions of public authority in countries that are apparently more male-dominated than our own. Part of the explanation might lie in the degree of separation between public and domestic domains in those countries, and in the fact that the roles women play in one arena do not impinge on their roles in the other (for examples from Turkey and Egypt, see respectively, Fallers and Fallers, 1976, and Mohsen, 1974).

Public and Private Social Spheres

A major point that has emerged from research into the social roles of men and women concerns the relative dimensions of men's and women's social worlds. It is commonly found that women's roles restrict them to a narrower social sphere, which can be characterized as "domestic" or "private," while men predominate in the wider circles of "public" life. This difference emerges from Young's (1965) comparative study of initiation rites, in which he concludes that men are generally initiated into the community as a whole, while women's initiations focus around incorporation into more restricted domestic groups.

Some anthropologists have seen the public/private dichotomy as a central dimension of women's social subordination, claiming that roles in the public domain are inevitably accorded higher prestige than roles in the private domain (see, for example, Rosaldo, 1974 and Rosaldo and Lamphere, 1974). Other anthropologists have adopted a critical attitude toward this dichotomy (Stack et al., 1975).

Friedl herself, in a publication antedating her general theory of sex-role differentiation, points out that societies vary with respect to the degree of separation between domestic and public spheres and the relative importance of each (Friedl, 1967). Following a line of reasoning that seems to be contradicted by her later thesis about the relationship between women's extradomestic exchange activities and their general status, she notes that in some societies (for example in rural Greece, where she did her own field work) the domestic sector is the center of resource allocation and significant decision-making. Male domination of the public sphere is thus an "appearance" that hides the "reality" of the important role women play in the family, which is pragmatically . . . the most significant social unit (Friedl, 1967, p. 97; see also Sweet, 1967, 1974).

Another perspective on the domestic vs. public dichotomy, and its meaning for the respective social experience of the sexes, is offered by Murphy and Murphy (1974), who focus not on power and decision-making, but on social solidarity, and suggest that while men's bonds may extend more widely, those of women are more enduring and cohesive.

Differences between men's and women's roles have also been analyzed in terms of their degree of formalization. Shapiro (1972, 1976b), in a study of the Yanomama Indians of South America, has shown that roles played by men are more structurally differentiated and ritualized than those played by women. The opposition between "formalized" and "nonformalized" roles has been developed most systematically by Beverly Chiñas (1973) in her study of Isthmus Zapotec women. The idea that women's roles tend to be less formally defined, as well as less public, than those of men has been used by one anthropologist to account for the male orientation of most social anthropological writings (Ardener,

1972). This criticism is appropriate to some traditions within anthropology—notably those that can be labeled "structuralist" —but the importance of studying the less formal dimensions of social life is not something that anthropologists in general have failed to recognize. What can be said is that the study of sex roles has called particular attention to this issue (Sweet, 1967; Friedl, 1967; Riegelhaupt, 1967).

Related to a categorization of roles in terms of how formalized they are is a consideration of types of control over the behavior of others. The usual distinctions are among authority (exercise of control in a way that is culturally recognized as legitimate), power (exercise of control that is not so recognized or that receives its legitimation at more covert levels of cultural patterning), and influence (usually conceived of as a means of affecting the behavior of others by convincing them that the behavior in question is in their own best interest). Women's roles are often said to differ from men's in the extent to which they are associated with the exercise of power or influence, rather than overt and legitimate authority (Sweet, 1974; Lamphere, 1974; Collier, 1974; Dole, 1974). It has also been pointed out that women's exercise of power frequently takes the form of subversion, of sabotaging the plans of those who hold authority over them by engaging in disruptive behavior (see, for example, Friedl, 1967; Shapiro, 1972; Dole, 1974). Women, more often than men, are in the position of having to achieve their ends through indirect means; they must work through others, sons or husbands for example, and as a result must learn the art of manipulation (Collier, 1974; Lamphere, 1974).

The notion of "manipulation" is itself treated in two different ways in the current anthropological literature on sex roles; on the one hand, it connotes indirectness, and on the other, enterprise. Given the value orientations of most of the authors whose work is under discussion here, manipulation in the first sense tends to be viewed negatively, while manipulation in the second sense prompts admiration. The two approaches may be combined within a single piece of analysis (Collier, 1974). The negative view of manipulation is represented in the collection of essays entitled *Many Sisters* edited by Carolyn Matthiasson, in which contributors' essays have been ordered into three sections according to whether women in the society each author is discussing are seen to be subordinate, equal, or superordinate to men; those societies in which women's position is judged to be inferior are labeled "Manipulative Societies." In a similar vein, Lamphere (1974) contrasts societies in which women are able to achieve their social goals directly with those in which they have to work through men; she uses the Navaho to illustrate the first type and various tribal African groups and peasant populations to represent the second.

A positive attitude toward the exercise of manipulative skills in social life is associated with attempts to see individuals not merely as playing out social roles as these are defined by the dominant norms of the sociocultural system, but shaping these roles to meet their own personal ends. This perspective is evident in *Woman, Culture, and Society,* a set of essays edited by Michelle Rosaldo and Louise Lamphere. In some of these essays, women are perceived as an interest group whose goals, which conflict with those of men, must be achieved without the kind of institutional support enjoyed by males. Jane Collier, in her essay on domestic politics in patrilineal societies, analyzed how women's interests grow out of their structural position in domestic groups, how these interests run counter to certain overt principles of patrilineal organization, and how women can prevail despite the fact that the deck of jural rights and legitimate authority patterns is stacked against them. Here the focus is on strategies employed generally by women in particular societies, or types of society. A more individualistically oriented analysis of how an exceptional woman can achieve a position of prominence by exploiting with special skill the structural possibilities of the social order in which she finds herself is presented in Carol Hoffer's description of Madam Yoko, ruler of the Kpa Mende Confederacy in West Africa.

In considering if, or when, it is appropriate to interpret sex-role differentiation in terms of social superiority and social inferiority, anthropologists have had to deal with the kinds of issues raised earlier in connection with economic approaches to sexual inequality. Several anthropologists have felt the need to emphasize that differences in the social roles of the sexes need not imply hierarchy, but instead may involve a complementarity in which neither side is higher than the other. This point is developed in several of the articles in Matthiasson's collection (H. Jacobson, Ebihara, Sweet, Richards), one section of which, entitled "Complementary

Societies," is devoted to societies in which the sexes are described as being social equals. Attention has also been drawn to general similarities in the culturally determined goals and values that men and women are trying to realize, each in the sex-appropriate manner (Albert, 1963). There are, however, cases in which it seems justified and, in fact, necessary to speak of sex-role differentiation in terms of ranking. One way of approaching this issue is through asymmetries in reactions toward the crossing of sex-role boundaries. If women who take on men's roles are admired, albeit with some degree of ambivalence, while men who take on women's roles are either ridiculed or discreetly ignored, would this not be an indication that we are dealing with a hierarchical system? Psychiatric and social psychological research in our own society has revealed a double standard in which attributes sex-typed as male, but not those sex-typed as female, are seen as generally desirable personal qualities when no explicit reference to sex is at issue. What we have here, in semiotic terms, is a case of markedness in which maleness, insofar as its features also constitute the more general category of humanity, is unmarked with respect to the more restricted, marked features of femaleness. In sociopolitical terms, a differential tolerance for the two directions in which sex-role lines can be crossed may mean that a system is threatened not when individuals strive to move up in it, but when they choose to move down.

Sex as a Cultural System

The studies I am considering here are concerned with cultural definitions of maleness and femaleness. In a sense, they are at the other end of the anthropological spectrum from those dealt with in the opening section, since they seek to understand other cultures from within, in terms of the set of shared values and understandings by which they are constituted. They do not have the behaviorist dimension of role analysis; the mental constructs they deal with are not rules that are thought to connect with action in some direct way, like the norms studied by sociologists, but ideas that serve to make action meaningful in a wider sense and enter into the construction of social reality itself.

The study of cultural definitions of sex involves both an investigation of ideas about what men and women are like and an understanding of the place that sexuality occupies in the general

289

world view of the people being studied. As a powerful natural symbol and binary opposition, sex may provide a metaphor for an entire cosmological system (Reichel-Dolmatoff, 1971). Michelle Rosaldo and Jane Atkinson's (1975) study of how the sexes are metaphorically linked to the plant world among the Ilongot of the Philippines, and Anthony Seeger's (1974) analysis of how the Suyá Indians of central Brazil compare men and women with various animals of the forest, provide insight into how sex differences are conceptualized and how they relate to the ordering of other areas of cultural experience. In the Ilongot case, a major contrast emerges between the life-giving properties of women and the life-taking properties of men. Among the Suyá, differences between men and women involve an opposition between the cultural world of the village and the natural (and also supernatural) world of the forest.

The symbolic association of men with culture and women with nature emerged as a central theme from Claude Lévi-Strauss's influential writings on the group of South American Indian societies to which the Suyá belong, and figures in Lévi-Strauss's more general theoretical reflections on the asymmetrical position of men and women in society (1949) and the meaning of sexual opposition in myth and cosmology (1962, 1964, 1966, 1967, 1971). Sherry Ortner (1974) has examined this Lévi-Straussian equation, considering the reasons for its possible universality and suggesting that, insofar as the opposition between culture and nature is invariably a hierarchical one, the symbolic identification of men with the first term and women with the second will involve concepts of female inferiority. This line of reasoning has also been developed by Rosaldo (1974), who connects the opposition between nature and culture to the dichotomy between private and public.

A common theme in the cultural complexes surrounding sex differences is that female sexuality represents a dangerous force that must be controlled. One variation on this theme that has received considerable attention in the anthropological literature is the so-called "honor and shame" complex found in Mediterranean societies (see Peristiany, 1966, for a general review and case studies dealing with this topic). Here, the elaborate precautions that are taken to insure the premarital chastity and the postmarital fidelity of women are related to beliefs about the weakness and sexual susceptibility of females and the rampant sexual aggressiveness of males. Since the honor of men resides in the purity of their kinswomen and wives, men must see to it that women are insulated from contact with males outside of the family circle. In the Muslim traditions of many Middle Eastern and North African societies, male control over female sexuality is justified through the idea that women are more sensual and less able to control their sexual desires than men, who possess greater reason and rationality (ʔaqel, in Arabic). The imposition of limitations on the sexuality of women finds its most extreme expression in the form of genital mutilation known as infibulation or pharonic circumcision, found among certain Muslim groups in northern Africa. (This operation is described by Hayes, 1975.)

A different version of the dangers inherent in female sexuality is expressed in the pollution beliefs characteristic of societies throughout Melanesia. Such beliefs, which are associated with ritualized patterns of sex antagonism, are portrayed in the following passage from an ethnography of the Mae Enga of Highland New Guinea:

> Men regard menstrual blood as truly dangerous. They believe that contact with a menstruating woman will, in the absence of counter-magic, sicken a man and cause persistent vomiting, turn his blood black, corrupt his vital juices so that his skin darkens and wrinkles as his flesh wastes, permanently dull his wits, and eventually lead to a slow decline and death. Menstrual blood introduced into a man's food, they say, quickly kills him, and young women crossed in love sometimes seek their revenge in this way. Menstrual blood dropped on the bog-iris plants (*Acorus calamus*) that men use in wealth-, pig- and war-magic destroys them; and a man would divorce, and perhaps kill, the wife concerned (Meggitt, 1964, p. 204).[5]

Anthropological accounts of the kinds of belief systems we have been discussing may be descriptive in their goal, the point being

5. Additional cases may be found in Goodale and Chowning, 1971, and the essays in Brown and Buchbinder, 1976. Goodale and Chowning point out, as does Faithorn (1975), that pollution beliefs should not be interpreted too one-sidedly, since men may also be thought of as polluting to women.

to penetrate another world of ideas and understand it in as rich and undistorted a manner as possible, or they may seek explanations for why particular sets of beliefs should appear in particular places. An explanation for the honor and shame complex in circum-Mediterranean societies has been offered by Jane Schneider (1971), who analyzes the restrictions on women in terms of competition between kin groups over resources, of which women are one. Rose Oldfield Hayes (1975), who has attempted to explain why infibulation continues to be practiced in the Sudan, claims that the practice functions to assert and maintain the integrity of patrilineal descent groups. Harriet Whitehead (1976) presents a comparative discussion of chastity requirements and female genital mutilation, attempting to bring different but related approaches into a more general framework. She notes that what is common to all cases is an attempt on the part of social groups to avoid status loss by restricting access to females.

Both Hayes and Whitehead also attempt to account for why women themselves should have an interest in perpetuating these practices. Both point out that, within the social universe defined by these cultural constructs, women wish to be proper exemplars of their sex and to enhance the status of the social group that defines their own place in society. In addition, Hayes notes that the women who perform the operation of infibulation occupy a position that carries with it considerable social prestige; abandonment of the practice would put an end to one of the more important roles attainable by women. Whitehead takes a different direction, suggesting that if sexual activity is culturally defined as a form of male domination over women, women may use any limitation on their ability to engage in sexual activity as a protection, or even a weapon, against men.

Melanesian pollution beliefs have been interpreted in demographic terms by Lindenbaum (1972), who views them as a significant factor in birth control. Demographic perspectives have also been brought to bear on the explanation of practices involving genital mutilation, including infibulation as well as various male operations like subincision. Birth control may indeed be a factor to keep in mind when considering the effects of these customs in societies lacking the technological devices that make birth control a safe and relatively easy matter; however, it should also be remembered that population control can be effected in a variety of ways among which elaborate pollution beliefs and radical and painful restructuring of genitalia hardly seem the most parsimonious.

Sociological explanations of pollution beliefs and sex antagonism in New Guinea have been proposed by Meggitt (1964) and Allen (1967). Meggitt attempts to show that the greatest development of ritualized fear and hostility between the sexes occurs among those Highlands peoples who intermarry with their enemies. Allen focuses on descent rather than alliance and claims that sexual hostility and distance varies directly with the strength of the localized patrilineal descent group. A study of how ideas about sex differences, including pollution beliefs, fit within a social structural context in one particular New Guinea society is provided in Strathern's (1972) monograph on the people of Mt. Hagen. Particularly interesting is her analysis of how the *noman* (translated as "mind," "disposition," or "will") of women is thought to differ from that of men in being less directed, less predictable, and more vacillating, a belief that Strathern ties to women's interstitial position between patrilineal descent groups and the women's divided loyalties.

That beliefs about sex differences, and the rituals through which they are communicated, not only reflect the social order, but also form a part of how it is created and maintained, is seen in L. L. Langness's (1974) analysis of secret male cults in Highland New Guinea. In the widespread *nama* cult, for example, "men regard women, and women tend to regard themselves, as (relatively) weak, more sexual, less intelligent, more inconsistent, dirtier, and in almost every way inferior" (p. 191). Langness believes that the cult must be interpreted in ideological terms, that is, as a symbolic means for the assertion of social control—in this case, control of women by men who wish to assure themselves both of access to women's labor power and to rights over children. The interpretation of cultural constructs in ideological terms involves, first of all, the idea that the beliefs in question benefit one segment of society more than another, and, second, that they represent a mystification, a masking of those social facts that are inconvenient to recognize, since they present a problem for the overt structures of domination.

For the men who participate in it, and as far as we know, for women as well, the *nama* cult is seen as necessary to the well-being of society as a whole. An anthropologist might be expected to adopt a similar viewpoint, since anthropological approaches to the interpretation of ritual have been heavily influenced by the holism and functionalism of the Durkheimian tradition. Langness, however, warns against accepting native perspectives uncritically; because a practice contributes to group survival or to social solidarity, it does not therefore follow that all members of the social group fare equally well within the system. The *nama* cult, he says, "promotes the solidarity of males at the expense of females" (p. 200). Yet women share these beliefs about female inferiority and see the practice as being in their own self-interest. In the view of Langness, this paradox illustrates the way in which ideologies operate to rationalize subordination to those at the bottom, as well as to those at the top.

If ideologies of male superiority serve their social function through a process of mystification, one must inquire into the nature of the facts that they mask. In the most general terms, one purpose they accomplish is to give a particular social system the aura of an immutable natural or supernatural system, hiding the fact that people could (and for that matter, sometimes do) behave in other ways. Langness points out that men might possibly be more attached to their mothers than is safe for a patrilineal descent rule or more loyal to their wives than is adaptive in a social system in which a man's allegiance must lie unequivocally with his male kinsmen. Langness says that "given the necessity for strength and cooperation among males," such attachments would create "an intolerable situation" (p. 208). What the ideology of the New Guinea secret men's cults attempts to hide is that it is perfectly reasonable for a man to feel close to his mother or his wife. If one goes a step beyond Langness and questions the "givenness" of the entire structure of male social bonds and activities in the societies of Highland New Guinea, then symbolic systems of the kind Langness is discussing serve a deeper and more powerful purpose than he himself has indicated. If it is not inevitable that individuals will develop the social sentiments appropriate to a given order, neither is it inevitable that the social order take the form it does.

Langness describes a situation in which men successfully establish a symbolic basis for their social power. Other analyses of the ideological dimensions of beliefs in male superiority reach a different conclusion. They see such beliefs, and the rituals in which they are acted out, as illusions that belie the reality of women's power, a cultural whistling in the dark whereby men hide from themselves, and they hope from women as well, their own sense of insignificance. This is the approach taken by S. Ardener (1973) in her analysis of beliefs in female pollution and by Friedl (1967) and Rogers (1975) in their explorations of the discrepancy between cultural concepts of male superiority and the actualities of women's social power in peasant societies. Michaelson and Goldschmidt (1971), in an overview of sex roles and ideologies of male dominance among peasants, connect the *machismo* complex to inheritance patterns that threaten the economic basis of male control. Other anthropologists have seen the strength of women as being rooted in their reproductive capacities, and have stressed the psychological dimensions of male insecurity.

Murphy and Murphy (1974) present a combination of social and psychological perspectives in their analysis of the Mundurucú Indians of central Brazil. In the Murphys' view, women enjoy the natural power of being creators of new life as well as the social power that comes from their independence from men in daily activities and from the bonds of solidarity they have with one another; men's insecurity comes from the fact that they cannot effectively exercise social control over women and from their own castration anxieties. The Murphys see these insecurities as lying behind the secret men's cult of the Mundurucú and the myth of role reversal associated with it, according to which women once controlled the cult through possession of the sacred flutes around which the cult is focused. Men, in the Murphys' analysis, rule symbolically by means of the flute (and naturally by means of the penis), but the flute (like the penis?) was once woman's possession and might possibly be lost again.[6] Bamberger (1974) presents a different analysis of this and other role-reversal myths

6. For a more extended discussion of the Murphys' book, *Women of the Forest*, see Shapiro, 1976a. Netting presents an analysis similar to that of the Murphys in his discussion of a Kofyar (African) myth in which God's wife is represented as having a penis. The Kofyar male, says Netting, believes that "at least he has what no woman can hope to possess, his manhood, his penis. But behind this brave assertion whispers the

associated with men's cults, saying that they provide a mythic charter for the social dominance of men by showing that women, for one reason or another, proved unfit to rule. Her approach is thus essentially similar to that of Langness.

A recurrent ideological connection between women and disorder, evident in role-reversal myths and in various other cultural constructs, can be interpreted as representing tensions inherent in a social order in a structurally convenient manner. Women, after all, do frequently engage in disruptive behavior. This behavior was analyzed earlier as an important tactic available to them, given their position in society; by transmuting it into a property of their natures, attention is deflected from the system as a whole and responsibility is fixed instead upon a subordinate subgroup within society. The function of blaming women for conflict and disharmony is particularly evident in patrilineal societies, since it preserves the social fiction that relations between male kinsmen are always harmonious (Wolf, 1968, especially Maurice Freedman's introduction; Collier, 1974; Denich, 1974). It also represents an attempt to deal with the structurally anomalous position of women in a society organized around descent through males, something that Denich refers to as "the patrilineal puzzle" (Denich, 1974, p. 260).

A more consistently Marxist interpretation of ideologies of sex differences is presented by Bridget O'Laughlin (1974) in an analysis of women's food taboos among the Mbum of Tchad. According to O'Laughlin, the Mbum social system is characterized by marked sexual asymmetry in relations of production and by the following "central contradiction": that "women have primary responsibility for both biological reproduction and socialization of children, but control over reproductive rights in women of the lineage, and authority derived from that control, are vested entirely in male elders" (p. 311). The ideological structures that "mediate" this contradiction are associated with a system of food taboos that, according to O'Laughlin, first of all, signify a metaphorical connection between women and certain domesticated animals, and second, carry with them the sanction of barrenness and other reproductive disorders. These beliefs serve to effect a

---

psyche of his society, the mythic presentiment, that perhaps she has that, too" (Netting, 1969, p. 1045).

symbolic transposition of women's place in a social system of production and reproduction to a level that is at once sacred and natural, and hence beyond question. In O'Laughlin's terms, "that which is arbitrary and culturally determined is morally linked to that which is biologically necessary, that women successfully bear children" (p. 316).

While ideologies of sex differences may serve to support a system of domination, it is also important to see how women can turn such beliefs to their own advantage. Goodale and Chowning (1971) show how pollution beliefs can be used by women as a source of power against men. S. Ardener (1973) gives an account of how women in the West Cameroons mobilize ideas about female sexuality in militant displays of their rights. Earlier the point was made that individuals do not merely conform to social roles, but actively shape them; similarly, cultural beliefs about sexuality constitute resources that can be drawn upon to serve a variety of purposes in the course of social life. And because the symbolic systems we call cultures are not monolithic, but present alternatives, contradictions, and loose ends, there is room for maneuvering in how individuals define themselves and their relationships to others.

Men, Women, and Knowledge

In the foregoing discussion, cultural views of sexual differentiation were treated as shared systems of belief. It is now necessary to look more closely at the notion of sharedness and to consider how sex differences constitute not only an object for cultural elaboration, but a basis for the differential allocation of knowledge. Can the sexes, in some measure, be seen as forming "subcultures"? This question fits within the more general investigation of intracultural variation, which has become a focus of interest as anthropologists have moved away from the traditional view of cultural systems as sets of beliefs and understandings that can be found in essentially the same form in the mind of each member of a particular society.[7]

7. The cultural anthropological interest in variation is related to similar trends in the field of linguistics. In the area of linguistic anthropology. some very interesting work has been done on differences between men's and women's speech. Pioneering research on this topic was carried

Differences between what men know and what women know (or, as may also be the case, between what men and women are permitted to show that they know) are central to the distribution of power and prestige in society. In most societies, men seem to have wider access to socially strategic information, allowing them to operate in a more extensive range of social settings. Riegelhaupt (1967) has analyzed a case in which the reverse is true in her study of Portuguese peasant women; here it is the men's economic activities that limit their experience to a narrower sphere, while women's participation in marketing takes them out of the local community and enables them to establish the contacts upon which the survival and well-being of their families depend.

What is significant is not just differences between what men know and what women know, but the differential prestige accorded to men's knowledge and women's knowledge. In societies where men have a virtual monopoly on the activities and information deemed sacred, possession of highly valued knowledge is a central component of male superiority. In South American societies such as the Yanomama, where access to a world of spirit beings is achieved with the aid of hallucinogenic drugs, the doors of perception that lead into the sacred realm remain closed to women because the drugs are taken only by men (Shapiro, 1972, 1976b). Privileged access to the realm of the sacred confers authority and prestige both because of the value attributed to what is learned, and because secrets serve to define an in-group and set it apart from outsiders. The way in which male control over the sacred serves to define the respective positions of the sexes has been noted in ethnographic accounts from many areas of the world (Warner, 1937; Langness, 1974; Murphy and Murphy, 1974; Shapiro, 1976b).

A controversial attempt to deal in a general way with differences in the world views of men and women is presented in an essay by Edwin Ardener, entitled "Belief and the Problem of Women" (E. Ardener, 1972, reprinted in S. Ardener, 1975). Ardener, who is concerned primarily with how societies are conceived of by their members, suggests that, for social structural

---

out by Edward Sapir (1929) and Mary Haas (1944). An extensive bibliography of recent work in this area can be found in Stack et al., 1975, pp. 153–156. See also Lakoff, 1975.

reasons, men tend to see society as a bounded entity set off from nature in a way that women do not. It is men who provide ethnographers with models that are used to characterize the society as a whole, while women constitute a "problem" for social anthropology in that they fail to articulate the kinds of perspectives on society that anthropologists find intellectually congenial and analytically manageable. Ardener's account, which incorporates Lévi-Straussian ideas about the opposition between nature and culture and its relation to sex, thus proposes an epistemological basis for male bias in anthropology.

Ardener's notion that women have been ignored because they are more ignorable seems an overly tidy and somewhat self-serving approach to the sexual asymmetry in social anthropological writings. One must also question the elevation to scientific status of the folk belief that women think in a basically different, less formal and articulate way than men do. In responding to criticisms of his work, Ardener (1975) emphasizes his concern with the nature of oppression, and with making analytic progress toward a proper understanding of the place of women in society.[8] He speaks of the need to recognize how "socio-intellectual structures . . . regularly assign contending viewpoints to non-real status; making them 'overlooked,' 'muted,' 'invisible': mere black holes in someone else's universe" (E. Ardener, 1975, p. 25; some may find the imagery of this last phrase intriguing from a Freudian perspective). What is most valuable in Ardener's approach is his insistence that domination should not always be understood in economic terms, as a function of "modes of production." In focusing on what he calls a "dominant communicative system" (1975, p. 22), Ardener relates inequality between men and women to differential access to and manipulation of symbolic resources. This approach, like those discussed in the preceding section, underlines the need for considering sex differences in the light of our species' uniquely characteristic activity: the creation of meaning and the imposition of value.

Cultural and Psychological Anthropology

The anthropological studies of sexual differentiation that have been reviewed and discussed here provide various perspectives on

8. Ardener is addressing himself particularly to the comments of Mathieu (1973).

the question of inequality between the sexes, which has again become a focus of concern in our own society in recent years. Relations of dominance and subordination between men and women have been defined in terms of such factors as differential access to and control over material resources; differences in role sets and social fields; relative placement in symbolic hierarchies; differential relationship to dominant ideologies; differential access to knowledge. Anthropologists have addressed the question of variation in the sociocultural patterning of sexual differentiation, some with a view toward explanation and others in the context of a relativistic commitment to understanding other cultures in their own terms, and have also considered universal features in the way sex differences are structured in social and cultural systems.

As a concluding point to this survey, I should like to call attention to the discontinuity between the work I have discussed and that done by psychological anthropologists. Psychological anthropology, including the phase in its development known as the "culture and personality" movement, has until recently constituted the single major contribution to the study of sex and gender within American anthropology and, moreover, has represented and generally continues to represent anthropology's contribution to this subject in the view of scientists in other disciplines. It is therefore necessary to explain why this body of literature has not been incorporated into the researches of those anthropologists whose work has been reviewed here.

Different investigators ask different kinds of questions, but this fact does not suffice as an answer. Indeed, it seems that the economic, sociological, symbolic, and communicational approaches outlined above have at times drawn covertly upon psychological principles that would be better developed overtly and systematically. The relationship between social roles and personality characteristics is touched upon in studies written from either an economic or a sociological perspective. Sweet, for example, characterizes the Middle Eastern women whose roles she is analyzing as "bold, outspoken, competent, and argumentative" (1974, p. 391); Paulme describes African women in terms of "their liveliness, their independent spirit, and their inexhaustible energy" (1963, p. 16) and suggests that women in a patrilineal-virilocal society gain independence and strength of character from the travels and adjustments that are required of them (p. 7). Cultural symbolic approaches would seem to benefit from a consideration of how the constructs they describe impinge upon the life experience of individuals, both as action strategies and as ingredients of identity; moreover, their focus on the human symbolic function provides an important link to the concerns of psychology. A recent observation by Langness is worth quoting in this context; it is made in the course of a concluding chapter to a set of essays on men and women in Highland New Guinea societies, and is directed to the relationship between the articles in the volume and earlier work by the same authors.

> Those who were yesterday social anthropologists and cultural ecologists have become today, and with no word of warning it appears, psychological anthropologists. The previous concentration on social structure has become an interest in culture. Although these papers are most properly considered currently as "symbolic anthropology," and their fundamental psychological character is clear, the latter consideration is ignored. This is terribly unfortunate, as until the relationship between symbolic anthropology and psychology is made explicit, it cannot possibly realize its potential (in Brown and Buchbinder, 1976, p. 102).

Behind Langness's criticism is the history of negative attitudes expressed toward psychological anthropology by anthropologists who have specialized in such areas as cultural ecology and the study of social structure; his point is that these anthropologists continue to avoid psychology even where their new interests make it intellectually problematic for them to do so. Looking at the issue from the other side, distrust of psychological approaches was understandable as a reaction to the ad hoc, intuitional approach of early culture and personality studies and to the uncritical application of Western psychological constructs, notably those of Freud, to other cultures. Many anthropologists continue to feel alienated from psychological anthropology, partly because psychological anthropologists tended to react against the early excesses of their field by operationalizing and objectifying their theories and methods to the point where their work lacks precisely the element of interiority one might expect from a psychological approach. To the degree that psychological anthropologists opt for behaviorist strategies, it makes little sense to assert that they and anthropologists interested in the study of symbolism have something to say to one another.

If psychological and cultural perspectives are to converge, as Langness suggests is necessary, the ground on which they will have to meet is a common concern with human action as a communicative process, involving patterning on both conscious and unconscious levels. Such an integration, or reintegration, would be oriented around an understanding that interpreting behavior is as important a goal as predicting it. The resulting contribution to the topic at hand would be to show how culturally shaped concepts about sexuality enter into the messages that individuals transmit to one another and into their attempts to make their own lives meaningful to themselves.

References

Albert, Ethel M. 1963. Women of Burundi: A study of social values. In *Women of tropical Africa,* ed. D. Paulme. Berkeley: University of California Press.

Allen, M. R. 1967. *Male cults and secret initiations in Melanesia.* Melbourne: Melbourne University Press.

Ardener, Edwin, 1972. Belief and the problem of women. In *The interpretation of ritual,* ed. J. S. LaFontaine. London: Tavistock.

————. 1975. The 'problem' revisited. In *Perceiving women,* ed. S. Ardener. New York: Wiley.

Ardener, Shirley G. 1973. Sexual insult and female militancy. *Man* (n.s.) 8:422–440.

————, ed. 1975. *Perceiving women.* New York: Wiley.

Aswad, Barbara C. 1967. Key and peripheral roles of noble women in a Middle Eastern plains village. *Anthropol. Quart.* 40:139–152.

Bamberger, Joan. 1974. The myth of matriarchy: Why men rule in primitive society. In *Woman, culture and society,* ed. M. Z. Rosaldo and L. Lamphere. Stanford: Stanford University Press.

Boserup, Ester. 1970. Women's role in economic development. London: G. Allen and Unwin.

Bossen, Laurel. 1975. Women in modernizing societies. *Am. Ethnol.* 2:587–601.

Briggs, Jean. 1974. Eskimo women: Makers of men. In *Many sisters: Women in cross-cultural perspective,* ed. C. J. Matthiasson. New York: Free Press.

Brown, Judith K. 1963. A cross-cultural study of female initiation rites. *Am. Anthropol.* 65:837–853.

———. 1970a. Economic organization and the position of women among the Iroquois. *Ethnohistory* 17:151–167.

———. 1970b. A note on the division of labor by sex. *Am. Anthropol.* 72:1073–1078.

Brown, Paula, and Buchbinder, Georgeda, eds. 1976. *Man and woman in the New Guinea highlands.* American Anthropological Association special publication no. 8.

Brown, Susan E. 1975. Love unites them and hunger separates them: Poor women in the Dominican Republic. In *Toward an anthropology of women,* ed. R. R. Reiter. New York: Monthly Review Press.

Chiñas, Beverly. 1973. *The isthmus Zapotecs: Women's roles in cultural context.* New York: Holt, Rinehart and Winston.

Collier, Jane Fishburne. 1974. Women in politics. In *Woman, culture and society,* ed. M. Z. Rosaldo and L. Lamphere. Stanford: Stanford University Press.

Denich, Bette S. 1974. Sex and power in the Balkans. In *Woman, culture and society,* ed. M. Z. Rosaldo and L. Lamphere. Stanford University Press.

Dole, Gertrude E. 1974. The marriages of Pacho: A woman's life among the Amahuaca. In *Many sisters: Women in cross-cultural perspective,* ed. C. J. Matthiasson. New York: Free Press.

Ebihara, May. 1974. Khmer village women in Cambodia: A happy balance. In *Many sisters: Women in cross-cultural perspective,* ed. C. J. Matthiasson. New York: Free Press.

Evans-Pritchard, E. E. 1940. *The Nuer: A description of the modes of livelihood and political institutions of a Nilotic people.* Oxford: Oxford University Press.

Faithorn, Elizabeth. 1975. The concept of pollution among the Kafe of the Papua New Guinea highlands. In *Toward an anthropology of women,* ed. R. R. Reiter. New York: Monthly Review Press.

Fallers, Lloyd A., and Fallers, Margaret G. 1976. Sex roles in Edremit. In *Mediterranean family structures,* ed. J. G. Peristiany. Cambridge: Cambridge University Press.

Friedl, Ernestine. 1967. The position of women: Appearance and reality. *Anthropol. Quart.* 40:97–108.

———. 1975. *Women and men: An anthropologist's view.* New York: Holt, Rinehart and Winston.

Goodale, Jane. 1971. *Tiwi wives: A study of the women of Melville Island, North Australia.* Seattle: University of Washington Press.

Goodale, Jane, and Chowning, Ann. 1971. *The contaminating woman.* Paper read at the American Anthropological Association annual meeting, November 1971, New York.

Goody, Jack, ed. 1958. The developmental cycle in domestic groups.

Cambridge papers in social anthropology, no. 1. Cambridge: Cambridge University Press.

Gough, Kathleen. 1971. Nuer kinship: A re-examination. In *The translation of culture: Essays to E. E. Evans-Pritchard,* ed. T. O. Beidelman. London: Tavistock.

————. 1975. The origin of the family. In *Toward an anthropology of women,* ed. R. R. Reiter. New York: Monthly Review Press.

Haas, Mary R. 1944. Men's and women's speech in Koasati. *Language* 20:142–149.

Hart, C. W. M., and Pilling, Arnold. 1961. *The Tiwi of North Australia.* New York: Holt, Rinehart and Winston.

Hayes, Rose Oldfield. 1975. Female genital mutilation, fertility control, and the patrilineage in modern Sudan: A functional analysis. *Am. Ethnol.* 2:617–633.

Hoffer, Carol P. 1974. Madam Yoko: Ruler of the Kpa Mende confederacy. In *Woman, culture and society,* ed. M. Z. Rosaldo and L. Lamphere. Stanford: Stanford University Press.

Jacobson, Doranne. 1974. The women of North and Central India: Goddesses and wives. In *Many sisters: Women in cross-cultural perspective,* ed. C. J. Matthiasson. New York: Free Press.

Jacobson, Helga E. 1974. Women in Philippine Society: More equal than many. In *Many sisters: Women in cross-cultural perspective,* ed. C. J. Matthiasson. New York: Free Press.

Krige, Eileen Jensen. 1974. Woman-marriage, with special reference to the Lovedu: Its significance for the definition of marriage. *Africa* 44:11–37.

Lakoff, Robin. 1975. *Language and woman's place.* New York: Harper Colophon.

Lamphere, Louise. 1974. Strategies, cooperation, and conflict among women. In *Woman, culture and society,* ed. M. Z. Rosaldo and L. Lamphere. Stanford: Stanford University Press.

Lancaster, C. S. 1976. Women, horticulture, and society in Sub-Saharan Africa. *Am. Anthropol.* 78:539–564.

Langness, L. L. 1974. Ritual, power, and male dominance. *Ethos* 2:189–212.

Leis, Nancy B. 1974. Women in groups: Ijaw women's association. In *Woman, culture, and society,* ed. M. Z. Rosaldo and L. Lamphere. Stanford: Stanford University Press.

LeVine, Robert A. 1966. Sex roles and economic change in Africa. *Ethnology* 5:186–193.

Lévi-Strauss, Claude. 1949. *Les Structures élémentaires de la parenté.* Paris. Presses Universitaires de France.

————. 1962. *La Pensée sauvage.* Paris: Plon.

―――. 1964. *Mythologiques I: Le Cru et le cuit*. Paris: Plon.

―――. 1966. *Mythologiques II: Du Miel aux cendres*. Paris: Plon.

―――. 1967. *Mythologiques III: L'Origine des manières de table*. Paris: Plon.

―――. 1971. *Mythologiques IV: L'Homme nu*. Paris: Plon.

Lindenbaum, Shirley. 1972. Sorcerers, ghosts, and polluting women: An analysis of religious belief and population control. *Ethnology* 11: 241–253.

Martin, M. Kay, and Voorhies, Barbara. 1975. *Female of the species*. New York: Columbia University Press.

Matthiasson, Carolyn J., ed. 1974. *Many sisters: Women in cross-cultural perspective*. New York: Free Press.

Mathieu, N. C. 1973. Homme-culture, femme-nature? *L'Homme* 13: 101–113.

Meggitt, M. J. 1964. Male-female relationships in the highlands of Australian New Guinea. *Am. Anthropol.* 66:204–224.

Michaelson, E. J., and Goldschmidt, W. 1971. Female roles and male dominance among peasants. *Southwest. J. Anthropol.* 27:330–352.

Mohsen, Safia K. 1974. The Egyptian woman: Between modernity and tradition. In *Many sisters: Women in cross-cultural perspective*. New York: Free Press.

Murphy, Yolanda, and Murphy, Robert F. 1974. *Women of the forest*. New York: Columbia University Press.

Nerlove, Sara B. 1974. Women's workload and infant feeding practices: A relationship with demographic implications. *Ethnology* 13:207–214.

Netting, Robert. 1969. Women's weapons: The politics of domesticity among the Kofyar. *Am. Anthropol.* 71:1037–1046.

O'Laughlin, Bridget. 1974. Mediation of contradiction: Why Mbum women do not eat chicken. In *Woman, culture, and society*, ed. M. Z. Rosaldo and L. Lamphere. Stanford: Stanford University Press.

Ortner, Sherry B. 1974. Is female to male as nature is to culture? In *Woman, culture, and society*, ed. M. Z. Rosaldo and L. Lamphere. Stanford: Stanford University Press.

Paulme, Denise, ed. 1963. *Women of tropical Africa*. Berkeley: University of California Press.

Peristiany, J. G., ed. 1966. *Honour and shame: The values of Mediterranean society*. Chicago: University of Chicago Press.

Radcliffe-Brown, A. R. 1950. Introduction. In *African systems of kinship and marriage*, ed. A. R. Radcliffe-Brown and Daryll Forde. Oxford: Oxford University Press.

Reichel-Dolmatoff, Gerardo. 1971. *Amazonian cosmos: The sexual and religious symbolism of the Tukano Indians*. Chicago: University of Chicago Press.

Reiter, Rayna R., ed. 1975. *Toward an anthropology of women*. New York: Monthly Review Press.

Remy, Dorothy. 1975. Underdevelopment and the experience of women. A Nigerian case study. In *Toward an anthropology of women*, ed. R. R. Reiter. New York: Monthly Review Press.

Richards, Audrey. 1956. *Chisungu: A girl's initiation ceremony among the Bemba of Northern Rhodesia*. London: Faber and Faber.

Richards, Cara E. 1974. Onondaga women: Among the liberated. In *Many sisters: Women in cross-cultural perspective*, ed. C. J. Matthiasson. New York: Free Press.

Riegelhaupt, Joyce F. 1967. Saloio women: An analysis of informal and formal political and economic roles of Portuguese peasant women. *Anthropol. Quart.* 40:109–126.

Rogers, Susan Carol. 1975. Female forms of power and the myth of male dominance: A model of female/male interaction in peasant society. *Am. Ethnol.* 2:727–756.

Rosaldo, Michelle Zimbalist. 1974. Woman, culture, and society: A theoretical overview. In *Woman, culture, and society*, ed. M. Z. Rosaldo and L. Lamphere. Stanford: Stanford University Press.

Rosaldo, Michelle, and Atkinson, Jane. 1975. Man the hunter and woman: Metaphors for the sexes in Ilongot magical spells. In *The interpretation of symbolism*, ed. Roy Willis. New York: Halstead Press.

Rosaldo, Michelle Zimbalist, and Lamphere, Louise, eds. 1974. *Woman, culture, and society*. Stanford: Stanford University Press.

Rubbo, Anna. 1975. The spread of capitalism in rural Colombia: Effects on poor women. In *Toward an anthropology of women*, ed. R. R. Reiter. New York: Monthly Review Press.

Sacks, Karen. 1976. State bias and women's status. *Am. Anthropol.* 78:565–569.

Sanday, Peggy R. 1973. Toward a theory of the status of women. *Am. Anthropol.* 75:1682–1700.

———. 1974. Female status in the public domain. In *Woman, culture, and society*, ed. M. Z. Rosaldo and L. Lamphere. Stanford: Stanford University Press.

Sapir, Edward. 1949. Male and female forms of speech in Yana (originally published in 1929). In *Language, culture and personality*, ed. David Mandelbaum. Berkeley: University of California Press.

Schlegel, Alice. 1972. *Male dominance and female autonomy: Domestic authority in matrilineal society*. New Haven: HRAF Press.

———. 1973. The adolescent socialization of the Hopi girl. *Ethnology* 12:499–462.

Schneider, Jane. 1971. Of vigilance and virgins: Honor, shame, and access to resources in Mediterranean society. *Ethnology* 10:1–24.

Seeger, Anthony. 1974. *Nature and culture and their transformations in the cosmology and social organization of the Suyá, a Gê-speaking tribe of Central Brazil.* Ph.D. dissertation, Department of Anthropology, University of Chicago.

Shapiro, Judith R. 1972. *Sex roles and social structure among the Yanomama Indians of Northern Brazil.* Ph.D. dissertation, Department of Anthropology, Columbia University.

————. 1975. Review of *Female of the species* by M. Kay Martin and Barbara Voorhies. *Science* 190:874–875.

————. 1976a. Review of *Women of the forest* by Yolanda Murphy and Robert F. Murphy. *Am. J. Sociol.* 81:981–983.

————.1976b. Sexual hierarchy among the Yanomama. In *Sex and class in Latin America,* ed. June Nash and Helen Icken Safa. New York: Praeger.

————. 1976c. Determinants of sex role differentiation: The kibbutz case. *Rev. Anthropol.* 3:682–692.

Silverman, Sydel. 1967. The life crisis as a clue to social function. *Anthropol. Quart.* 40:127–138.

Slocum, Sally. 1975. Woman the gatherer: Male bias in anthropology. In *Toward an anthropology of women,* ed. R. R. Reiter. New York: Monthly Review Press.

Stack, Carol; Caulfield, Mina Davis; Estes, Valerie; Landes, Susan; Larson, Karen; Johnson, Pamela; Rake, Juliet; and Shirek, Judith. 1975. Anthropology (review essay). *Signs* 1:147–159.

Strathern, Marilyn. 1972. *Women in between: Female roles in a male world: Mount Hagen, New Guinea.* New York: Seminar Press.

Sweet, Louise. 1967. Introduction to special issue on Appearance and reality: Status and roles of women in Mediterranean societies. *Anthropol. Quart.* 40:95–96.

————. 1974. In reality: Some Middle Eastern women. In *Many sisters: Women in cross-cultural perspective,* ed. C. J. Matthiasson. New York: Free Press.

Talmon, Yonina. 1965. Sex-role differentiation in an equalitarian society. In *Life in society,* ed. Thomas Lasswell, John Burman, and Sidney Aronson. Glenview, Ill.: Scott, Foresman.

————. 1972. *Family and community in the kibbutz.* Cambridge: Harvard University Press.

Tiger, Lionel. 1969. *Men in groups.* New York: Random House.

Tiger, Lionel, and Fox, Robin. 1971. *The imperial animal.* New York: Holt, Rinehart and Winston.

Warner, W. Lloyd, 1937. *A black civilization: A social study of an Australian tribe.* New York: Harper and Brothers.

Whitehead, Harriet. 1976. *The dynamics of chastity and the politics of mutilation.* Paper read at the Symposium on Social Structure, Ideology and Women's Choices, American Anthropological Association annual meeting, November 17–21, 1976, Washington, D.C.

Whiting, J. W. M.; Kluckhohn, R.; and Anthony, A. S. 1958. The function of male initiation ceremonies at puberty. In *Readings in social psychology,* 3d edition, ed. E. E. Maccoby, T. M. Newcomb, and E. I. Hartley. New York: Wiley.

Wolf, Margery. 1968. *The house of Lim.* New York: Appleton-Century-Crofts.

Young, Frank W. 1965. *Initiation rites: A cross-cultural study of status dramatization.* Indianapolis: Bobbs-Merrill.

Anthropology and Sex: Developmental Aspects

Robert A. LeVine

The usual approach of psychological anthropology to the understanding of a behavioral domain in human development proceeds as follows: (1) Ethnographic cases are adduced which show behavior in that domain to be more variable cross-culturally than psychologists and psychiatrists had assumed. (2) A review of diverse ethnographic evidence leads to the identification of some universal features. (3) The universals are attributed to certain biosocial constants for the human species, while the variables are correlated (in statistical or informal comparison) with variations in cultural ecology, social structure, and values. (4) The variable aspects of the domain are shown to require, for their maintenance in a specific culture, their introduction into psychological ontogeny at an early stage in the life of the individual. (5) Studies are then conducted that seek to show how cross-cultural variations in childhood environments influence psychological development to produce behavioral variation in that domain.

In the case of sexuality and sex roles in human development, we are faced with a paradox: on the one hand, it seems that we went through the above process a long time ago, beginning (let us say) in 1935 with Margaret Mead's *Sex and Temperament in Three Primitive Societies* and ending in 1966 with Roy D'Andrade's article, "Sex Differences and Cultural Institutions." To go over that ground again would be redundant. On the other hand, hardly any of the issues raised during those thirty years have been resolved empirically, and in the last decade more problems than data have accumulated. A review of cross-cultural evidence concerning the psychological and developmental aspects of sexuality and sex roles would certainly reveal a body of data inadequate to answer the more urgent questions of behavioral scientists. The discussion that follows calls attention to issues that deserve further investigation.

Erotic and Reproductive Behavior

As Judith Shapiro's paper indicates, there have been many recent additions to the ethnographic record on the roles and relations of men and women in diverse societies. By excluding from her review consideration of erotic and reproductive behavior, Shapiro conforms fairly closely to the literature she is reviewing, which is concerned with issues of labor, status, domination, antagonism, and symbolic communication in relations between males and females—but not with their sexual relations. This approach represents the viewpoints of the anthropologists of particular theoretical schools or persuasions (Marxist, structuralist, symbolic, feminist), but it does not necessarily represent the viewpoints of the peoples the authors are writing about.

When anthropologists omit erotic and reproductive goals and interests from their ethnographic accounts of sex roles and relations, it is not because such goals and interests are absent from the experience of sex roles and relations among the people described. On the contrary, erotic and reproductive factors play a great part in the way most peoples experience and react to sex and gender (however defined). The omission occurs only when the ethnographer chooses to omit the aspect of sex and gender.[1] My impression is that the recent literature falls into two categories: one (covered by Shapiro) in which the ethnographer, having a strong theoretical position that accords no place to the erotic side of life, prefers to ignore it (in this, puritanical radicalism and sociological estheticism coincide); the other (much smaller) in which the ethnographer describes some aspects of sexual behavior and experience but without a coherent theoretical analysis. Both categories of literature reflect the absence in contemporary anthropology of a coherent theoretical framework in which to collect and analyze cross-cultural data regarding human sexual behavior.

1. Professor Shapiro points out that this explanation does not take into account the difficulties young single women anthropologists would face were they to carry out research on erotic behavior in most field settings, and the more general problems of lack of institutional support and concerns about legitimacy surrounding such work. [Ed.]

Sex Differences in Development

There has been at least one significant comparative study of sex differences in behavioral development. Whiting and Edwards (1973) compared the observed social behavior of children drawn from seven communities (two in Africa, three in Asia, one in Mexico, and one in the United States). They sought to find the extent to which the sex differences conformed to those of standard stereotypes, whether such differences were replicated across the seven samples at different age levels (suggesting universality), whether universal differences were present at the earliest age level (suggesting genetic influence), and whether age differences for a sex in a sample could be related to environmental factors distinctive to the community from which that sample was drawn. The findings are summarized as follows:

> (a) There are universal sex differences in the behavior of children 3-11 years of age, but the differences are not consistent nor as great as the studies of American and Western European children would suggest, (b) socialization pressure in the form of task assignment and the associated frequency of interaction with different categories of individuals—i.e., infants, adults and peers—may well explain many of these differences, (c) aggression, perhaps especially rough and tumble play, and touching behavior seem the best candidates for biophysical genesis; (d) all of the behaviors which are characteristic of males and females seem remarkably malleable under the impact of socialization pressures, which seem to be remarkably consistent from one society to another; and (e) the difference in many of the types of behavior seems to be one of style rather than intent—i.e., seeking help ("feminine") rather than attention ("masculine"), and justifying dominance by appealing to the rules ("feminine") rather than straight egoistic dominance ("masculine") (Whiting and Edwards, 1973, p. 188).

Culturally Defined Stereotypes

One way of conceptualizing the potential contribution of anthropology to the scientific understanding of sex and gender is by showing how psychosocial elements that form parts of an influential sexual stereotype in our culture are disaggregated and assembled quite differently in some other cultures. One example is the sexual stereotype of *macho* or *machismo*, widely recognized to be characteristic of North American culture as well as of the more

311

expressive Latins who contributed the terms we use to describe it. The stereotype consists of the following parts:

First, a constant concern with projecting a masculine appearance, which in turn has several parts: (a) desire to display secondary sexual characteristics (muscular physique and physical strength; hair on face, chest, arms); (b) swagger or other characteristic gait or posture thought to display masculine strength or self-confidence); (c) an unyielding or "tough" reaction to being publicly challenged, even on a trivial matter, thought to suggest a ferocious bellicosity being held in check; (d) concern with prowess in sexual performance, relating this conceptually to physical strength; (e) pride in biological paternity as evidence of virility; (f) fear of being seen as feminine, manifested by exaggerated rejection of activities, emotions, or clothing remotely associated with the appearance of femininity.

Second, there is the assumption that the successful projection of a masculine appearance makes a man sexually attractive to women; this belief is a conscious motive for maintaining masculine appearance.

Third, there is the sexually exploitative attitude toward women, seeing them as "sex objects" and seeking to prove one can attract them away from other men and "conquer" as many women as possible.

Fourth, there is the jealous protectiveness concerning women under one's own control by virtue of consanguinity or marriage.

And finally, there is the concern with male dominance in relations with females.

This stereotype as I have sketched it may be an accurate characterization of a psychosocial style that is variably legitimized in Western cultural settings ranging from Italian society to cowboy films and affecting areas as diverse as the socialization of small children and opposition to gun control laws. On the other hand, it may be an inaccurate portrayal, at best a caricature of psychosocial reality, constructed by feminists to ridicule certain opponents and attack the sexual status quo. In either case, the stereotype is an organization of ideas that function together in a mutually consistent manner and attain an ideological coherence within the confines of our culture. But the macho stereotype does not coincide with the concept of masculinity in other cultures, such as the African ones I have worked in. A major reason for this seems to lie in a different set of relationships between social structure, social appearances, and the sexual motives of individuals.

In many African societies, for example, male dominance and sexual access to women are established as aspects of social structure, either as general properties of sex status or as prerogatives of high position. In either case, they are removed from the field of visible competitive interaction among males, and it is almost inconceivable that a man would try to project an appearance of greater masculinity than other men in order to command respect from women or attract them sexually. Among some of these peoples, men are primarily concerned to display the distinctive tokens of age status or wealth, by growing beards when their hair has turned white and growing fat to show their greater leisure and food resources. Where age and girth lead to prestige, older and fatter men have an edge in competition for women, whom they implicitly offer a share in their wealth, rather than romance. Sexual attractiveness, sexual prowess, and biological paternity are of minor importance as matters of invidious comparison among men. Ethnobiological beliefs do not link masculine physique with sexual performance and fertility, and ethnopsychological beliefs do not relate sexual performance to bellicosity and self-confidence.

While the macho syndrome as such does not exist, none of its elements are entirely absent in African societies; they are embedded in different cultural styles and play different parts in the individual's goal structure, self-concept, and psychosocial development. These variable connections between cultural standards, individual experience, and biological events in the sexual development of children and adults are precisely what anthropology can and should be illuminating.

Protest Masculinity

Though cultural styles of masculinity and femininity vary considerably, there are striking recurrences among peoples otherwise remote from each other in distance and historical background. One recurrent pattern that has been studied comparatively and developmentally is the "protest masculinity" of young men who engage in violence of one kind or another as an exaggerated display of male aggressiveness (without necessarily erotic implications). John W. M. Whiting and his associates have been investigating this phenomenon cross-culturally for many years, beginning with a study of the function of male initiation ceremonies (Whiting, Kluckhohn, and Anthony, 1958).

The latest and most comprehensive study in this series is that of Whiting and Whiting (1975). Their theory is that in male-dominant societies boys whose fathers interact with them very little in early childhood form an unconscious identification with their mothers that they seek to counteract in young adulthood through hyperaggressive behavior, which may be legitimized in the military role of warrior or expressed in crimes of violence. The Whitings support this formulation with correlational evidence from a large sample of diverse societies, calling particular attention to the psychological consequences of institutionalized housing arrangements in which men sleep and eat apart from their wives and children, leaving the latter to be reared in a world of women. Though direct developmental evidence is lacking and the links with sexuality have yet to be spelled out, "protest masculinity" remains the most intriguing hypothesis concerning psychosocial aspects of masculinity that has been explored so far in cross-cultural research.

There is an enormous amount of research to be done. The peoples of the world have much to teach us about the cultural integration of sexual development with other aspects of psychosocial adaptation—if we would let them. Here, for example, are the observations of a missionary on the Asmat people in West Irian (formerly Netherlands New Guinea):

> Headhunting is required for the bodily development of young men and for their sexual maturation. The Asmat is inclined to consider that things having a similarity in shape or otherwise [are] related. . . . The decapitated head of a victim is laid between the out-spread legs of the initiate, almost touching the genitals of the boy who is about to mature sexually. I have repeatedly been told that after this ceremony the boys grow very fast. . . . [As] the human head is associated with fruit, the Asmat expect that the germinative power of the head (fruit) will be transferred to the boy's genitals by the ritual of placing it between his legs, and thus that it will enable him to reproduce (Zegwaard, 1959, p. 1039).

> . . . In Asmat society all prestige, and therefore all authority, is ultimately derived from achievements in war. It is impossible to be a man of social standing without having captured a few

heads. A bunch of skulls at the door post is a measure of status (Zegwaard, 1959, p. 1040).

. . . An Asmat can marry without having acquired a single head, even without initiation, but he will be constantly reminded of his nothingness. His opinion will not be asked in the bachelor's house; his own wife will pay little attention to him. . . . He is not considered a real man; he belongs to the category of women and children. . . . As a result, he may work himself into a frenzy and go out and kill. Then he can look eye to eye with the other men and has the admiration of the women and children, for he has proven that he too has a soul. . . . There is also a vague relationship between headhunting and sexual intercourse, which seems to follow from the manner in which headhunting contributes to manliness. Mention has been made of the cry of the headhunters at the beginning of the attack: "I am your husband from Sijuru." It seems to me that the enemy is called woman for more than one reason. But undoubtedly, headhunting is drawn into the sexual sphere. There is a story telling how some men were decapitated and how their heads were miraculously restored, but this was a secret the women were not to know. When the secret was given away by a child, the men were unmanned and transformed into dolphins (which have a hole in the nape of the neck and a skull that shows a striking resemblance to the human skull) (Zegwaard, 1959, p. 1041).

In the face of such data, the highest priorities for a psychological anthropology of sex are (1) to understand the diverse meanings that cultures give to the universals of sex and gender, (2) to find out how these meanings function in the responsiveness and regulations of men and women as they organize their interpersonal relationships and their sexual conduct, and (3) to discover how these meanings, and the patterns of responsiveness and regulation observed in adults, are acquired by children. In the files of anthropologists there is in fact a great deal more information concerning the first two of these points than has found its way into print, and Robert Edgerton and Robert Stoller have been attempting to assemble a volume that brings some of it out into the open for scientific examination.

In addition to deepening the psychological relevance of ethnographic data on sex and gender, as Edgerton and Stoller are doing, anthropologists have the opportunity to use their access to the phenomena of social change—which usually affects sex roles, gender identities, and sexual conduct—to disentangle some of the elements inevitably confounded in synchronic analysis, with the goal of identifying environmental factors that influence sexual development. Causal links that would otherwise escape notice might be identified by comparing individuals of different generational cohorts within the same community, whose early learning environments contained different cultural standards of acceptable feminine, masculine, and erotic behavior or differential exposure to male and female role models.

Sex and Its Psychosocial Derivatives

Studies of other cultures provide data that can be used extensively in testing our hypotheses about gender identity, sexual behavior, and sex roles. The importance of cross-cultural studies can be illustrated by several issues that arose during the conference on Sex and Its Psychosocial Derivatives: (1) overt behavior vs. subjective meaning in the study of human sexuality; (2) critical periods in the formation of gender identity; (3) the politics of scientific research on human sexual behavior.

Behavior and Meaning

There is no necessary opposition between approaching human sexuality as overt behavior and also in terms of its subjective meanings; both aspects are required in comparative and developmental investigations. We can construct transcultural categories based on universal human activities that recur, though at varying rates and in varying situations, through the life course:

1. sexual arousal and orgasm;
2. reproductive activities (including conception, contraception, pregnancy, birth);
3. interpersonal relationships (such as stable and short-term, heterosexual and homosexual, kin-based and associational);
4. economic activities, and so on. Each of these categories represents an aspect of the life history in which a lifespan activity career could be described in terms of overt behavior, for an individual and for aggregates or populations of individuals.

Each culture as a collective system of beliefs and values includes a conceptual organization of these activity careers and ideals concerning them at different phases of the lives of man and woman. Different cultures offer differing beliefs about how sex, reproduction, and interpersonal relationships are related to each other and to gender-specific role behavior, and differing ideals about how these activity careers should be related. To describe a culture's beliefs and values on these topics is to explicate the cultural meanings of sex and gender that are represented in the subjective experience of the individual.

The varying ways in which cultures combine or segregate sex, reproduction, and marital relationships can be illustrated by considering some of the polygynous societies of Africa in which husband-wife social and sexual relations are organized around reproductive goals to such a degree that they virtually cease once the wife reaches menopause, after which she devotes herself to independent economic activity and grandmotherhood (with its vicarious reproductiveness), while the husband devotes his attention to younger wives.

In some cases the meanings in these relationships become evident to the outside observer only when examined from a life-course perspective that includes the later years. In tracing the trajectories of activity careers through ideal and actual life histories, both the cultural and the personal meanings of overt behavior, sexual and gender-related, can become objects of empirical study.

The Critical-Period Hypothesis

In her review of clinical research and developmental studies on the formation of gender identity, Zella Luria found evidence to support the notion of a critical period for the development of core gender identity between the ages of 18 and 36 months. Luria notes as aspects of this development the linguistic use of gender labels, the choice of same-sex playmates and gender-coded toys, and the expectancies (and pressures) of parents and peers. My colleagues and I have recently completed a longitudinal study of twenty-eight African children (fourteen of each sex) over much of this age span. Our data raise many questions about the hypotheses outlined by Luria.

Our study was conducted among the Gusii people of southwestern Kenya, whose early learning environment for children has the following features relevant to hypotheses concerning the formation of gender identity:

317

1. The Gusii speak a Bantu language which, like all Bantu languages has no gender in the linguistic sense, that is, no pronominal forms coded by sex. Thus, when Gusii children learn to use third-person pronouns, they are not simultaneously learning to assign gender labels to persons and objects in their environment. Does the absence of gender labels make a difference in the age and stage at which children become aware of themselves as boys or girls?

2. Gusii children are reared in small mixed groups of siblings and half-siblings, often with no possibility of choosing playmates close in age by sex. Whether choice is possible or not, they do not seem to show same-sex preference at ages two or three—a point that can be empirically tested in our observational data. This finding might bear on the universality of same-sex preference in playmates at this age.

3. Gusii children have few toys, and there is little evidence that toys are sex-coded or that boys and girls express different preferences. Does culture make a difference?

4. Although the gender roles of Gusii men and women are strongly differentiated, and Gusii parents view the potential value of male and female children very differently, we saw few signs of differential treatment of or attitude toward boys and girls in infancy and early childhood. Furthermore, the early environment of children seems much less fraught with pressures toward sex-role conformity or stigma for deviance than ours is. It will be interesting to see how many of the sex differences we usually attribute to environmental pressure manifest themselves among the Gusii children.

Luria's contribution thus brought a number of developmental issues into comparative focus for me, and I hope we can analyze our data so as to throw cross-cultural light on the issues mentioned above. In any event, the questions raised by the Gusii example illustrate the continuing relevance of data from other cultures for the testing of developmental hypotheses concerning sex roles.

References

LeVine, R. A. 1959. Gusii sex offenses: A study in social control. *Am. Anthropol.* 61:965–990.

Whiting, B., and Edwards, C. 1973. A cross-cultural analysis of sex differences in the behavior of children aged three through eleven. *J. Social Psychol.* 91:171–188.

Whiting, J.; Kluckhohn, R.; and Anthony, A. 1958. The function of male initiation ceremonies at puberty. In *Readings in social psychology,* ed. E. Maccoby, T. Newcomb, and E. Hartley. New York: Holt.

Whiting, J., and Whiting, B. 1975. Aloofness and intimacy of husbands and wives: A cross-cultural study. *Ethos* 3:183–207.

Zegwaard, G. 1959. Head-hunting practices of the Asmat of Netherlands New Guinea. *Am. Anthropol.* 61:1020–1041.

Contributions of Anthropology to the Study of Gender Identity, Gender Role, and Sexual Behavior

Beatrice B. Whiting

Judith Shapiro has presented a comprehensive review of recently published anthropological monographs that discuss the hierarchical status of women, especially their relative position in the power structure vis-à-vis men; she has reviewed the diversity of role definitions that are sex-linked; she has summarized some of the most recent studies of beliefs about the nature of men and women, their relation to each other and to the universe. Her summary is essentially a modern version of cultural relativism. The works reviewed are descriptive and interpretive. There are new data, particularly in the realm of ethnopsychology, and countless new and not-so-new hypotheses as to the interrelationship between economics, social structure, politics, and ideology.

Shapiro's presentation is stimulating, and it reminds us of the plasticity of human beings; but its relevance or possible contribution to the study of sexuality is oblique. The authors whose work she presents have been content to rest their case on coherence truth; they eschew correspondence truth. They use psychological theories to support their interpretations but, as Shapiro points out, do not scrutinize these theories or consider them in the context of alternatives. Too frequently they fall into the error of drawing conclusions from the comparison of two naturally occurring cases.

Granted that cultural relativism broadens our vision, what insights can we get from this new generation of anthropologists? Two areas discussed in the Shapiro paper are especially relevant to papers presented by other authors in this volume. The first is

320

the analysis of the changing roles of men and women during the life span and the presence or absence of rituals and feelings of anguish during the transitions. The second is the review of new detailed data collected by anthropologists on the concepts of the nature of men and women and their relationship to each other.

LeVine's approach is of particular relevance to the research aspirations expressed by Sears and others. He is interested in life-span psychology, the life-course patterns of an individual from infancy to old age. In common with psychologists interested in life careers, LeVine seeks to relate the experiences of infancy to the emotions stated and observed in later life. He observes the rituals performed in his African cultures at the transitions between life stages and attempts to show how these sequential experiences shape the marital, reproductive, and later life careers of men and women. LeVine takes an essentially clinical approach, treating each culture as a case and monitoring the sequential experiences of males and females.

Unlike many of the anthropologists described by Shapiro, LeVine believes there are transcultural categories for career lines, universal principles that underlie the progression through the life course, and that these can be discovered by cross-cultural comparisons. Such comparisons require that researchers agree to collect comparable data, an anathema to more humanistic anthropologists who, as Shapiro states, are not interested in prediction.

Gender Identity

My work and that of John Whiting is more similar to LeVine's in that we are committed to prediction and detailed cross-cultural comparison. Of our work, John Whiting's research on cross-sex identity is the most relevant to the theme of this volume (Whiting, Kluckhohn, and Anthony, 1958; J. Whiting, 1960; Burton and Whiting, 1961; B. Whiting, 1965). This work is worth presenting in somewhat more detail as it relates to research on the age at which gender identity is established and the possibility of reassignment.

John Whiting's research suggests that in some societies there is a radical shift in gender identity between infancy and adulthood, often accompanied by elaborate rituals. As LeVine has mentioned, in many societies, especially in those that are polygynous and situated in the tropics, fathers remain aloof from domestic tasks and seldom handle infants. Until the age of four or five, children spend most of their time with women and other children. Frequently there is no generic kinship term such as *parent* that includes both the father and the mother, and often young boys as well as girls are labeled by a term that includes adult females. Using a theory of status envy, John Whiting (1960) has hypothesized that young boys reared under these conditions have an early identification with women. This self-concept of being like a woman is associated with labels and grammatical forms that do not clearly distinguish the gender of young children. In societies of this type in East Africa, where we have observed the social behavior of boys and girls between the ages of two and seven, there are comparatively few sex differences (Whiting and Edwards, 1973; Whiting and Whiting, 1975). In this type of society, the well-known male initiation rites that include hazing, genital operations, and bonding to males serve the avowed purpose of changing the boy's status from that of "woman-child" to adult male. If this native theory is accepted, it implies that a boy's early gender identity as woman-child is established before he is aware of the hierarchical status of males in his society and before he is aware that he will one day join this status group.

By five or six in many of these societies, the young boys are encouraged to move out of their mother's sleeping quarters and join their fathers or older brothers. In some New Guinea societies the first transition rites take place at this time; the male child is placed between his mother's legs and then removed from this position by an adult male. A second transition is marked by a rebirth ceremony that occurs at eight or nine, at which time the male child crawls through a basket woven in the shape of a vagina.

These cross-cultural data suggest that certain rituals may act as a form of therapeutic "brainwashing" helping the young male make the transition to a new gender identity with new role expectations. In societies in which the father remains aloof in infancy and no transitional rituals occur, the culture may permit males to act out latent feminine identity by practices such as the couvade (Munroe, Munroe, and Whiting, 1973; Munroe and Munroe, 1971; Munroe, Munroe, and Nerlove, 1973).

If further research validates these findings, we can infer that gender identity may be established at an early age, as Luria suggests, but gender identity does not necessarily correspond to sex identity; contrary to the evidence Luria has presented, initial gender identity may be pressured to change at a later point in the life span. In such cases, however, group norms and rituals are involved, rather than aberrant or deviant individuals. As suggested by Maccoby, the possibility of reassignment of gender identity is clearly an area in which further cross-cultural research would be valuable.

Studies of the effect of father salience on gender identity in our own society have fallen into disrepute because the data have been used to stereotype and derogate Black families. The new research on the effects of divorce on children of various ages and the growing number of White families headed by females may make it possible to resume research to explore the effects of male and female salience on the development of gender identity.

In research on the effect of father absence carried out at the Laboratory of Human Development at Harvard during the sixties by Roy D'Andrade and Lyn Kuchenberg Carlsmith, age two through three was the critical age for predicting differences in gender-relevant behavior (D'Andrade, 1973; Carlsmith, 1973).

Related is the cross-cultural research that John Whiting and I have been conducting on dimensions of aloofness and intimacy in husband-wife relations and their association with patterns of child rearing and adult male and female bonding (Whiting and Whiting, 1975). Intimacy is found in the most simple and the most complex societies, whereas aloofness is common among hoe and digging-stick agriculturalists and pastoralists. Associated with husband and wife aloofness is strong same-sex bonding.

A similar relationship between husband-wife aloofness and same-sex bonding has been reported in recent studies in England (Bott, 1972; Young and Willmott, 1957). The effect of same-sex bonding on male and female self-concept, role behavior, and affective and heterosexual behavior seems a promising area for research.

Sexual Behavior

Although there is little new ethnographic data on sexual behavior —for the reasons discussed by Judith Shapiro—Gwen Broude (1975), George Goethals (1971), John Whiting (manuscript), and George P. Murdock (1964), using the existing published data, have explored the correlation of premarital sexual permissiveness with other aspects of culture. Early correlations reported relate the presence of castes and social classes to restrictive practices, ostensibly to prevent girls from being impregnated by males of a lower-ranking social group. A paper by Broude (1975) reports a strong correlation between close body proximity with caretakers in infancy and permissiveness in premarital relations, and suggests that anxiety about intimate sexual relations may be greatest in adults whose early experience has been that of the "bundled" baby, living in cribs and baby carriages, sleeping alone, and not spending periods of the day in close body contact with others.

Other cross-cultural studies relevant to sexuality include the work of Barbara Ayers (1967) on pregnancy taboos and their possible relation to premarital norms of sexual behavior and sex anxiety, as well as Stephens' (1967) studies of the relation of menstrual taboos and postpartum sex taboos to attitudes and rules concerning sexual behavior.

Two types of cross-cultural research strategies are available for the study of sexual behavior and its association with gender identity and gender-role behavior. The first type is based on published ethnographic data. In addition to an ever-growing body of detailed accounts of customary life in hundreds of societies, some of the sociological and cultural information has been coded and is published in the *Ethnographic Atlas* (Murdock, 1967). There are codes for economic variables, types of social groups, forms of marriage, types of marriage contracts, residence rules, and many other background variables, as well as some rituals and child-training practices. When used with methodological constraints such as sample selection, quality control, and detailed knowledge of the development of the codes, this body of data is useful in exploring hypotheses about the interrelationship of identifiable life-cycle events, such as the relations of father's salience in infancy, culturally prescribed male dominance in the adult world, same-sex bonding, and male initiation rites. Although these studies are constrained by the nature of the ethnographic data, they are useful for jeopardizing hypotheses and exploring new hunches. Since they are correlational, they can only suggest causal relationships.

A second strategy is the planning and carrying out of field

research testing the relation between variables judged by other research to be interrelated. Of particular importance is the selection of societies that can be compared on the basis of either the presence or the absence of predictor variables or variation in points on a delineated measure of independent and/or dependent variables. In these societies, as LeVine has outlined, one can follow the life career lines of men and women and test the applicability of transcultural categories for their descriptions.

Over the years social scientists have been establishing research bases in various parts of the world, where local behavioral scientists have been either directly involved or trained as apprentices by working in collaboration with Europeans and Americans. (For a description of one such project financed by Carnegie Corporation, see J. Whiting, 1970.) The study of sexual behavior might profit from work in these locations through the collaboration of an insider who understands the subtleties of language, symbols, and body language with an outsider who has a comparative perspective.

The aims of such research are to collect comparable data and to encourage young investigators to replicate studies in various cultural contexts. An example of this type of research is a data "potlatch" financed by the Ford Foundation. Sixteen anthropologists and psychologists have agreed to code data that has been collected using similar formats and to analyze this data in a similar manner in order to test hypotheses concerning sex differences in children's activities and social behavior by replicating the comparisons in each society. We have comparable data on children aged two through eleven in eighteen samples, including families in West, South, and East Africa, Mexico, Guatemala, India, the Philippines, Okinawa, and the United States.

Unfortunately, none of us has tried to code sexual behavior in children. It is my opinion, however, that two of our social-interaction categories, both involving body contact, have sexual components—rough-and-tumble play, and seeking and offering physical contact. The former, which is more prevalent in boys, is associated with sociability but may end in an aggressive exchange. Seeking and offering physical contact is more frequent in girls and is associated with seeking and offering comfort and types of behavior that have often been labeled "dependency." If it were possible to untangle the components of these observed behaviors, we might be able to explore the parameters of early sexual development.

Sexual learning in these societies has been sadly neglected by researchers. Jane Lancaster has mentioned the training of girls among the Goba in Zambia. There is published data on the Kpelle bush schools in Liberia, some information in detailed accounts of male and female initiation in Melanesia and Africa. *Patterns of Sexual Behavior* by Ford and Beach is an excellent summary of this data.

Although young people learn about sexual behavior in all societies, frequently members of the grandparental generation, rather than parents, are the instructors and there is a culturally proscribed avoidance of discussion of sex between adjacent generations. Assuming the wisdom of cultures, it is worth exploring how other societies have transmitted information about sexual behavior and their beliefs, values, and sexual appetites.

Directions for New Research

Since in our society research on sexuality is undoubtedly biased by norms and values about appropriate sexual and gender-specific behavior, it seems clear, as Shapiro, LeVine, and others have advised, that we should look at relevant data from other cultures.[1] Unfortunately the data is not extensive. Its paucity is undoubtedly due in part to the age and reticence of ethnographers, but also in large part to universal cultural taboos that surround the discussion of sexual matters. I know of no society where copulation is public. Although some societies are more open than others both in the degree of sexual foreplay displayed in public and in the discussion of erotica, probably there will always be a wall of reserve and even suspicion that makes the interchange of information between members of different social groups difficult.

For these reasons I suggest that we solicit the help of the social scientists of other countries. There are, for example, educated women from various parts of the world who, being aware of the sexual and marital problems arising from industrialization, might well join with us as colleagues in this investigation. Women

1. These comments are based upon the author's discussions with Robert LeVine and Judith Shapiro.

from developing nations in the Third World are concerned with the changing relationship between men and women and are questioning existing sexual mores. They could become good colleagues in our exploration of sexual and reproductive careers by collecting data from their social groups.

Chester Pierce has cautioned us to approach this research with sensitivity to the fact that, except for the U.S. White middle class, few societies can afford to give high priorities to this topic.[2] For Blacks and other minorities, far more important subjects call for research and policy action. The economic status of Blacks and minority groups is salient. The differential ability of Black men and women to get prestigious jobs is of great concern and has a powerful effect on the relationship between the sexes. Black women are finding it easier than Black men to move into status positions. Pierce's caution should alert us to the fact that sexual mores cannot be studied in a vacuum, but must be considered in relation to maintenance systems, economic and political institutions, and cultural codes that are not, at first glance, related to sexual behavior.

Responding to Chester Pierce's caution that the publishing of research on sexual behavior will involve knotty problems of human consent and arouse political reverberations, LeVine suggests that the research be given institutional support, and that it be legitimized by the international scientific community. Since rapid social change is affecting marriage customs and sexual mores in many countries, and premarital teenage pregnancies and population control are becoming world-wide problems, possibly one branch of an international institute concerned with such problems could be dedicated to the study of erotic behavior and to sexual and reproductive careers.

"Scientific research on human sexual behavior remains a neglected and vulnerable enterprise, lacking in personnel, continuous activity, funds, and public support," LeVine comments.

There are only a few outstanding investigators who have devoted substantial portions of their careers to it. Large-scale investigations occur sporadically and are never properly replicated, leaving questions unanswered for decades. Young investigators make a few contributions and then move on to less

2. Remarks made at the Conference on Sex and Its Psychosocial Derivatives, January 30, 1977, Stanford, California.

sensitive research areas, leaving the field open to commercial exploitation. Our society has not yet decided whether research on human sexuality is good, at least good enough to be legitimized as an aspect of science, a field of study from which benefits might be expected. Although all psychosocial research is potentially offensive to some individuals and groups, our public agencies in their commitment to free speech and the beneficial expansion of science have given institutional sanction to psychological and social research on many topics, but sexual research remains unprotected. If and when the makers of public policy decide that human sexual research should be encouraged, they will have to recognize its controversial nature and provide safeguards to facilitate its development.

Given the type of support proposed by LeVine, what areas of research should be given priorities? First and foremost, to ensure that comparable data is gathered in a variety of societies, we need the delineation of transcultural dimensions that describe sexual and gender-appropriate behavior over the entire life span. Within the life span we should explore (1) changes in the conception of, labels for, and symbols of gender identity; (2) the possibility of a critical age for establishing gender identity; (3) the early environmental influences on the formation of gender-identity, such as the availability of appropriate role models and the growing child's perception of the power structure, both of which may vary during the life span; (4) cultural taboos on the discussion of sex between adjacent generations; (5) institutions which function to teach appropriate sexual behavior or to restructure or emphasize gender identity; and (6) changes during the life span in sexual and gender-specific behavior and its relation to reproductory and economic careers. Both LeVine and Shapiro have stressed the importance of studying sexual symbols. Shapiro has described the insights to be gained from analyzing concepts of maleness and femaleness.

If research is limited to American and Western European cultures that share many of the same beliefs and values about appropriate gender and sexual behavior, we will never know to what extent our findings are culture specific rather than universally human. By attempting to account for observed societal differences in the life course of identity formation and sexual behavior and norms, we may gain insight into those experiences that shape gender and sexual careers.

Professor Shapiro believes that the cultural anthropological approach has important implications for sex research in the United States. Her comments follow:

One of the most important benefits of doing research in a different cultural setting is that our own culture becomes less transparent, less something that can be treated as a "natural" order. Thus, with an anthropological perspective, the study of sexuality in our own society must properly become the study of a particular, culturally patterned form of sexuality—something that sex researchers may tend to lose sight of. I do not agree with Professor Whiting that the concept of cultural variation, or cultural relativism, is something we have all understood and need no longer focus upon *per se.* On the contrary, it seems to me that the significance and implications of this concept are commonly not realized. If they were, more sex researchers would be engaged in attempting to interpret sexual and other gender-related behavior in terms of the set of conventions that render such behavior meaningful, as well as attempting to explain such behavior in terms characteristic of the natural sciences.

To give an example of how such a perspective might contribute to research on sexuality in American society, it is important to have a more systematic understanding of how the value concept of "achievement" enters into American ideas and feelings about erotic and reproductive behavior, gender identity, and sex roles. One might, for example, expect that sex, insofar as it is ascribed, presents a contradiction to the notion of individual freedom to achieve; thus, the question of ascribed versus achieved statuses, in relation to sex, becomes not only a matter for general sociological inquiry, but a problem in American culture. The importance of considering sexuality in the context of concepts of achievement has been raised in this volume by Jean Lipman-Blumen and Harold Leavitt. However, while Lipman-Blumen and Leavitt begin by giving cultural data on the connection between sex and achievement in American society, they go on to construct an abstract typology of achievement orientations—a legitimate and valuable endeavor, but one that differs from what is being suggested here, namely, an investigation of how communications members of a particular society enter into with regard to sex are interpretable in terms of the understandings they share, or, for that matter, disagree about. Such an approach, which is contained in Professor LeVine's contribution to this volume, could bear additional emphasis.

References

Ayers, Barbara. 1967. Pregnancy magic: A study of food taboos and sex avoidances. In *Cross-cultural approaches,* ed. Clellan S. Ford. New Haven: HRAF Press.

Bott, Elizabeth. 1972. *Family and social network,* 2d ed. New York: Free Press.

Broude, Gwen. 1975. Norm of premarital sexual behavior: A cross-cultural study. *Ethos* 3:381–402.

Broude, Gwen, and Greene, Sarah J. 1976. Cross-cultural codes on twenty sexual attitudes and practices. *Ethnology* 15:409–429.

Burton, Roger V., and Whiting, John W. M. 1961. The absent father and cross-sex identity. *Merrill-Palmer Quart.* 7:85–95.

Carlsmith, Lyn. 1973. Some personality characteristics of boys separated from their fathers during World War II. *Ethos* 1:466–477.

D'Andrade, Roy G. 1973. Father absence, identification, and identity. *Ethos* 1:440–445.

Ford, Clellan S., and Beach, Frank A. 1951. *Patterns of sexual behavior.* New York: Harper and Brothers.

Goethals, George W. 1971. Factors affecting rules regarding premarital sex. In *Studies in the sociology of sex,* ed. James M. Hauslen. New York: Appleton-Century-Crofts.

Munroe, R. L., and Munroe, Ruth. 1971. Male pregnancy symptoms and cross-sex identity in three societies. *J. Social Psychol.* 84:11–25.

Munroe, R. L.; Munroe, R. M.; and Nerlove, Sara B. 1973. Male pregnancy symptoms and cross-sex identity: Two replications. *J. Social Psychol.* 89:147–148.

Munroe, R. L.; Munroe, R. M.; and Whiting, J. W. M. 1973. The couvade: A psychological analysis. *Ethos* 1:30–74.

Murdock, G. P. 1964. Cultural correlates of the regulation of premarital sexual behavior. In *Process and pattern in culture: Essays in honor of Julian H. Stuard,* ed. Robert A. Manners. Chicago: Aldine.

————. 1967. Ethnographic atlas: A summary. *Ethology* 6:109–236.

Stephens, W. N. 1967. A cross-cultural study of menstrual taboos. In *Cross-cultural approaches,* ed. Clellan S. Ford. New Haven: HRAF Press.

Whiting, Beatrice. 1965. Sex identity and physical violence: A comparative study. *Am. Anthropol.* 67:123–140.

Whiting, Beatrice, and Edwards, Carolyn. 1973. A cross-cultural analysis of sex differences in the behavior of children aged 3–11. *J. Social Psychol.* 91:171–188.

Whiting, Beatrice, and Whiting, John W. M. 1975. *Children of six cultures: A Psycho-cultural analysis.* Cambridge: Harvard University Press.

Whiting, J. W. M.; Kluckhohn, Richard; and Anthony, Albert S. 1958. The function of male initiation ceremonies at puberty. In *Readings in social psychology,* ed. E. E. Maccoby, T. Neucomb, and E. Hartley. New York: Holt, Rinehart and Winston.

———. 1960. Resource mediation and learning by identification. In *Personality development in children,* ed. I. Iscoe and H. Stevenson. Austin, Texas: University of Texas Press.

———. 1970. *Progress report.* Child Development Research Unit. Harvard University and University College, Nairobi, Kenya (pamphlet).

Whiting, J. W. M., and Whiting, B. B. 1975. Aloofness and intimacy of husbands and wives: A cross-cultural study. *Ethos* 3:183–207.

Young, M., and Willmott, P. 1957. *Family and kinship in East London.* London: Routledge and Kegan Paul.

Appendix: Conference on Psychosocial Derivatives of Sexuality

January 28–30, Stanford, California

List of Participants

Richard D. Alexander
Professor of Zoology
University of Michigan

Frank A. Beach
Professor of Psychology
University of California at Berkeley

Julian M. Davidson
Associate Professor of Physiology
Stanford University

Anke A. Ehrhardt
Psychiatric Institute
Division Child Psychiatry
Columbia University

John H. Gagnon
Visiting Professor, 1978–1979
Graduate School of Education
Harvard University
Professor of Sociology
State University of New York at
    Stony Brook

Richard Green
Professor of Psychiatry, Behavioral
    Science, and Psychology
State University of New York at
    Stony Brook

Albert H. Hastorf
Professor of Psychology
Stanford University

Herant A. Katchadourian
Professor of Psychiatry and
    Behavioral Sciences
Vice Provost and Dean of
    Undergraduate Studies
Stanford University

Jane B. Lancaster
Assistant Professor
Department of Anthropology
University of Oklahoma

Robert A. LeVine
Roy E. Larsen Professor of
    Education and Human
    Development
Chairman, Laboratory of Human
    Development
Harvard University

Harold J. Leavitt
Kilpatrick Professor of
    Organizational Behavior and
    Psychology
Graduate School of Business
Stanford University

Jean Lipman-Blumen
Director of Women's Research
National Institute of Education

Zella Luria
Professor of Psychology
Tufts University

333

Eleanor E. Maccoby
Professor of Psychology
Stanford University

John A. Martin
Graduate Student
Department of Psychology
Stanford University

Patricia Y. Miller
Associate Director of Research
Institute for Urban Studies
University of Houston

Chester M. Pierce
Professor of Education
and Psychiatry
Harvard University

Lee Rainwater
Professor of Sociology
Harvard University

Robert R. Sears
David Starr Jordan Professor
of Psychology, Emeritus
Stanford University

Judith R. Shapiro
Assistant Professor of
Anthropology
Bryn Mawr College

William Simon, Director
Institute for Urban Studies
University of Houston

Beatrice B. Whiting
Professor of Education and
Anthropology
Harvard University

Participant-Observers from the Project on Human Sexual Development

Barbara D. Finberg
Program Officer
Carnegie Corporation of New York

Ann Gillis
Project Manager

Marie Harleston
Member, Board of Directors
Population Education, Inc.

William Houlton
Project Staff

David Kent Kline
Associate Professor of Education
Harvard University

Philip R. Lee
Director, Health Policy Program
University of California, San
Francisco
Chairperson, Board of Directors
Population Education, Inc.

Valarie Munden
Project Staff

Elizabeth J. Roberts
Executive Director
Project on Human Sexual
Development
President, Population
Education, Inc.

Alberta E. Siegel
Professor of Psychology
Department of Psychiatry and
Behavioral Sciences
Stanford University
Member, Board of Directors
Population Education, Inc.

Faustina Solis
Deputy Director, Department
of Health
State of California
Member, Board of Directors
Population Education, Inc.

Gwill York
Vice-chairman, Board of
Directors
The Cleveland Foundation

Board of Directors of Population Education, Inc.

336

Index

Aberle, D. F., on parental contribution to gender role, 171
Achievement motivation, 219
  child-rearing experience and, 210
Achievement orientation, sexual behavior as expression of, 246–56
  typology of achievement orientations, 246–54, 249 fig.
    direct achievement orientations, 247, 251–52
    salience, flexibility, range, and intensity, 253–54
    sex roles and achievement roles, 247, 248–51
    sexuality achievement scoring mechanism, 248 fig.
    vicarious achievement orientations, 247, 248–51
Adolescence
  in formation of gender role and gender identity, 229–30, 282, 283
  and homosexual commitments, 239
  masturbation and gender roles during, 233–35
Adrenocorticotropic hormone (ACTH), 126
Adrenogenital syndrome. *See* Virilizing adrenogenital syndrome
Africa
  characterization and status of women in, 284–85, 300–1
  formation of gender identity in, 322
  importance of female bonds in, 282
  initiation rites in, 282–83, 285–86 326
  macho stereotype absent in, 312–13
  study of critical-period hypothesis for gender; identity formation in, 317–18
  tribal kinship studies in, 279–81

women as "husbands" in, 283–84
Age, high status and, among primates, 65–66
Aggression
  changing significance of, with age of child, 215
  child-rearing experience and, 210, 212
  sex-typing and, 219
Agricultural systems. *See also* Horticultural societies
  technology of, and sexual differentiation, 272
Aldrich-Blake, F. P. G., on evolutionary theory and female choice of mating partners, 69
Alexander, M.
  dominance study of rhesus monkeys by, 61
  on male mating preference in baboons, 65
Alexander, Richard D.
  on correlation between harem sizes and degree of sexual dimorphism in body length in mammalian groups, 81–82
  on evolutionary importance of male parental care, 89–90
Allen, M. R., on pollution beliefs in New Guinea, 293
Altruistic vicarious orientation, 248–49
Androgen
  activational effects of, 143–47
  bisexual effect on female rhesus, 142
  deficiency of, and homosexuality, 120, 139
  effect on female fetuses of rhesus monkeys, 116–17
  gender role behavior and, 152–54, 170–71

337

insensitivity to, and gender identity, 168–69

libido-enhancing quality of, 158

necessary for sexual behavior in males, 140

and "prone head reaction," 121

role in sexual differentiation, 136–38, 165

  in brain mechanisms, 137

  in genital functions, 136

suggested research on, 157, 158

virilizing adrenogenital syndrome caused by, 117

Androsterone-etiocholanolone urine ratio, sexual orientation and, 128

Animal models for human behavior, 98–111

constraints on interspecific comparisons, 99–103

directions for new research

  comparative and longitudinal studies of female sexuality, 106–7

  human sexuality and evolutionary models, 107–11

  molecular analysis of sexual behavior, 105–6

and female orgasm, 103–5

limitations on applicability to human behavior, 138–39

uncertain role of primate data, 139–42

  lack of androgenation studies on adults, 140

  lack of comparability between animals and endocrinologically emancipated human females, 141

Anthropology, study of sex through

behavioral approach and, 309

contributions in study of

  changing sex roles during life span, 321

  gender identity, 321–23

  sex roles, 28

  sexual behavior, 323–26

directions for new research, 326–29

research areas for developmental aspects, 309–18

  culturally defined stereotypes, 311–12

erotic and reproductive behavior, 310

protest masculinity, 313–16

sex and psychosocial derivatives, 316–18

sex differences in development, 311

women as focus of research, 269

Antibiotics, and fetal development, 157

Ardener, Edwin, and study of sex differences in perceptions of society, 298–99

Ardener, S.

analysis of pollution beliefs by, 295

study of women's activism in West Cameroons, 297

Asexuality, transsexualism and, 182

Asmat people (West Irian), protest masculinity among, 314–15

Aswad, Barbara C., study of roles of public women in Middle East, 284

Atkinson, Jane, study of Ilongot people, 290

Australian aborigines, sexual differentiation among, 280

Autoerotic behavior

as direction of sexual striving, 37–40

origin of term *autoerotic*, 37

sex differences in, 124–25

Ayers, Barbara, study of pregnancy taboos, 324

Baboons, dominance study of, 60. *See also* Chacma baboons; Hamadryas baboons; Olive baboons; Savannah baboons; Yellow baboons

Bach, George, and use of "cultural sex typing," 29n

Bamberger, Joan, study of role-reversal myths, 295–96

Bamileke people, women's kin roles among, 280–81

Barbiturates, and fetal development, 157

Bauer, H. R., on chimpanzee intrasexual bonding, 71

Beach, F. A., on use of term *sexuality*, 12, 150

346

Design	Dave Comstock
Composition	Freedmen's Organization
Lithography	Edwards Brothers
Binder	Edwards Brothers
Text	Compugraphic Times Roman
Display	Compugraphic Times Roman
Paper	50 lb EB Book Natural
Binding	Holliston Roxite B 51549 Vellum